5(

MW01040363

# *Best of Our*

# *Favorite Recipes*

First Printing, March 1996
Second Printing, July 1996
Third Printing, November 1996
Fourth Printing, January 1997
Fifth Printing, April 1997
Sixth Printing, July 1997
Seventh Printing, October 1997
Eighth Printing, January 1998
Ninth Printing, September 1998
Tenth Printing, January 1999
Eleventh Printing, September 1999
Twelfth Printing, June 2000

**Maui Association for Family and
Community Education**
formerly
**Maui Extension Homemakers Council**
and
**Maui Home Demonstration Council**
Kahului, Maui, Hawaii 96733

# Foreword

University Extension Clubs were organized as educational groups of homemakers who were interested in learning how to improve their homes, how to be better citizens, and how to work with others for the improvement of their communities.

During the past 50 plus years, members have thus participated in informal educational programs provided by county agents charged with the responsibility to provide practical information in agriculture, families, and related subjects.

The foundation for home demonstration work on Maui was established by Miss Gertrude Gage. During the 1929-30 extension year, Ms. Gage organized clubs mainly by working through the younger generation, sending messages home from school and through the Parent Teacher Associations.

The first University Extension Club was organized on Puukolii where 24 women attended three meetings on food and three on clothing. Keokea, Paia, Kealahou, and Haliimaile were other communities where home demonstration groups were formed. The food programs were simple and fundamental. Many women were learning about certain foods for the first time.

Home demonstration work then expanded, and clubs were organized from Honokohua to Hana and throughout Central Maui. By 1946, many groups were ready to affiliate as a county-wide council. Through the encouragement of Home Agent Mary Ann Amoss, the Maui Home Council was organized to plan programs and activities on a county-wide basis.

Throughout the past 50 years, members continued to provide leadership and educational opportunities. They responded to new initiatives and developed innovative programs to meet the changing needs of Maui's families and communities.

Through partnerships with the University of Hawaii-Cooperative Extension and allied agencies and organizations, the Council helped to meet many challenges and changes. Members journeyed together from the kitchen to the capitol as they established the Family Community Leadership Program. Throughout the decades, their image from cooking and sewing was changed. Today, the organization is recognized as the Association for Family and Community Education.

For many years, Maui Extension Homemakers' Council (MEHC) and now Maui Association for Family and Community Education (MAFCE) has sponsored the Homemakers' Exhibit at the Maui County Fair. This is its largest undertaking each year. The association has spearheaded the seat belt requirement in Hawaii. Most recently, they have provided baby blankets for Kauai after Hurricane Iniki, huggy dolls and animals for distressed children and lap blankets for the frail elderly. Storybook aprons and books for preschools and kindergartens were also provided. Members help the charities of their own choice.

Together, members and their families have made a difference through education, leadership, and community service. Hundreds of people throughout the many years have been served by the extension homemakers/U.E. Club members. The quality of life on Maui was thus enhanced by 50 years of their commitments, cooperation and caring.

Over the years, the Maui Extension Homemakers' Council had published five cookbooks. The first, "Our Favorite Recipes," was published in 1957. Proceeds from all of the cookbook sales have been used to finance programs in community services, continuing education, and leadership training.

The Maui Association for Family and Community Education is to present its "50th Anniversary Best of our Favorite Recipes." We sincerely express our Aloha and appreciation to all who so kindly donated their favorite recipes and may all enjoy this cookbook.

# DEDICATION

This 50th Anniversary Favorite Recipes cookbook is dedicated to all past and present members of Maui Home Demonstration Council, Maui Extension Homemakers' Council, and Maui Association for Family and Community Education; to all Maui Home Demonstration Agents, Extension Home Economists and University of Hawaii Extension Specialists who have advised us and provided educational programs to help to improve the family life and community betterment of Maui during the past 50 years. Special thanks are extended to those who have accepted leadership roles in the University Extension Clubs, Council, and Association to carry on the programs.

# APPRECIATION

The cookbook committee would like to thank all members and friends who generously contributed recipes and who assisted in compiling them or in any way contributed to the publication of our 50th Anniversary cookbook.

We have tried to include our best or favorite recipes, including those from the past five cookbooks and from the past University Extension club lessons. A new section for Microwave Cooking and Special Dietary needs have been added.

| | |
|---|---|
| Our Favorite Recipes | (Yellow) |
| More of Our Favorite Recipes | (Red) |
| Still More of Our Favorite Recipes | (Green) |
| Still Many More of Our Favorite Recipes | (Blue) |
| Our Golden Anniversary Favorite Recipes | (Gold) |

(Golden Anniversary of Cooperative Extension Service in Hawaii)

# COOKBOOK COMMITTEE

| | |
|---|---|
| Ludvina Abrew | Virginia Newgent |
| Kimiko Anzai | Jean Okada |
| Mabel Ito | Lillian Takabayashi |
| Patsy Nakamura | Grace Tanimoto |

Divider artwork by Irene Machida of Pukalani FCE

Any mention of a commercial product is not intended as an endorsement, nor is it to be discriminatory to other products with similar characteristics.

Maui Home Council Board of Directors Meeting
February 1, 1947
Old Wailuku Community Center

# MAFCE PRESIDENTS

| | |
|---|---|
| 1946-47 | Eva Muller* |
| 1947-48 | Edith Izumi |
| 1948-49 | Lillian Takabayashi |
| 1949-50 | Mary Oda* |
| 1950-51 | Virginia Kunz |
| 1952 | Rose Tagami* |
| 1953 | Helen Burden* |
| 1954 | Emma Ambrose |
| 1955 | Mary Soon |
| 1956-57 | Mary Oda* |
| 1958-59 | Yukie Ueoka |
| 1960-61 | Eleanor Sato |
| 1961-62 | Gladys Lai |
| 1963-64 | Eleanor Sato |
| 1964-65 | Haruko Kanemitsu |
| 1966-67 | Julia Souza |
| 1968-69 | Kiyoko Saito |
| 1970-71 | Rebecca Keala |
| 1972-73 | Lillian Coelho* |
| 1974-75 | Ludvina Abrew |
| 1976-77 | Grace Tanimoto |
| 1978-79 | Mary Monden |
| 1980-81 | Patsy Nakamura |
| 1982-83 | Beatrice Barboza |
| 1984-85 | David Keala |
| 1986-87 | Pasita Pladera |
| 1988-89 | Lynn Barut |
| 1990-91 | Mary Monden |
| 1992-93 | Katsuko Enoki |
| 1994-95 | Virginia Newgent |
| 1996- | Pasita Pladera |

*Deceased

# TABLE OF CONTENTS

# FAVORITE RECIPES
## FROM MY COOKBOOK

| Recipe Name | Page Number |
|---|---|
| | |
| | |
| | |
| | |
| | |
| | |
| | |
| | |
| | |
| | |
| | |
| | |
| | |
| | |
| | |
| | |
| | |
| | |
| | |
| | |
| | |
| | |
| | |
| | |
| | |
| | |
| | |

# APPETIZERS,

## PICKLES & RELISHES

# FOOD QUANTITIES FOR 25, 50, AND 100 SERVINGS

| FOOD | 25 SERVINGS | 50 SERVINGS | 100 SERVINGS |
|---|---|---|---|
| Rolls | 4 doz. | 8 doz. | 16 doz. |
| Bread | 50 slices or 3 1-lb. loaves | 100 slices or 6 1-lb. loaves | 200 slices or 12 1-lb. loaves |
| Butter | ½ lb. | ¾ to 1 lb. | 1½ lb. |
| Mayonnaise | 1 c. | 2 to 3 c. | 4 to 6 c. |
| Mixed filling for sandwiches (meat, eggs, fish) | 1½ qt. | 2½ to 3 qt. | 5 to 6 qt. |
| Mixed filling (sweet-fruit) | 1 qt. | 1¾ to 2 qt. | 2½ to 4 qt. |
| Jams & preserves | 1½ lb. | 3 lb. | 6 lb. |
| Crackers | 1½ lb. | 3 lb. | 6 lb. |
| Cheese (2 oz. per serving) | 3 lb. | 6 lb. | 12 lb. |
| Soup | 1½ gal. | 3 gal. | 6 gal. |
| Salad dressings | 1 pt. | 2½ pt. | ½ gal. |
| **Meat, Poultry, or Fish:** | | | |
| Wieners (beef) | 6½ lb. | 13 lb. | 25 lb. |
| Hamburger | 9 lb. | 18 lb. | 35 lb. |
| Turkey or chicken | 13 lb. | 25 to 35 lb. | 50 to 75 lb. |
| Fish, large whole (round) | 13 lb. | 25 lb. | 50 lb. |
| Fish, fillets or steaks | 7½ lb. | 15 lb. | 30 lb. |
| **Salads, Casseroles, Vegetables:** | | | |
| Potato salad | 4¼ qt. | 2¼ gal. | 4½ gal. |
| Scalloped potatoes | 4½ qt. or 1 12x20" pan | 8½ qt. | 17 qt. |
| Mashed potatoes | 9 lb. | 18-20 lb. | 25-35 lb. |
| Spaghetti | 1¼ gal. | 2½ gal. | 5 gal. |
| Baked beans | ¾ gal. | 1¼ gal. | 2½ gal. |
| Jello salad | ¾ gal. | 1¼ gal. | 2½ gal. |
| Canned vegetables | 1 #10 can | 2½ #10 cans | 4 #10 cans |
| **Fresh Vegetables:** | | | |
| Lettuce (for salads) | 4 heads | 8 heads | 15 heads |
| Carrots (3 oz. or ½ c.) | 6¼ lb. | 12½ lb. | 25 lb. |
| Tomatoes | 3-5 lb. | 7-10 lb. | 14-20 lb. |
| **Desserts:** | | | |
| Watermelon | 37½ lb. | 75 lb. | 150 lb. |
| Fruit cup (½ c. per serving) | 3 qt. | 6 qt. | 12 qt. |
| Cake | 1 10x12" sheet cake 1½ 10" layer cakes | 1 12x20" sheet cake 3 10" layer cakes | 2 12x20" sheet cakes 6 10" layer cakes |
| Whipping cream | ¾ pt. | 1½ to 2 pt. | 3 pt. |
| **Ice Cream:** | | | |
| Brick | 3¼ qt. | 6½ qt. | 12½ qt. |
| Bulk | 2¼ qt. | 4½ qt. or 1¼ gal. | 9 qt. or 2½ gal. |
| **Beverages:** | | | |
| Coffee | ½ lb. and 1½ gal. water | 1 lb. and 3 gal. water | 2 lb. and 6 gal. water |
| Tea | 1/12 lb. and 1½ gal. water | ⅙ lb. and 3 gal. water | ⅓ lb. and 6 gal. water |
| Lemonade | 10 to 15 lemons, 1½ gal. water | 20 to 30 lemons, 3 gal. water | 40 to 60 lemons, 6 gal. water |

# APPETIZERS, PICKLES AND RELISHES

## ABURAGE TAEGU

1 to 2 pkg. aburage
¼ c. green onions or
   chives, chopped
2 to 3 cloves garlic, grated
2 Tbsp. sugar
2 Tbsp. sesame oil

3 Tbsp. shoyu
1½ Tbsp. white vinegar
2 Tbsp. sesame seeds,
   roasted and ground
¼ tsp. chili pepper flakes

Cut aburage in thin slices. Mix rest of the ingredients in a bowl. Add aburage and mix thoroughly.

*Kiyomi Ito, Kimiko Anzai*

## AGE YUBA

Use 1 block of yuba (dried bean curd). Cut into 2 inch pieces or break into bite-size pieces. Deep-fry over medium heat. Drain on paper towel. Sprinkle salt (optional).

## CHINESE FISH CAKE

2 Tbsp. cornstarch
1 tsp. sugar
1 Tbsp. oil
1 Tbsp. water
1 Tbsp. chopped green
   onion
1 Tbsp. minced Chinese
   parsley

1 lb. raw Chinese fish cake
2 Tbsp. minced water
   chestnuts
¼ c. minced cooked ham
2 Tbsp. minced Chinese
   mushrooms

Condiments:

**Mustard**

**Soy sauce**

Combine all ingredients and mix well. Drop small amounts into 400°F. oil; fry until brown. Serve on cocktail picks and dip into mustard and soy sauce. Makes about 40 portions.

# CHINESE RUMAKI
## (Broiled Chicken Livers)

½ lb. chicken livers          ½ lb. bacon
1 (8 oz.) can water
   chestnuts

Drain water chestnuts; dry on paper towels. Place chicken livers on broiler tray. Run under broiler flame for a few minutes to set blood, but *do not actually cook.* Cut set livers into 3 (4 inch) pieces. Cut chestnuts in halves crosswise. Cut bacon slices in halves crosswise.

Put 1 chicken liver and 1 chestnut half on each half-slice of bacon. Roll up and fasten with toothpicks. Return to broiler tray and broil under a moderate flame until bacon is crisp and livers cooked. *Do not overcook.* Drain on paper towels and serve hot. Makes 15 to 17 pupus.

Uncooked rumaki may be frozen for later use. *Do not* store frozen for more than 2 weeks.

# CRABMEAT-STUFFED MUSHROOMS

1 lb. fresh mushrooms          2 Tbsp. seasoned bread
   (large size)             crumbs
¼ c. butter          ¼ lb. crabmeat, shredded,
1 Tbsp. round onion,             or 1 (6 oz.) can
   chopped             crabmeat
2 Tbsp. celery, diced

Wash mushrooms. Remove stems and finely chop. Heat butter in frying pan. Cook stems and onions and celery. Add bread crumbs and shredded crabmeat. Stuff mushroom caps with mixture; brush with butter to keep moist during baking. Place in greased pan. Bake at 300° for 15 minutes.

*T. Oki*

# HOT CRAB CANAPES

1 c. flaked crabmeat
¼ c. mayonnaise
1 tsp. tarragon vinegar
½ tsp. dry mustard
¼ tsp. salt
1 Tbsp. minced parsley
1 Tbsp. minced chives
Thin bread slices or
   crackers
Grated cheese
Paprika

Combine the first 7 ingredients and set aside. Toast small rounds (2 inch diameter) bread on 1 side only. Spread crab mixture on the untoasted side. Top with grated cheese and paprika. Place on cookie sheet and broil about 3 inches below broiler flame until brown. Makes about 36.

# JAPANESE CRAB TIDBITS

1 Tbsp. butter or margarine
1 Tbsp. flour
½ c. milk
1 (6½ oz.) can crabmeat
½ tsp. salt
½ c. cornstarch
Oil (for frying)

Condiments:

Soy sauce                    Mustard

Melt the butter, then add flour and stir until smooth. Slowly add milk and stir to make a thick cream sauce. Bring sauce to a boil and add crabmeat and salt. Remove from heat and chill mixture. When chilled thoroughly, form into balls the size of a walnut and roll in cornstarch. Deep-fry in hot oil. Serve hot with condiments of soy sauce and mustard. These crab tidbits may be prepared an hour or so in advance and then reheated in a hot 400° oven. Makes about 30 balls.

# CRISP WUN TUN

½ lb. pork, ground
4 medium size shrimp, cooked and shelled
4 water chestnuts
½ tsp. salt
1 stalk green onion, chopped fine
½ tsp. monosodium glutamate
¼ tsp. sugar
1 pkg. wun tun wrappers
Oil (for frying)

Combine all ingredients, except wrappers, and chop to a hash. Place ½ teaspoon of this mixture in each wun tun wrapper; dampen edges and (1) fold diagonally. Dampen the 2 opposite corners of this triangle; (2) fold the two narrow ends together in center and press tightly. (3) Fold the third and center corner back to stand up and away from the filled part. Fry in deep fat until a light, golden brown. Drain on paper and serve hot. Makes about 60 wun tun.

These Crisp Wun Tun may also be served with Chinese meat and vegetable dishes. Or, for soups, drop the folded wun tun into boiling water and when they float to the top, remove and place in a soup bowl. Use with Chinese noodles or a plain prepared soup of chicken or beef broth.

Wun tun wrappers may be purchased from a store, about 60 in a package, for approximately 30 cents. If not available, prepare the wrappers in advance from this recipe.

Wun Tun Wrappers:

1½ c. flour
½ tsp. salt
¼ c. water
1 egg (unbeaten)

Sift flour and salt into a bowl. Add water and egg; mix well. Knead dough until smooth and not sticky. Roll out dough paper thin on a floured board. Cut into 3 inch squares. Makes about 50 wrappers.

*Green*

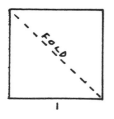 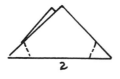

# SPAM WUN TON

3 Kamaboko, grated
1 can Spam, grated

1½ pkg. cream cheese
3 pkg. wun ton pi

Mix together and fill; seal edges with water and deep-fry in pan of oil until golden brown.

*Caroline Yoshioka*

# FRIED CHICKEN BALLS

1 lb. ground chicken
½ medium onion, chopped
1 Tbsp. sugar
2½ Tbsp. mirin
2 Tbsp. shoyu

1 egg
3½ Tbsp. water
1½ Tbsp. sherry or sake
   wine
2 Tbsp. salad oil

Combine chicken, onion, sugar, 1½ tablespoons mirin, 1 tablespoon shoyu, and egg. Mix and roll into bite-size balls; flatten slightly. Heat oil in pan. Brown meat balls on all sides.

Combine 3½ tablespoons water, 1½ tablespoons sake or sherry, and 1 tablespoon shoyu. Add to meat and cook until almost evaporated. Do not overcook.

# KIM CHEE OGO

1 lb. ogo (seaweed)
1 to 2 cloves garlic,
   chopped fine
1 Tbsp. ginger, chopped
   fine
¼ c. vinegar
1 Tbsp. goma (sesame
   seed), toasted

½ c. shoyu
1 Tbsp. mirin
1 or 2 chili peppers
3 stalks green onion,
   chopped, or 1
   medium Kula onion,
   chopped

Clean ogo and shred to bite-size pieces. Rinse well to get all the sand out. Pour boiling hot water over ogo. After a minute or 2, drain and run under cold water. Mix with other ingredients and chill.

*Katsuko Enoki*

# LITTLE LINKS

1 c. brown sugar
3 Tbsp. flour
2 tsp. dry mustard
1 c. pineapple juice

½ c. vinegar
1½ tsp. soy sauce
3 pkg. (5 oz.) smoked
   cocktail sausages

In a skillet, combine brown sugar, flour, mustard, pineapple juice, vinegar, and soy sauce. Bring to a boil, stirring constantly, and boil 1 minute. Stir in sausages. Cook slowly 5 minutes or until heated through. Keep warm over low heat. Use food picks for serving. Makes about 3 dozen.

*L. Takabayashi*

# LOMI SALMON

½ lb. salt salmon
2 large ripe tomatoes,
   diced
1 small round onion,
   chopped

1 sprig green onion,
   chopped
2 cubes ice

Select salmon with thick meat. Soak in cold water overnight and drain. Take off skin and free from bones. Pick into small pieces and put in bowl. Add tomatoes, onion, and ice and lomi with hands until all are in small pieces. Chill until watery. Serves 6.

*Ludvina Abrew*

6

# LUMPIA LABONG
## (Fried Rolls with Bamboo Shoot Filling)

1 Tbsp. salad oil
6 cloves garlic, minced
1 onion, minced
½ lb. pork, thinly sliced
½ lb. shrimp, thinly sliced
1 tsp. monosodium
    glutamate (optional)

¾ tsp. salt
¼ tsp. pepper
1 Tbsp. soy sauce
3 c. slivered bamboo
    shoots
Deep fat (for frying)
24 lumpia wrappers

Heat oil in saucepan. Saute garlic and onion. Stir in pork, shrimp, monosodium glutamate, salt, pepper, and soy sauce. Cover and simmer until pork is tender. Add bamboo shoots and cook 3 to 4 more minutes; cool. Heat deep fat to 375°F. Put 1 to 2 tablespoons of filling about 2 inches from the nearest edge of each wrapper. Fold edge of wrapper over filling. Fold right and left sides toward center to completely enclose filling in envelope fashion. Roll toward open end, moistening edge with water for sealing. Fry in deep fat until lightly browned. Serve with dipping sauce if desired. Makes 24 lumpia.

Lumpia wrappers may be purchased or make from recipe in Miscellaneous Section of this cookbook.

Dipping Sauce for Lumpia:

3 cloves garlic
¼ c. cider vinegar

Dash of salt

Press garlic through garlic press. Stir in vinegar and salt. Makes ¼ cup.

# PICKLED OAMA WITH ONIONS

1⅔ c. distilled vinegar
4 Tbsp. sugar
⅛ c. (or less) water
4 (or less) chili peppers
1 Tbsp. salt

1 medium round onion,
  minced
60 to 70 oama, cleaned,
  head and entrails
  removed

Combine vinegar, sugar, water, peppers, salt, and onions. Mix thoroughly. Add fish and marinate in the refrigerator for 1 or 2 days before serving.

How to clean oama: To remove scales, put oama into a large container with pebbles and coarse sand. Stir until the scales are loosened or rubbed off, then rinse in sea water. Cut off the head and remove the entrails. Rinse again before using in a recipe.

# PORK DUMPLINGS
## (Gyoza)

¼ lb. ground pork
½ lb. ground beef
1 egg, beaten
2 shiitake, soaked and
  minced
¼ tsp. salt
1 Tbsp. shoyu
1 Tbsp. mirin (rice wine)
¼ tsp. monosodium
  glutamate

¼ tsp. sesame seed oil
2 Tbsp. green onion or
  chives, minced
1 c. cabbage, finely minced
  (optional)
3 doz. gyoza no kawa (won
  ton pi or wrapper)
1 qt. oil (for frying)

Combine first 11 ingredients and mix thoroughly. Fill each gyoza wrapper with 1 tablespoon filling mixture. Moisten edges of wrapper; fold in half and flute edges to seal. Fry in oil heated to 375°F. on gas thermostatically controlled top burner for 1 to 2 minutes or until golden brown. Gyoza may also be steamed for 20 to 30 minutes instead of frying. Drain and serve with Ponzu Sauce if desired. Yield: Approximately 3 dozen.

*Ludvina Abrew*

# EBI NO MINO AGE

Mino is a straw cape used in rural Japan for protection from rain.

12 shrimp (cuttlefish, aji, or any small fish may be used)
1 medium size Irish potato
½ c. Katakuri (potato starch, cornstarch may be used)

½ c. flour
2 egg whites

Peel potato and cut into very fine strips (like shoestring potatoes). Soak in water for awhile; drain and dredge with Katakuri. Clean shrimp. Remove tails; slit from back and pound lightly with knife.

Dredge shrimp with flour; dip in slightly beaten egg whites. Roll in potato and deep-fry for 375°.

Serve with grated turnip and tempura sauce.

*Mabel Ito*

# MARINATED SHRIMP

5 lb. medium shrimp with shells
1 bottle Italian dressing

½ c. dry sherry
1 tsp. pepper
½ tsp. basil

Soak shrimp overnight in the mixture of Italian dressing, sherry, pepper, and basil, turning occasionally. Cook on barbeque grill.

*L. Takabayashi*

# SHRIMP WRAPPED IN BACON

Remove shell and head of small shrimp (leave tails intact). Remove veins. Wrap with thin slices of bacon. Fasten with tooth-pick. Bake in 350° oven for 20 minutes.

# INDONESIAN SHRIMP BALLS

2 c. cooked shrimp, minced
2 eggs, beaten
1 clove garlic, minced
¼ c. bread crumbs
⅛ tsp. pepper
½ tsp. salt
1 Tbsp. minced parsley
Few grains of nutmeg
Oil (for frying)

Mix all ingredients well. Form into balls the size of a large marble and deep-fry at 375°F. until a golden brown. Serve on cocktail picks. Makes about 60.

May be prepared ahead of time, frozen, and for later use, reheated in an oven.

# SHOYU-LEMON SQUID

3 lb. Calamari squid
1 c. shoyu
Juice of 2 lemons
¼ c. sesame oil
1 Tbsp. sesame seeds,
     toasted
1 small onion, sliced thin
MSG to taste (optional)
9 squirts of Tabasco or 2
     chili peppers, sliced

The day before, clean squid by inserting knife into the body cavity and slitting it open. Clean the inside, removing the center membrane and everything else in it. Discard what you remove, except the legs, cutting just below the eyes. Separate legs by cutting into 3 to 4 separate groups. Bring medium pot of water to a rolling boil. Place squid into pot, stirring to cook all the pieces. As soon as the squid starts to curl, it will take only a few seconds. Drain into a colander and run under the faucet to stop cooking process. Drain well. Cut the body pieces in halves lengthwise and slice across the body into 18 (¼ inch) strips.

Prepare marinade with remaining ingredients. Add the squid. Refrigerate overnight. Makes about 1½ quarts.

# MARINATED SQUID

3 lb. squid (fresh or frozen)
¼ c. olive oil (for marinade)
2 Tbsp. olive oil (for
    cooking squid)

¼ c. vinegar or lemon juice
2 cloves fresh garlic
1 tsp. salt

Optional (cut in bite-size):

Mushrooms
Olives
Onions

Pimento
Parsley
Green pepper

Clean the squid by removing skin, head, and insides (keep tentacles). Cut into ½ inch rings.

In a heavy pan, put 2 tablespoons olive oil, 1 crushed garlic clove, and 1 teaspoon salt. Add the squid. Put a lid on and simmer for about 20 minutes, until tender. Remove lid and let water evaporate, but do not let it get too dry. Transfer to a bowl and let cool. Add the rest of the ingredients and more salt if desired. Let it marinate for at least 4 hours, preferably overnight, in refrigerator. Take out of refrigerator 1 hour before serving.

*Mabel Ito*

# BAKED TARO PUFFS

Taro root

Butter

Boil taro until soft in salted water. Peel and put through a ricer or mash well. Mix with a little water, using only enough to make a smooth dough. While hot, form into small cakes and place in a buttered pan. Make a dent in top and add a dollop of butter. Bake in a 375° oven until browned. Serve hot with butter.

# TEX MEX
## (It's like a taco, but in a won ton pi)

1 lb. ground beef
1 pkg. taco mix
½ can (16 oz.) refried beans
½ c. shredded Cheddar
    cheese

2 pkg. won ton pi (40 to 50
    pieces)

Brown ground beef. Drain oil. Add taco mix, beans, and cheese. Mix well. Wrap in won ton pi. Deep-fry. Eat with taco sauce or salsa.

# PORK ROLLS

2 eggs
2 Tbsp. soy sauce
1 lb. lean ground pork
¾ c. minced green onion
2 Tbsp. sugar
6 water chestnuts, minced

¼ c. Chinese cabbage,
    minced
¼ tsp. salt
½ c. flour
2 Tbsp. sherry

Beat eggs; add soy sauce, sugar, and sherry. Add pork, green onion, water chestnuts, and cabbage and mix until well blended. Add salt and flour. Form into balls the size of walnuts. Fry in hot oil about 1 inch deep. Drain on paper towels. Serve on cocktail picks.

Can be made in advance and refrigerated or frozen.

*Helen Apana*

# SPINACH ROLL

1 c. sour cream
1 c. mayonnaise
1 pkg. Hidden Valley
   (original)
½ jar Bac-Os bits

6 stalks green onion,
   chopped
2 boxes chopped frozen
   spinach, defrosted
1 pkg. tortilla

   1. Place sour cream, mayonnaise, Hidden Valley, Bac-Os bits, and green onion in a bowl.

   2. Squeeze out water from spinach and add to preceding mixture.

   3. Mix ingredients together until completely blended.

   4. Divide mixture into 10 parts and place on tortilla and spread evenly.

   5. Roll up tortilla like rolling sushi.

   6. Wrap each roll individually in wax paper.

   7. Refrigerate. Cut when ready to serve.

*Helen Kawahara*

# STUFFED CELERY

3 stalks celery, cut into 1½
   inch lengths
½ kamaboko, grated
2 Tbsp. mayonnaise
2 pinches of sugar

1 tsp. round onion, finely
   chopped
Few drops of
   Worcestershire
   sauce

   Mix kamaboko with mayonnaise, Worcestershire sauce, sugar, and onion. Stuff this mixture on celery stalks and serve.

*Gold*

# TOFU POKE

1 block firm tofu
2 tsp. toasted sesame
  seeds
¼ c. ogo (add more as
  desired)
2 tsp. chopped green
  onions

1 tsp. grated ginger
½ large red chili pepper,
  chopped
¼ c. shoyu
1 Tbsp. sesame oil

Cut tofu into 1 inch cubes and drain well. Parboil ogo and chop coarsely. Mix shoyu and sesame oil and pour over rest of ingredients. Toss lightly and chill ½ hour before serving.

*Lillian H. Kobayashi*

# TUNA PUPUS

2 cans tuna
2 eggs
2 Tbsp. minced onion
2 Tbsp. grated lemon peel

2 Tbsp. lemon juice
2 Tbsp. minced parsley
½ c. flour

Combine preceding ingredients in a bowl. Drop by teaspoonful into hot oil and fry until golden brown. Serve with tartar sauce or with shoyu and mustard.

*Thelma Iwami*

14

# WARABI APPETIZER

1 lb. warabi
1 c. boiling water
1 Tbsp. Hawaiian salt
1 (4 oz.) pkg. codfish,
    shredded

1 onion, thinly sliced
2 tomatoes, cubed

Sauce:

¼ c. shoyu
⅓ c. fresh lemon juice
½ c. sugar

¼ tsp. garlic salt
¼ tsp. MSG

Wash and cut warabi in 1 inch length. In a saucepan of boiling water, add salt and cook warabi until it comes to a boil. Drain immediately under cold running water until cool.

Heat codfish in saucepan on medium heat for 2 minutes. Cool. Combine warabi, codfish, onion, and tomatoes in mixing bowl.

Combine sauce ingredients and pour over warabi mixture. Toss gently. Yield: 8 servings.

# PARTY MIX

1 any size bag plain M&M's
    candies
1 any size bag pretzel
    sticks
1 any size can peanuts

1 to 2 c. raisins
Approx. ½ box cheese
    flavored crackers
    (such as Cheez-its or
    Goldfish)

Combine all ingredients in a bowl and serve.

The amount of each ingredient depends on personal preference. If you are an M&M's freak, use a large size bag or if you're nuts over peanuts, use a big size can, etc.

# CRABMEAT DIP

1 stick butter
A small bunch of green
  onions
½ c. fresh chopped parsley
2 Tbsp. flour
1 pt. half & half
½ lb. grated Swiss cheese
2 Tbsp. dry sherry
Salt and pepper to taste
1 lb. white fresh crabmeat

Melt butter in heavy saucepan. Saute onions until clear. Slowly blend in flour and cream, then cheese. Stir until melted. Add other ingredients. Serve in chafing dish with Melba toast.

# EGGPLANT DIP

3 to 4 long eggplants
½ c. chopped onion
¼ c. chopped parsley
1 clove garlic, minced
¼ tsp. freshly ground
  pepper
1 tsp. Italian seasoning
1 Tbsp. olive oil
2 tsp. fresh lemon juice

Prick eggplants several times with fork. Place on double thickness of paper towel. Microwave 8 to 12 minutes until soft. Remove from oven. Let cool. When cool, halve lengthwise and scoop out flesh. Place in bowl of food processor. Add onion, parsley, garlic pepper, and Italian seasoning. Process until coarsely chopped.

Transfer to serving bowl. Stir in oil and lemon juice. Serve at room temperature with vegetable dippers, crackers, or pita bread.

*Marlene Curtis*

# ONION DIP

1 pkg. whipped cottage
  cheese
¼ c. milk
½ pkg. dehydrated onion
  soup

Stir until smooth. Allow flavor to develop for at least 30 minutes before serving.

May be thinned more with milk if a softer dip for potato chips is desired.

*Ludvina Abrew*

# GUACAMOLE

Aguacate is the Spanish word for alligator pear. When served as a sandwich spread, dip, or pupu, it is called guacamole.

2 medium to large ripe
   avocados
½ c. tomato, diced
¼ c. onion, chopped
2 green chiles, chopped

½ tsp. salt
¼ tsp. black pepper
¼ tsp. garlic salt
2 Tbsp. lemon juice

In salad bowl, mash avocados with fork; add remaining ingredients to taste. Serve on lettuce with Fritos or corn chips as garnish.

Variations: Substitute Tabasco sauce for green chiles. Use 1 clove garlic, pressed, for garlic salt. Add 1 teaspoon Worcestershire sauce instead of lemon juice. Use green onions instead of round onions. Blend or sieve avocado for smoother texture. Smooth top and cover with mayonnaise.

# POOR MAN'S CRAB

⅔ c. sour cream (small ctn.)
1 (3 oz.) pkg. cream cheese
2 tsp. lemon juice

1 (.75 oz.) pkg. dry Italian
   dressing mix
1 (6 oz.) can tuna, drained

Mix well, adding tuna last. Let stand in refrigerator overnight before serving with crackers.

*Vera Reid*

# PICKLES

## CABBAGE TSUKEMONO
### (Pickle)

1 small cabbage, cut into
  wedges

1 slice fresh ginger,
  chopped fine

Combine following and bring to a boil:

2 Tbsp. salt
4 Tbsp. sugar

¼ c. vinegar
¼ c. water

Pour hot solution over cabbage and ginger. Cool and bottle. Keep in refrigerator. Turn bottle occasionally to keep cabbage in solution.

*Blue*

## CHINESE APRICOT PRESERVES

2 (12 oz.) pkg. dried
  apricots
¾ c. Hawaiian washed raw
  sugar (more if
  needed)
1 c. water
2 Tbsp. light or dark
  molasses

¼ tsp. Chinese Five Spices
  (more if desired)
1 Tbsp. rock salt
⅛ tsp. Star Seed (ground)
2 tsp. lemon juice
2 tsp. chopped Chinese
  preserved lemon peel

Combine all ingredients, except apricots. Bring to a boil and add apricots. Cook about a minute or 2, longer if apricots are hard dried. Remove apricots from syrup and drain. Store in sterilized jars. Recipe yields about 2 pints.

If a juicy apricot preserve is desired, do not drain syrup.

*Blue*

# CUCUMBER PICKLES

3 lb. cucumber — ¼ c. Hawaiian salt

Slice cucumber and salt. Leave for 3 hours salted.

Boil for 5 minutes:

1 c. vinegar — 1⅔ c. sugar
½ c. water — 1 Tbsp. mustard seed

Take vinegar sauce off from fire.

Add:

1 round onion, sliced — ¼ tsp. paprika
1¼ tsp. celery seed

Wash and squeeze cucumber to drain off excess water. Pour hot vinegar mixture over cucumber. Put into bottles and refrigerate to keep.

*Red*

# EGGPLANT PICKLE (JAPANESE STYLE)

2 lb. Long eggplants — ¾ c. sugar
¼ c. dry mustard — ¼ c. miso
½ c. shoyu — ½ c. sake (Japanese wine)

Cut eggplants in halves lengthwise and into small triangles. Soak in salt water with weight overnight. Place eggplants in colander and pour boiling water over them. Let stand till cool. Squeeze out water. Mix and make paste with rest of ingredients. Add eggplant and let stand overnight. Pack in jars and cap tightly.

*Blue*

# MANGO STRIPS

Use 1 gallon green mango strips; partially dry in hot sun for 1 day, turning at intervals.

Syrup:

1 box brown sugar
2 c. washed sugar
¼ c. lemon or lime juice
(increase if mangoes
are sweet)

½ c. water
1 Tbsp. salt

Mix together and bring to boil till sugar melts.

Add:

½ tsp. five spices
½ tsp. red food coloring
1 tsp. sodium benzoate
(preservative, optional if
to keep long
unrefrigerated)

Add mango strips into syrup and cook for about 15 minutes, or until syrup is absorbed and thickened.

*Green*

# MANGO STRIPS
## (Chinese shredded mango)

8 c. green mangoes, peeled
and cut into strips
2 Tbsp. salt
1½ c. brown sugar or raw
sugar (or ½ each)
6 Tbsp. vinegar

½ tsp. Five Spices
(Chinese)
½ tsp. licorice or anise
½ tsp. red coloring
1 Tbsp. molasses
(optional)

Sprinkle salt over mango strips; mix and soak overnight. Drain, using cloth to squeeze out as much liquid as possible. Cook for 15 minutes in sauce made of the rest of ingredients. Stir constantly, especially toward the end when syrup thickens.

Lay strips in 1 layer on baking pan. Drizzle syrup if any is left. Cover with net or screen. Dry in sun all day or use dehydrator.

*Mabel Ito*

# SHREDDED MANGO

1 doz. green hayden
   mangoes, cut in strips
   and salt overnight
   (rinse and drain)
¼ c. Hawaiian salt

2½ c. raw sugar
2 boxes dark brown sugar
½ orange rind, minced
1 tsp. red food coloring
2 tsp. 5 spices

Put all together. Bring to boil; lower to medium and cook for ½ hour. Cool and pack in jars.

*Green*

# PICKLED MANGOES

Use 1 gallon green mangoes, peeled and cut.

Boil and cool:

4 c. raw (brown) sugar
2 c. vinegar

¼ c. Hawaiian or crude salt

Add red food coloring to the cooled syrup and mix. Pour the syrup into the gallon of mangoes. Shake the jar occasionally. Let stand for a day or 2 and refrigerate.

*Stella Yamamoto*

# PICKLED MANGO

1 gal. green tender
   mangoes
4 c. water
4 c. brown raw sugar

2 c. vinegar
¾ c. salt (Hawaiian)
2 Tbsp. red coloring

Wash and slice mango in half. Mix all the other ingredients and boil. When cool, add the mangoes. Store in jars.

*Yellow*

# PEACH UME

1 gal. peaches
6 c. vinegar (white)
6 c. sugar
½ bottle red coloring

3 c. Hawaiian salt (to be
used to soak the
peaches)

Wash and soak peaches in salt water for about 1½ days and dry it for 1 day. Boil rest of the ingredients and cool. Put the dried peaches in a gallon jar and pour the syrup and let stand for a week or longer.

*Yellow*

# PINEAPPLE PICKLES

1 fresh pineapple (4 to 6 c.)
2 c. sugar
2 c. water
Dash of salt

1 c. vinegar
1 (2 inch long) stick
cinnamon
2 to 4 whole cloves

Peel pineapple and cut crosswise into 1 inch thick slices. Remove core and cut into sections about 1 inch wide. Mix sugar and water in saucepan; add pineapple pieces and boil for about 10 minutes. Remove pineapple. To the syrup, add vinegar and spices. Boil until syrup is thickened. Add pineapple back into syrup and boil for about 5 minutes. Pour into hot sterilized jars and seal. Yield: 1 to 1½ pints.

*LRA*

# SAN BAI ZUKE - JAPANESE SHOYU PICKLE

5 c. daikon
4 c. cucumber
1 c. carrots
2 c. eggplants
1½ c. shoyu
2 c. sugar

3 Tbsp. vinegar
1 Tbsp. ajinomoto
    (optional)
Chili pepper (optional)
Ginger (optional)

Cut daikon, cucumber, carrot, and eggplant in thin slices and soak overnight in ¼ cup salt. Drain and pour water; squeeze hard. Boil rest of the ingredients. When it starts to boil, put the vegetables and mix and drain, but save the liquid. Boil this same liquid for 1 to 2 minutes; add vegetables and mix. Pour in a jar and refrigerate.

*Yellow*

# SAN BAI ZUKE

3 large daikon
2 large cucumber
1 small carrot
1 medium eggplant

1 medium hasu, sliced and
    boiled
¾ tsp. ajinomoto (optional)
Sesame seeds

Syrup - Boil together:

1 c. shoyu
2 c. brown sugar
½ c. vinegar

Small piece of ginger
Small hot pepper

Slice the vegetables thin; put in a pan and salt with ¼ cup Hawaiian salt. Leave about ½ day; mix or rub 2 or 3 times at intervals, then squeeze or drain well. Add boiled, cooled syrup, and hasu (lotus root), ajinomoto, and sesame seeds. Pour in container and refrigerate.

*Red*

# SWEET TAKUAN

2 large Japanese daikon
1¼ c. sugar
1 c. water
¼ c. vinegar

1 tsp. salt
1 tsp. ajinomoto (optional)
¼ tsp. yellow coloring
1 chili pepper (optional)

Cut daikon into round pieces and soak in ¼ cup salt overnight. Drain and pour water. Squeeze hard. Put daikon in the jar.

In the meantime, boil all the ingredients and when it cools, pour over the daikon. Makes 1 quart. Keep in the refrigerator.

*Yellow*

# TAKUAN - PICKLED TURNIPS

10 lb. turnips or daikon
4 c. sugar
½ c. salt

¾ c. vinegar
Drop of yellow food
coloring

Slice turnips and leave overnight on dish towel. Mix turnips and preceding ingredients all together in bowl. Let stand. Stir occasionally and leave it out 1 day, then pack in jars.

*Doris Mori*

# TSUKEMONO
## (Pickled Vegetables)

1¾ c. water
1 (5 inch) piece dashi
kombu
1½ to 3 Tbsp. rock salt
1½ Tbsp. sugar

½ tsp. shoyu
1½ tsp. rice vinegar
1½ tsp. sake
¼ tsp. monosodium
glutamate (optional)

Suggested Vegetables:

Turnips
Radishes
Head cabbage
Cucumbers

Eggplants
Celery cabbage
Chinese mustard cabbage
Carrots

Combine ingredients and add desired vegetables. Let stand 1 to 2 days in refrigerator or at room temperature with 3 to 5 pound weight. Serve with shoyu. Yield: Approximately 2 cups solution.

*Ludvina Abrew*

# TSUKEMONO - DAIKON AND MUSTARD CABBAGE

2 pkg. Sengiri daikon,
    soaked ½ hour

3 mustard cabbages, cut
    and salted

Sauce:

1 c. white sugar
1 c. shoyu
¼ c. vinegar
Few drops of sesame oil
Sesame seeds

Kim Chee powder (sprinkle
    to taste)
Monosodium glutamate
    (optional)

*Green*

# FILIPINO CHERRY SEED

1 qt. Filipino cherries
1 c. white or raw sugar
¼ tsp. five spices

¼ tsp. red coloring
1 Chinese salted lime

Soak the cherry seeds in salted water (must cover the seeds); soak for several hours and drain. Dry in sunlight for at least 1 day. If drying in electric oven, turn heat to 400° and let oven heat. Turn oven off, then put seeds in oven. Leave in oven until seeds are as dry as you want. When oven cools and seeds are quite not dry enough, repeat heating process. If you have a gas stove, the heat from the pilot light is sufficient to dry the seeds.

Over high heat, cook cherries in sauce for about 10 minutes, stirring frequently with a wooden spoon.

When cooked, put seeds in covered jar and let stand in own juice for 3 to 4 days.

Drain seeds and lay in pan lined with layer of newspaper covered with paper towels. Put dried seeds in container and let stand again. If not sweet enough, add more sugar.

Seeds can be packaged and frozen if desired.

*Frances Kawaguchi*

# Notes

# BREADS & ROLLS

# APPROXIMATE 100 CALORIE PORTIONS

Almonds (shelled)—12 to 15 nuts
Angel cake—1¾ inch cube
Apple—1 large
Apple pie—⅓ normal piece
Apricots—5 large
Asparagus—20 large stalks
Bananas—1 medium
Beans—⅓ cup canned baked
Beans—green string, 2½ cups
Beets—1⅓ cups sliced
Bread—all kinds, slice ½ inch thick
Butter—1 tablespoon
Buttermilk—1⅛ cups
Cabbage—4 to 5 cups shredded
Cake—1¾ inch cube
Candy—1 inch cube
Cantaloupe—1 medium
Carrots—1⅔ cups
Cauliflower—1 small head
Celery—4 cups
Cereal—uncooked, ¾ cup
Cheese—1⅛ inch cube
Cottage cheese—5 tablespoons
Cherries—sweet fresh, 20 cherries
Cookies—1 to 3 inches in diameter
Corn—⅓ cup
Crackers—4 soda crackers
Crackers—graham, 2½ crackers
Cream—thick, 1 tablespoon
Cream—thin, 4 tablespoons
Cream sauce—4 tablespoons
Dates—3 to 4
Doughnuts—½ doughnut
Eggs—1⅓ eggs
Fish—fat, size of 1 chop
Fish—lean, size of 2 chops
Flour—4 tablespoons
Frankfurter—1 small
French dressing—1½ tablespoons
Grapefruit—½ large
Grape juice—½ cup
Grapes—20 grapes
Gravy—2 tablespoons
Ice cream—½ cup
Lard—1 tablespoon
Lemons—3 large

Lettuce—2 large heads
Macaroni—¾ cup cooked
Malted milk—3 tablespoons
Marmalade and jelly—1 tablespoon
Marshmallows—5 marshmallows
Mayonnaise—1 tablespoon
Meat—cold sliced—⅛ inch slice
Meat—fat, size of ½ chop
Meat—lean, size of 1 chop
Milk—⅝ cup (regular)
Molasses—1½ tablespoons
Onions—3 to 4 medium
Oranges—1 large
Orange juice—1 cup
Peaches—3 medium fresh
Peanut butter—1 tablespoon
Pears—2 medium fresh
Peas—¾ cup canned
Pecans—12 meats
Pie—¼ ordinary serving
Pineapple—2 slices 1 inch thick
Plums—3 to 4 large
Popcorn—1½ cups
Potatoes—sweet, ½ medium
Potatoes—white, 1 medium
Potato salad—1 cup
Prunes—dried 4 medium
Radishes—3 dozen red button
Rhubarb—stewed and sweetened,
  ½ cup
Rice—cooked, ¾ cup
Rolls—1 medium
Rutabagas—1⅔ cups
Sauerkraut—2½ cups
Sherbet—4 tablespoons
Spinach—2½ cups
Squash—1 cup
Strawberries—1⅓ cups
Sugar—brown, 3 tablespoons
Sugar—white, 2 tablespoons
Tomatoes—canned, 2 cups
Tomatoes—fresh, 2 to 3 medium
Turnips—2 cups
Walnuts—8 to 16 meats
Watermelon—¾ slice 6 inches diameter

# BREADS AND ROLLS

## BANANA BREAD

1¾ c. flour, sifted
2¾ tsp. baking powder
½ tsp. salt
2 eggs

⅓ c. shortening
⅔ c. sugar
3 to 4 ripe bananas

Sift together flour, baking powder, and salt. Beat shortening in mixer bowl until creamy. Add sugar and eggs. Continue beating at medium speed 1 minute or 150 strokes by hand beater. Peel bananas and mash; add to egg mixture. Mix until blended. Do not overbeat. Scrape bowl and beater once or twice. Turn into greased loaf pan and bake in a moderate oven, 350°, about 1 hour and 10 minutes, or until bread is done.

Variations - To egg mixture, add either: 1 cup coarsely chopped nuts, 1 cup seedless raisins, or 1 cup finely chopped dates.

*Yellow, Red*

## LIGHT BANANA BREAD

1 c. sugar
½ c. butter or margarine
2 eggs
1 tsp. vanilla
1 c. bananas, mashed

¼ c. buttermilk
½ c. chopped nuts
1⅔ c. flour
1 tsp. baking soda
½ tsp. salt

Preheat oven to 350°. Grease 9x9 inch square pan or loaf pan. Combine sugar, butter, eggs, and vanilla in large mixer bowl; cream on high 1½ minutes. Add banana, buttermilk, and nuts. Add flour, baking soda, and salt, a little at a time. Beat on low speed ½ minute. Bake in square pan, takes about 30 to 35 minutes. Loaf pan takes 50 minutes to 1 hour to bake. Test with toothpick.

*Yoshiko Maeda*

2821-95

# THE NEW BANANA BREAD
## ("Light Banana Bread")

1½ c. flour
½ tsp. baking soda
½ tsp. cinnamon
¼ tsp. baking powder
¼ tsp. nutmeg
⅛ tsp. salt

Nonstick spray coating
2 egg whites
1 c. sugar
1 c. mashed banana
¼ c. oil
½ c. currants

Mix flour, baking soda, cinnamon, baking powder, nutmeg, and ⅛ teaspoon salt. Beat egg whites, sugar, and banana. Add oil and mix well. Stir flour mixture into banana mixture. Gently fold in currants. Spray an 8x4x2 inch loaf pan with nonstick spray and pour batter in pan. Bake at 350° for 55 to 60 minutes. Cool in pan for 10 minutes, then cool thoroughly on wire rack.

# QUICK BANANA BREAD

Sift into bowl:

1½ c. all-purpose flour
¾ c. sugar
1½ tsp. baking powder

¾ tsp. soda
½ tsp. salt

Add:

1 c. banana pulp
2 Tbsp. lemon juice

1 egg
4 Tbsp. salad oil

Barely mix. Don't beat. Pour into greased, floured loaf pan. Bake at 350° for 1 hour. Add nuts or cherries if desired.

*Green*

# BUTTER BREAD

2 c. + 3 c. flour, divided
¼ c. sugar
1 Tbsp. salt
2 Tbsp. yeast (or 2 env.)
½ c. water
1 tsp. sugar

1 (12 oz.) can evaporated milk
1 (4 oz.) block butter, melted
1 egg, beaten

Sift together 2 cups flour, sugar, and salt. Dissolve yeast in sugar-water mixture. Allow it to rise for 5 minutes. Add to the dry flour mixture. Mix milk, butter, and egg together. Add to flour mixture and mix to make a batter. Add 3 cups flour slowly to batter. Batter will become stiff dough.

Sprinkle a smooth surface with flour. On it, knead dough to smooth consistency for 10 minutes. Add gradually up to 1 cup of flour to reduce stickiness of dough.

Shape dough into ball. Place in oiled bowl. Cover with a cloth. Place in an oven with its light on. For 1 hour allow dough to rise and double.

Punch dough down. Knead. Shape into ball. Place on foiled cookie sheet. Let the dough rise for 5 minutes. Bake at 375° for 20 to 25 minutes.

To test for doneness, listen for a hallow-hollow sound as you tap the bottom. Cool on wire rack. When cooled, wrap tightly in plastic and place in Ziploc bag. Store in the refrigerator or freezer. Set outside for ½ hour before serving.

*Maysie Tam, Hanalima Club*

# CORN BREAD

2 blocks butter or margarine, melted
4 eggs, slightly beaten
2 c. milk
1 c. corn meal

4 c. Bisquick mix
1 tsp. baking powder
½ tsp. baking soda
1 c. sugar

Mix ingredients together. Bake in 9x13 inch greased pan at 325° for 35 to 40 minutes, or until done.

*Kimie Tanaka*

# CORN BREAD

1½ c. corn meal
½ c. flour
4 tsp. baking powder
½ tsp. salt

1 c. milk
1 egg, beaten
¼ c. melted fat or oil
¼ c. sugar (if desired)

Mix corn meal, flour, baking powder, and salt. Mix together milk and egg and add fat. Add milk mixture to corn meal mixture. Stir only enough to mix. Fill greased baking pan half full. Bake at 425°F. (hot oven) about 25 minutes, or until lightly browned. Makes 6 servings.

Corn Meal Muffins: Use recipe for corn bread. Fill greased muffin pans half full of corn meal mixture. Baking time will be 15 to 20 minutes. Makes 12 muffins.

# CORN CAKE

3 c. biscuit mix
1 block butter
½ tsp. baking soda
1½ c. milk

1½ c. sugar
1 block margarine
3 eggs
¼ c. corn meal

Mix biscuit mix, baking soda, and corn meal; set aside. Cream butter and margarine; add sugar. Add eggs whole, 1 at a time. Add dry ingredients alternately with milk. Bake 40 minutes at 350°.

*Green*

# GOOD SHEPHERD'S BREAD

Use 1 boule French bread or 1 round loaf bread.

Filling:

**1 clove garlic, minced**
**½ round Kula onion,**
   **chopped**
**1 (approx. 16 oz.) brick**
   **Monterey Jack cheese,**
   **grated**

**1 (approx. 16 oz.) brick**
   **Pepper Jack cheese,**
   **grated**
**2 c. mayonnaise**

Optional additions to filling:

**Bacon bits**
**Ham bits**
**Crabmeat, shrimp, etc.,**
   **cooked**

**Spices (tarragon,**
   **marjoram)**

Cover a cookie sheet with foil. Place the boule on the sheet. Slice the top of the boule to make a lid. Cut ½ inch border from the crust sides. To hollow out, gently pull up the inside circle of bread. Slice the inside circle of bread into ½ inch cubes. Place around the boule.

Mix the filling ingredients together and fill the hollowed bread. Replace the lid on the boule. Bake at 325° for 25 to 30 minutes. Serve hot.

Fresh vegetable sticks can also be served like the bread cubes as edible dippers.

*Maysie Tam, Hanalima Club*

# MANGO BREAD

3 sticks butter or margarine
2½ c. sugar
6 eggs
2 tsp. vanilla extract
½ tsp. coconut extract
4 c. sifted all-purpose flour

1 tsp. salt
4 tsp. baking soda
3 tsp. cinnamon
4 c. diced mango
1 c. chopped nuts
  (optional)

Cream butter; add sugar gradually and beat until fluffy. Add eggs, 1 at a time, and beat well. Add flavoring. Sift dry ingredients and mix into egg mixture alternately with the mango. Add nuts. Bake in 5 medium pans for 40 to 45 minutes or in 4 large loaf pans for about an hour at 350°.

*Blue*

# ZUCCHINI BREAD WITH WHEAT GERM

3 eggs
1 c. salad oil
1 c. granulated sugar
1 c. firmly packed brown
  sugar
1 Tbsp. maple flavoring
2 c. coarsely shredded
  zucchini (about 4
  medium size)

1 c. finely chopped walnuts
2½ c. all-purpose flour
½ c. toasted wheat germ
2 tsp. soda
2 tsp. salt
½ tsp. baking powder
¼ c. sesame seeds

With rotary mixer, beat the eggs to blend; add the oil, sugar, and maple flavoring and continue beating until mixture is thick and foamy. Using a spoon, stir in the shredded zucchini and walnuts. Combine the flour, wheat germ, soda, salt, and baking powder. Stir gently into zucchini mixture just until blended.

Divide the batter equally between 2 greased and flour dusted 5x9 inch or 3 (3x7 inch) loaf pans. Sprinkle the sesame seeds evenly over tops of each. Bake in a 350° oven for 1 hour or until done. Cool in pan 10 minutes. Turn out on wire racks to cool thoroughly. Makes 2 or 3 loaves.

*Mabel Ito*

# BISCUITS

3 c. flour
½ c. sugar
3 eggs
4 tsp. baking powder

Dash of salt
5 Tbsp. shortening
½ to 1 c. milk

Sift together all dry ingredients. Add to dry mixture the shortening and mix well, then add eggs and milk. Roll on floured board and cut. Bake at 400° for 10 to 12 minutes.

*Yellow*

# BUTTER BISCUITS

Sift:

3 c. flour
⅛ tsp. salt

6 Tbsp. sugar
2 Tbsp. baking powder

Cut into dry ingredients ½ cup butter to pea size.

Add:

1 c. milk

2 eggs

Mix. Melt ½ cup butter in a 9x13 inch pan. Drop dough by tablespoons to make 12 biscuits. Bake for 15 minutes in 450° oven.

# TARO BISCUITS

1 c. mashed cooked taro
1½ c. flour
3 tsp. baking powder
2 tsp. sugar

¼ c. shortening
½ tsp. salt
¼ c. milk
1 egg, beaten

Combine taro and shortening and mix until well blended. Sift dry ingredients together and add to preceding mixture. Add the beaten egg and milk and mix thoroughly.

On a slightly floured surface, place dough and pat it with finger to about ½ inch thickness. Cut with biscuit cutter and place on slightly greased pan. Bake at 350° for 15 to 20 minutes.

# ANDAGI

Also called Sugar Tempura and Okinawan Doughnut.

3 eggs, slightly beaten
1 c. milk
3 c. flour
1 tsp. salt
3½ tsp. baking powder

1 c. sugar
3 Tbsp. goma (sesame
   seeds, roasted,
   optional)
Oil (for deep-fat frying)

Beat eggs and milk together. Sift flour, salt, and baking powder together. Add sugar and goma and mix well. Fold into beaten egg and milk mixture. Let dough rest 10 to 15 minutes. While dough is resting, heat deep oil to 360°. Fill oiled ice cream scoop ½ full of dough and release into hot oil. These doughnuts will turn all by themselves. Fry until golden brown. Makes 2 dozen doughnuts.

*Thelma Oshiro*

# BREADFRUIT FRITTERS

1 c. breadfruit (uncooked),
   pulp or grated
   (depending on
   ripeness of fruit)
1⅓ c. flour (unsifted)

3 tsp. baking powder
1 tsp. salt
2 eggs, well beaten
⅔ c. milk

Pour flour into sifter with baking powder and salt. Add to breadfruit and mix thoroughly. Beat eggs until light and fluffy and add milk. Combine with flour and breadfruit mixture. Drop from tablespoon or teaspoon into deep, hot fat, 365° to 375°, 2 to 5 minutes. Drain on absorbent paper. Dust with powdered sugar or serve with honey or maple syrup.

May be served as part of main course, or when sweetened, as a dessert. Serves 4 to 6.

# BREADFRUIT SPICED DROP DONUTS

1 c. ripe breadfruit pulp
(uncooked)
1 egg, beaten
2 Tbsp. shortening
1 c. flour (unsifted)

¼ tsp. nutmeg
½ tsp. cinnamon
½ tsp. salt
1 Tbsp. sugar
3 tsp. baking powder

Combine beaten egg, breadfruit pulp, and shortening. Mix well either by hand beater or electric beater. Sift flour, sugar, baking powder, salt, and spices. Stir into egg mixture. When thoroughly mixed, drop by spoonfuls into hot, deep fat, 360°F., and fry until brown. Drain on absorbent paper; dust with confectioners sugar or granulated sugar. Makes 18 to 20 donuts.

# JAPANESE DOUGHNUT
## (Sato Dango)

3 c. flour
1 c. sugar
4½ tsp. baking powder

½ tsp. salt
3 eggs, slightly beaten
1 c. milk

Sift dry ingredients together. Combine eggs and milk; add to dry ingredients. Mix thoroughly. Drop by teaspoonfuls into oil heated to 375°F. Cook about 2 minutes, or until golden brown. Drain on paper towel and roll in sugar if desired. Yield: 2½ to 3 dozen doughnuts.

# MALASSADAS
## (Portuguese Doughnuts)

1 pkg. active dry yeast
1 Tbsp. sugar
⅓ c. warm water
8 c. flour
½ c. sugar
1 tsp. salt

2 c. milk, scalded
½ c. butter or margarine, melted
8 eggs, beaten
Deep fat (for frying)

Dissolve yeast and the 1 tablespoon sugar in water. Let rise until doubled. In a large mixing bowl, combine flour, sugar, and salt; make a well in the center. Add milk, butter, eggs, and yeast mixture. Beat thoroughly to form a soft smooth dough. Cover and let rise until doubled. Heat deep fat to 375°F. Spoon teaspoonfuls of dough into fat and fry until browned. Drain on absorbent paper; shake in a bag with sugar and serve hot. Makes 5 dozen.

# MALASADAS

1 pkg. active dry yeast
1 tsp. sugar
¼ c. warm water
6 eggs
6 c. flour
½ c. sugar

¼ c. butter, melted
¼ tsp. nutmeg
1 c. evaporated milk
1 c. water
1 tsp. salt
Deep fat (for frying)

Dissolve yeast and the 1 teaspoon sugar in warm water. Beat eggs until thick. Measure flour into a large bowl. Make a well in center. Add yeast, eggs, and remaining ingredients; beat thoroughly to form a soft smooth dough.

Cover and let rise until doubled. With a circular motion following the outer edge of bowl, turn dough and let rise until doubled. Heat deep oil to 375°. Spoon teaspoonfuls of dough carefully from bowl to keep risen dough from falling. Drop into fat and fry till brown. Drain on absorbent paper. Shake in bag with granulated sugar and serve hot. Makes about 7 dozen.

*Leo Asuncion*

# POTATO CAKE DOUGHNUTS

1 c. sugar
2 Tbsp. vegetable oil
2 eggs
1 tsp. vanilla
1 c. buttermilk or sour milk
1 tsp. salt

2 tsp. baking powder
1 tsp. nutmeg or cinnamon
1½ c. potato flakes
4 c. flour
1 tsp. baking soda

Mix sugar, vegetable oil, and eggs; beat for 1 minute. Add vanilla and milk; mix. Add flour, potato flakes, baking soda, baking powder, salt, and cinnamon (or nutmeg); blend together and roll on floured board until ⅓ inch thick. Cut with doughnut cutter and fry in hot oil on both sides until brown. Leave plain or while doughnuts are still warm, roll in sugar or powdered sugar.

*Doris Mori*

# FILIPINO PANCAKES

Sift:

2 c. flour
¾ c. sugar

2 tsp. baking powder

Add:

2 eggs

1 c. milk

Batter will be thick. Fry in ¼ inch oil on medium heat. Yield: 16 (4 inch) pancakes.

# BRAN MUFFINS

2 c. Nabisco Bran
2 c. boiling water
1 c. shortening
1½ c. brown sugar
1½ c. white sugar
4 eggs, beaten

1 qt. buttermilk
4 c. Kellogg's All-Bran
5 c. flour
5 tsp. baking soda
1 tsp. salt
½ lb. raisins

Pour boiling water over Nabisco Bran and let stand. Cream shortening, sugar, and eggs. Add buttermilk and Kellogg's Bran. Let stand. Sift flour, soda, and salt. Add buttermilk mixture and then fold in Nabisco Bran and raisins.

Keep in refrigerator overnight before using. Bake at 400° for about 15 minutes. Batter keeps in refrigerator in a covered bowl for about 6 weeks. Makes dozens.

# MAPLE BRAN MUFFINS

1⅔ c. buttermilk or sour
    milk*
2⅔ c. whole bran cereal
½ c. whole wheat flour or
    all-purpose flour
½ c. all-purpose flour
1¾ tsp. baking powder
¼ tsp. baking soda
⅓ c. margarine or butter

⅓ c. packed brown sugar
2 eggs
¼ c. maple syrup or maple
    flavored syrup
¾ c. mixed dried fruit bits
    or light raisins
Maple syrup or maple
    flavored syrup
    (optional)

In a medium mixing bowl, pour buttermilk or sour milk over the bran cereal; let stand for 5 to 10 minutes or till cereal is softened. In a small mixing bowl, stir together the flours, baking powder, and baking soda; set aside. In a large mixing bowl, beat margarine or butter and sugar for 30 seconds or till fluffy. Add eggs, 1 at a time, and the ¼ cup maple syrup; beat till combined. Add the cereal mixture and flour mixture, stirring just till combined. Stir in dried fruit. Spoon batter into 6 greased 3½ inch muffin cups. (Cups will be almost full.) Bake muffins in a 350° oven for 30 minutes or till tops are golden and centers are firm to the touch. Remove from pan; brush lightly with maple syrup if desired. Serve warm. Makes 6 large muffins.

The batter can be poured into 18 (2½ inch) greased muffin cups and baked for 22 to 25 minutes or till done.

* Note: To make sour milk, combine 5 teaspoons lemon juice or vinegar with enough milk to equal 1⅔ cups. Let stand for 5 minutes before using.

# OAT BRAN MUFFINS

4 c. oat bran cereal flakes
¼ c. brown sugar
½ c. raisins
2 c. skim milk
3 egg whites

3 Tbsp. salad oil
2 c. flour
2 Tbsp. baking powder
½ tsp. salt
Dash of cinnamon

Preheat oven to 375°F. Grease 12 muffin pans. In a large mixing bowl, combine cereal, sugar, raisins, and milk. Add egg and oil; beat well. Sift flour with baking powder, salt, and cinnamon. Add to bran mixture, stirring only until mixture is moistened. Spoon batter into prepared pans. Bake for 25 to 30 minutes or until golden brown. Makes 12 muffins.

# ONO BANANA MUFFINS

1½ c. sugar
¾ c. oil
4 eggs
2½ c. flour
½ tsp. baking powder

2 tsp. baking soda
1 pkg. instant vanilla
    pudding mix
3 c. bananas, mashed
1 c. chopped walnuts

Mix together oil, sugar, and eggs. Sift in flour, baking powder, baking soda, and pudding mix. Blend in banana and walnuts. Fill paper lined muffin pan ⅔ full. Bake at 375° for 15 to 20 minutes.

# PINEAPPLE BRAN MUFFINS

1 egg
2 Tbsp. melted shortening
¾ c. crushed pineapple
1¼ c. enriched flour
6 Tbsp. sugar

1½ tsp. baking powder
¼ tsp. soda
¾ tsp. salt
½ c. bran flakes
⅓ c. chopped walnuts

Beat the egg; add the melted shortening and undrained pineapple. Sift together the flour, sugar, baking powder, soda, and salt; stir into the pineapple mixture. Add the bran flakes and nuts. Pour into well oiled muffin pans and bake at 375° for 30 minutes. Yield: 12 muffins.

# JELLIES, JAMS

# & PRESERVES

# APPLE VARIETIES

| NAME | SEASON | COLOR | FLAVOR/ TEXTURE | EATING | PIE |
|------|--------|-------|-----------------|--------|-----|
| Astrachan | July-Aug | Yellow/ Greenish Red | Sweet | Good | Good |
| Baldwin | Oct-Jan | Red/ Yellowish | Mellow | Fair | Fair |
| Cortland | Oct-Jan | Green/Purple | Mild, tender | Excel. | Excel. |
| Delicious, Red | Sept-June | Scarlet | Sweet, crunchy | Excel. | Good |
| Delicious, Golden | Sept-May | Yellow | Sweet, semifirm | Excel. | Excel. |
| Empire | Sept-Nov | Red | Sweet, crisp | Excel. | Good |
| Fameuse | Sept-Nov | Red | Mild, crisp | Excel. | Fair |
| Granny Smith | Apr-Jul | Green | Tart, crisp | V. Good | V. Good |
| Gravenstein | July-Sept | Green w/red stripes | Tart, crisp | Good | Good |
| Ida Red | Oct | Red | Rich | Good | Good |
| Jonathan | Sept-Jan | Brilliant red | Tart, tender, crisp | V. Good | V. Good |
| Macoun | Oct-Nov | Dark red | Tart, juicy, crisp | Excel. | Good |
| McIntosh | Sept-June | Green to red | Slightly tart, tender, juicy | Excel. | Excel. |
| Newtown Pippin | Sept-June | Green to red | Slightly tart, firm | V. Good | Excel. |
| Northern Spy | Oct | Red | Crisp, tart | V. Good | V. Good |
| Rhode Island Greening | Sept-Nov | Green | Very tart, firm | Poor | Excel. |
| Rome Beauty | Oct-June | Red | Tart, firm, slightly dry | Good | V. Good |
| Stayman- Winesap | Oct-Mar | Red | Semifirm, sweet, spicy | V. Good | Good |
| Winesap | Oct-June | Red | Slightly tart, firm, spicy | Excel. | Good |
| Yellow Transparent | July-Aug | Yellow | Tart, soft | Poor | Excel. |

# JELLIES, JAMS AND PRESERVES

## BANANA BUTTER

4 hands ripe bananas
1 c. cranberry or orange
   juice

2½ c. sugar
5 Tbsp. white vinegar
1½ tsp. ground cardamom

1. Mash bananas and add juice. Bring to boil; reduce heat and cook for about 30 minutes.

2. Remove from heat and process in food processor until smooth.

3. Return banana puree to pot and add remaining ingredients. Cook on low heat until of desired thickness. Keep lid on pot, partially ajar, to prevent spattering. Stir frequently.

4. Remove from heat and pack into jars. Process as for jam or jelly. Makes 4 to 6 half pints.

*Marlene Curtis*

## LILIKOI BUTTER

½ c. lilikoi juice
4 c. sugar

4 eggs, beaten
1 stick butter

Melt butter over medium heat. In a large bowl, measure 4 cups sugar; add beaten eggs. Mix well. Add lilikoi juice slowly, stirring constantly. Add mixture to melted butter, stirring constantly. Bring to a full boil (still at medium heat so that eggs don't coddle). Cook for 5 to 10 minutes for desired consistency. Strain out any congealed eggs. Pour into clean containers (six 4 ounce baby food jars). Keep refrigerated. Perfect on toast, biscuit, or muffin.

Note: Can substitute 4 lemons to make lemon butter, or use other fruit juices. If fruits tend to be sweet, lessen amount of sugar to taste. For instance, guava may require less than 3 cups sugar.

# MULBERRY JAM

4 c. (2 lb.) prepared fruit          1 bottle liquid pectin
2 Tbsp. lemon juice
7½ c. (3¼ lb.) granulated
    sugar

    To prepare the fruit: Pull out stems; crush thoroughly about 2 quarts fully ripe mulberries. Measure 4 cups into a very large saucepan. Squeeze the juice from 1 medium size lemon. Measure 2 tablespoons lemon juice into saucepan.

    To make the jam: Add sugar to fruit in saucepan and mix well. Place over high heat; bring to a full rolling boil and boil hard 2 minutes, stirring constantly. Remove from heat and at once stir in pectin, then stir and skim by turns for 5 minutes to cool slightly, to prevent floating fruit. Ladle quickly into sterilized jars. Paraffin at once. Makes about 11 (6 ounce) glasses of jam.

*Ludvina Abrew, Red*

# PINEAPPLE AND PAPAYA JAM

4 c. pineapple, chopped          8 c. sugar
6 c. papaya, chopped             1 pkg. Sure-Jell
½ c. lemon juice

    Mix fruits; add lemon juice, sugar, and Sure-Jell. Cook 3 minutes to rolling boil. Remove from heat and pour in sterilized jars. Process as for jam and jelly.

*Irene Brittain*

# PINEAPPLE-PAPAYA-GINGER CONSERVE

2 c. shredded fresh
   pineapple (firm ripe)
2 c. diced fresh papaya
   (firm ripe)

4 c. sugar
4 tsp. grated fresh ginger
   root

Peel pineapple; shred by running a fork from top to bottom of fruit. Discard core. If you leave top on, it will serve as a hand grip for the shredding process. Peel papaya and dice. Peel and grate fresh ginger. Measure equal amounts of each fruit. Add sugar (use 1 cup sugar per each cup of fruit) and grated ginger (about 1 teaspoon per each cup of fruit). Cook briskly in a large kettle until mixture boils, then reduce heat, and stir frequently until thick. Pour into hot, sterilized jars and cover with paraffin. Yield: 4 (6 ounce) glasses.

Good to serve on vanilla ice cream, thin hot toast, or hot biscuits.

*Ludvina Abrew*

# MANGO CHUTNEY

2 c. vinegar
5½ c. sugar
10 c. green mango slices
1 tsp. salt
½ c. chopped green ginger
   root
1 clove garlic, chopped fine

4 red peppers (chili), seeds
   removed
3 c. seedless raisins
1 large onion, sliced
¼ c. fresh orange peel
⅔ c. blanched chopped
   almonds

Boil vinegar and sugar about 5 minutes. Add sliced mangoes and other ingredients. Mix all ingredients and boil slowly, stirring frequently until thick (about ½ hour). Place in sterilized jars and seal tightly. Yield: 4 quarts.

*Yellow*

# RIPE MANGO CHUTNEY

6 c. firm ripe slices of
   mango
2½ c. sugar
1 c. + 2 Tbsp. vinegar
1 small onion, minced
1 clove garlic, minced
2 fresh chili peppers,
   seeded and minced
¼ c. preserved ginger,
   minced

1 c. seedless raisins
1 c. almonds, blanched and
   sliced
2 Tbsp. ginger, finely
   minced
2 c. orange rind, sliced (2
   medium oranges)
¼ c. lemon rind, sliced

Boil sugar and vinegar for 10 minutes. Add other ingredients and add mango last. Cook on low flame for about 1 hour or until mango is tender. Pour into sterilized jars and seal with paraffin or cap.

*Eunice Arakawa*

# HOME CANNING

10 Easy Steps in Canning:

1. Collect, test, and get ready equipment, jars, lids, and other supplies needed.

2. Gather products; sort and cool. Work fast and can promptly.

3. Sterilize jars and bottles. Keep them in the sterilizer until ready to fill.

4. Wash and prepare product.

5. Precook.

6. Pack quickly into hot jars. Wipe sealing edge and adjust lid.

7. Process for the time recommended.

8. Remove from cooker and let cool in a place where no draft will strike jars. Do not touch lids unless they are of the type needing tightening. You may break the seal if you try tightening metal flat tops.

9. The next day, check the seal by inverting jars and watching for leaks, then label and store. Use food immediately if jar is leaking.

10. Check within the first week and then again once a month to see if any jar is not sealed.

# SELECT THE RIGHT METHOD OF CANNING
## FOR EACH FOOD

1. *Pressure-cooker canning.* For corn, peas, beans, and other common vegetables (except tomatoes) - use a steam pressure canner. They require a temperature higher than boiling to process these foods safely in a reasonable time. It takes 240° or higher. The only way to get these high temperatures is to hold steam under pressure.

2. *Water-bath canning.* Fruits can be successfully canned by this method. There is less waste of food and food values when fruit is canned in this way than when the open kettle method is used. The fruits more nearly keep the original flavor and color, too. When fruit is canned by this method, it is usually partly cooked to shrink the product. It is then packed into jars, and cooking is completed in the water bath.

3. *Open-kettle canning.* Use this method for preserves, jams, jellies, pickles, and other foods with enough sugar or vinegar to help keep them from spoiling. In emergencies, when equipment for water-bath canning is not available, the open kettle method is used for fruits to avoid complete waste of the surplus. When canned this way, food is cooked in an ordinary kettle, then packed into hot sterilized jars and sealed. To sterilize a jar; cover with water and boil for 20 minutes.

# PROCESSING

Using a water-bath canner: Have water in the canner hot. Put jars into canner as soon as packed. Add boiling water, if needed, to bring water level over jar tops at least an inch. Put lid on canner. Count time as soon as water comes to a rolling boil. Keep boiling steadily for as long as the time table directs for the food you are canning. Add boiling water, if needed, to keep the jar tops covered.

Using a pressure canner: Follow the manufacturer's directions for your canner. Here are general pointers: Before you put in jars, have enough boiling water in canner so it won't boil dry and be damaged. The water should not come up over the jars. Place hot, filled jars on rack. Don't let them touch or tip over. Steam must flow around and over each jar. Fasten the canner cover securely so that no steam escapes, except at the open pet cock. Watch until steam pours steadily from pet cock or weighted-gage opening. Let it pour 10 minutes or more so all air is driven from canner, leaving only steam inside, then close the pet cock or put on the weighted gage and let pressure rise to number of pounds desired. Begin counting time. Hold at constant pressure for time required, then remove from heat and allow pressure to return to zero before lifting gage or opening pet cock.

2821-95

# CANNING FRUITS
## (Table of Sirups for Fruits)

Thin sirup: Use 1 cup sugar to 4 cups fruit juice or water.

Moderately thin sirup: Use 1 cup sugar to 3 cups fruit juice or water.

Medium sirup: Use 1 cup sugar to 2 cups fruit juice or water.

Allow approximately ¾ to 1 cup sirup per quart jar of fruit.

Following is kind, how to prepare, and time table for hot water bath:

Mangoes - Wash, peel, and halve or slice. Precook ripe mangoes for 5 minutes and half ripe ones 10 minutes in a medium syrup. Pack; fill with the syrup to within ½ inch of top and remove air bubbles. Wipe, sealing edge, and adjust lid. Process for 15 to 20 minutes.

Pineapple - Wash, slice, and peel. Cut into long or small wedges as desired. Precook for 2 to 4 minutes in medium syrup. Pack into clean hot jars and add syrup to within ½ inch of top. Remove air bubbles and adjust lid. Process for 15 minutes.

Tomatoes - Choose fully ripe, firm tomatoes. Scald and remove stem ends. Peel and quarter. Bring to rolling boil. Stir just enough to heat all portions. Pack hot; add 1 teaspoon salt to each quart. Fill to within ½ inch of top. Wipe sealing edge and adjust lid. Process for 10 minutes.

Bamboo shoots - Select bamboo sprouts when they are young and tender. Wash and cut into desired pieces. Precook in water, covering all pieces. Drain; cover with cold water and leave to soak overnight. Fill jars and add hot water to within ½ inch of top. Remove air bubbles; wipe, sealing edge, and adjust lid. Process pints (10 pounds) for 45 minutes, or quarts (10 pounds) for 50 minutes.

# CANNED TUNA

Use 18 pounds tuna for 7 flat 1 pint jars.

Bone and clean; cut up to 3 inch thickness. Steam until cooked and cool. Sterilize jars. Pack jars with tuna, leaving ½ inch at top.

Add:

**½ tsp. salt**                    **2 Tbsp. salad oil**

Swish lids in boiling water. Cover tight and twist back about ¼ circle. Place 7 jars in 16 quart pressure cooker and cook for 1½ hours at 15 pounds pressure.

# Notes

# SOUPS, SALADS

## & VEGETABLES

# A HANDY SPICE AND HERB GUIDE

**ALLSPICE-**a pea-sized fruit that grows in Mexico, Jamaica, Central and South America. Its delicate flavor resembles a blend of cloves, cinnamon, and nutmeg. USES: (Whole) Pickles, meats, boiled fish, gravies; (Ground) Puddings, relishes, fruit preserves, baking.

**BASIL-**the dried leaves and stems of an herb grown in the United States and North Mediterranean area. Has an aromatic, leafy flavor. USES: For flavoring tomato dishes and tomato paste, turtle soup; also use in cooked peas, squash, snap beans; sprinkle chopped over lamb chops and poultry.

**BAY LEAVES-**the dried leaves of an evergreen grown in the eastern Mediterranean countries. Has a sweet, herbaceous floral spice note. USES: For pickling, stews, for spicing sauces and soup. Also use with a variety of meats and fish.

**CARAWAY-**the seed of a plant grown in the Netherlands. Flavor that combines the tastes of anise and dill. USES: For the cordial Kummel, baking breads; often added to sauerkraut, noodles, cheese spreads. Also adds zest to French fried potatoes, liver, canned asparagus.

**CURRY POWDER-**a ground blend of ginger, turmeric, fenugreek seed, as many as 16 to 20 spices. USES: For all Indian curry recipes such as lamb, chicken, and rice, eggs, vegetables, and curry puffs.

**DILL-**the small, dark seed of the dill plant grown in India, having a clean, aromatic taste. USES: Dill is a predominant seasoning in pickling recipes; also adds pleasing flavor to sauerkraut, potato salad, cooked macaroni, and green apple pie.

**MACE-**the dried covering around the nutmeg seed. Its flavor is similar to nutmeg, but with a fragrant, delicate difference. USES: (Whole) For pickling, fish, fish sauce, stewed fruit. (Ground) Delicious in baked goods, pastries, and doughnuts, adds unusual flavor to chocolate desserts.

**MARJORAM-**an herb of the mint family, grown in France and Chile. Has a minty-sweet flavor. USES: In beverages, jellies, and to flavor soups, stews, fish, sauces. Also excellent to sprinkle on lamb while roasting.

**MSG (MONOSODIUM GLUTAMATE)-**a vegetable protein derivative for raising the effectiveness of natural food flavors. USES: Small amounts, adjusted to individual taste, can be added to steaks, roasts, chops, seafoods, stews, soups, chowder, chop suey, and cooked vegetables.

**OREGANO-**a plant of the mint family and a species of marjoram of which the dried leaves are used to make an herb seasoning. USES: An excellent flavoring for any tomato dish, especially pizza, chili con carne, and Italian specialties.

**PAPRIKA-**a mild, sweet red pepper growing in Spain, Central Europe, and the United States. Slightly aromatic and prized for brilliant red color. USES: A colorful garnish for pale foods, and for seasoning Chicken Paprika, Hungarian Goulash, salad dressings.

**POPPY-**the seed of a flower grown in Holland. Has a rich fragrance and crunchy, nut-like flavor. USES: Excellent as a topping for breads, rolls, and cookies. Also delicious in buttered noodles.

**ROSEMARY-**an herb (like a curved pine needle) grown in France, Spain, and Portugal, and having a sweet fresh taste. USES: In lamb dishes, in soups, stews, and to sprinkle on beef before roasting.

**SAGE-**the leaf of a shrub grown in Greece, Yugoslavia, and Albania. Flavor is camphoraceous and minty. USES: For meat and poultry stuffing, sausages, meat loaf, hamburgers, stews, and salads.

**THYME-**the leaves and stems of a shrub grown in France and Spain. Has a strong, distinctive flavor. USES: For poultry seasoning, croquettes, fricassees, and fish dishes. Also tasty on fresh sliced tomatoes.

**TURMERIC-**a root of the ginger family, grown in India, Haiti, Jamaica, and Peru, having a mild, ginger-pepper flavor. USES: As a flavoring and coloring in prepared mustard and in combination with mustard as a flavoring for meats, dressings, salads.

# SOUPS, SALADS AND VEGETABLES

## BREADFRUIT CHOWDER

1 green breadfruit
5 slices bacon, chopped
1 large onion, chopped
2 c. water
3½ c. milk

1 (12 oz.) can corn Niblets
1 tsp. salt
Dash of pepper
Chopped parsley

Pare breadfruit; cut into lengthwise quarters. Remove core and dice. In a large Dutch oven, fry bacon until crisp. Add onion and saute lightly. Add breadfruit and water and cook until breadfruit is tender. Stir in milk and corn. Heat thoroughly. Season with salt and pepper. Serve with chopped parsley. Makes 6 servings.

## BREADFRUIT CHOWDER

2 thin strips bacon
⅓ c. sliced onion
2 c. diced raw green
　　breadfruit

½ c. diced raw carrots
2 tsp. salt
3 c. boiling water
1⅓ c. milk

Cut bacon into small pieces and fry until light brown. Add onion and cook until light brown. Add vegetables, salt, and water. Boil until vegetables are tender. Add milk and serve hot. Yield: 6 servings.

# CHICKEN SOUP

1 lb. chicken, cut into pieces
1 clove garlic, finely minced
2 large onions, cut into small pieces
2 medium size potatoes, cut into small pieces
2 tomatoes, cut into small pieces
2 carrots, cut into small pieces
2 stalks local green celery, coarsely chopped

Tie up in a small piece of muslin:

10 peppercorns
2 cloves
1 small piece cinnamon (size of green pea)
1 piece nutmeg (size of green pea)

Remaining ingredients:

2 dessert spoons vegetable oil (or 1 spoon oil and 1 spoon butter)
Salt to taste
2 dessert spoons finely sliced onion, fried golden brown (for garnishing)

Heat oil in deep pan. Brown garlic; add chicken and fry for 3 minutes. Add 3½ cups water, bag of spices, and salt and boil till chicken is tender, then add all other ingredients, adding more water, if necessary, and simmer till vegetables are cooked.

Serve in large dish or in individual cups, garnishing top with fried onions.

Note:

1. Substitute for vegetables 20 medium size dried mushrooms, previously soaked in boiling water and from which stalks have been removed, whole or cut into quarters.

2. If vegetables are used, you can substitute beef for chicken.

*Lynn Nakamura Tengan*

# CHINESE MOCK BIRD'S NEST SOUP

1 bundle long rice
4 dried mushrooms
6 c. canned chicken broth
⅛ tsp. MSG
1 tsp. salt
1 c. ground pork
½ c. ground ham

½ c. chopped water
  chestnuts
2 egg whites, slightly
  beaten
Chopped Chinese parsley
  or green onions

Soak long rice bundle in hot water for 30 minutes; chop in ¼ inch lengths. Soak mushrooms in warm water until soft; wash thoroughly and remove stems. Chop mushroom caps fine. To the broth, add mushrooms, seasonings, meat, and water chestnuts; simmer for 30 minutes. Add long rice and simmer 5 minutes more. Remove from heat and stir in egg whites. Serve hot with chopped parsley or onion sprinkled on top. Yield: 12 servings.

*Blue*

# CHINESE RICE SOUP
## (Chuk)

Left over turkey bones
6 qt. water
1 chung choi (preserved
  turnip)
2 c. rice, washed and
  drained
2 stalks celery, cut in
  halves

1 (13¼ oz.) can clear
  chicken broth
2½ tsp. salt
1 tsp. ajinomoto
2 stalks green onion,
  chopped
1 lettuce, shredded

In a large pot, add turkey bones, chung choi, celery, and water. Cook for 1 hour. Remove bones, chung choi, and celery. Debone meat. Strain stock and return to pot. Add rice, salt, and meat and cook for 1½ hours. Add chicken broth and cook for another ½ hour. Add green onion and ajinomoto and stir. Turn heat off. Serve garnished with lettuce. Serves 8 to 10.

*Janet Yayoshi*

# CLAM AND CORN CHOWDER

1 medium round onion, chopped
½ c. chopped celery
2 Tbsp. margarine
¼ c. all-purpose flour
1 tsp. dried dill weed
1 (6½ oz.) can chopped clams
½ tsp. Worcestershire sauce
¼ tsp. salt
3½ c. milk
1 can whole kernel corn

In a 3 quart saucepan, cook onion and celery in the margarine over medium heat. Stir in flour, dill weed, Worcestershire sauce, and salt. Add milk and stir over medium heat until thickened. Stir in the corn and clams until heated through. Serve with crackers.

*T. Oki*

# FISH CHOWDER

1 lb. semi-thawed minced fish
2 Tbsp. oil or shortening
½ c. chopped onion
2 c. water
2 c. diced raw potatoes
1½ tsp. salt
3 Tbsp. flour
3 c. milk
1 Tbsp. minced parsley

Cook onion in oil until lightly browned. Add fish and cook, stirring frequently, until color has changed. Add water, potatoes, and salt. Cover and simmer until potatoes are tender. Stir about ½ cup of the milk into the flour; add to the fish mixture. Bring to a boil and simmer 1 to 2 minutes. Add remaining milk and heat to boiling. Sprinkle parsley on the bowls of soup before serving. Makes 6 to 8 servings.

# IMITATION CHINESE BIRD NEST SOUP

1 bundle long rice (bean
   thread)
1½ tsp. salt
¼ tsp. ve-tsin
   (monosodium
   glutamate)
5 c. soup stock or water

2 eggs, well beaten
½ c. pork
½ c. ham
1 c. bamboo shoots
½ c. mushrooms
½ c. green onion

Soak long rice in boiling water for ½ to 1 hour. Drain and cut into very small pieces. Chop pork, ham, bamboo shoots, and mushrooms. Add all of the ingredients (except eggs and onion) to stock and simmer for 15 to 20 minutes.

Just before serving, add beaten eggs and green onion. Yields 6 to 8 (¾ cup) servings.

# GRACE'S PORTUGUESE SOUP
## (Pressure Cooker Method)

1 c. kidney beans
4 c. water
1 ham bone or hock
1 small soup bone
1 onion, chopped
2 carrots, sliced
2 stalks celery, chopped
1 salad potato (optional)
1 small cabbage
1 clove garlic
⅛ c. green pepper, minced

½ c. tomato puree
2 peppercorns
1 clove
Minced parsley
⅛ tsp. mustard
1 bay leaf
4 to 8 oz. hot Portuguese
   sausage, sliced in ½
   inch pieces
Salt and pepper to taste

Wash beans; cover with water and soak overnight. Drain. Place all ingredients in pressure cooker; cover and cook 30 minutes with steam at "cook."

If you don't use a pressure cooker, cook all ingredients in a heavy pot over low-medium heat for at least 6 hours. Add water as needed.

*Blue*

# MOCK PORTUGUESE SOUP

1 linguesa
1 (10¾ oz.) can minestrone
   soup

1 (15½ oz.) can kidney
   beans
1 can water

Slice, then fry sausage (linguesa). Add soup and beans and cook all together. Add water also. May add 1 can tomatoes, (14½ ounces), some spaghetti noodles, or chopped cabbage.

*Jean Okada*

# PHO (VIETNAMESE BEEF NOODLE SOUP)

Broth:

5 c. beef stock
1 inch fresh ginger
3 star anise

2 green onions
3 Tbsp. fish sauce

Soup:

8 oz. rice sticks or
    cellophane noodles
1 onion
12 basil leaves

6 to 8 oz. beef tenderloin or
    sirloin, partially
    frozen

Garnish:

2 c. fresh mung-bean
    sprouts
8 sprigs fresh basil (Thai)
2 jalapeno or serrano
    chilies, thinly sliced

1 lime, quartered
Hoisin sauce
Hot chili sauce

Combine the beef stock, ginger, star anise, green onions, and fish sauce and gently simmer for 30 minutes. Remove the ginger, anise, and green onions. Soak the rice sticks in warm water for 30 minutes.

Slice the green onions, onion, and basil leaves as thinly as possible. Slice the beef as thinly as possible across the grain. (Meat can be sliced using a meat slicer. It helps to partially freeze the meat before slicing.)

Bring 4 quarts water to a boil. Arrange the sprouts, mint sprigs, chilies, and lime on a platter.

Just before serving, bring the broth to a boil. Cook the rice sticks in boiling water for 30 seconds, then drain. Divide the noodles among 4 large bowls. Arrange the scallions, onion slices, and beef slices on top. Spoon the boiling broth on top; the heat of the liquid should be sufficient to cook the meat.

Serve the soup at once, with the garnish platter on the side. Let each person add sprouts, mint, chilies, lime, and hoisin and/ or chili sauce to taste. Makes 4 servings.

*Lynn Nakamura Tengan*

# PORTUGUESE COMFORT SOUP

1 can Spam, cubed
2 Tbsp. olive oil
2 cloves garlic
½ c. Madeira wine
1 Maui onion, diced
6 potatoes, peeled and
    quartered
2 Tbsp. butter

1 c. milk
1 bunch kale or Swiss
    chard
Dash of pepper (¼ tsp.)
Dash of cayenne pepper (¼
    tsp.)
Dash of nutmeg (¼ tsp.)
Salt to taste

Cover potatoes in salted water; boil until tender. Add butter and milk to water and mash. In soup pot on medium high heat, add olive oil, Spam, garlic, onion, pepper, cayenne, nutmeg, and ¼ cup Madeira. Cook until Spam browns, about 15 minutes.

Deglaze soup pot with remaining Madeira. Add potato mixture and bring to boil. Reduce heat and add kale or Swiss chard (chopped and deveined). Let cook for 15 minutes.

*Richard Santo*

# PORTUGUESE FISH SOUP - SOPA DE PEIXE

1 (2 lb.) whole fish
¼ c. salad oil
2 onions, minced
2½ qt. water
1 tomato, chopped
1 to 2 tsp. salt

¼ c. rice
2 potatoes, cubed
3 cloves garlic, minced
3 Tbsp. white wine
Lemon wedges

Scale and clean fish. In a large saucepan, heat 3 tablespoons of the oil. Saute onion until transparent. Add the water, fish, tomato, and salt. Cover; bring to a boil. Lower heat to medium; cook for 30 minutes. Carefully remove fish from pan. Strain broth; return to pan. Bring broth to a boil; add rice and potatoes. Cover and cook for 30 minutes or until rice is done.

In a skillet, heat remaining 1 tablespoon oil; saute garlic and pan-fry fish with wine. Discard skin and bones; shred fish. Add to broth; simmer for 20 minutes. Serve with lemon. Makes 6 servings.

# PORTUGUESE RED BEAN SOUP

3 good size ham shanks
1 medium size linguesa
1 small soup bone
2 c. dried, quick cooking
   red beans
2 large potatoes, diced

1 can tomato sauce
¼ tsp. Portuguese spice
2 Tbsp. oil
1 medium size round onion
3 Tbsp. minced parsley

Boil ham shanks, linguesa, and soup bone in enough water to cover. When meat is almost done, add beans and cook until done. Add tomato sauce and spice. Fry onion slices and parsley until tender. Add to soup stock. Add potatoes and cook until done. Salt to taste.

Other vegetables, such as cabbage, watercress, carrots, etc., may be added to this soup.

# SEAFOOD SINIGANG - SEAFOOD SOUP

1 lb. mussels
½ lb. shrimp
3 c. water
1 tomato, sliced
1 small onion, sliced
1 small piece ginger root,
   crushed

½ tsp. salt
1 bunch watercress or
   swamp cabbage, cut
   into 3 inch lengths

Scrub mussels well; rinse in water several times to remove sand and grit. Remove and discard beard from mussels. Wash shrimp, leaving shells on.

In a large saucepan, combine water, tomato, onion, ginger, and salt. Cover and bring to a boil; lower heat and simmer 5 minutes. Add mussels; cook until mussels open. Add shrimp and watercress or swamp cabbage; cook 1 minute. Serve immediately. Makes 6 servings.

May omit mussels and add more shrimp. *Filipino dish.*

# TURKEY CHUK

1 turkey carcass
1½ c. uncooked rice or 3 c.
    cold cooked rice
4 qt. water
1 (2 inch) piece ginger,
    crushed

1 (6 inch) piece chung choi
1 small can water
    chestnuts, chopped
1 Tbsp. Hawaiian salt

Garnish:

Green onion, minced
Chinese parsley
Shredded lettuce

Finely chopped chung choi
    (rinse first)
Dash of shoyu

Remove any meat from turkey carcass; chop and refrigerate until almost ready to serve.

In large pot, place the bones, water, rice (washed), ginger, and chung choi. Boil, then simmer about 1 to 1½ hours. (If using cooked rice, boil bones, etc. about ½ hour before adding rice, then cook another hour.)

Discard bones, ginger, and chung choi. Add the water chestnuts, the reserved turkey meat, and more salt if necessary. Serve with desired garnish.

*Mary Soon*

# SALADS

## AHI SALAD WITH MISO DRESSING

1 medium daikon, cut crosswise into ¼ inch slices
1 lb. makina (celery cabbage), blanched
½ lb. warabi (fern shoots), blanched
1 bunch horenso (spinach), blanched
1 Tbsp. salad oil
1 long eggplant, cut diagonally into ¼ inch slices
6 (3 oz.) pieces ahi fillets
Salt
Freshly cracked black pepper
Chopped green onions
Black sesame seed
¼ c. miso
¼ c. peanut oil
¼ c. salad oil
2 Tbsp. vinegar
1 Tbsp. soy sauce
1 Tbsp. mirin
2 Tbsp. sugar
2 tsp. grated ginger root
2 tsp. toasted and ground sesame seed

Blanch daikon slices. Cut makina, warabi, and horenso into 2½ inch lengths. In a skillet, heat the 1 tablespoon oil. Fry eggplant; drain on paper towels. Arrange all vegetables on a platter. Season ahi with salt and pepper; fry in skillet until lightly browned, adding oil if necessary. Arrange on vegetables. Garnish with green onions and sesame seed. Combine remaining ingredients; mix well. Serve over salad. Makes 6 servings. *Okinawan.*

## BEAN SALAD

1 can Northern beans (undrained)
1 can chili beans (undrained)
1 can kidney beans, drained
½ c. catsup
⅓ c. brown sugar
½ tsp. ground ginger

Mix all together and heat 30 minutes.

You can add hot dogs or sausage to this dish.

*Leo Hubbard*

# BEAN SALAD

1 can kidney beans
1 can garbanzo beans
1 can green beans
1 can wax beans
1 onion, sliced thin

1 green pepper, sliced thin
½ c. salad oil
¾ c. sugar
2 tsp. salt

Drain and rinse all the beans. Add onions and green pepper. Add the oil, sugar, and salt. Marinate overnight in the refrigerator.

# THREE BEAN SALAD

1 can French cut (or
    regular) green beans
1 can yellow wax beans
1 can red kidney beans
½ c. diced green pepper
½ c. diced onion

½ c. salad oil
¾ c. granulated sugar
½ c. cider vinegar
1 tsp. salt
½ tsp. pepper

Drain wax and green beans. Wash and drain kidney beans. Mix beans, onions, and green peppers. Mix well the oil, salt, black pepper, sugar, and vinegar. Pour over beans. Let stand overnight in refrigerator.

*Eleanor Dickie Robertson, Green*

# BREADFRUIT SALAD

3 c. cooked breadfruit
    (green ripe)
1 (7 oz.) can crabmeat,
    tuna, or any other fish
    meat, bacon, ham, or 3
    hard cooked eggs,
    chopped
½ c. chopped celery

½ c. grated carrot
½ c. shredded cabbage
½ tsp. salt, or to suit taste
Salad dressing or
    mayonnaise to
    moisten
2 Tbsp. green onions,
    chopped

Combine breadfruit, fish, celery, carrot, cabbage, and onion. Mix lightly with salad dressing or mayonnaise. Serve on lettuce leaves garnished with parsley and sprinkle of paprika. Serves 6 to 8.

*Green*

# BREADFRUIT SALAD

1 green breadfruit
2 Tbsp. minced onion
2 Tbsp. chopped green
    pepper
2 Tbsp. chopped parsley
1 medium carrot, grated

2 Tbsp. chopped pickles
¾ c. mayonnaise
1 tsp. prepared mustard
1 tsp. vinegar
1 tsp. pickle juice

Pare breadfruit; cut into lengthwise quarters. Remove core and dice. Cook in salted water until tender; drain and cool. Stir in onion, green pepper, parsley, carrot, and pickles. Combine remaining ingredients; pour over salad and mix well, using only enough dressing to thoroughly moisten salad. Chill before serving. Makes 6 servings.

# BROCCOLI SALAD

4 c. broccoli flowerettes
    (you can use peeled
    stems, too)
½ c. raisins
½ c. red onions (you can
    use white)

1 c. cashew nuts (you can
    use toasted slivered
    almonds)
½ c. bacon bits

Toss all ingredients together; let stand while mixing dressing.

Dressing - Mix:

¾ c. mayonnaise
¼ c. sugar

2 Tbsp. vinegar

Place on top of salad ingredients and toss.

## CABBAGE BEAN SPROUT SALAD

½ head medium cabbage,
   shredded
1 small carrot, slivered
1 cucumber, sliced thin
1 pkg. bean sprouts
2 tsp. sesame oil

2 tsp. lemon juice
1 tsp. sugar
2 tsp. mild vinegar
1 Tbsp. sesame seed
1 chili pepper

In a large bowl, combine cabbage, carrot, and cucumber. Sprinkle 2 to 3 tablespoons salt. Mix well and let set for about ½ hour. Drain well. Add bean sprouts and rest of the ingredients to preceding mixture. Mix well.

If you like it hot, 1 chili pepper may be added. Chill. Serves 6.

## CARROT RAISIN SALAD

1 c. grated carrot
1 c. shredded cabbage
¼ c. raisins
½ tsp. salt

2 Tbsp. lemon juice
1 Tbsp. sugar
¼ c. mayonnaise

Toss and combine well the carrot, cabbage, raisins, salt, lemon juice, and sugar. Refrigerate until ready to serve.

Just before serving, toss with mayonnaise. Makes 4 servings.

*Patsy Takushi*

# CHINESE CHICKEN SALAD

1 or 2 chicken breasts, boiled in water with salt, cooled, and shredded
1 (2 oz.) bundle Chinese long rice (deep-fry long rice until brown)

1 head lettuce, shredded
3 to 4 stalks green onions, chopped
2 Tbsp. toasted almonds, chopped
2 Tbsp. toasted sesame seed

Dressing:

2 to 3 Tbsp. sugar
1 tsp. salt
½ tsp. pepper

¼ c. salad oil
3 to 4 Tbsp. white vinegar
1 to 2 Tbsp. sesame oil

Combine all ingredients in jar. Shake well. Refrigerate. Combine all salad ingredients. Add dressing and toss lightly. Serve immediately.

*Katsuko Enoki, Blue*

# CHINESE CHICKEN SALAD

1½ lb. chicken, cooked and shredded
1 medium head lettuce, shredded
2½ c. slivered celery
2 bunches Chinese parsley, chopped
¼ c. sugar
6 Tbsp. vinegar
½ c. salad oil

2 Tbsp. sesame oil
2 tsp. salt
1 tsp. pepper
½ c. finely chopped peanuts
1 Tbsp. toasted sesame seed
1 (3½ oz.) pkg. wun ton chips

In a large bowl, combine chicken, lettuce, celery, and parsley. Combine sugar, vinegar, oils, salt, and pepper.

Just before serving, pour dressing over salad. Top with peanuts, sesame seed, and wun ton chips. Makes 8 servings.

# CHINESE CHICKEN SALAD

This salad makes a beautiful and different dish, either as a side dish or a main dish.

1 (2½ lb.) broiler-fryer
1 Tbsp. salt
1 carrot, chopped
1 onion, coarsely chopped
1 stalk celery, chopped
2 c. peanut oil
½ c. Chinese sai fun (bean threads)

3 c. shredded iceberg lettuce
½ c. chopped green onions
1 Tbsp. sesame seeds
½ c. chopped Chinese parsley

Place the chicken in a large pot with water to cover. Add the salt, carrot, onion, and celery. Simmer until chicken is tender. Remove chicken from the pot; take off the skin, and cut meat from the bones in ½ inch slivers.

Heat the peanut oil and quickly fry chicken slivers until crisp, 1 or 2 minutes. Remove and drain on paper towels. Next, drop the Chinese bean threads into the hot peanut oil, stirring constantly for a few seconds, until the bean threads are crisp but not brown. (They look like thin crisp noodles.) Remove bean threads from oil and combine with the shredded lettuce, green onions, chicken slivers, and sesame seeds. Top with Chinese parsley.

Just before serving, add the following dressing - Sesame Seed-Oil Dressing:

½ tsp. sesame seed oil
3 Tbsp. Chinese plum sauce
1 Tbsp. sugar

1 Tbsp. white wine vinegar
1 Tbsp. salad oil
½ tsp. dry mustard

Blend all ingredients and mix with Chinese Chicken Salad.

## CHICKEN SALAD

5 c. cooked chicken, cut in
    chunks
2 Tbsp. salad oil
2 Tbsp. orange juice
2 Tbsp. vinegar
1 tsp. salt
3 c. cooked rice
1½ c. small green grapes

1½ c. sliced celery
1 (13½ oz.) can pineapple
    tidbits, drained (1 c.)
1 (11 oz.) can mandarin
    oranges, drained
1 c. toasted slivered
    almonds
1½ c. mayonnaise

Combine chicken, salad oil, orange juice, vinegar, and salt; let stand while preparing remaining salad ingredients (or you can refrigerate mixture overnight). Gently toss together all ingredients just before serving. Makes 12 servings.

## MANDARIN CHICKEN SALAD

3 c. diced cooked chicken
1 c. diced celery
2 Tbsp. finely chopped
    onion
¾ c. mayonnaise
1 (11 oz.) can mandarin
    oranges, drained

1 c. seedless grapes,
    halved
1 tsp. lemon pepper
½ c. toasted pecans

In medium bowl, combine the first 7 ingredients. Mix well; cover and chill for 1 to 2 hours. Fold in pecans just before serving.

*Helen Misner*

# COLD SOMEN SALAD

1 (9 oz.) pkg. somen*
¼ c. sugar
1 c. chicken broth
¼ c. soy sauce
¼ c. rice vinegar
2 Tbsp. sesame oil

1 small cucumber, slivered
2 c. shredded lettuce
½ block kamaboko,
   slivered**
¼ lb. ham, slivered
¼ lb. char siu, slivered***

Cook noodles according to package directions; rinse and drain. Chill. In a saucepan, combine sugar, chicken broth, soy sauce, vinegar, and sesame oil. Bring to a boil; lower heat and simmer for 5 minutes. Chill. Place somen on a large platter. Garnish with lettuce, kamaboko, ham, and char siu. Serve with broth mixture. Makes 6 to 8 servings.

* Somen - narrow wheat noodles.

** Kamaboko - Japanese fishcake.

*** Char Siu - Sweet roast pork.

*Gold*

# COLE SLAW

This is an adaptation of a Frugal Gourmet (Jeff Smith) recipe. It is delicious the second and third day.

1 (2½ to 3 lb.) head cabbage
2 bell peppers

2 small sweet onions
¼ c. sugar

Dressing:

2 Tbsp. sugar
2 tsp. celery seed
2 tsp. dry mustard
2 tsp. salt

⅔ c. vinegar
2 Tbsp. olive oil
½ c. salad oil

In a large bowl, shred cabbage; slice peppers into thin strips. Cut onions in halves and slice very thin. Toss vegetables with ¼ cup of sugar; let stand while preparing the dressing. Combine sugar, celery seed, dry mustard, and salt; add vinegar. Bring these ingredients to a boil; cook 1 minute and let cool. When cool, beat in the oil. Place dressing on vegetable and refrigerate until ready to serve. Yields 15+ servings.

## COOKIE SALAD

1 large box instant vanilla
    pudding
2 c. buttermilk
1 (8 oz.) Cool Whip

1 pkg. fudge stripe cookies,
    broken up
2 cans mandarin oranges,
    drained

Mix pudding, buttermilk, and Cool Whip. Add oranges. Cover and refrigerate.

Before serving, stir crumbled cookies into mixture.

*Lois Farrington*

## CREAMY FRUIT SALAD

1 pkg. strawberry jello
1 c. boiling water
1 c. tap water
½ c. mayonnaise
1 (1 lb. 1 oz.) can fruit
    cocktail, drained

1 can mandarin oranges,
    drained and strained
1 c. small marshmallows
½ c. chopped walnuts

Dissolve jello in boiling water; stir in tap water and mix. Chill to slightly set. Beat mayonnaise and add to jello. Fold fruit cocktail into the jello mixture. Add marshmallows and nuts. Pour into a mold. Add oranges on top and chill until firm.

*Janet Yayoshi*

2821-95

# SUNSET SALAD

1 pkg. lemon flavored
    gelatin
2 Tbsp. lemon juice (or
    vinegar)

1½ c. grated raw carrots
1¼ c. well drained canned
    crushed pineapple*

Prepare gelatin according to directions on package. Add the lemon juice or vinegar. Chill, and when partially set, add grated carrots and crushed pineapple. When partially set again, pour into a ring mold (8½ inches in diameter and 2½ inches deep) or 8 to 10 individual molds. Chill until firm. Unmold on large chop plate or individual salad plates. Garnish with crisp lettuce or lacy watercress.

Serve with appropriate dressing: Mayonnaise or salad dressing thinned with a little cream. Serves 8 to 10.

* If fresh pineapple is used, cook and sweeten to taste before adding to gelatin.

*Ludvina Abrew*

# CRUNCHY FRUIT SALAD

2 (3 oz.) cans chow mein
    noodles
2 qt. assorted fresh fruit
    chunks and/or slices

½ c. Passion Fruit French
    Dressing

Put noodles on a platter. Arrange fruit on noodles. Before serving, pour dressing over fruit. Makes 8 servings.

Passion Fruit French Dressing:

1 (6 oz.) can frozen passion
    fruit juice, thawed
¾ c. salad oil
1 clove garlic

1 tsp. paprika
½ tsp. salt
½ tsp. celery seed

Put all ingredients into blender. Cover and blend well. Makes 1½ cups.

# PINEAPPLE SALAD

1 large can chunk
  pineapple
1 can mandarin oranges
2 c. miniature
  marshmallows
1 c. nutmeats
1 c. whipped cream or 1
  env. Dream Whip (do
  not use Cool Whip)

2 Tbsp. flour
½ c. sugar
2 eggs
Pinch of salt

1. Drain juice (1 cup) from pineapple and place in double boiler.

2. When hot, add sugar, flour, salt, and eggs which have been beaten together. Cook until thick.

3. Cook this mixture a day ahead and let it get cold in the refrigerator.

4. Whip the cream and fold into pudding mixture.

5. Pour over fruit.

6. Add nuts and stir.

7. Let stand in refrigerator for 1½ hours or overnight.

*Doris Wetters*

# CUCUMBER SEAWEED NAMASU

3 medium size cucumbers
3 c. prepared limu (limu
  manauea)
½ c. sugar
½ tsp. salt
½ tsp. MSG (optional)

½ c. Japanese vinegar
2 Tbsp. shoyu
1 tsp. chopped ginger
½ (No. 1 size) can abalone
  juice
½ can abalone, slivered

Prepare limu by washing thoroughly. Break or cut into small pieces. Pour boiling water over limu. Drain; press water from limu. Slice cucumbers. Sprinkle with salt; let stand 20 minutes. Drain; press out excess water.

Meanwhile, measure sugar, salt, and MSG in bowl. Add vinegar, shoyu, abalone juice, and ginger. Mix well until sugar is dissolved. Add abalone, cucumber, and seaweed. Toss well and chill.

## CUCUMBER SEAWEED NAMASU

2 medium cucumbers
1 (¾ lb.) pkg. ogo
1 small carrot, sliced
1 kamaboko, sliced
1 can Kogai baby clams

6 Tbsp. sugar
6 Tbsp. vinegar
2 tsp. salt
½ tsp. MSG (optional)

Cut cucumbers into halves lengthwise, and remove seeds. Slice thinly. Pour boiling water over ogo; drain and rinse in cold water. Drain well and cut into 2 inch pieces.

In a large bowl, combine cucumbers, ogo, carrot, kamaboko, and clams. Mix the remaining ingredients and pour over the vegetables. Serve cold.

*T. Oki*

## DANCE OF DRAGON AND PHOENIX SALAD

1 lettuce head
1 chicken breast
2 c. shrimp
2 stalks green onions, chopped
2 stalks chives, chopped

1 (10 oz.) pkg. frozen peas
1 (8 oz.) can mandarin oranges, drained
1 (4 oz.) pkg. fried wun ton chips
1 c. almonds, toasted

Sauce:

2 Tbsp. sesame seeds, toasted
4 Tbsp. sugar
2 Tbsp. oil
2 Tbsp. rice vinegar

4 Tbsp. shoyu
½ tsp. sesame oil
1 slice ginger, minced
1 clove garlic, minced

Thinly shred lettuce. Place in serving bowl. Toss onion, chives, and oranges with lettuce. Defrost frozen peas. Add to lettuce.

Steam chicken breast 5 to 8 minutes until done. Cool and shred into strips. Add to lettuce. Steam shrimp in shell. Plunge in cold water. Remove shell. Add to lettuce.

Add dressing to individual servings, then sprinkle almonds and chips to each serving.

*Maysie Tam, Hanalima Club*

# FIRE-AND-ICE TOMATOES

6 large tomatoes
1 green pepper
1 Maui onion
¾ c. white vinegar
1½ tsp. celery salt
1½ tsp. mustard seed

½ tsp. salt
4½ tsp. sugar
⅛ tsp. cayenne
⅛ tsp. pepper
¼ c. water
1 cucumber

Pare and quarter tomatoes. Slice green pepper into strips. Slice onion and separate into rings. Put vegetables into a bowl.

In a saucepan, combine vinegar, seasonings, and water. Bring to a boil and boil hard for 1 minute. Pour over vegetables; chill.

Just before serving, pare and slice cucumber. Stir in gently. Makes 6 servings.

*Ludvina Abrew*

# GREEK STYLE SALAD

3 tomatoes, cut into
  wedges
1 medium zucchini, cut into
  julienne strips
1 cucumber, sliced
1 red onion, cut into rings
1 c. pitted olives

½ lb. Feta cheese, cubed
1 (6 oz.) jar marinated
  artichoke hearts
  (undrained)
¼ c. red wine vinegar
Freshly ground pepper

In a large bowl, combine tomatoes, zucchini, cucumber, and onion rings. Add olives and Feta cheese. Top with artichoke hearts. Pour vinegar over salad; sprinkle with pepper and toss well. Chill several hours, tossing occasionally. Makes 6 servings.

# GREEN BEAN-SESAME SALAD

½ lb. green beans, sliced
1 red pepper, julienned

½ medium onion, sliced
2 Tbsp. sesame seed

Dressing:

¼ c. sesame oil
2 Tbsp. rice vinegar
1 tsp. grated ginger

1 tsp. minced garlic
1 tsp. shoyu

Slice green beans into 2½ to 3 inch long pieces. Steam 3 to 4 minutes until cooked, but still crunchy. Immediately plunge into bowl of ice water for 10 minutes until cold. Drain. Remove stem, membrane, and seeds from peppers. Slice into strips 2½ inches long. Slice onion thinly.

Whisk dressing ingredients together. Put green beans, peppers, onions, and sesame seeds in bowl. Toss with dressing. Serve well chilled with sesame seed. Garnish if desired. Serves 4.

*Marlene Curtis*

# GREEN SALAD

1 medium size cabbage
   (won bok), sliced
1 medium size head
   lettuce, sliced
2 c. head cabbage, sliced

¼ c. green onion, chopped
   fine
1 medium tomato, sliced
1 pkg. won ton chips,
   crushed

Dressing:

1 clove garlic, minced
½ c. salad oil
½ c. sugar
½ c. white vinegar

1 tsp. salt
¼ tsp. white pepper
¼ c. mayonnaise

Combine vegetables and the won ton chips in a bowl. Mix the dressing ingredients in a bottle and shake well.

Just before serving, pour over vegetables.

*Kimiko Anzai*

# HAWAIIAN SEAFOOD SALAD

1 head lettuce, torn
1 cucumber, thinly sliced
1 green pepper, thinly
  sliced
½ lb. imitation crab, cut
  into bite-size pieces
1 (6 oz.) pkg. fried fish cake,
  slivered
3 green onions, minced
1 Maui onion, minced
½ lb. ahi or aku, cubed

½ lb. ocean vegetable
  salad
1 Tbsp. chopped limu kohu
½ Tbsp. ground roasted
  kukui nuts
1 Hawaiian red pepper,
  seeded and minced
½ tsp. Hawaiian salt
2 Tbsp. sesame oil
1 Tbsp. soy sauce

In a large bowl, combine lettuce, cucumber, green pepper, crab, fish cake, and onions. Chill. Combine remaining ingredients; mix well and chill.

Just before serving, add fish mixture to salad greens; toss gently. Makes 8 servings.

# IMITATION HOT CRAB SALAD

½ lb. imitation crab
2 c. thinly sliced cabbage

Pinch of salt
2 Tbsp. mayonnaise (light)

Mix ingredients in bowl. Pour mixture into a shallow dish (9 inch pie dish). Seal top of mixture lightly with heaping 2 tablespoons of mayonnaise. Broil (not bake) until mayonnaise gets golden and spotted with brown spots (watch closely when broiling).

Note: Amount of mayonnaise and cabbage varies - use judgment for best amount.

*Daisy Takayesu*

## KHONG NAMUL
### (Korean Bean Sprout Salad)

1 (1 lb.) pkg. bean sprouts
2 small green onions,
    chopped
¼ tsp. pepper
Dash of monosodium
    glutamate (optional)
1¼ tsp. salt

1½ tsp. sugar
2 Tbsp. soy sauce
1½ Tbsp. vinegar
1 small Hawaiian red
    pepper, crushed
1 Tbsp. toasted sesame
    seeds

Wash bean sprouts; place in boiling water. Drain and cool. Combine green onions, pepper, monosodium glutamate, salt, sugar, soy sauce, vinegar, and red pepper. Pour over bean sprouts and sprinkle with sesame seeds. Chill for 1 hour. Makes 6 servings.

## LONG RICE SALAD

3 (1⅞ oz.) pkg. long rice
1 egg, beaten
1 cucumber, thinly sliced
2 stalks green onions,
    finely chopped
¼ lb. thinly sliced ham
1 c. shredded cabbage
½ lb. imitation crab legs,
    shredded

⅓ c. vinegar
⅓ c. sugar
2 Tbsp. soy sauce
1 tsp. ginger or garlic juice
    or puree
2 tsp. sesame oil

Cook long rice in salted boiling water until tender, about 10 to 15 minutes. Drain and rinse with cold water; cut into 3 inch lengths. Fry egg in a thin sheet. Cut cucumber, eggs, onions, and ham into thin strips; mix with long rice. Stir in crab and cabbage. Combine remaining ingredients and pour over mixture, tossing gently. Makes 6 servings.

# OGO (SEAWEED) NAMASU

1 pkg. seaweed (about 4 or
 5 c.)
2 medium firm ripe
 tomatoes

1 cucumber
½ medium onion, sliced
 thin

Marinade:

¼ c. vegetable oil
¼ c. cider vinegar
3 Tbsp. shoyu
2 tsp. salt

Dash of Tabasco sauce
1½ Tbsp. sugar
¼ to ½ tsp. minced ginger

Blanch seaweed in boiling water; drain and cut in small pieces. Cut tomato, onion, and cucumber in strips. Add all ingredients and marinate. Let stand for about 2 hours before serving.

Opihis may be added, should you have some on hand.

*Blue*

# FRESH OGO, CUCUMBER, AND CRAB SALAD

½ lb. fresh ogo (seaweed)
2 medium Japanese
 cucumbers
½ lb. crabmeat, shredded
3 Tbsp. rice vinegar
3 Tbsp. soy sauce

1 Tbsp. sugar
2 tsp. toasted and ground
 sesame seed
½ tsp. ground red pepper
¼ tsp. salt

Wash and blanch ogo; cut into 2 inch lengths. Pare and cut cucumbers in halves lengthwise; thinly slice crosswise. In a large bowl, combine ogo, cucumbers, and crab.

To make dressing, combine remaining ingredients. Just before serving, pour dressing over ogo mixture; mix well. Makes 6 servings.

# OKINAWAN SEAWEED SALAD

1 (2 oz.) pkg. kurome (dried seaweed)
2 Tbsp. salad oil
1 (6 oz.) pkg. gobo tempura fishcake, slivered
1 (10 oz.) pkg. konyaku (gelatinous sheet from a tuberous root), slivered

1¼ c. water
¼ c. soy sauce
2 Tbsp. mirin
2 Tbsp. sake
2 Tbsp. sugar
¼ tsp. dashi-no-moto (soup base granules)
½ block firm tofu, well drained

Soak kurome in water for 20 minutes; drain. In a large skillet, heat the oil. Saute kurome, fishcake, and konyaku for 3 minutes. Add remaining ingredients, except tofu. Cook on medium heat, stirring frequently, until liquid evaporates. Cool. Cut tofu into strips and add to salad; toss lightly. Makes 6 servings.

# OVERNIGHT LAYERED GREEN SALAD

1 small head iceberg
  lettuce, shredded
Alfalfa sprouts
1 c. celery, thinly sliced
½ c. green onions,
  chopped
1 can water chestnuts,
  sliced
1 (10 oz.) pkg. frozen peas/
  carrots, thawed
2 c. mayonnaise
2 tsp. sugar

½ c. Parmesan cheese,
  grated
1 tsp. seasoned salt
¼ tsp. garlic powder or
  garlic salt
½ lb. bacon, crisply cooked
  and crumbled
3 hard cooked eggs,
  chopped
2 medium tomatoes, cut in
  wedges

Place lettuce on bottom of an 11x7 inch glass baking dish. Layer in order, alfalfa sprouts, green onions, celery, water chestnuts, and peas. Spread with mayonnaise; sprinkle with sugar, cheese, seasoned salt, and garlic powder. Cover and chill for 24 hours.

Just before serving, sprinkle with eggs and bacon. Arrange tomatoes around salad.

Note: Half of a green pepper, sliced, and 1 cup roasted blanched peanuts may be added when layering the vegetables. Also, the mayonnaise, sugar, cheese, seasoned salt, and garlic powder may be combined and spread over the layered ingredients.

*Lei Matsumura*

# POTATO AND CABBAGE SALAD

2 medium potatoes,
  cooked and cubed
2 c. head cabbage,
  shredded
½ c. celery, sliced thin

¾ c. imitation crabmeat
⅓ c. mayonnaise
1 tsp. sugar
Dash of salt and pepper

In a bowl, combine potato, cabbage, celery, and crabmeat. Add mayonnaise, sugar, and dash of salt and pepper.

*Kimiko Anzai*

## POTATO AND MACARONI SALAD

5 lb. salad potatoes
1 Tbsp. salt
2 lb. salad macaroni
1 doz. hard cooked eggs,
    chopped
4 c. finely chopped celery
2 c. shredded carrots

1 c. finely chopped onions
2 (10 oz.) pkg. frozen peas,
    thawed
3 (7 oz.) cans tuna, drained
1½ tsp. pepper
2½ qt. mayonnaise

Cook potatoes until tender; peel and dice. Sprinkle with salt; set aside. Cook macaroni following package directions; drain well.

In a large bowl, combine all ingredients; mix lightly, adding additional mayonnaise if desired. Refrigerate several hours before serving. Makes 50 (¾ cup) servings.

## SPAM AND POTATO SALAD

1 or 2 cans Spam
6 hard-boiled eggs
3 lb. steamed potatoes
String beans
1 c. chopped celery
1 medium round onion,
    chopped

1 c. packed shredded
    cabbage (head)
1 c. grated carrots
1 pt. mayonnaise
Salt and pepper to taste

Peel and slice potatoes in halves and steam for 20 minutes. Place washed and cleaned string beans in same steamer. When beans are just about done, add the Spam, sliced in halves, above the beans. Turn heat off and let cool off. While the potatoes, etc. are being steamed, prepare the rest of the vegetables. Combine all chopped vegies and eggs in a bowl; add sliced beans. Add mayonnaise and seasoning, then add cubed potatoes and Spam, saving some Spam for garnish.

*Gladys Lai*

# SPAM POTATO SALAD

12 medium boiled
  potatoes, cubed
8 boiled eggs, chopped or
  diced
1 c. shredded imitation
  crabmeat
1 can Spam, thinly sliced
  and chopped
1 c. frozen peas, cooked
1 qt. mayonnaise
Salt and pepper to taste

Combine all ingredients. Serves 6.

*Patricia S. Moniz*

# WARM SHRIMP AND POTATO SALAD

2 potatoes, cut into ¼ inch
  slices
1 lb. shrimp, shelled and
  deveined
3 Tbsp. vegetable oil
2 Tbsp. lemon juice
2 tsp. grated ginger
1 tsp. sesame oil
½ tsp. salt
⅛ tsp. pepper
1 c. fresh spinach leaves
½ c. cherry tomatoes,
  halved
2 green onions, thinly
  sliced

1. In a 9 inch microwave-safe pie plate, arrange potato slices. Cover loosely with plastic wrap. Cook on HIGH 8 to 10 minutes or until potatoes are tender, stirring once. Place shrimp on top of potatoes.

2. In a bowl, combine vegetable oil, lemon juice, ginger, sesame oil, salt, and pepper. Pour over shrimp and potatoes. Recover. Cook on HIGH 4 to 6 minutes or until shrimp are pink, gently stirring once.

*T. Oki*

# SAIMIN SALAD

¼ c. sliced almonds
8 stalks green onions,
    finely sliced
¼ c. sesame seeds
1 medium head cabbage,
    finely chopped

2 pkg. (3 oz.) Nissin Ramen
    noodles (uncooked),
    broken into small
    pieces

Dressing:

¼ c. sugar
1 tsp. salt
6 Tbsp. rice vinegar

1 tsp. black pepper
1 c. salad oil
2 tsp. MSG (optional)

Toast almonds and sesame seeds in oven until golden brown. Cool. Mix first 5 ingredients together. Mix well.

Make dressing by mixing all ingredients together. Mix cabbage mixture with dressing. Serve immediately before noodles become soft.

*Mabel Domae*

# SHRIMP AND WATERCRESS SALAD

3 bunches fresh
    watercress
1 lb. bay shrimp

1 red onion, minced
1 tomato, peeled and
    minced

Dressing:

1¼ c. mayonnaise
1 lemon (squeeze for juice)
10 tsp. sugar

1½ tsp. dill weed (dried)
Salt
Pepper

Wash and cut watercress into 1 inch pieces. Drain, then combine the rest and chill. Mix dressing and add before serving.

*L. Takabayashi*

# SWEET POTATO SALAD

4 to 5 sweet potatoes
1 c. celery, chopped
¼ c. green onion, chopped
1 can mandarin oranges,
    drained

½ c. sour cream or yogurt
¼ c. mayonnaise
Salt and pepper

Microwave sweet potatoes in ¼ cup water. Peel and dice potatoes into bite-size pieces. Combine sweet potatoes with mandarin oranges. Add green onions. Mix sour cream and mayonnaise. Add a little salt if you wish and combine all ingredients.

Chopped walnuts may be added.

# TACO SALAD

1 lb. ground beef or turkey
1 (1.25 oz.) pkg. taco
    seasoning mix
1 (1 lb.) can refried beans
6 fluted tortilla shells or 1
    lb. taco chips
1 head lettuce, shredded

1 large tomato, diced
½ c. sliced black olives
1½ c. shredded Cheddar
    cheese
Salsa
Guacamole
Sour cream

Prepare ground meat according to directions on taco seasoning package. Heat refried beans. In each tortilla shell, layer beans, beef, lettuce, tomato, olives, and cheese. Serve with salsa, guacamole, and sour cream. If using taco chips, layer ingredients for each serving on a bed of chips. Makes 6 servings.

# TERIYAKI TOFU-BEAN SALAD

1 (16 oz.) pkg. fresh bean curd (tofu), cubed (3 c.)
1 (15 oz.) can garbanzo beans, drained
1 small green pepper, cut into bite-size pieces
1 small tomato, seeded and chopped
¼ c. olive or salad oil
2 tsp. Dijon style mustard
½ tsp. ground ginger
¼ c. snipped parsley
¼ c. red wine vinegar
½ tsp. salt
⅓ c. sliced green onion
Leaf lettuce
1 clove garlic, minced
2 c. sliced fresh mushrooms
Sesame seed (optional)
½ c. soy sauce, more or less to taste depending on type of soy sauce

In a large bowl, combine bean curd, garbanzo beans, mushrooms, green onion, green pepper, tomato, and parsley. Set aside.

In screw-top jar, combine garlic, wine vinegar, oil, mustard, soy sauce, ginger, and salt. Shake well. Pour over salad; toss. Cover and chill several hours or overnight.

To serve, use a slotted spoon to arrange mixture atop lettuce. Sprinkle with sesame seed if desired. Makes 4 or 5 servings.

# TOFU SALAD

1 block tofu, cubed
Sliced Kula onions
2 sliced tomatoes
1 can tuna or salmon, drained

Place in bowl.

Sauce - Heat:

½ c. cooking oil
2 cloves garlic (until dark brown)

Cool oil.

Add:

½ c. soy sauce
⅔ c. green onions

Mix well in bottle. Pour over tofu salad just before serving.
*Lei Matsumura*

# TOFU SALAD

1 (1 lb. 4 oz.) block firm tofu, drained and cubed
1 (1 lb.) can salmon, drained and flaked
1 large tomato, diced
1 small onion, chopped
1 (12 oz.) pkg. bean sprouts
1 bunch watercress, cut into 1½ inch pieces
¼ c. chopped green onions
2 Tbsp. salad oil
1 clove garlic, minced
½ c. soy sauce

On a large platter, layer tofu, salmon, tomato, onion, bean sprouts, watercress, and green onions. Heat salad oil and garlic for a few minutes; add soy sauce and mix well. Pour dressing over salad; serve immediately. Makes 8 servings.

# WARABI SALAD

2 lb. warabi, parboiled
1 kamaboko, sliced thin
1 red onion, sliced thin
1 tomato, chopped in wedges
1 pkg. shiofuki konbu
1 Tbsp. sesame seed oil
2 Tbsp. vegetable oil

Cut warabi in 1½ inch pieces. Toss in bowl with all other ingredients. Refrigerate and serve.

*L. Takabayashi*

# GUAVA DRESSING

1 c. mayonnaise
1 c. tomato catsup
¼ c. vinegar
½ c. salad oil
1 tsp. dry mustard
2 tsp. lemon juice
½ c. guava jelly or jam
½ tsp. garlic salt
1 tsp. dried basil

Combine ingredients and beat with rotary beater or use blender. Chill. Serve on greens.

# VEGETABLES

## BAKED BREADFRUIT

1 very ripe breadfruit      ½ c. butter or margarine
1 c. water

Place breadfruit in a shallow pan; add water. Bake at 350°F. in electric oven for 1 hour or until tender. Pull out stem and core; cut breadfruit into 6 sections. Top with butter. If preferred, remove stem and core before baking. Put 1 tablespoon butter and 1 tablespoon sugar into cavity. Replace stem before baking. Makes 6 servings.

## CABBAGE NO MIDORIZU HITASHI

1 small cabbage      Beni-shoga (red pickled
1 small green cucumber      ginger)

     Sauce:

3 Tbsp. vinegar      1½ tsp. salt
3 Tbsp. sugar      ¼ tsp. ajinomoto (optional)

Separate cabbage leaves and soak in salt water for a few minutes. Cut off hard part; shred and sprinkle salt. Mince beni-shoga. Grate cucumber; squeeze lightly. Mix cabbage, cucumber, and beni-shoga with vinegar sauce and let stand 5 minutes before serving.

Shredded boiled ham may be added.

# COOKED PUMPKIN DISH - NANKWA UMBUSHI

2 lb. pumpkin
1 c. water
1½ Tbsp. salad oil
1½ Tbsp. soy sauce
1 Tbsp. sake

1½ Tbsp. dried shrimp,
　　chopped
1 Tbsp. sugar
1½ tsp. grated ginger root
½ tsp. salt

Remove seeds from pumpkin; cut pumpkin into 2 inch pieces. In a large saucepan, combine remaining ingredients. Cover and bring to a boil; simmer for 5 minutes. Add pumpkin. Tossing occasionally, cook, uncovered, for about 10 minutes or until pumpkin is tender and liquid evaporates. Makes 6 servings.

## GRANDMA'S TOFU

1 block tofu
½ Tbsp. minced garlic
1 Tbsp. minced ginger
1 Tbsp. hot bean paste
1 Tbsp. shoyu

½ Tbsp. oyster sauce
½ Tbsp. mirin
½ Tbsp. sesame oil
½ c. stock or water
2 tsp. corn starch

Rinse and drain tofu. Cut in ¾ inch squares. Mix remaining ingredients and simmer in pot. Add tofu and stir gently till hot. Add water as needed.

Garnish with chopped scallions or cilantro.

*Becky Lau*

2821-95

# GREENS WITH SESAME SEED DRESSING

Aemono are vegetables, fish, or shellfish which are boiled or rubbed with salt and mixed with dressing made of sesame seed, miso, or tofu with seasoning of vinegar, shoyu, salt, or sugar.

The sesame seeds are toasted in frying pan and ground in suribachi (earthenware mortar), then mixed with shoyu or miso.

**1 lb. spinach or cabbage**          **3 Tbsp. shoyu**
**3 Tbsp. sesame seeds**

Boil spinach or cabbage for a few minutes. Cut into 1½ inch lengths. Press out the water. Toast sesame seed; grind fine and add shoyu. Mix spinach in sesame and shoyu dressing. Serve in small bowls.

# HARVARD BEETS

**6 c. cooked sliced beets**          **3 Tbsp. catsup**
**1 c. sugar**                        **3 Tbsp. cooking oil**
**¾ c. vinegar**                      **1½ c. beet juice**
**2 Tbsp. cornstarch**                **½ tsp. salt**
**24 whole cloves**

Mix all ingredients in a saucepan, including beets. Cook for 3 minutes over medium heat or until mixture thickens. Cool. Pack in jars and refrigerate.

*Yoshiko Maeda*

# IMO (SWEET POTATO) TEMPURA

Batter - Mix together:

½ c. water
½ c. sugar
1 tsp. salt

1 egg
4 Tbsp. sake (optional)

Mix together and add to above ingredients:

¾ to 1 c. flour                3 Tbsp. cornstarch

Slice about 4 potatoes about ¼ inch thick. Dip potato in batter and deep-fry until brown, about 4 to 5 minutes.

Note: Potato can be rolled in sesame seeds before frying for extra special flavor.

*Green*

# JAPANESE WATERCRESS TEMPURA

1 bunch watercress          Oil (for frying)
Tempura Batter

Break off tops of watercress into 3 inch lengths. Wash and pat almost dry between paper towels. Dip into Tempura Batter and deep-fry.

Tempura Batter:

1 small egg
1¾ c. water

2 c. flour
2 tsp. baking powder

Beat egg; add 1 cup of the water. Now, add the dry ingredients sifted together, then add the remaining ¾ cup of water. Makes 2 cups batter.

Suitable for any type tempura - seafood or vegetable.

# KINPIRA GOBO

Gobo (approx. 18 inches long)
2 Tbsp. oil
2 Tbsp. sugar
3 Tbsp. shoyu

1 chili pepper
1 Tbsp. dashinomoto
½ tsp. monosodium glutamate

Scrape skin off gobo and wash. Cut into 2 inch pieces, then to matchstick size. Soak in water for ½ hour. Drain well. Heat oil in frying pan; chop pepper and fry. Turn heat on high; add gobo and stir-fry. Add seasoning and cook till dry at medium heat.

# MISO AE

Variation for vegetables: 1 pound spinach, string beans, carrots, broccoli, mustard cabbage, or bean sprouts.

Ae Sauce:

1 Tbsp. sesame seeds, toasted
3 Tbsp. sugar
3 Tbsp. miso, ground

3 Tbsp. shoyu
Dash of monosodium glutamate (optional)

Grind or crush sesame seeds in suribachi until fine. Add sugar, miso, and shoyu. Mix well. Add any of the preceding vegetables (cooked and cut in 1½ inch strips) to sauce and mix well.

*Green*

# NASU SHIGIYAKI - EGGPLANT

Use 1 pound nasu.

Sauce:

3½ Tbsp. water
½ Tbsp. sake or mirin
½ Tbsp. shoyu
2 Tbsp. dashi no moto

4 Tbsp. Hawaiian miso
½ tsp. ajinomoto
1 Tbsp. sugar

Cut eggplant and soak in water for a few minutes and drain. Heat oil in fry pan; add eggplant and heat until light brown.

Mix sauce ingredients together in a bowl; add to eggplant. Raise heat and cook for 2 to 3 minutes, stirring constantly.

Optional: Konyaku and bell pepper may be added.

# OKARA WITH VEGETABLES

3 Tbsp. oil
1 medium gobo (burdock, slivered, soaked in water, and drained)
1 medium carrot, slivered
5 to 6 string beans, chopped
2 aburage, sliced thin

½ stick kamaboko, slivered
1 pkg. okara
4 green onions, chopped
1 tsp. salt
1 can chicken broth
2 Tbsp. raw sugar
2 Tbsp. shoyu

Spray a large frying pan with vegetable spray. Add oil and on medium heat, stir-fry gobo, carrots, and string beans until crisp tender. Add kamaboko and aburage. Mix with vegetables and push to one side. Add okara and cook until heated through. Add seasoning. Mix together with vegetables. Sprinkle with chopped green onions. Serve hot.

# ONION PIE

½ c. oleo, melted (reserve small amount to pour over top)
1½ c. crushed soda crackers
2 c. chopped onion
1 c. milk
½ tsp. salt
Dash of pepper
2 eggs, beaten
1 can mushrooms, drained
1½ c. grated Cheddar cheese

1. Mix cracker crumbs and oleo (save a few to put on top).
2. Put in baking dish and make crust.
3. Saute onions in oleo.
4. Warm the milk, salt, and pepper.
5. Add eggs, mushrooms, cheese, and onions.
6. Pour mixture on crust and bake at 350° for 30 minutes.

Serves 6.

*Doris Wetters*

# PAPRIKA POTATOES

½ c. butter
¼ c. flour
¼ c. grated Parmesan cheese
1 Tbsp. paprika
¾ tsp. salt
⅛ tsp. pepper
Pinch of garlic salt or onion salt
6 medium potatoes, peeled and quartered lengthwise

Melt butter in 9x13 inch baking pan. Combine the next 6 ingredients in a large plastic bag. Rinse the potatoes under cold water and drain well. Place half the potatoes in the above bag. Shake well to coat. Place in a single layer in the baking pan. Repeat with the remaining potatoes. Bake, uncovered, at 350° for 50 to 60 minutes or until tender, turning once after 30 minutes.

*Helen Misner*

# PINACBET
## (Filipino Mixed Vegetables)

3 long eggplants
2 bitter melons or 1 (10 oz.)
    pkg. frozen whole
    okra, thawed
¼ lb. thinly sliced pork

1 small onion, sliced
1 clove garlic, crushed
3 medium tomatoes, sliced
1½ Tbsp. bagoong
1 c. water

Cut eggplants and bitter melons into 2 inch pieces. In an electric skillet, saute pork, onion, garlic, tomatoes, and bagoong. Add eggplants, bitter melons, and water. Cover and simmer for 15 minutes. Makes 6 servings.

# RENE POHOLE SALAD

1 lb. pohole shoots
1 large onion, thinly diced
(preferably Maui
onion)
½ lb. your choice of dried
cuttlefish, dried
shrimp, or sauteed
shrimp, cut into ½ inch
pieces

2 large tomatoes, diced

Dressing:

1 c. mayonnaise
1 oz. rice vinegar

1 oz. sesame seed oil

Clean pohole by washing off hairs. Use portion of stalk where it breaks off easily (as with asparagus), and *break* into 1 inch pieces. Add balance of salad items and toss. Blend dressing ingredients and pour over salad.

Sauteed Pohole: Saute cleaned *pohole* pieces with garlic, onion, or any vegetables. Excellent served with all fish.

About pohole: Pohole should be kept cold and moist at all times before use. If it is allowed to warm or dry out, it will spoil. If stored cool and moist, it will have a shelf life up to 10 days. Clean pohole by washing off hairs, using portion of stalk where it breaks off easily (as with asparagus) for salads, whole for cooking.

The secret of perfect pohole: Blanche shoots by immersing in boiling water for 1 minute and then quickly immersing in very cold water. For salads, be sure to serve cold.

*Eileen Comeaux*

# GRAND PACIFIC POHOLE

2 lb. pohole
1 Tbsp. sugar
1 Tbsp. sesame seeds

½ c. natural soy sauce
1 tsp. sesame oil
Bonito flakes

Remove the tough fibrous portion of the pohole. Wash and break in 1 inch lengths. Wash and break in 1 inch lengths. In a medium size pot, bring salted water (about 2 cups) to a boil. Add pohole pieces and cook until tender. Drain and immediately rinse with cold water to stop further cooking.

Heat sesame seeds in a cast iron skillet until golden brown. To the skillet, add soy sauce, sugar, sesame oil, stirring quickly, then add pohole pieces and toss lightly. Sprinkle with shaved Bonito.

Steamed Pohole: Steam whole cleaned stalks for several minutes (al dente). Serve as asparagus with hot lemon butter. Use some of the tightly curled fern tips as an elegant garnish.

*Eileen Comeaux*

# KOREAN STYLE POHOLE

2 lb. pohole
2 stalks green onion
¼ c. dried shrimp
1 Tbsp. sushi vinegar
1 Tbsp. sesame seeds
2 Tbsp. sesame oil

½ tsp. sugar
1 tsp. chopped ginger
1 clove chopped garlic
Kogeejam (season to
   taste)*

Remove the tough fibrous portion of the pohole. Wash and break in 1 inch lengths. Wash green onion and cut into 1 inch lengths, also. Blanch pohole and onion pieces in boiling water; drain and immediately rinse with cold water to stop further cooking.

Combine vinegar, sesame oil and seeds, Five Flavor Sauce, and fried shrimp. Mix well with fern and onion. Refrigerate. Serve as an antipasto.

* Kim Chee base.

*Eileen Comeaux*

2821-95

# POTATO DISH TO TAKE

2 lb. hash brown frozen
    potatoes, thawed
1 (8 oz.) ctn. sour cream
1 (8 oz.) pkg. grated
    Cheddar cheese
1 (10 oz.) can cream of
    potato soup

1 (10 oz.) can cream of
    mushroom soup
½ c. minced round onion
Grated Parmesan cheese

Combine all ingredients, except the Parmesan cheese. Put mixture into a 13x9 inch pan. Sprinkle Parmesan cheese over top. Bake at 350° for about 1 hour. Serves 8 to 10 persons.

*Carol Abrew Graetz*

# POTATO SKINS

1 (8 oz.) sour cream
1 c. mayonnaise
1 pkg. (dry) vegetable soup
1 (10 oz.) pkg. chopped
    spinach, thawed and
    drained

1 c. water chestnuts
Shredded Cheddar or
    Mozzarella cheese
Potato skins

Mix the preceding 5 ingredients and refrigerate at least 2 hours or overnight. Bake potato skins for 3 to 5 minutes in 350° oven to dry. Fill skins and top with cheese. Bake for 15 to 20 minutes.

# QUICK CANDIED SWEET POTATOES

¾ c. brown sugar, packed
½ c. water
½ tsp. salt
2 Tbsp. butter or margarine

Dash of cinnamon
1 (1 lb. 2 oz.) can sweet
potatoes

In large skillet, simmer together for 5 minutes, ¾ cup brown sugar, packed, ½ cup water, ½ teaspoon salt, 2 tablespoons butter or margarine, and dash of cinnamon. Add 1 (1 pound 2 ounce) can sweet potatoes.

Turn heat low; cook, uncovered, turning occasionally, 15 to 20 minutes, or until potatoes are well glazed. Or, place potatoes in greased shallow baking pan; add syrup. Bake, uncovered, turning now and then, at 400°F. for 20 to 25 minutes. Makes 5 or 6 servings.

*Masami Imada*

# SPINACH LASAGNE

1 pkg. lasagne noodles
1 (30 oz.) prepared
   spaghetti sauce
1 pkg. frozen spinach
1 c. Ricotta cheese
1 c. small curd cottage
   cheese

1 c. Mozzarella cheese,
   grated
Salt and pepper to taste
Parmesan cheese to taste

Cook lasagne noodles as directed on package. Drain; set aside.

Spread thin layer of sauce on bottom of 9x13 inch pan. Mix rest of sauce and remaining ingredients in bowl. Layer noodles and spread half of mixture on top. Make 2 layers. Bake at 350° for 30 to 45 minutes.

*Shirley Ann Kimizuka*

# STIR-FRY VEGETABLES WITH LUP CHONG

Lup chong (amount to your
    desire)
2 carrots
1 round onion

2 broccoli stems
4 celery tops with leaves
1 Tbsp. oyster sauce

Slice lup chong. Stir-fry in pan. Drain oil and discard. Add carrots and onions, cut in thick julienne style. Cut other vegetables the same way. Stir-fry all together. If too dry, add a little water. Add oyster sauce. Serve.

You may also add string beans or any other vegetable you like. Use lup chong (how much you like), 1 per person or 1 per 2 people. Vegetables, you may add more or less, depends on how many you feed.

*Beatrice Barboza*

# STUFFED EGGPLANT

6 medium size eggplants
½ onion, chopped
½ lb. ground chicken
½ c. bread crumbs
½ tsp. salt

1 Tbsp. water
Cornstarch
1 ginger root, chopped or
    grated

Remove stem of eggplants. Slice lengthwise in halves. Leave about ½ inch intact on the stem side. Soak in salted water. Wipe off moisture from eggplants; sprinkle cornstarch on cut surface. Stuff eggplants with meat mixture. Deep-fry until meat is well done. Serve with shoyu and ginger sauce.

Three tablespoons chopped cheese may be added (optional).

## STUFFED HASU (LOTUS ROOT)

1 large piece hasu
1 Tbsp. green onion,
   chopped
¾ lb. fish cake paste
1 egg

1 Tbsp. chopped round
   onion
⅓ c. water
1 carrot, grated

Peel and slice hasu about ⅜ inch thick. Mix the remaining ingredients and stuff the hasu. Coat with a package of vegetable batter mix. Deep-fry in oil. Dip into tempura sauce (optional).

## STUFFED ZUCCHINI

2 medium size zucchini
½ lb. ground chicken or
   turkey
½ tsp. salt
½ tsp. sugar
2 Tbsp. shoyu

1 egg, slightly beaten
1 pkg. dashi-no-moto or 1
   bouillon cube
Water (enough to ¼ inch in
   frying pan)
1 beaten egg

Slice zucchini lengthwise in halves. Scoop out seeds. Mix ground chicken with salt, sugar, shoyu, and 1 slightly beaten egg. Stuff zucchini. Add water to frying pan to about ¼ inch. Add dashi-no-moto or bouillon cube. When it starts to simmer, lay your stuffed zucchini in pan. Simmer 15 to 20 minutes or until done.

If using pork hash, cook it before stuffing.

# SZECHUAN STYLE EGGPLANT

1¼ lb. eggplant
1 tsp. minced garlic
6 Tbsp. vegetable oil
1 piece pork or top sirloin
1 Tbsp. fresh ginger,
   chopped
1 Tbsp. hot bean sauce
1½ tsp. Hoi Sin sauce

2 tsp. rice vinegar
2 Tbsp. shoyu
1 tsp. sugar
½ tsp. salt
½ c. chicken broth
1½ tsp. sesame oil
1 Tbsp. chopped green
   onion

Fry garlic and ginger in hot oil. Add beef or pork and then add other ingredients. Thicken with cornstarch and water. Put aside.

Cut eggplants in 4 inch long pieces. Cut in halves. Brown on both sides and lay in dish. Pour meat mixture over eggplant, then serve.

*Janice Toguchi*

# THE USES OF TARO

Taro has long been a staple food of the natives of all Polynesian islands as well as in the West Indies and the Orient. Some varieties are used as cooked table taro or for making poi; others are raised primarily for their leaves which are used for luau. The stalks of some are also cooked. There are a great many different varieties but all may be divided into 2 groups.

The Polynesian group includes the so called Hawaiian and Chinese taros. They are used as cooked table taro or for luau. Hawaiian taros are also used for poi. The corm, popularly known as the root, is somewhat tough, spongy, with numerous fibers. The root is an energy food. It may be used in place of rice in the diet. The food value of the root is very similar to that of sweet potatoes. The stalk contains good amounts of calcium and iron and gives variety to the meal. The leaves are very similar to spinach.

# TARO CAKE

2 c. diced taro (½ inch cubes)
½ c. cooked diced pork
½ c. chopped green onions
2 Tbsp. chopped larm see (salted black olives)
1 c. flour
2 tsp. sesame seed

½ c. chopped dried shrimp
¼ c. finely diced ham
2 Tbsp. chopped Chinese parsley
¾ c. water
1 tsp. salt
2 Tbsp. scrambled egg

Fry taro cubes in 2 tablespoons oil. Cover and simmer 15 minutes. Combine flour and water to form a paste. Add all ingredients, including taro, to the paste mixture. Grease an 8 inch cake pan and spread mixture in pan. Place in a steamer and steam 25 minutes. Garnish with sesame seeds and shredded egg.

## TARO CHIPS 1
### (Use Chinese Taro)

Peel raw taro and cut into *very thin* slices. Soak them for 1 hour in cold water, then drain and dry on a towel. Fry in deep fat (395°F.) a few slices at a time until a very light brown. Keep them in motion so that each slice will cook evenly. Lay them on clean paper to drain. Sprinkle lightly with salt. If not used immediately, store in a dry tightly covered tin and set in a cool place.

## TARO CHIPS 2

Cook taro in boiling water until tender but firm; drain and set in a cool place until thoroughly cooled. Slice very thin. Fry in deep fat (390°F.) until light brown.

2821-95

# TARO FRITTERS

1 c. mashed boiled taro
1 egg, separated
¼ c. milk

¼ c. flour
1 tsp. baking powder
½ tsp. salt

Beat egg yolk; add milk and add mixture to taro, blending well. Add dry ingredients sifted together. Fold in stiffly beaten egg white. Drop by tablespoons into hot fat or oil heated to 365°F. Cook until puffy and golden brown, turning once. Yield: 4 servings.

Note: Taro may be more easily mashed by cutting in small pieces and heating in the top of a double boiler or by grating on a coarse vegetable grater.

# TOFU BURGERS

1 block tofu, mashed
1 medium carrot, grated
½ zucchini, grated
½ yellow pepper, diced
½ green or red pepper, diced
½ red or yellow onion, diced
3 cloves garlic, pressed or minced

1½ c. cooked brown rice
2 c. cooked couscous (see directions following)*
⅓ c. burger mix*
⅓ c. TVP (texturized vegetable protein)*
⅓ c. grated Parmesan cheese
¼ c. sesame seeds
2 Tbsp. shoyu or tamari

1. Combine all the preceding ingredients in bowl. Form mixture into patties.

2. Heat 2 tablespoons olive oil in frying pan. Saute 2 to 3 patties at a time, cooking about 5 minutes on each side until golden brown and crispy. Continue cooking all the patties, adding oil as necessary so patties do not stick to pan. When cooled, patties can be frozen for future use. Serve as you would any burger, on a bun with melted cheese, sliced tomato or onion, lettuce or sprouts, with mustard, catsup, or relish if desired.

To cook couscous: In 1 cup water, add 1 vegetable cube and 2 teaspoons Italian spice. Bring to a boil and add 1 cup couscous. Cover pot and turn off heat. After 5 minutes, fluff with fork.

* These products are all available in health food stores in the bulk food section.

*Marlene Curtis*

# VEGETABLE TEMPURA

1 c. flour
1 tsp. sugar
1 tsp. salt
1 tsp. baking powder
1 egg
¾ c. water
Oil (for deep-frying)
½ c. carrots, julienned

1 c. string beans, julienned
½ c. gobo, julienned
¼ c. parsley, chopped
¼ c. chives, chopped
3 stalks green onion, chopped
½ kamaboko (red), julienned

Heat oil. In a fairly large bowl (2 quart size), add dry ingredients. In ¾ cup water, add egg and stir to mix. Add to dry ingredients and mix until well blended. Add prepared vegetables and kamaboko. Mix until vegetables are coated with batter. Drop by spoonfuls or hashi (chopstick) into hot oil. Drain on paper towel. Serve hot.

*Yoshiko Maeda*

# *MAIN DISHES*

# MEAT ROASTING GUIDE

| Cut | Weight Pounds | Approx. Time (Hours) (325° oven) | Internal Temperature |
|---|---|---|---|
| **BEEF** | | | |
| Standing rib roast | | | |
| (10 inch) ribs | 4 | 1¾ | 140° (rare) |
| (If using shorter cut (8-inch) | | 2 | 160° (medium) |
| ribs, allow 30 min. longer) | | 2½ | 170° (well done) |
| | 8 | 2½ | 140° (rare) |
| | | 3 | 160° (medium) |
| | | 4½ | 170° (well done) |
| Rolled ribs | 4 | 2 | 140° (rare) |
| | | 2½ | 160° (medium) |
| | | 3 | 170° (well done) |
| | 6 | 3 | 140° (rare) |
| | | 3¼ | 160° (medium) |
| | | 4 | 170° (well done) |
| Rolled rump | 5 | 2¼ | 140° (rare) |
| (Roast only if high quality. | | 3 | 160° (medium) |
| Otherwise, braise.) | | 3¼ | 170° (well done) |
| Sirloin tip | 3 | 1½ | 140° (rare) |
| (Roast only if high quality. | | 2 | 160° (medium) |
| Otherwise, braise.) | | 2¼ | 170° (well done) |
| **LAMB** | | | |
| Leg | 6 | 3 | 175° (medium) |
| | | 3½ | 180° (well done) |
| | 8 | 4 | 175° (medium) |
| | | 4½ | 180° (well done) |
| **VEAL** | | | |
| Leg (piece) | 5 | 2½ to 3 | 170° (well done) |
| Shoulder | 6 | 3½ | 170° (well done) |
| Rolled shoulder | 3 to 5 | 3 to 3½ | 170° (well done) |

# POULTRY ROASTING GUIDE

| Type of Poultry | Ready-To-Cook Weight | Oven Temperature | Approx. Total Roasting Time |
|---|---|---|---|
| **TURKEY** | 6 to 8 lb. | 325° | 2½ to 3 hr. |
| | 8 to 12 lb. | 325° | 3 to 3½ hr. |
| | 12 to 16 lb. | 325° | 3½ to 4 hr. |
| | 16 to 20 lb. | 325° | 4 to 4½ hr. |
| | 20 to 24 lb. | 300° | 5 to 6 hr. |
| **CHICKEN** | 2 to 2½ lb. | 400° | 1 to 1½ hr. |
| (Unstuffed) | 2½ to 4 lb. | 400° | 1½ to 2½ hr. |
| | 4 to 8 lb. | 325° | 3 to 5 hr. |
| **DUCK** | 3 to 5 lb. | 325° | 2½ to 3 hr. |
| (Unstuffed) | | | |

NOTE: Small chickens are roasted at 400° so that they brown well in the short cooking time. They may also be done at 325° but will take longer and will not be as brown. Increase cooking time 15 to 20 minutes for stuffed chicken and duck.

# MAIN DISHES
## BEEF

### CABBAGE ROLLS

1½ lb. hamburger
1 egg
1 grated onion
1 grated garlic
2 Tbsp. Wesson oil
2 Tbsp. uncooked rice

1 large can solid pack tomatoes
Parsley to taste
Salt and pepper to taste
1 medium size cabbage, parboiled

Mix all ingredients, except cabbage, tomatoes, and egg. Roll in cabbage leaves. Put in pot and pour solid pack tomatoes over. Season to taste. Add beaten egg when almost done.

*Yellow*

# CABBAGE STUFFED WITH GROUND MEAT

12 large cabbage leaves
2 Tbsp. butter or margarine
1 large onion, chopped
1 (16 oz.) can tomato sauce
    or diced tomatoes
2 tsp. brown sugar
Salt
Pepper
1½ lb. lean ground beef or
    turkey

1 c. cooked rice
1 slice bread, crumbled
1 egg
½ tsp. basil
1 tsp. Worcestershire
    sauce
1 small garlic clove,
    crushed

1. In covered 12 inch skillet, cook cabbage leaves in 1 inch boiling water for 5 minutes; drain and set aside.

2. In same skillet over medium heat, in hot butter or margarine, cook onion 5 minutes or until tender, stirring occasionally. Add tomato sauce, brown sugar, ½ teaspoon salt, and ¼ teaspoon pepper; mix well and set aside.

3. In large bowl, combine remaining ingredients and ½ teaspoon salt and ¼ teaspoon pepper.

4. In center of each cabbage leaf, place portion of meat mixture. Fold 2 sides of leaf toward center, from one narrow edge of leaf, and roll up. Place filled leaves, seam sides down, in sauce in skillet. Over medium heat, heat sauce and filled leaves to simmer. Reduce heat to low; cover and simmer 45 minutes. Makes 6 servings.

*Virginia Newgent*

# DAD'S SPECIAL CASSEROLE

1 lb. ground round
½ c. chopped onions
1 (10 oz.) can cream of
   celery soup
½ c. milk
½ tsp. salt

¼ tsp. pepper
¼ tsp. thyme
1 (8 oz.) pkg. sharp cheese,
   grated
4 c. uncooked wide
   noodles

Brown meat; add onions and stir until tender. Stir in cream of celery soup, milk, salt, pepper, and thyme. Cook noodles according to directions. Layer 1 cup noodles in a 2 quart casserole, ½ meat sauce, and ½ (8 ounce) package cheese. Repeat layers. Bake at 350° for 20 minutes. Add remaining cheese and bake for 10 minutes to melt cheese.

*Misae Kameya*

# HAMBURGER-VEGETABLE CASSEROLE

1¼ lb. hamburger
1 c. diced carrots
1 c. peas
4 medium potatoes, diced

1 small onion
½ stalk celery
1 can tomato soup
Salt and pepper to taste

Brown meat, onion, and celery in a little fat. Add salt and pepper. Put ⅓ of meat in buttered casserole, layer of potatoes, then layer of carrots and peas. Repeat, finishing with meat layer. Pour soup, undiluted, over the top and bake approximately 1½ hours at 350°.

This can be hurried by precooking potatoes and carrots while meat is browning. Left over vegetables, including corn, may be used.

*Ludvina Abrew*

# LUCKY CASSEROLE

1 lb. ground beef
1½ c. Cheddar cheese,
   shredded
½ c. dry bread crumbs
⅓ c. milk
¼ c. chopped onion
1 egg
4 c. thin potato slices

1 (9 oz.) frozen cut green
   beans, thawed
⅓ c. flour
1 tsp. salt
⅛ tsp. pepper
1 (15 oz.) can tomato sauce
½ tsp. ground sage

Combine meat, ¾ cup cheese, crumbs, milk, onion, and egg. Mix lightly. Shape into 24 (1½ inch) balls. Combine potatoes, beans, remaining cheese, flour, salt, and pepper. Place in buttered 9x12 inch baking dish. Combine tomato sauce and sage; pour half of sauce over potato mixture. Bake in preheated oven at 350° for 20 minutes. Place meat balls on potato mixture; top with remaining sauce. Bake 45 to 50 minutes, until potatoes are soft.

*Leonilda Hubbard*

# CRESCENT ROLL TACOS

2 (8 oz. tube) rolls crescent
   rolls
1 lb. hamburger
1 can tomato sauce
Grated Cheddar cheese

1 pkg. taco sauce mix
Olives and canned
   mushrooms
   (optional)

Grease a 9x13 inch pan with oil. Divide 1 tube rolls into 4 rectangles. Line the pan. Brown hamburger and drain the oil. Add taco package, tomato sauce, and ⅓ cup water. Simmer for 5 minutes. Pour hamburger mix over crescent rolls in pan. Put cheese, olives, and mushroom over. Open second can of rolls; divide into 4 rectangles and put over hamburger mix. Bake at 425° for about 15 minutes.

# EASY LOCAL-STYLE CHILI

10 lb. ground beef
3 (7 oz.) pkg. Portuguese
  sausage, sliced
3 onions, chopped
2 stalks celery, chopped
10 (1.25 oz.) pkg. chili
  seasoning mix
2 Tbsp. salt

4 tsp. cumin
1 Tbsp. brown sugar
4 (20 oz.) cans stewed
  tomatoes
5 (6 oz.) cans tomato paste
8 (15 oz.) cans kidney
  beans

In a large sauce pot, brown beef lightly. Add sausage and brown. Add onions and celery; cook about 5 minutes. Stir in seasoning mix, salt, cumin, and brown sugar. Add stewed tomatoes, tomato paste, and liquid from beans. Bring to a boil; lower heat and simmer for 10 minutes. Stir in beans and simmer for 10 more minutes. Makes 50 (1 cup) servings.

# EASY SPAGHETTI

1 lb. hamburger or ground
  round
½ c. chopped round onion
½ c. chopped green pepper
1 (10¾ oz.) can cream of
  mushroom soup

1 can tomato soup
½ lb. spaghetti, cooked
½ c. shredded Cheddar
  cheese

Fry hamburger or ground round until browned. Add the round onion and green pepper and cook for 5 minutes. Add the mushroom soup and tomato soup and cook for 10 minutes. Spread the cooked spaghetti in a baking pan, 9x13 inches, and pour the hamburger sauce over it. Top with the shredded cheese. Bake in moderate oven at 350° for 30 minutes.

*Kimiko Anzai*

# HAMBURGER BY THE YARD

Mix:

1 lb. ground chuck
1 (12 oz.) can Mexican style
   corn, drained
½ c. chopped onion
1 egg

1 Tbsp. prepared mustard
1 tsp. salt
⅛ tsp. pepper
1 tsp. MSG (optional)

Remaining ingredients:

1 loaf French bread, cut in
   half lengthwise

6 slices cheese

Forty-five minutes before dinner, heat oven to 350°. Mound mixture evenly on cut side of each French bread half. Bake 35 minutes. Cut cheese slices into 3. Top with cheese. Bake 5 minutes or until cheese melts. Cut diagonally. Yield: 4 super size servings.

# HAMBURGER CURRY

1 lb. hamburger
1 medium size round
   onion, chopped
1 (No. 2) can peas and
   carrots

1 to 2 Tbsp. curry powder
Salt and pepper
2 c. water

Fry onion in 1 tablespoon oil until onion clears. Add hamburger and fry until evenly browned. Add water and can of peas and carrots. Bring to a boil. Add curry powder and salt and pepper to taste and simmer awhile. Thicken gravy with flour.

When fresh carrots and beans are used, increase water to 3 cups. Add carrots and beans before adding water.

*Yellow*

# HELEN'S HAMBURGER AND MACARONI

1 lb. pkg. macaroni or other
  pasta
1 lb. hamburger
1 onion, chopped
1 Tbsp. Worcestershire
  sauce

Salt to taste
1 can tomato soup
1 can cheese soup
½ to 1 small bottle catsup

Boil macaroni until done. Fry hamburger; add chopped onions. Add tomato and cheese soups, flavoring, and cooked macaroni. Mix together and add catsup. Bake in casserole dish at 350° for 20 minutes.

# HUNGARIAN GOULASH

2 Tbsp. salad oil
1 medium onion, chopped
1 lb. ground beef
2 (8 oz.) cans tomato sauce
1 medium carrot, grated

1 (No. 303) whole kernel
  corn
1 tsp. salt
¼ tsp. pepper

Fry onion in hot oil; add beef. Cook, stirring, until light brown. Stir in tomato sauce, carrot, corn, and seasoning. Simmer for 5 minutes. Yield: 8 servings.

*Natsue Kametani*

# ITALIAN DELIGHT

½ lb. spaghetti
½ c. shortening
1 onion, chopped
1 clove garlic, chopped fine
1 green pepper, diced

½ lb. hamburger
1 can tomato soup
1 can corn (cream style)
Salt and pepper to taste

Cook spaghetti and drain. Fry onion, garlic, and green pepper in shortening. Add hamburger. Fry awhile; stir, then add tomato soup, corn, and seasoning to the preceding mixture. Cheese may be added. Cook for 10 minutes on medium heat; remove from fire and add drained spaghetti. Mix well. Turn into baking dish and bake for 30 minutes at 350°.

*Red*

# EASY LASAGNA

1 lb. ground beef or turkey
1 (32 oz.) jar prepared
   spaghetti sauce
1 (8 oz.) pkg. lasagna
   noodles
1 lb. Ricotta or cottage
   cheese

¾ lb. Mozzarella cheese,
   thinly sliced
¾ c. grated Parmesan
   cheese

In a skillet, brown ground beef or turkey; drain. Add spaghetti sauce and mix thoroughly. Cook noodles according to package directions. Drain and rinse with cold water. Mix noodles with a little salad oil to keep pieces from sticking together. Place a few spoonfuls of spaghetti sauce mixture in the bottom of a 15x10x3 inch baking dish. Layer half of the noodles, cheeses, and sauce in dish. Repeat layers. Bake at 375°F. for 40 to 45 minutes. Makes 8 servings.

# ONE STEP LASAGNA

½ to 1 lb. ground beef
½ c. water
1 (32 oz.) jar spaghetti
   sauce
8 oz. lasagna noodles

1 c. small curd cottage
   cheese
12 oz. Mozzarella, sliced
¼ c. grated Parmesan
   cheese

Brown meat and drain off excess oil. Add water and spaghetti sauce and bring to boil. In a 2 quart flat baking dish or 9x13 inch pan, layer sauce, uncooked noodles, ½ of the cottage cheese, ½ of the Mozzarella cheese, and more sauce. Repeat layers, ending with sauce. Cover pan lightly with foil and bake at 375° for 1 hour. Sprinkle with Parmesan cheese. Let lasagna stand 10 minutes before cutting. Serves 6 to 8.

# SKILLET LASAGNA

1 lb. ground beef
2 Tbsp. olive oil or fat
1 (2½ oz.) pkg. spaghetti
   sauce mix
1 lb. or 2 c. cottage cheese
3 c. medium noodles
   (uncooked)

1 Tbsp. basil
1 Tbsp. parsley or flakes
1 (No. 2½) can tomatoes
   (3½ c.)
1 c. cold water
8 oz. shredded Mozzarella
   cheese

1. Heat meat in fat in 12 inch electric skillet at 350°F. (other skillet could be used if with tight lid).

2. Sprinkle ½ package spaghetti sauce mix over meat.

3. Add all of cottage cheese in layer.

4. Add noodles (spread on top).

5. Add remaining spaghetti sauce mix, basil, parsley, and salt.

6. Add tomatoes with liquid and water. Be sure all is moistened. Cover and set heat minder at 250° and cook 30 to 35 minutes or until noodles are done; close vent on cover part of time.

7. Sprinkle cheese over top. Add cover.

8. Let stand 10 to 15 minutes before serving. Yield: 8 servings.

*Doris Wetters*

# BARBECUED MEAT BALLS

1 lb. ground beef
1 tsp. salt
⅛ tsp. pepper

⅔ c. milk
¾ c. oatmeal (uncooked)
2 Tbsp. oil

Combine all ingredients, except fat, and mix well. Shape into 12 balls. Brown meat balls in hot fat in skillet. While meat browns, prepare barbecue sauce.

Barbecue Sauce:

½ c. catsup
2 Tbsp. brown sugar
2 Tbsp. cider vinegar
1 Tbsp. Worcestershire
     sauce

1 Tbsp. shoyu
2 tsp. prepared mustard

Combine all ingredients for sauce and pour over meat balls. Cover pan and cook until meat balls are done (about ½ hour).

*Yellow*

# MEATBALL CASSEROLE

2 lb. ground beef
½ c. commercial sour
   cream
3 Tbsp. dried onion soup
   (mix well before
   measuring)
1 egg, slightly beaten
1½ c. soft bread crumbs

¼ c. butter or margarine
1 (8 oz.) can whole or sliced
   mushrooms and
   liquid
1 (10½ oz.) can cream of
   chicken soup
1⅔ c. water

Mix ground beef, sour cream, onion soup, egg, and soft bread crumbs and form into 16 balls. Brown slowly in margarine. Mix mushrooms, chicken soup, and water and add to meat balls. Simmer 20 minutes, adding more water if needed. Place in 3 quart casserole.

Make butter dumplings and place on top of hot meat and gravy. Bake, uncovered, at 400° for 20 to 25 minutes until dumplings are golden. Makes 8 servings.

If extra sauce is desired, simmer 1 can cream of chicken soup flavored with ¼ teaspoon poultry seasoning and 1 teaspoon onion flakes. Stir in ½ cup sour cream and reheat.

Butter Crumb Dumplings:

2 c. sifted flour
4 tsp. baking powder
1 Tbsp. poppy seeds
1 tsp. celery salt
1 tsp. poultry seasoning
2 tsp. dried onion flakes

¼ c. oil
¾ c. plus 2 Tbsp. milk
¼ c. melted butter or
   margarine
2 c. soft bread crumbs

Mix first 6 ingredients together. Mix in oil and milk. Stir melted butter into crumbs. Drop dough by tablespoons in 12 equal portions into buttered crumbs and roll to cover with crumbs.

*Virginia Newgent*

# MEAT BALLS WITH FRENCH CREAM

1 lb. ground beef
8 stuffed green olives
Seasoned flour
1 Tbsp. butter or margarine
Hot buttered pilaf or rice
1 Tbsp. Worcestershire
    sauce

2 tsp. onion juice
½ tsp. dried whole thyme
1 c. light cream or half &
    half
½ tsp. lemon juice

Form meat in 8 balls, shaping each around an olive. Roll meat balls in seasoned flour. Brown in butter, then reduce heat and cook 10 to 12 minutes, turning frequently. When meat balls are done to your liking, lift from skillet and place atop hot buttered pilaf or fluffy rice.

Pour off fat; to browned bits of meat in skillet, add Worcestershire sauce, onion juice, and thyme. Cook 1 minute. Add cream; cook and stir over low heat only until hot through. Remove from heat and add lemon juice. At once pour the sauce over the meat balls. Makes 4 servings.

# ITALIAN MEAT BALLS

1 lb. ground beef
1 clove garlic, minced
Chopped parsley (fresh or
    dried, optional)
¾ c. grated cheese
    (Parmesan)
¾ c. bread crumbs
½ c. boiling water

2 Tbsp. cooking oil
1 (1 lb. 13 oz.) can tomatoes
2 eggs
1 (8 oz.) can tomato sauce
1 (6 oz.) can tomato paste
1½ (1 lb. 13 oz.) cans water
    (use tomato can)
Salt and pepper to taste

1. Combine beef, eggs, garlic, parsley, cheese, crumbs, boiling water, salt, and pepper.
2. Shape into balls.
3. Heat oil in pan. Brown meat balls; set aside.
4. Drain fat from pan into large saucepan. Add tomatoes, tomato sauce, and tomato paste and 1½ cans water. Bring to boil; simmer 45 minutes.
5. Add meat balls and simmer 45 minutes longer.

*Helen Apana*

# SWEET-SOUR MEATBALLS

¾ lb. ground beef
¾ c. fine dry crumbs
⅛ c. sesame seeds, toasted
Dash of monosodium
    glutamate (optional)
1 small can pineapple
    chunks

1 small onion, minced
1 egg, beaten
⅙ c. salt
Dash of pepper
1 Tbsp. salad oil

Sweet-Sour Sauce:

2 Tbsp. cornstarch
½ c. sugar
¼ c. white vinegar

¼ c. pineapple juice
2 tsp. shoyu sauce
¼ c. water

Combine beef, crumbs, onion, egg, sesame seeds, salt, monosodium glutamate, and pepper. Shape meat mixture into balls, putting a chunk of pineapple in the center of each meatball. Heat oil in skillet; saute meatballs, a few at a time, browning well on all sides. Cover and cook on low heat till meatballs are done (a few minutes).

While the meatballs are cooking, make the Sweet-Sour Sauce in a small pan. Cook about 5 minutes, stirring constantly, till thickened. (Pineapple chunks may be added to sauce if desired.) Pour the sauce over the meatballs and serve. Serves 4.

*Green*

# TERIYAKI MEATBALLS

1½ lb. ground beef
¼ c. finely chopped onion
1 egg
½ tsp. salt

2 Tbsp. soy sauce
½ tsp. grated fresh ginger
1 clove garlic, grated

Combine ingredients together and mix well. Shape into 1 inch meatballs and place it in a glass baking dish. Cover with plastic wrap.

Sauce:

½ c. soy sauce
1 Tbsp. sake
3 Tbsp. sugar
1 tsp. ginger, grated

1 clove garlic, grated
1 tsp. cornstarch, mixed
    with water

Combine all the ingredients for the sauce in a glass bowl. Microwave on HIGH until sauce boils. Microwave meatballs on ROAST for 5 to 6 minutes or until piping hot.

*Gold*

# TERIYAKI MEAT ROLLS

1 egg
1 lb. lean ground meat
1 pkg. teriyaki sauce
    powder
¼ c. grated carrots

1 small round onion,
    chopped
4 sheets sushi nori
Bread crumbs
Oil

Mix ground meat, egg, seasoned powder, carrots, and onion. Divide into 4 equal parts. Spread each portion onto 1 sheet of nori as you would when rolling sushi, starting with a thin layer closest to you and ending about 1 to 1½ inches from the top end of the nori. Refrigerate rolls to get them firm, about 2 to 3 hours, or freeze them if you are in a hurry. Cut each roll into 10 to 12 slices. Coat cut ends with bread crumbs and fry until nicely browned.

Note: This can be made ahead and frozen; cut when partially thawed and fried. They may also be fried and then frozen for ready pupu on hand.

# MEAT LOAF - BARBECUE STYLE

1½ lb. ground beef
½ c. finely chopped onion
½ c. fresh bread crumbs
1 egg, beaten
1½ tsp. salt
¼ tsp. pepper
2 (8 oz.) cans tomato sauce

3 Tbsp. vinegar
3 Tbsp. sugar
2 Tbsp. prepared mustard
2 tsp. Worcestershire
   sauce
½ c. water

Mix together beef, bread crumbs, onion, beaten egg, salt, pepper, and ½ can tomato sauce. Form into loaf and put in shallow pan (about 7x10 inches). Combine the rest of the tomato sauce and all other ingredients. Pour over loaf. Bake in moderate oven at 350° for 1 hour and 15 minutes. Baste occasionally. Makes 4 to 6 servings.

*Ruth Inouye*

# EASY MEAT LOAF

2 lb. hamburger
2 cans vegetable soup
3 handfuls oatmeal
1 round onion, chopped

4 eggs
¾ tsp. salt
¼ tsp. pepper

Mix all ingredients and put in greased loaf pan. Bake at 350° for 1 hour.

*Blue*

# VEGETABLE MEAT LOAF

2 lb. ground beef
2 eggs
½ c. chopped onion
2 tsp. salt

¼ tsp. pepper
1 can vegetable soup
1¼ c. rolled oats
¼ c. catsup

Mix ingredients thoroughly. Press into loaf pan and bake in 400° oven for 1 hour. Unmold on platter and serve in slices.

*Red*

# FREEZER MEAT SAUCE

⅓ c. salad oil
3 cloves garlic, minced
3 green peppers, chopped
3 large onions, sliced
3 lb. chuck, ground
2 c. boiling water
4 (8 oz.) cans tomato sauce
3 (6 oz.) cans tomato paste
   (2 c.)

1 Tbsp. salt
1 Tbsp. paprika
1 tsp. celery salt
1 tsp. garlic salt
1 tsp. chili powder
2 Tbsp. Worcestershire
3 Tbsp. bottled thick meat
   sauce
3 Tbsp. chili sauce

In hot oil in large kettle, cook garlic, peppers, and onions 5 minutes. Add meat; cook over high heat until all red color disappears. Add water and rest of ingredients; simmer, uncovered, 2 hours. Cool quickly. Freeze in 1 pint freezer containers. Makes 7 pints.

To thaw: Place container under hot water long enough so that contents will slip out. Or, let container stand at room temperature several hours, then heat sauce in double boiler.

# ONE-DISH MEAL

1 lb. hamburger
1 medium onion, chopped
1 can green peas

1 can tomato soup
½ soup can cold water
4 to 5 potatoes, sliced

Fry hamburger until browned; add remaining ingredients. Stir gently; cover and cook slowly over low heat for 20 to 30 minutes, stirring occasionally. Yield: 4 to 5 servings.

*Gold*

# HAMBURGER PATTIES

1 lb. ground round (may substitute ground turkey or chicken)
2 slices bread, shredded
½ c. milk
1 medium round onion, chopped

1 tsp. garlic salt
1 Tbsp. oyster sauce
1 Tbsp. mayonnaise
2 Tbsp. onion soup mix
2 eggs
Pepper

Mix all the ingredients together and form into patties. Fry in a little oil in pan.

*Audrey Kong*

# KOREAN MEAT PATTIES

1 lb. ground round or meat of your choice
1 egg, slightly beaten
2 Tbsp. milk
2 tsp. sugar
½ tsp. (or more) salt
⅛ tsp. pepper (black)

1 Tbsp. plus 1½ tsp. shoyu
1 Tbsp. sesame seed, toasted and crushed
1 small clove of garlic, minced
¼ c. chopped onions
¾ c. day old bread crumbs

Combine all ingredients, except ground meat, and mix thoroughly. Add ground meat and blend; handle mixture lightly. Shape into 6 patties and broil. Serves 6.

*Green*

# WHOPPER-BURGERS

Two juicy meat patties in one - and there's a surprise in between.

**2 lb. ground beef**                    **Prepared mustard**
**Salt and pepper**

Pickle Filling:

**Pickle relish**
**½ inch cubes sharp**
    **process American**
    **cheese**

Or, fill each with a thin onion slice, and a round of smoky cheese.

Using a ⅓ cup measure, divide ground beef in 10 mounds. Flatten each mound between squares of waxed paper to a 4 inch patty. Set half the patties aside for "lids."

Sprinkle remaining patties with salt and pepper, then spread with prepared mustard, leaving ½ inch margin for sealing. Top with a mound of Pickle Filling. Cover the filling with "lids," sealing edges well.

Place on greased grill or spread both sides with soft butter or margarine. Season top with salt and pepper. Broil over hot coals about 10 minutes; turn and broil about 10 minutes more or till done to your liking. Season second side. Slip patties into hot buttered buns. Makes 5 Whopper-Burgers.

*Ludvina Abrew*

# PINEAPPLE MEAT RINGS

1 lb. ground beef
½ c. bread crumbs
1 beaten egg
1 c. milk
1¼ tsp. salt
3 Tbsp. minced onion

⅛ tsp. pepper
¼ tsp. dry mustard
⅛ tsp. sage
1 tsp. curry (optional)
10 pineapple slices

Combine all ingredients, except pineapple slices. Divide meat mixture into 10 equal portions; shape like a doughnut and arrange on individual pineapple slices. Place on a rack in pan and bake at 350°F. for 45 minutes. Garnish with stuffed olive and parsley in center of each ring. Makes 10 rings.

An excellent oven meal served with green beans baked in mushroom soup, a green salad, hot French bread, a simple dessert as ice cream or sherbet, and coffee.

*Ludvina Abrew*

# BEEF BROCCOLI

1 lb. meat, sliced
2 tsp. sugar
2 Tbsp. shoyu
1 Tbsp. crushed ginger
2 Tbsp. sherry or whiskey

2 Tbsp. flour
2 lb. broccoli, sliced
½ c. water
½ tsp. salt

Marinate meat with sugar, shoyu, ginger, sherry, and flour. Heat 1 teaspoon oil and stir-fry broccoli; add salt and water. Simmer until tender, then take out. Stir-fry meat in 1 tablespoon heated oil for 2 minutes. Add broccoli and serve.

*Blue*

# BEEF WITH LONG RICE

1 lb. beef
½ bundle of long rice
2 round medium onions

½ head lettuce
1 piece ginger
Green onions

Marinade:

2 Tbsp. flour
1 Tbsp. sugar
½ tsp. ginger juice

1 Tbsp. shoyu
½ tsp. salt

Gravy:

2 tsp. cornstarch
1 Tbsp. shoyu
¼ tsp. ajinomoto

¾ c. water
½ tsp. salt

Slice beef into 2 inch strips; marinate in sauce. Cut dry long rice into 3 inch lengths. Deep-fry a small handful of long rice at a time; rice deep-fries instantly and becomes puffy and crispy. Fry both sides of long rice and drain, then place on platter lined with shredded lettuce. Slice onions and stir-fry in 1 tablespoon oil for 2 minutes, then remove from pot. Stir-fry marinated meat in 1 tablespoon oil for 2 minutes and remove. Mix meat with onions and place on crispy long rice.

Mix gravy ingredients and bring to a boil. Pour gravy over meat.

# BEEF WITH NOODLES

8 oz. Chinese style thin egg
   noodles, cooked and
   drained
½ c. water
3 tsp. shoyu
¼ tsp. salt
2 tsp. instant chicken
   bouillon granules

1 lb. uncooked teriyaki
   meat
6 Tbsp. vegetable oil
4 pieces green onions,
   sliced diagonally
1 piece fresh ginger, sliced
2 cloves garlic, crushed

Spread cooked noodles evenly over towel to dry. Combine water, 2 teaspoons of shoyu, salt, and bouillon in bowl. Slice meat about 2 inches long. Heat 4 tablespoons oil in wok over high heat. Add noodles and stir-fry 3 minutes.

Pour water mixture over noodles; toss until noodles are coated. Place noodles in serving plate and keep warm. Heat remaining 2 tablespoons oil in wok over high heat. Add beef, onions, ginger, garlic, and remaining 1 teaspoon shoyu. Stir-fry until beef is cooked, about 5 minutes. Spoon meat mixture over noodles.

*T. Oki*

# OYSTER SAUCE BEEF AND CHINESE PEAS

1½ lb. beef
1 Tbsp. cornstarch
1 Tbsp. sugar
1 tsp. shoyu
2 tsp. sherry
¼ c. oyster sauce

2 Tbsp. corn oil
1 clove garlic, minced
½ c. thinly sliced onion
1½ c. Chinese peas,
   blanched*

Cut meat in thin strips. Combine cornstarch, sugar, shoyu, sherry, oyster sauce, and 1 tablespoon of oil. Mix with meat. Heat remaining tablespoon of oil in a saucepan and brown garlic. Add meat mixture and onion; stir-fry 1 minute. Add peas and cook 1 more minute. Makes 4 to 6 servings.

* To blanch, pour hot water over the peas in their pods. Drain before adding pods to the rest of the ingredients.

*Blue*

# BEEF WITH STRING BEANS

½ lb. tender beef
1 lb. string beans, cut into
    1 inch lengths

1 clove garlic, crushed
1 sliced ginger, crushed

Seasoning - Mix in bowl:

1 Tbsp. shoyu
½ tsp. sugar
1 tsp. wine

1 tsp. salt
1 Tbsp. cornstarch

Slice beef very thin and flat. Add beef to seasoning; let stand for 10 to 20 minutes. Bring to a boil, 1 cup water and add 1 teaspoon salt. Add string beans and boil for 4 minutes without lid. Do not strain. Heat pan with oil. Brown ginger and garlic; fry meat for 2 minutes, until almost done. Add beans with liquid and cook for 1 minute. Add more cornstarch if thicker gravy is desired. Serve hot.

*Blue*

# BEEF TOMATOES

2 stalks celery
3 or 4 tomatoes
1 stalk green onion
3 or 4 green peppers

1 or 2 onions
1 lb. beef slices, soaked in
    the following mixture for
    ½ hour before cooking

Mixture:

1 tsp. wine
2 Tbsp. oil
2 tsp. shoyu

2 tsp. sugar
1 tsp. cornstarch

Gravy:

1 tsp. corn starch
1 tsp. shoyu
1 Tbsp. catsup

2 tsp. sugar
½ tsp. Worcestershire
    sauce

Cook soaked beef; remove from pan. Cook vegetables; put beef back in pan and add gravy and cook for a minute.

*Yellow*

# BUTTER YAKI

2 lb. tender thinly sliced
   meat
2 lb. vegetables (wonbok,
   watercress, green
   onion, bean sprout),
   cut in 2 inch lengths

1 block butter
1 can Japanese
   mushrooms, sliced
   lengthwise

Sauce:

1 c. shoyu
¼ c. mirin (Japanese wine)
½ c. grated daikon (using
   Japanese grater)

¼ c. sugar
½ tsp. ajinomoto
2 limes, cut in halves

Fry meat in butter, using electric skillet at dinner table. Serve as it is done, dipping in individual dishes of prepared sauce. Fry vegetables and mushrooms and serve same as meat. Eat while it is hot.

For sauce: Heat shoyu, sugar, and mirin. Cool and serve in individual dishes. Individuals to squeeze in own lime juice and add own grated daikon before dipping meat and vegetables.

*Red*

# BROILED CHUCK STEAK

With these seasonings, it tastes like a T-bone!

2½ lb. chuck steak (½ inch
   thick)
½ c. chopped onion
½ c. lemon juice
¼ c. salad oil
½ tsp. salt

½ tsp. celery salt
½ tsp. pepper
½ tsp. thyme
½ tsp. oregano
½ tsp. rosemary
1 clove garlic, minced

Combine all ingredients, except steak. Marinate steak in mixture 1 to 2 hours, turning several times. Broil 2 inches from heat for 15 minutes. Turn. Broil 15 minutes more. Baste with marinade during broiling. Serves 4.

*Ludvina Abrew*

# FOIL WRAPPED CHUCK STEAK SUPPER

1 (6 oz.) can sliced
    mushrooms
1 env. (½ pkg.) onion soup
    mix
1 Tbsp. Worcestershire
    sauce
3 lb. chuck steak, cut 1 inch
    thick

3 medium carrots,
    quartered
2 stalks celery, cut into
    sticks
3 medium potatoes,
    quartered
2 Tbsp. oil
½ tsp. salt

Drain mushrooms, saving liquid. Combine liquid with onion soup mix and Worcestershire sauce. Tear off a 2½ foot length of 18 inch width aluminum foil. Put half of soup mixture in center of foil; add meat. Put remaining soup mixture on top. Add mushrooms and vegetables. Brush with oil and sprinkle with salt. Fold foil over and seal securely to hold juices in. Place in shallow baking pan. Bake at 375°F. for 2½ to 3 hours. Makes 9 servings of 3 ounce protein each.

# POLISH BEEF ROLL-UPS

2 lb. steak, cut ¼ inch thick
2 tsp. salt
½ tsp. pepper
2 c. soft bread crumbs
1 small minced onion

1 slightly beaten egg
½ c. butter
Flour
2 c. water or beef stock

Cut steak into strips about 4½ x 2 inches. Use part of salt and pepper on meat. Pound meat. Make dressing of bread crumbs, onion, egg, ¼ cup melted butter, and remaining salt and pepper. Spread dressing on meat and roll up. Secure with toothpicks or skewers. Roll in flour and brown in remaining butter. Add liquid. Cover and simmer until tender. Remove skewers and pour gravy over roll-ups on serving plate. Serves 5 to 6.

Ideal for wild meat. For wild meat, use a little sage.

*Lei Matsumura*

# MORCON
## (Stuffed and rolled flank steak)

1 lb. flank steak
½ c. lemon juice
2 tsp. soy sauce
½ tsp. salt
¼ tsp. pepper
¼ c. ground ham
¼ lb. ground pork
¼ c. chopped sweet pickles
2 Tbsp. raisins

1 egg, beaten
2 hard cooked eggs
1 Tbsp. salad oil
2 c. water
¼ c. vinegar
1 small onion, sliced
2 cloves garlic, crushed
½ c. tomato sauce
1 bay leaf

To butterfly steak, slit horizontally from 1 long side to within ½ inch of the other side; open and pound until about ¼ inch thick. Combine lemon juice, 1 teaspoon of the soy sauce, the salt, and pepper; pour over steak. Marinate for 1 hour, turning once.

Combine ham, pork, pickles, raisins, and beaten egg; spread over steak to within ½ inch of edges. Cut eggs into quarters; arrange crosswise over meat mixture about 2 inches from nearest edges. Roll with the grain like jelly roll; secure with string.

In a large saucepan, heat oil; brown meat roll on all sides. Add remaining 1 teaspoon soy sauce and all remaining ingredients. Cover; bring to a boil and simmer 1½ hours or until tender. Thicken pan liquid if desired. Slice crosswise and serve with pan liquid. Makes 6 servings.

# POT ROAST

4 lb. chuck steak
¼ c. shoyu
1 Tbsp. mirin
⅓ c. water

¼ c. brown sugar
¼ c. catsup
1 tsp. grated ginger
1 tsp. minced garlic

Brown chuck steak. Add other ingredients; simmer for 2 hours.

*Vicky Malaqui*

# CHINESE POT ROAST

1 clove garlic, minced
1½ tsp. minced ginger root
¼ tsp. heong liu fun
1 tsp. salt
4 lb. chuck roast
2 Tbsp. brown sugar
1 Tbsp. sherry
¼ c. soy sauce

2 Tbsp. oil
1½ c. water
3 carrots, pared
3 potatoes, pared
1 onion, peeled
1 stalk celery
2 Tbsp. cornstarch
2 green onions, chopped

Combine garlic, ginger, heong liu fun, and salt; rub over roast. Mix sugar, sherry, and soy sauce; pour over roast and let stand 30 minutes; turn once. Heat a large skillet; add oil and brown roast. Pour marinade over roast; add 1¼ cups of water. Cover and simmer 2 hours. Cut vegetables into serving pieces and add to roast; simmer 30 minutes longer or until tender. Remove roast and vegetables.

To make gravy, mix cornstarch with remaining ¼ cup water; stir into the sauce left in skillet. Add green onions; cook until mixture thickens. Makes 12 servings of 3 ounces protein each.

# BAKED SHORT RIBS

5 lb. short ribs, cut into
    serving pieces
2 Tbsp. Worcestershire
    sauce
¾ c. catsup
2 Tbsp. brown sugar
2 tsp. salt

Dash of pepper
2 cloves garlic, minced
2 Tbsp. vinegar
1 tsp. paprika
1 tsp. chili powder
¾ c. water
2 large onions, sliced

Combine all ingredients with exception of the onions and let stand for ½ hour or longer. Place in a large casserole and spread onions on top. Cover and bake in 350° oven for 2 hours or until meat is tender.

*Thelma Iwami*

# BARBECUED SHORT RIBS

3 lb. beef short ribs
3 Tbsp. oil
1 onion, chopped
3 to 4 Tbsp. vinegar
2 Tbsp. sugar
⅓ c. water

3 Tbsp. Worcestershire
  sauce
1 tsp. prepared mustard
½ c. sliced celery
2 tsp. salt
1 c. catsup

Melt oil in a heavy skillet. Brown the short ribs and onion. Add all remaining ingredients; cover and cook slowly for 1½ to 2 hours or until tender or bake in a moderate oven (350°). Yield: 4 servings.

*Red*

# SHORT RIBS DELIGHT

2¾ lb. short ribs
Salt and pepper to taste
¼ c. catsup
1 (8 oz.) can tomato sauce
1 Tbsp. sugar
1 piece garlic, minced
¼ c. packed brown sugar

3 Tbsp. shoyu
1½ Tbsp. vinegar, lime or
  lemon juice
1½ Tbsp. wine or any other
  liquor
1½ Tbsp. Worcestershire
  sauce

Brown meat well with a little salt and pepper and place in roasting pan. Mix all other ingredients together and pour over meat. Cover pan with foil before roasting. Roast for 2 hours at 325°F.

Note: Heavy skillet may be used. Cook for 1½ hours or until tender.

*Gold*

# KOREAN SHORT RIBS

Use 4 pounds short ribs.

Sauce:

½ c. shoyu
1 Tbsp. sugar
2 cloves garlic, crushed
1 Tbsp. honey
Ginger, finely sliced

2 stalks green onion,
    chopped
1 tsp. sesame oil
1 tsp. oil

Slice meat 1½ inches. Combine sauce ingredients and marinate meat for a couple of hours. Broil to desired doneness.

*T. Oki*

# KOREAN SHORT RIBS

3 lb. short ribs
3 Tbsp. sesame seeds
3 Tbsp. salad oil
¼ c. shoyu

¼ c. chopped green onion
1 clove garlic, crushed
1 slice ginger, slivered
2 tsp. sugar

Combine toasted sesame seeds with oil, shoyu, green onions, garlic, ginger, and sugar.

Marinate meat overnight in refrigerator. Broil in oven, or over charcoal.

# KOREAN SHORT RIBS

3 lb. short ribs
½ c. shoyu
1 tsp. vegetable oil or
    sesame oil
1 clove garlic
½ c. green onions,
    chopped fine

2 Tbsp. sesame seeds,
    toasted and crushed
5 Tbsp. sugar
½ tsp. salt
¼ tsp. cayenne or 1 small
    chili pepper

Combine preceding ingredients. Soak overnight. Broil in oven or charcoal broil.

*Betsy Arakawa*

# EASY STEW

Combine:

1½ lb. stew meat
2 carrots, cut in chunks
1 to 2 stalks celery, sliced
2 potatoes, cut in chunks
String beans, cut in thirds
1 (28 oz.) can crushed
    tomatoes
1 can cream of mushroom
    soup

1 c. water
1 can tomato sauce or
    tomato soup
1 tsp. salt
¼ tsp. garlic powder
⅛ tsp. black pepper
1 bay leaf

Put in a casserole and bake at 350° for 2½ to 3 hours. Or, cook in a slow cooker at LOW for 8 hours.

# NOUVELLE BEEF STROGANOFF

1 lb. beef tenderloin (lean
   beef round)
2 c. sliced mushrooms
1 onion, sliced
3 Tbsp. polyunsaturated
   vegetable oil
3 Tbsp. enriched all-
   purpose flour

2 c. beef broth
2 Tbsp. tomato paste
1 tsp. dry mustard
¼ tsp. oregano
¼ tsp. dill weed
2 Tbsp. dry sherry
⅓ c. lowfat yogurt, drained
½ tsp. pepper

Remove all the visible fat from the meat and cut into thin strips about 2 inches long. Grind the pepper into the meat and let stand 2 hours. Put the oil into a heavy skillet and saute the onion; add the beef and then the mushrooms. Brown quickly and remove all the ingredients from the pan. Blend the flour into the oil left in the pan and add the broth, stirring constantly until smooth and slightly thick. Add the tomato paste, dry mustard, oregano, dill weed, and sherry. Blend well. Add the meat, mushrooms, and onion back to the sauce and cook 20 minutes. Beat the drained yogurt and add some of the hot sauce to the yogurt to warm it up. Lower the heat of the skillet and slowly add the yogurt to the pan about 5 minutes before serving. Serves 6.

Nutrients per serving: 334 calories, 21 g fat, 7 g carbohydrates, 70 mg cholesterol.

*Ludvina Abrew*

# SUKIYAKI

1 tsp. fat
1 c. sliced onion
1 lb. beef, sliced thin
4 tsp. sugar
½ c. shoyu
1 c. sliced bamboo shoots
½ block tofu, cubed

½ c. sliced mushrooms
2 c. watercress, cut in 1½ inches
½ bunch long rice, washed, soaked in hot water for ½ hour, and cut in 4 inch lengths

Melt fat in skillet on thermostatically controlled burner set at 200°F. Add sliced onion and stir. Stir in beef and brown. Stir in sugar and shoyu. Add bamboo shoots, tofu, and mushrooms. Cook 2 to 4 minutes.

Before serving, stir in and heat watercress, green onion, and long rice. Serves 6.

*Blue*

# SUKIYAKI OR HEKKA

Definition: Beef, pork, or chicken in shoyu sauce with a variety of vegetables added.

Bamboo shoots, celery, garland chrysanthemum, green onions, mushrooms, onions, tomatoes, and watercress are used. Soybean curd (tofu) and konnyaku are frequently added. This dish is usually prepared at the table over a charcoal brazier. The hot sukiyaki may be served in a bowl into which a raw egg has been broken. The hot mixture cooks the egg as the two are mixed with chopsticks.

2 Tbsp. salad oil
½ c. sugar
1⅛ c. shoyu
1 bunch green onions, cut in 1½ inch lengths (with tops)
2 medium size onions, sliced thin
1 (10½ oz.) can bamboo shoots, sliced thin
1 block tofu, cut in 1 inch cubes (if desired)
1 bundle long rice (bean thread), soaked in water until soft and cut into 1½ inch lengths

1½ lb. round steak, sliced diagonally in very thin slices
1 c. water or mushroom stock
½ lb. watercress or spinach, cut into 2 inch lengths
1 (10½ oz.) can mushrooms, sliced thin
1 c. celery, sliced diagonally in 1½ inch pieces

Heat oil in a heavy iron or aluminum frying pan. Fry ⅓ of the meat slightly, then add 2 tablespoons sugar. Three minutes later, add ½ cup soyu; cook 3 minutes, then add ⅓ of the onions.

When the onions are soft, add ⅓ of the celery, mushrooms, long rice, and bamboo shoots, and ½ cup water or mushroom stock, and cook 3 minutes. Add ⅓ of the green vegetables and green onions. Add ⅓ cup more shoyu, and more sugar and water if necessary. Add the tofu and serve immediately. Yield: 6 servings.

*(Continued on next page)*

*(Continued from previous page)*

The Japanese custom is to prepare sukiyaki in a frying pan over a charcoal brazier at the table. Approximately ⅓ of the ingredients are cooked at the beginning and more added as the individual bowls are filled from the frying pan. Fu (gluten cakes) may be substituted for the tofu. Konnyaku may be added. Serve hot with rice.

*Red*

## TERIYAKI

1 or 1½ lb. sliced beef or chicken
½ c. shoyu
½ c. sugar (or less to suit one's taste)
2 Tbsp. mirin or sherry wine
1 clove garlic, chopped very fine
1 inch piece ginger, crushed

Combine ingredients and let beef or chicken soak for at least 1½ to 2 hours. Broil in oven or over charcoal.

For Korean style sauce, add:

2 Tbsp. sesame seed oil
1 tsp. sesame seeds
A little chili pepper
¼ c. chopped green onions

*Green*

## TERIYAKI BEEF

3 lb. barbecue beef
⅓ c. sugar
½ c. soy sauce
1 clove garlic, crushed
1 (½ inch) piece ginger root, crushed
¼ tsp. monosodium glutamate (optional)

Place beef in bowl. Combine sugar, soy sauce, garlic, ginger, and monosodium glutamate. Marinate beef for at least 30 minutes. Place beef on rack of broiling pan; broil 3 inches from unit in electric oven for 3 to 5 minutes on each side. Serve immediately. Makes 6 servings.

# PINEAPPLE TERIYAKIS

1 lb. tender top round or sirloin of beef, cut ¾ inch thick
2½ c. (one No. 2 can) pineapple chunks, drained
½ c. syrup drained from chunks
¼ c. soy sauce
1 clove garlic, chopped fine
1 tsp. chopped fresh ginger root or ¾ tsp. ground ginger
1 small jar stuffed olives, drained (about 22)
22 short wooden or metal skewers (about 4 inches long)

With a sharp knife, cut meat into bite-size pieces, about the same size as the pineapple chunks. Combine pineapple syrup, soy sauce, garlic, and ginger; pour over meat cubes and set aside at room temperature for at least 1 hour. Alternate cubes of meat and pineapple chunks on skewers, then finish off with a stuffed olive. Broil 3 inches from heat, turning once, for 10 to 12 minutes. Serve very hot. This recipe makes 20 to 22 servings, sufficient as an appetizer for 8 to 10 persons.

Teriyakis are equally good to serve with rice and a salad for luncheon or supper. In that case, cut meat in larger pieces, or use longer skewers. The amounts given will be adequate for 4 to 5 persons.

*Ludvina Abrew*

# CORNED BEEF PATTIES

1 can corned beef
1 medium onion, chopped fine
⅓ c. minced parsley
6 eggs, slightly beaten
1 tsp. salt
¼ tsp. pepper

Combine and stir until well blended. Drop by spoonful into well greased frying pan and fry.

*Green*

# CALIFORNIA SAUCE

Laura's Ono-licious marinade for shish-kabobs.

1 c. salad oil
¾ c. shoyu
¼ c. lemon juice
¼ c. Worcestershire sauce
¼ c. prepared mustard

1 to 2 tsp. coarse black
  pepper
2 cloves garlic, mashed
2 Tbsp. sugar

Soak meat in sauce for half a day. May also soak mushrooms and round onions in sauce with meat. Yield: Enough for 4 to 6 pounds meat.

# PORK

## BASIC PORK (OR CHICKEN) ADOBO

3 lb. pork, cut in serving
    pieces
1 tsp. peppercorns
1 tsp. salt
4 Tbsp. shoyu (optional)
1 bay leaf (optional)

4 cloves garlic, mashed
1 c. vinegar or enough to
    cover meat
½ medium onion, chopped
Water (if meat is tough)

1. Combine ingredients in a heavy saucepan.
2. Simmer until meat is tender. If meat is still tough and there is no more stock, add ½ cup of hot water and continue simmering.
3. When meat is tender, the meat is browned slightly in its own fat.
4. Serve hot with hot rice. Serves 6.

Note: Cook *slowly* on a very *low* heat until meat becomes tender and brown in the fat when the vinegar and water has been absorbed in the meat and evaporated.

## BAKED LUNCHEON MEAT

2 (12 oz.) cans luncheon
    meat
1 small can crushed
    pineapple

1 c. brown sugar
Whole cloves

Place meat in baking dish and stud with cloves. Top with sugar and pineapple and bake in 350° oven for ½ hour.

Canned yams may be placed around meat the last 10 minutes of baking.

*Red*

# BAKED PORK AND BEANS

1 (1 lb. 15 oz.) can pork and
  beans
⅓ c. catsup
¼ c. minced onions

1 tsp. dry mustard
⅓ c. sugar
2 slices bacon

Mix all ingredients. Put in baking dish with bacon slices on top. Bake 45 minutes at 325°F.

*Green*

# BAKED SPARERIBS

3 lb. spareribs
¼ c. Worcestershire sauce
¾ c. catsup
2 Tbsp. sugar
Ajinomoto

½ tsp. salt
Dash of pepper
1 piece garlic, crushed
1 piece ginger, crushed

Combine all ingredients and let stand for ½ hour or longer. Bake in 350° oven for 1 hour.

*Red*

# BARBECUED RIBS

3 lb. lean pork ribs
1 (1 inch) piece ginger,
  grated or thinly sliced
1 clove garlic, pureed
1 Tbsp. sherry
½ c. soy sauce

1 c. tomato ketchup
1 tsp. salt
⅓ c. vinegar
Dash of Tabasco
  (according to taste)

Boil ribs in water. Simmer for about 1 hour or until meat is tender but will not fall off bones. Drain. Combine remaining ingredients; marinate ribs in sauce for at least 30 minutes. Broil in oven or over charcoal.

# BARBEQUE SPARERIBS

4 to 5 lb. spareribs
1 onion, chopped
1 c. catsup
1½ c. water
2 tsp. salt

2 Tbsp. Worcestershire
   sauce
¾ c. brown sugar
1 tsp. prepared mustard
½ tsp. ajinomoto (optional)

Cut spareribs 3 inches wide and 5 inches long. Brown onion in a baking pan over low heat on stove. Combine the remaining ingredients and pour over the ribs. Cover. Bake in a 350° oven for 2 hours. Spoon the sauce over the ribs 2 or 3 times during baking. Bake, uncovered, 15 minutes.

*Janet Yayoshi*

# BARBECUE SPARERIBS

3 to 4 lb. spareribs (baby
   back ribs are good)

1 c. vinegar
Water

Cook spareribs in vinegar and water to cover for about 15 minutes. Drain.

Mix together:

1 c. ketchup
1 c. sugar

1 c. shoyu

Pour mixture over meat. Bake in oven about 1 hour at 400°.

# BARBECUED SPARERIBS - DAE JI KALBI GUI

3 lb. slab lean spareribs,
  cut crosswise
  through bones
¾ c. soy sauce
⅓ c. ko choo jung
¼ c. sake
½ c. honey
½ c. brown sugar

½ c. chopped green onions
1 Tbsp. chopped garlic
1 Tbsp. minced ginger root
2 Tbsp. toasted sesame
  seed
2 Tbsp. sesame oil
½ tsp. pepper
¼ c. salad oil

Place spareribs in a large saucepan; add water to cover. Bring to a boil; lower heat and simmer for 1 hour. Drain. Combine ½ cup of the soy sauce, the ko choo jung, sake, ¼ cup of the honey, brown sugar, green onions, garlic, ginger, sesame seed, sesame oil, and pepper. Add spareribs and marinate overnight in refrigerator. Place spareribs on rack of a baking pan and bake in an electric oven at 325°F. for 30 minutes.

While spareribs are cooking, make a basting sauce by combining the remaining ¼ cup soy sauce, the remaining ¼ cup honey, and the ¼ cup salad oil. Turn spareribs and baste with sauce. Cook for 30 more minutes, turning and basting several times with sauce. To serve, cut ribs between the bones. Makes 6 servings.

# BLACK BEAN SPARERIBS

2 lb. spareribs, cut up          3 Tbsp. oil

    Black Bean Mixture:

3 Tbsp. salted black beans       6 cloves garlic
1 tsp. hot bean sauce

    Broth: Use 1 can chicken broth.

    Cornstarch:

¼ c. cornstarch                  ¼ c. water

    Garnish:

½ c. green onions, cut fine      Chinese parsley

1. Parboil spareribs for 20 minutes. Rinse and drain well.
2. Wash and soak black beans for 3 minutes. Combine black bean mixture and mash into a paste.
3. Heat oil in a Dutch oven pot. Stir-fry the black bean mixture for 2 minutes, then add the spareribs and stir to coat.
4. Add broth. Bring to a boil and simmer, covered, for 40 minutes.
5. Thicken with cornstarch mixture.
6. Garnish.

# EASY SPARERIBS

2 to 3 lb. ribs                  ¼ c. shoyu
4 cloves garlic                  Hawaiian salt to taste
½ c. vinegar                     Pineapple chunks (save
¾ c. brown sugar                   the juice)

Brown ribs. Add the sauce ingredients and simmer until cooked. Thicken the pineapple juice with flour and add to ribs.

*Audrey Kong*

# SPARERIBS HAWAIIAN

2½ to 3 lb. meaty pork
    spareribs (or lamb
    breast)
Salt and pepper
¼ c. chopped onion
¼ c. thinly sliced celery
¼ c. green pepper, cut in ½
    inch squares
2 Tbsp. margarine or butter
    or pork fat
1 Tbsp. cornstarch
2½ c. (one No. 2 can)
    pineapple chunks or
    tidbits
¼ c. vinegar
1 Tbsp. soy sauce

Arrange spareribs (or lamb breast), meaty-side up, in shallow pan; salt and pepper lightly. Roast in fairly hot oven (400°F.) 30 minutes.

Meanwhile, cook chopped onion, celery, and green pepper in margarine or pork fat 5 minutes; sprinkle with cornstarch, then stir in 1 cup syrup drained from pineapple chunks, and cook, stirring, until transparent. Add vinegar and soy sauce. Add pineapple chunks. Pour off fat from roasting pan; pour pineapple and liquid over meat. Reduce heat to 350°F. and cook about 45 minutes or until done, basting with liquid in pan. Serves 4 to 6.

*Ludvina Abrew*

# HONEY-GLAZED SPARERIBS

2 lb. pork spareribs, cut
  into 2 to 3 inch widths
¼ c. plus 1 Tbsp. shoyu
3 Tbsp. hoisin sauce
3 Tbsp. dry sherry, divided
1 Tbsp. sugar

1 tsp. minced fresh ginger
2 cloves garlic, minced
¼ tsp. Chinese five spice
2 Tbsp. honey
1 Tbsp. cider vinegar
Green onion (for garnish)

For marinade: Combine ¼ cup of the shoyu, the hoisin sauce, 2 tablespoons of the sherry, sugar, ginger, garlic, and five spice in a bowl; mix well. Pour marinade over ribs and refrigerate overnight, mixing occasionally.

In a foil-lined baking pan, place rack in pan and place ribs on rack. (Reserve marinade.) Bake in 350° oven for ½ hour. Turn ribs over and brush with marinade and bake till ribs are tender.

For glaze, combine honey, vinegar, and remaining 1 tablespoon shoyu and 1 tablespoon sherry. Brush over ribs and broil 2 to 3 minutes. Turn over and do the same.

*T. Oki*

# ISLAND SPARERIBS

¼ c. sugar

1 tsp. salt

Rub both sides of 4 pounds of pork spareribs ribs. Let stand for 2 hours.

Island Barbecue Sauce:

½ c. soy sauce
½ c. catsup

1 egg-size ginger root
3 Tbsp. brown sugar

Mix night before using. Makes 1 cup sauce. Let stand for 1 hour longer. Place, meaty side up, on rack in shallow pan. Bake at 450° for 15 minutes; pour off fat. Bake for 1 hour at 350°, turning and brushing a few times.

*Doris Mori*

# OKINAWAN SPARERIBS

3 lb. lean spareribs  
⅔ c. sugar

⅓ c. sake  
⅔ c. soy sauce

Cut spareribs into 2x2 inch pieces. Place in a saucepan; add water to cover. Cover and simmer until spareribs are tender. Drain all but 1 cup liquid from spareribs. Add sugar and sake. Cook, uncovered, until liquid is reduced to half. Add soy sauce and cook until most of liquid is gone, turning spareribs occasionally to glaze. Makes 6 servings.

# SPARERIBS WITH PINEAPPLE

2 lb. spareribs  
1 clove garlic, crushed  
1 (1 inch) piece ginger,  
    crushed

1 tsp. Hawaiian salt

Place in cold saucepan or pressure cooker and brown on high heat. Pour off accumulated fat.

Add:

3 Tbsp. cider vinegar  
3 Tbsp. washed sugar  
1 Tbsp. shoyu

⅛ tsp. 5 spices  
¼ tsp. ajinomoto

Cover and cook on low heat until done, about 30 to 40 minutes. For pressure cooker, cook 10 minutes at 15 pounds pressure; cool immediately.

Gravy:

1 tsp. cornstarch  
½ c. juice from small can  
    of pineapple chunks

Mix and add to cooked spareribs. Before serving, mix pineapple chunks with spareribs; place on platter and garnish with Chinese parsley.

*Red*

2821-95

# SWEET SOUR SPARERIBS

1½ to 2 lb. spareribs
⅓ c. flour
⅓ c. shoyu
⅓ c. vinegar
1½ c. water
½ c. brown sugar

1 tsp. salt
1 Tbsp. fat
1 clove garlic, crushed
1 (1 inch) piece ginger,
   crushed

Chop spareribs into small pieces. Mix flour and shoyu and soak spareribs in this mixture for about ½ hour. Heat fat. Add garlic and ginger. Brown ribs; add vinegar, water, salt, and sugar. Allow to simmer for 1 hour. Serve on Pickled Turnips and Carrots.

Pickled Turnips and Carrots:

1 medium turnip
1 medium carrot
½ Tbsp. salt

1 tsp. sugar
¼ c. water
2 Tbsp. vinegar

Peel and cut turnip and carrot into very thin slices. Add salt and sugar and mix well. Let stand 30 minutes, then press out excess liquid. Add water and vinegar and allow to stand 30 minutes. Drain and arrange on platter. Pour hot spareribs over vegetables.

*Red*

# TERIYAKI SPARERIBS
## (Butaniku No Teriyaki)

3 to 4 lb. spareribs       Water

Teriyaki Sauce:

2 c. shoyu
1 c. brown sugar, packed
1 clove garlic, crushed

1½ tsp. fresh ginger, grated
½ c. sake or mirin (rice
   wine)

Simmer spareribs in water to cover for 20 to 30 minutes. Drain. Marinate in Teriyaki Sauce for 30 minutes or longer. Broil, basting frequently and turning occasionally, for 20 to 30 minutes or until done. Yield: 4 to 6 servings.

*Ludvina Abrew*

# CHINESE MEAT BALLS

2 eggs
1 Tbsp. soy sauce
1 Tbsp. sugar
1 lb. lean pork, ground
¾ c. minced green onions
¼ c. minced Chinese
    cabbage (may
    substitute head
    cabbage)

1 tsp. salt
¼ tsp. monosodium
    glutamate
¼ c. flour
Oil (for frying)

Beat eggs; add soy sauce and sugar. Add pork, green onions, and cabbage and mix until well blended. Add salt, monosodium glutamate, and flour and knead until mixed well. Form into balls the size of a walnut. Fry in hot oil about 1 inch deep. Drain on paper towels. Serve on cocktail picks. Makes about 60 balls.

These meatballs may be prepared in advance and refrigerated or frozen, then reheated just before use.

# HELEN'S BAKED BEANS

1 (No. 2½) can (3½ c.) pork
    and beans
1 link linguisa
1 medium onion, chopped
1 Tbsp. prepared mustard

½ to 1 small (14 oz.) bottle
    catsup
1 Tbsp. Worcestershire
    sauce

Pierce sausage with fork and cook in a little water until water evaporates and sausage browns. Slice sausage and return to pan; fry onion in oil of sausage. Add beans and flavoring. Add catsup; mix together and bake in casserole dish at 350° for 20 minutes.

# EASY KALUA PUA'A
## (Hawaiian Roast Pork)

3 lb. boneless shoulder
  pork roast
1 Tbsp. Hawaiian salt
1½ Tbsp. monosodium
  glutamate
¼ c. soy sauce
1 tsp. Worcestershire
  sauce

1 clove garlic, crushed
1 small piece ginger root,
  crushed
Liquid smoke
4 large ti leaves

Place roast into a plastic bag; set in a bowl. Combine salt, monosodium glutamate, soy sauce, Worcestershire sauce, garlic, ginger, and a few drops of the liquid smoke. Seal bag and marinate overnight in refrigerator, turning occasionally. Wash ti leaves and remove fibrous part. Place 2 ti leaves vertically and the third leaf horizontally in the center between the other 2 leaves. Place the fourth leaf horizontally next to the third leaf. Place roast in the center of the leaves. Baste with marinade. Wrap and secure with string. Place in an 8 inch square baking dish. Roast pork in electric oven at 325°F. for 2½ hours or until done. Makes 6 servings.

# KALUA PIG IN POT

3 lb. Boston butt
1 Tbsp. Hawaiian salt
1 Tbsp. liquid smoke

6 ti leaves
Foil
6 sweet potatoes

Rub pork with salt. Brush with smoke. Wrap in ti leaves and foil. Place on rack in large, deep pot. Add 1 inch of water. Simmer for 3 hours. Replenish water when necessary. Open foil; place sweet potatoes around pork. Seal again. Steam 1 hour longer. Shred pork; toss with 1 teaspoon Hawaiian salt. Pour juice from foil package over the pork. Garnish with sliced sweet potatoes. Serves 6.

Hint: If pork is dry, add water and salt. Heat thoroughly.

*Ludvina Abrew*

# ONO OVEN KALUA PIG

4 to 6 lb. pork butt (if frozen,
   thaw and score)
2 Tbsp. liquid smoke
2 to 3 Tbsp. crude salt
14 to 16 ti leaves, stems cut
   off (more or less
   leaves, depending on
   width and length)          **Heavy aluminum foil**

   Wash ti leaves and arrange them in a circular pattern overlapping leaves.

   In a container, place scored butt and rub all sides with salt
and liquid smoke. Place butt, fat side up, on the ti leaves. Fold or
wrap butt with ti leaves to completely cover and tie securely with
string. Place the wrapped butt on foil and seal well so no steam
escapes. Place the prepared butt in a shallow roasting pan and
roast in a preheated 450° oven. After 1 hour, reduce heat to 400°
and cook from 3 to 4 hours longer or until done.

   Serve with poi, baked sweet potatoes, lomi salmon, etc.

*Blue*

# KONBU MAKI WITH PORK CENTER
# (SEAWEED ROLL)

8 oz. nishime or dashi
   konbu
1 lb. pork
Kampyo or string to tie

⅓ c. shoyu
1 tsp. salt
3 Tbsp. sugar
½ tsp. gourmet powder

   1. Wash sand off konbu and cut into 5 or 6 inch lengths
(2½ inches wide).
   2. Cut pork into strips ½ x ½ x 2½ inches.
   3. Place a piece of pork on one end of the konbu strip; roll
and tie with Kampyo or string.
   4. Put the konbu maki in a saucepan; add water to cover
and cook until tender (3 hours).
   5. Add shoyu, salt, sugar, and gourmet powder and cook
for another 30 minutes.

*Yellow*

2821-95

# LAULAU

7 lb. brisket, cut in 2 inch
   pieces
3 lb. pork butt or belly, cut
   in 2 inch pieces
¾ c. Hawaiian salt
2 Tbsp. liquid smoke

60 to 70 luau leaves, stems
   stripped
40 ti leaves
String
10 sweet potatoes,
   scrubbed

Add ½ cup salt and 1 tablespoon smoke to beef; mix thoroughly. Mix pork with remaining ¼ cup salt and 1 tablespoon smoke. Remove stems from luau leaves; wash leaves thoroughly. Strip skin from stems with knife. Arrange 3 luau leaves, the largest on the bottom, on the palm of the hand. Place pork and beef cubes in center of leaves. Top with 4 or 5 stems and 2 more leaves.

Prepare each ti leaf by cutting partially through the stiff back rib about ½ way up. Strip down to stem. Place laulau on the end of a ti leaf and wrap tightly. Wrap another ti leaf around in opposite direction, forming a flat package. Tie with string or fibrous part of ti leaves. Steam 4 to 6 hours. Add sweet potatoes for last hour. Makes 20 laulaus.

Note: To steam in electric roaster, add 3 quarts water. Set temperature control at 350°; place rack above water and put laulaus on rack when steaming point is reached. When steaming thoroughly, lower temperature to 300°. Replenish water at end of 2½ hours.

*Ludvina Abrew*

# LAULAUS

1 lb. fresh pork
1 lb. brisket stew meat
¾ lb. salted salmon or
    butterfish

3 lb. taro leaves
24 ti leaves
Salt

Wash the taro leaves (luau); remove stem and tough fibrous part of the rib. Prepare ti leaves, removing stiff rib from underside of the leaf. Wash the leaves.

Divide pork, meat, and fish into 12 parts. Salt to taste, depending on saltiness of fish. Wrap a piece of pork, meat, and fish in 8 to 10 taro leaves.

Place the wrapped bundle in the center of the ti leaves. Pull up the ti leaves and tie the ends securely with stem end of the ti leaves. If preferred, the laulau may be wrapped in 1 large leaf with another leaf around it in the opposite direction, making a flat package. This should be tied securely with string. Steam the laulau 4 hours or longer in a covered steamer in the oven at 300°F. Sweet potatoes and baking bananas may be steamed with the laulau during the last 2 hours of baking.

Laulaus may be cooked in the pressure cooker for 1½ hours at 15 pounds pressure.

*Yellow*

# LUP CHONG AND BROCCOLI

1 (1 lb.) pkg. lup chong
½ tsp. shoyu

1 large bunch broccoli
½ c. water

Clean broccoli. French cut both the lup chong and broccoli. Fry lightly. Add broccoli, shoyu, and water in skillet and cover. Cook 3 to 4 minutes or until broccoli is cooked.

## MARUNGAY BEANS WITH PORK

3 c. marungay beans
1 lb. pork (in ½ inch pieces)
2 cloves garlic
1 medium tomato (in 1 inch pieces)

1 Tbsp. shoyu
1 tsp. salt
1 c. water
1 tsp. MSG

Peel beans and cut in small pieces. Brown pork and garlic in saucepan. Stir in tomato and shoyu. Add beans and salt. Stir to blend seasonings. Add water and cook for 3 to 5 minutes. Sprinkle with MSG.

*Ludvina Abrew*

## NISHIME

½ lb. cut-up pork
2 strips nishime konbu
3 pieces dried mushrooms (soak, wash, and cut in 1 inch pieces)
2 konyaku, sliced
3 aburage (fried tofu)
1 c. daikon (turnip), cut in stew pieces
2 c. araimo (Japanese taro), cut in 1½ inch pieces
1 c. takenoko (bamboo shoot), cut in stew pieces

1 c. carrots, cut in stew pieces
1 c. gobo (burdock), cut in ¼ inch thick diagonal slices and soaked in water until used
2 Tbsp. oil
1½ c. water
½ c. shoyu
⅓ c. sugar
½ tsp. salt
1 tsp. ajinomoto (optional)

Soak konbu and mushrooms in water for 10 minutes or until soft. Wash and strip konbu down center, lengthwise, if too wide (more than 3 inches). Tie in knots about 2 inches apart. Cut between knots. Fry pork in oil until light brown. Add water, mushrooms, aburage, and konbu. Cover; cook for 10 minutes. Add seasoning and cook for 5 minutes. Add daikon, carrots, and gobo; cook for 15 minutes. Add taro and cook until taro is done (about 15 minutes).

Chicken may be used with or instead of pork.

*Red*

## OKINAWA-STYLE PORK

10 lb. Boston butt
4 c. shoyu
⅓ c. vinegar
2¼ c. brown sugar
3 Tbsp. salt

3 tsp. monosodium
glutamate (optional)
3 ginger
3 garlic

Combine preceding ingredients. Put pork into mixture and cook for 1 to 1½ hours on medium heat until mixture boils, then on low until pork is cooked.

*Blue*

## POOR MAN'S PIZZA

French bread
⅔ c. Parmesan cheese
1 c. mayonnaise
¼ c. chopped green onion

Portuguese sausage (slice
thin or chop it very
fine)

Slice French bread 1 inch thick. Blend the Parmesan cheese, mayonnaise, and the green onions together. Spread the cheese mixture on the slices of bread. Spread the Portuguese sausage. Bake the *pizza* at 350° for 15 minutes or broil for 5 minutes.

*Blue*

## PORK ADOBO

2 to 3 lb. pork with skin and
fat
½ c. vinegar
1 bay leaf

1 tsp. salt
3 cloves garlic, mashed
1 tsp. peppercorns

Cut pork into 2 inch cubes. Combine meat, vinegar, and ingredients in a deep skillet. Marinate 10 to 15 minutes. Cook at medium heat until it boils. Reduce heat and cook until tender and oil is extracted from meat. Stir occasionally to avoid sticking.

*Vicky Malaqui*

# PORK CHOP SUI

1 lb. pork, sliced thin
1 medium carrot
3 stalks celery
½ lb. string beans or
    Chinese peas
¾ c. soaked ear fungus
3 stalks green onion

3 Tbsp. peanut or salad oil
1 Tbsp. cornstarch
1 Tbsp. shoyu
1 tsp. sugar
Salt
Water

Slice pork into thin 2 inch strips. Cut vegetables into thin slices. Mix cornstarch, sugar, and shoyu with pork. Add oil and salt to heated fry pan. Add vegetables, 1 at a time, in the order of the length of cooking necessary. Stir constantly until all vegetables are partially cooked. Remove vegetables from fire.

To the fry pan, again add oil and salt. Fry pork for 25 minutes; add cooked vegetables. Make a smooth paste by combining 1 tablespoon flour, 1 teaspoon sugar, 1 tablespoon shoyu, and ⅔ cup water. Add this to the vegetable-pork mixture and thicken. One cup canned bamboo shoots may be added.

Chop sui is not a typical Chinese dish but the name means a mixture of meat and vegetables so that the combination of meat and vegetables may be varied to suit the taste.

*Yellow*

# PORK WITH EGGPLANT

2 to 3 long eggplants
¾ lb. ground pork or
   ground chicken
3 Tbsp. dried mushroom,
   soaked and chopped
1½ tsp. minced garlic
2 to 2½ Tbsp. vegetable oil
Oil (for frying)

2 to 3 Tbsp. soy sauce
1½ Tbsp. sherry
1 tsp. cornstarch
Dash of pepper
1 tsp. salt
1 tsp. sugar
1 tsp. sesame or salad oil

Cut eggplant into ¾ inch slices. Deep-fry eggplant for 2 minutes. Set aside.

Combine soy sauce, sherry, and cornstarch and mix with ground pork, mushroom, and garlic. Heat the oil and saute pork mixture for 2 to 3 minutes over medium heat. Add fried eggplant and mix well. Add pepper, salt, and sugar and stir well. Stir in salad or sesame oil.

# PORK HASH

1 lb. ground pork
2 Tbsp. chopped chung-
   choy

½ lb. sanbai zuke, chopped
2 Tbsp. chopped green
   onions

Mix well; place in dish and steam until done, about 40 minutes.

*Red*

# PORK HASH WITH PEANUTS

1 lb. hamburger

½ lb. pork hash

Fry pork hash; drain oil. Fry hamburger together with pork.

Add:

4 Tbsp. shoyu
1 Tbsp. sugar
½ c. green onion, chopped

1 can salted peanuts
4 to 5 eggs, beaten

Steam awhile.

*Natsue Kametani*

# PORK ROAST (WITH MISO)

5 lb. pork
1 (2 or 3 inch) piece ginger,
    mashed
2 cloves garlic, mashed

¾ c. miso
½ c. sugar
¾ c. shoyu
½ tsp. ajinomoto

Mix miso, shoyu, and sugar well in a large pot, then add your ginger and garlic and mix well. Place your pork in the pot and simmer for 2½ to 3 hours until done and well soaked in. Serve hot.

*Yellow*

# PORK TOFU

½ lb. lean pork, sliced thin
2 Tbsp. fat
1 medium round onion,
    sliced thin
8 to 10 green onions, with
    tops cut in 1½ inch
    lengths

¼ tsp. monosodium
    glutamate
2½ Tbsp. sugar
⅓ c. shoyu sauce
4 to 5 thin slices ginger root
1 sq. cubed tofu

Brown pork in fat. Add shoyu sauce, sugar, ginger slices, and monosodium glutamate. Cook until sauce bubbles. Add onions and cook over low flame. Add tofu cubes and cook until tofu absorbs shoyu sauce and turns light brown. Serve hot with rice.

Variations: Crush tofu before adding. Just before serving, add 3 beaten eggs. Mix slightly and cook over low flame until eggs are firm. Serve hot.

Optional:

¼ c. sliced string beans
¼ c. sliced carrots
¼ c. bamboo shoots

¼ c. mushrooms
¼ c. watercress

*Blue*

# PORTUGUESE PICKLED PORK
## (Carne de vinha D'alhos)

3 to 4 lb. pork shoulder or
    butt
1½ c. vinegar
1½ tsp. salt
2 red peppers or 3 chili
    peppers

3 cloves garlic
1 Tbsp. shortening
Potatoes, peeled and
    quartered

Pork may be cut up into small pieces or left in 1 large piece. Combine vinegar, salt, peppers, and garlic with meat. Cover and allow to stand overnight in a cool place, turning occasionally to permit seasoning to penetrate the meat evenly. Melt shortening in pot or pan and brown meat on all sides. Add a little water to meat; cover and simmer 1¾ to 2 hours (35 to 40 minutes per pound). Meat may be roasted in oven at 350°. About ¾ hour before meat is cooked, add potatoes and cover with meat's juice.

*Yellow*

# PORTUGUESE SAUSAGE (LINGUISA)

2 lb. lean pork
¼ c. water
1 Tbsp. vinegar
8 cloves garlic, minced
2 Hawaiian red peppers,
    minced

1 tsp. salt
¼ tsp. pepper
⅛ tsp. paprika
⅛ tsp. monosodium
    glutamate
Few drops of liquid smoke

Chop pork into ¼ inch pieces. In a bowl, combine remaining ingredients. Add meat and refrigerate for 2 days, stirring occasionally. Form into small thin patties and fry until browned on both sides and cooked throughout. Makes 8 servings.

2821-95

## SAUSAGE AND APPLES

1 lb. fresh pork sausage
    links
6 medium cooking apples
    (2 lb. total)

3 Tbsp. brown sugar
1 Tbsp. lemon juice
¼ tsp. salt
⅛ tsp. pepper

Cook sausage in a 12 inch skillet over medium heat about 10 minutes or till no longer pink. Drain well and discard juices. Cut sausage links crosswise in halves. Return sausage links to the skillet. Core apples and cut each apple into 8 wedges. Add apple wedges to sausage. Sprinkle with brown sugar, lemon juice, salt, and pepper. Cover and cook over medium-low heat for 10 to 15 minutes or till apples are just tender, gently stirring once or twice. Makes 6 servings.

## SPAM AND PINEAPPLE

2 cans Spam
½ c. brown sugar

½ c. pineapple juice
12 whole cloves

Stick cloves in Spam. Mix sugar and juice and pour over Spam. Simmer for 20 minutes or bake in a casserole dish at 325°F. for 30 minutes. Yield: 6 servings.

*Blue*

# VEGETABLE SPAM DELIGHT

Spam, cut ¼ inch thick
Velveeta cheese, sliced ¼
  inch thick
Green Italian tomato, sliced
  ¼ inch thick

Eggplant, sliced diagonally
  ¼ inch thick

Batter:

1 c. sifted flour
2 tsp. baking powder
1½ Tbsp. sugar
1 tsp. salt

3 to 4 drops of yellow
  coloring
¾ c. water

Layer eggplant, cheese, Spam, cheese, Italian tomato. Fold together and hold with a toothpick. Dip into batter and sprinkle with white bread crumbs. Deep-fry in hot oil for 1 minute or to light brown in color.

*Karen Suzuki-Kawahara (first place)*

# TERIYAKI SPAM STIR-FRY

1 can Spam
1 (2 oz.) pkg. long rice
¾ c. red bell pepper
½ large onion
2 c. snow peas
1 large carrot
1 (5 oz.) can water
  chestnuts, drained
1½ c. teriyaki sauce

8 to 10 medium
  mushrooms
¾ c. yellow bell pepper
¾ c. broccoli
¾ c. water
1 medium Italian squash
1 (8 oz.) can baby corn,
  drained

Cut Spam into strips. Marinate Spam in teriyaki sauce for 2 hours. Slice carrot and onion. Chop all other vegetables. Before cooking, put long rice in warm water for 2 minutes, then drain. Cook Spam, teriyaki sauce, and long rice over medium heat for 5 to 7 minutes. Add all vegetables, except for corn and water chestnuts; add water and cook for 10 minutes or until tender. Add corn and chestnuts; cover and cook 2 more minutes. Serve over rice or noodles. Add chow mein noodles for crunch. Serves 6 to 8.

*Karyn Hermo (second place)*

# SPAM VEGETABLE TEMPURA

1 (12 oz.) can Spam
2 pkg. beans, sliced

3 carrots, sliced
1 stalk gobo, sliced

Batter:

1 c. flour plus 3 Tbsp.
   cornstarch
¼ c. sugar
¼ c. sake

½ c. water
1 egg
1 tsp. salt

Mix batter together, then add vegetables to batter. Heat oil in deep pan. Be sure oil is hot. Drop mixture by tablespoon. Fry until light brown color. Place on paper towel until it cools off.

*Sandra Suzuki (third place)*

# SPAM CHINESE STIR-FRY

1 (12 oz.) Spam
2 Kula round onions
2 Kula carrots
2 stalks Kula celery

½ lb. Kula Chinese snow
   peas
2 cloves garlic

Sweet and Sour Sauce Mix:

1 c. vinegar
1½ c. water
1½ c. Hawaiian (Maui Brand
   raw sugar)

3 Tbsp. cornstarch
2 Tbsp. ketchup

Prepare mix. Pour over and mix into Spam and vegetables.

*Cindy S.L. Ching*

# STUFFED WON BOK

1 lb. pork hash
1 can water chestnuts,
   minced
1 chung choi, soaked and
   minced

3 shiitake, soaked and
   sliced
2 Tbsp. oyster sauce
1 egg

Split won bok in half and wilt in boiling salted water. Mix all remaining ingredients. Stuff cabbage leaves and place in casserole dish. Steam for 30 to 45 minutes. Cool and slice. Thicken remaining sauce in pan with cornstarch. Sprinkle with chopped green onions and Chinese parsley.

# YOGURT-MINT PORK KABOBS

1 (16 oz.) container plain nonfat yogurt
2 Tbsp. lemon juice
2 to 4 cloves garlic, minced
2 tsp. dried oregano, crushed
1 tsp. dried mint, crushed
1½ lb. boneless pork loin, cut into 1 inch cubes
½ c. seeded, finely chopped tomato
½ c. seeded, finely chopped cucumber
4 c. desired fresh vegetables (such as eggplant, zucchini, yellow summer squash, red onion, and mushrooms), cut into 1 inch pieces
Olive oil flavored nonstick spray coating

In a medium bowl, combine yogurt, lemon juice, garlic, 1 teaspoon of the oregano, and mint. Divide mixture in half. Stir the pork cubes into half of the yogurt mixture. Cover and chill meat and remaining yogurt mixture for 1 to 4 hours.

For sauce, up to 1 hour before serving, stir tomato and cucumber into the remaining half of the yogurt mixture. Cover and chill till serving time.

In a large bowl, combine the desired vegetables. Lightly spray vegetables with nonstick spray coating, tossing to coat. Stir in remaining 1 teaspoon oregano. Set aside.

Drain pork. Alternately thread pork and vegetables onto 12 (6 inch) long skewers. Grill kabobs on the rack of an uncovered grill directly over medium coals for 12 to 14 minutes or till pork is tender and juices run clear, turning once halfway through grilling. Service kabobs with sauce and hot cooked saffron rice (made from a mix).

# POULTRY

## ADOBO
### (Vinegared Chicken and Pork)

1 lb. chicken
1 lb. lean pork
2 Tbsp. minced garlic
3 bay leaves

6 Tbsp. vinegar
1½ tsp. salt
6 peppercorns
½ c. boiling water

Cut chicken and pork into serving pieces. In a skillet, combine chicken, pork, garlic, bay leaves, vinegar, salt, and peppercorns. Let stand for 10 minutes. Add enough boiling water to nearly cover meat. Cover and simmer until water is evaporated, about 1½ hours. Brown meat in skillet, adding more fat if necessary. Makes 6 servings.

## BARBECUE CHICKEN

3 to 5 lb. chicken parts
1 c. ketchup
⅓ c. oyster sauce

1 c. raw sugar
¾ c. shoyu
3 cloves garlic, crushed

Combine ingredients, except chicken. Mix well until sugar is dissolved. Marinate chicken overnight. Bake in oven at 350° for 20 minutes, turning over after 10 minutes. Broil for browning. May be placed on charcoal grill for added flavor.

*Shirley Ann Kimizuka*

# CHAWAN-MUSHI

Chicken Stock: Use 1 pound chicken breast. Separate the meat and bone. (Meat can be used for teriyaki.) Crack the bones and wash. In saucepan, add 2 cups water and washed bones. Bring to a boil. Reduce the heat to low and cook for 35 to 40 minutes. Strain through cheesecloth and cool.

While making the stock, prepare the following:

**8 slices breast meat (1x2 inch pieces, ¼ inch thick)**
**4 slices kamaboko (⅜ inch thick)**
**4 small shiitake, softened with water**
**4 shrimp, cleaned with tail left on**
**12 ginko nuts or 8 leaves of spinach which have been boiled**
**8 leaves of mitsuba or Japanese parsley**

Soak chicken meat and shiitake in 2 tablespoons of sake with ½ teaspoon shoyu for 15 to 20 minutes.

After shrimp have been cleaned, make 4 or 5 crosscuts on the underside of each. Insert a toothpick through each shrimp, lengthwise. The toothpick prevents shrimp from curling. Steam the shrimp at high heat for 2 minutes. After steamed, remove the toothpick.

In Chawan-Mushi bowl, put chicken, shiitake, kamaboko, shrimp, and ginko nuts or spinach. Beat 2 eggs in a mixing bowl, and add 2 cups of the chicken stock seasoned with 1½ teaspoon shoyu, ½ teaspoon salt and ½ teaspoon sugar. Pour this mixture over the ingredients in Chawan-Mushi bowl, leaving a margin of about ½ inch at top of bowl.

Bring steamer to high heat. Place the bowl in steamer. Cover the top with a paper towel, then close the bowl cover. Put lid on the steamer. Steam for 2 minutes at high heat. Reduce to low heat and steam for 18 to 20 minutes more. Remove contents from steamer at once. Remove the paper towel and serve.

*Ludvina Abrew*

166

# CHICKEN A LA KING

1½ c. cooked chicken,
    turkey, or seafood,
    cubed
3 Tbsp. chicken fat or
    butter
1 c. fresh mushrooms or 1
    (14 oz.) can, sliced
    and drained

4 Tbsp. flour
1 c. chicken stock or milk
1 c. thin cream or top milk
½ tsp. salt
⅛ tsp. pepper
1 whole canned pimiento,
    cut in strips

1. Cook fresh mushrooms in fat about 4 minutes. (If canned mushrooms are used, they will be added later with chicken and pimiento.)
2. Add flour to fat and mushrooms and blend well.
3. Add stock and cream or top milk.
4. Cook on low heat until thick, stirring constantly.
5. Add chicken (mushrooms if canned), pimiento, and seasonings.
6. Cool before packaging and place in freezer. Yield: 5 servings.

# CHICKEN AND BAMBOO

2 lb. chicken thighs
¾ c. shoyu
2 Tbsp. white sugar
1 clove garlic, crushed
2 c. sliced bamboo shoots

1 (6⅓ oz.) can button
    mushrooms
2 c. watercress, cut in 1
    inch pieces (optional)

Remove skin from chicken thighs. Heat fry pan to 300° or low heat on range. Put chicken on ungreased, hot surface. Cook 5 minutes, then turn chicken over. Combine shoyu, sugar, and garlic. Pour over chicken. Cook 20 minutes or until chicken is done. Stir in bamboo shoots and mushrooms. Cook another 5 minutes. Stir in watercress. Remove from heat. Serve hot with rice. Serves 4.

*Blue*

# CHICKEN AND LONG RICE

1 (2½ lb.) deboned stewing
   chicken, cut in 1½
   inch pieces
2 Tbsp. butter
4 c. water

1 Tbsp. salt
1 tsp. shoyu
1 bundle long rice, soaked
   in water as bundled

Saute chicken in butter or chicken fat. Add 4 cups water and cook until tender (2½ hours). Season with salt and shoyu. Cut long rice by strings and add to chicken and cook 10 minutes more. Serves 10.

*Ludvina Abrew*

# CHICKEN AND LONG RICE

2½ to 3 lb. stewing chicken,
   cut in pieces
2 Tbsp. oil
1 clove garlic
1 (1 inch) piece ginger
4 c. water
1 stalk green onion

1 bundle long rice, soaked
   in hot water and cut
   into 3 to 4 inch lengths
1 Tbsp. salt
Dash of pepper
1 Tbsp. shoyu
2 eggs

Fry garlic and ginger in 2 tablespoons oil (chicken fat may be used) until brown. Take out garlic and ginger; add chicken and fry until slightly browned. Add water and cook until chicken is tender (about 2 to 2½ hours). Add long rice and seasonings. Cook 10 minutes longer.

Beat eggs lightly. Add chopped green onions. Season with salt and pepper. Fry into thin sheets. Cut in ½ inch squares and add to chicken and long rice.

*Red*

# CHICKEN AND RICE CASSEROLE

5 lb. chicken thighs
1½ c. uncooked rice, washed

1 pkg. onion soup mix
2 cans cream of mushroom soup

Spread raw rice on bottom of large baking pan. Sprinkle soup mix over rice. Add 2¾ cups water. Salt chicken; place, meat side up, on rice so that rice is covered. Pour mushroom soup over chicken. Bake at 350° for 2 hours, uncovered.

*T. Oki*

# CHICKEN CURRY

3 lb. chicken (2 pkg. frozen packaged)
Boiling water
1 Tbsp. salt
3 c. shredded fresh or packaged coconut
1½ pt. milk
2 Tbsp. butter
1 Tbsp. lemon juice

1 c. chopped onion
1 tsp. chopped garlic
1 tsp. chopped fresh ginger root or ½ Tbsp. dried ginger root soaked in 2 Tbsp. water
1½ Tbsp. curry powder
2 Tbsp. flour
3 Tbsp. water

Clean the chicken; partially cover it with boiling water. Add the salt and simmer until the chicken is tender but do not cook until the meat falls from the bone. Cook; drain and remove the meat from the bone. Cut the chicken into ½ inch pieces.

Soak the coconut in 2 cups milk for 15 minutes. Fry the onion, garlic, and ginger in butter until they are a golden brown. Add the curry powder and mix thoroughly. Add 1 cup milk, a small amount at a time; simmer 5 minutes, then add the remaining milk and coconut and simmer 30 minutes. Do not allow the mixture to boil as it may curdle. Cool it and strain through a poi cloth or several thicknesses of cheesecloth. Squeeze out as much liquid as possible. Discard the coconut, onion, and ginger mixture.

Heat the liquid; stir in the paste made of flour and water, and cook until it has thickened. Add the chicken and simmer for 20 minutes. Season with salt and lemon juice if necessary. Serve the curry with hot rice.

*Yellow*

# CHICKEN DRUMETTES

Use 3 pound chicken (drumettes).

Mix:

¼ c. melted butter      3 Tbsp. prepared mustard
½ c. honey      2 Tbsp. shoyu

Drizzle mix over drumettes and bake at 350° for 35 to 45 minutes.

*T. Oki*

# CHICKEN LUAU

1 (2½ lb.) deboned stewing      1 tsp. salt
    chicken, cut in 1½      50 luau leaves
    inch pieces      1 Tbsp. salt
2 Tbsp. butter      2 c. water
4 c. water      3 c. coconut milk

Saute chicken in butter. Add 4 cups water and simmer until tender (2½ hours). Season with salt. Remove stems from luau leaves; wash thoroughly. Strip skin from stem with knife. Cook leaves with 2 cups water and salt over medium heat for 1 hour; drain. Combine chicken, luau leaves, and coconut milk. Heat thoroughly and serve. Serves 10.

*Ludvina Abrew*

# CHICKEN LUAU (TARO LEAVES)

1 to 4 lb. chicken,
    disjointed and cut in
    small pieces

3 c. coconut milk
2 lb. luau
3 tsp. salt

Place pieces of chicken in large kettle; cover with hot water and add salt. Bring to boil; pour off and save liquid. Rinse chicken in warm water and drain off. Replace chicken in liquid and simmer until tender. Wash luau leaves thoroughly; chop the stem. Place in separate covered saucepan; add 1 cup water and cook until wilted. Drain; add fresh hot water and continue cooking. Drain; add water again. Cook until tender and drain. Draw a knife through luau leaves to cut into small pieces. Add coconut milk and cook awhile until luau is heated through with coconut milk. Place chicken in a serving dish with hot broth (excess fat removed); add luau on one side of the chicken and serve hot.

# CHICKEN ONO LOA

3 or 4 lb. chicken
3 Tbsp. fat
1 Tbsp. finely chopped
    garlic
1 Tbsp. chopped ginger

6 Tbsp. vinegar
1 Tbsp. soy sauce
2 tsp. salt
⅛ tsp. pepper
Boiling water

Prepare chicken by grooming, drawing, and cutting into pieces. Heat fat in large, heavy skillet and brown chicken. Combine all seasonings and add to chicken. Add enough boiling water so that it may be just seen around chicken. Cover skillet and simmer until the chicken is tender and liquid has cooked away (about 2 hours). Serve hot. Serves 6.

*Yellow*

# CHICKEN TERIYAKI

Use 12 chicken thighs.

Sauce:

5 Tbsp. peanut butter
1 stalk celery, minced
1 small round onion,
   minced
½ c. mirin (sweet wine)

5 Tbsp. shoyu
1 Tbsp. sugar
Sprinkle of monosodium
   glutamate

Bone thighs and make several incisions to flatten the meat. Combine all ingredients for sauce; mix well to blend peanut butter. Soak thighs in sauce for 30 minutes or longer. Broil in oven or over charcoal, basting 2 or 3 times during broiling. Yield: 6 or 4 servings (depending on size of thighs).

For hors d'oeuvres, cut into tidbits.

*Red*

# CHICKEN STEW WITH MARUNGAY LEAVES

3 lb. frying chicken *or*
   stewing chicken
1 (13¾ oz.) can chicken
   broth to use with
   frying chicken
1 Tbsp. finely chopped
   onion

1 Tbsp. finely chopped
   ginger
2 tsp. finely chopped garlic
1 (4 oz.) can mushrooms
2 c. marungay leaves

Cut chicken into small pieces. If using frying chicken, heat broth in large saucepan, then add chicken. If using stewing chicken, cover with water and simmer until tender, then add onion, ginger, and garlic. Cover and simmer about 30 minutes until chicken is tender and flavored. Stir in mushrooms. Bring to a boil; stir in leaves and cook 5 minutes. Serve with rice. Paper thin lemon slices, chutney, or chopped peanuts are accompaniments for this dish. Serves 6.

*Ludvina Abrew*

# CHICKEN TERIYAKI

1 Tbsp. shoyu
1 Tbsp. mirin
1 Tbsp. sugar
½ Tbsp. ginger liquid (grate root and strain)
½ tsp. ajinomoto (optional)

2 tsp. ground sesame seeds
White part of green onion, cut into 1 inch long pieces

Cut the chicken into 1 inch square pieces. Soak the chicken in preceding mixture for 30 minutes. Skewer on onion pieces alternately and broil. If you wish, you may sprinkle more sesame seeds on the chicken before broiling.

*Ludvina Abrew*

# CHICKEN TERIYAKI

Use 12 chicken thighs.

Sauce:

5 Tbsp. peanut butter
1 piece celery, minced
1 small round onion, grated

½ c. mirin
5 Tbsp. shoyu
1 Tbsp. sugar

Bone thighs and make several incisions. Combine all ingredients for sauce and mix well.

Soak thighs in sauce for at least 30 minutes and broil until done, basting 2 or 3 times during broiling. Test for doneness with fork or chopstick.

# CHICKEN TINOLA
## (Stewed Chicken with Papaya)

3 lb. stewing chicken
2 Tbsp. salad oil
1 small piece ginger root, crushed
1 clove garlic, crushed
4 c. chicken broth
2 tsp. salt
⅛ tsp. pepper
2 green papayas

Cut chicken into serving pieces. In large skillet or Dutch oven, heat oil. Brown chicken, ginger, and garlic. Add broth, salt, and pepper. Cover and simmer for 2½ hours or until chicken is tender.

Pare papayas; remove seeds and cut papayas into 1 inch cubes. Just before serving chicken, add papayas and cook for 5 more minutes. Makes 6 servings.

# CHICKEN TOFU

½ lb. chicken breast, thinly sliced
1½ Tbsp. salad oil
2½ Tbsp. sugar
⅓ c. shoyu
¼ tsp. monosodium glutamate (optional)
2 thin slices fresh ginger root, crushed
1 Tbsp. mirin
1 medium carrot, cut in thin strips
3 stalks green onion, cut in 1 inch lengths
1 small round onion, sliced
1 block tofu, cut in 1 inch cubes

Stir-fry chicken in hot oil. Add sugar, shoyu, monosodium glutamate, ginger, and mirin; cook 2 minutes. Add carrots, green onion, and round onion; cook additional minute. Add tofu; cook 1 minute or until tofu is heated. Yield: 4 servings.

*Ludvina Abrew*

# CHICKEN WINGS

Use to 3 to 4 pounds chicken wings.

Marinade:

| | |
|---|---|
| 1 Tbsp. sesame seed oil | 8 Tbsp. cornstarch |
| 4 Tbsp. flour | 5 Tbsp. shoyu |
| 4 Tbsp. sugar | 2 stalks green onions, |
| 3 tsp. garlic salt | chopped |
| 2 eggs, beaten | 2 Tbsp. sesame seeds |
| 1 clove garlic, minced | |

Combine marinade ingredients well and marinate chicken wings overnight. Deep-fry until they are cooked and nicely browned.

*Gold*

## CHICKEN WINGS WITH JAPANESE SOY BEANS

| | |
|---|---|
| 2 lb. chicken wings | 1 Tbsp. shoyu |
| 8 oz. Japanese soy beans | 4 Tbsp. oil |
| (Asahi Sakura brand) | 3 Tbsp. shoyu |
| 4 shiitake (soak in water) | 3 Tbsp. sugar |
| 1 small can takenoko | 2 Tbsp. sake |
| (bamboo shoots) | 1 tsp. ajinomoto (optional) |
| 1 slice ginger | 1 c. water |
| 1 stalk green onion | 2 Tbsp. sherry |

1. Wash soy beans and soak them overnight. Rinse; cook for 10 minutes and drain.

2. Cut chicken wings in halves and marinate with 1 table-spoon shoyu. Chop green onion and ginger.

3. Fry chicken wings with oil until brown. Add chopped green onion, ginger, takenoko, shiitake, and Japanese soy beans.

4. Add all seasonings; cook at high heat until it boils. Turn to medium high heat and cook for about 20 minutes till the gravy is absorbed.

Optional: Add string beans and carrots 10 minutes before done.

*Ludvina Abrew*

# CHICKEN WINGS WITH SAUCE

Batter:

| | |
|---|---|
| **1 c. flour** | **1½ tsp. baking powder** |
| **½ c. cornstarch** | **½ tsp. salt** |

Combine ingredients listed preceding. Add enough water so that batter is a little thicker than the consistency of pancake batter. Dip wings in batter and deep-fry.

Sauce:

| | |
|---|---|
| **1 c. pineapple juice** | **3 Tbsp. vinegar** |
| **1 Tbsp. salad oil** | **6 Tbsp. water** |
| **3 Tbsp. cornstarch** | **½ c. sugar** |
| **1 Tbsp. shoyu** | |

Dissolve ingredients together over low heat. Add ½ teaspoon red food coloring. Serve with sesame seeds. Use about 20 wings per recipe.

*Green*

# CHICKEN WITH PINEAPPLE

| | |
|---|---|
| **4 cloves garlic** | **¼ c. shoyu** |
| **½ c. vinegar** | **A little Hawaiian salt** |
| **¾ c. brown sugar (packaged)** | **3 or 4 lb. chicken, cut into pieces** |

Sauce:

**1 Tbsp. cornstarch**
**2 tall cans pineapple chunks**

Mix everything in pot and simmer until tender. Remove fat. When tender, add cornstarch mixed in pineapple syrup from 2 tall size chunks. Add all the syrup and pineapple.

*Katsuko Enoki*

# CHICKEN WITH POTATOES

5 lb. chicken thighs

2 cans small potatoes

Sauce:

½ c. shoyu
½ c. ketchup
¾ c. white sugar

3 oz. sherry wine or ⅓ c.
   sake
½ tsp. salt

Boil sauce, then add potatoes (drained) and chicken. Simmer for 1 hour. Turn chicken over after ½ hour.

*Tomie Kawawaki*

# COUNTRY CAPTAIN 1

1 (1½ lb.) chicken, cut into
   pieces
2 cloves garlic, ground
1 tsp. black peppercorns,
   ground
½ inch piece dry turmeric,
   ground
½ teacup small onions,
   sliced fine and fried
   brown

2 cloves garlic, sliced fine
   and fried brown
1½ teacups thick coconut
   milk (from ¾
   coconut)
Salt to taste
Juice of 1 lime

Rub ground ingredients over the chicken; add all the coconut milk and salt, and let this simmer gently, till chicken is tender and dry. Fry sliced onions and garlic in oil and add to the chicken. Season with lime juice.

This is a dry curry and is like spiced fried chicken.

*Lynn Nakamura-Tengan*

# COUNTRY CAPTAIN 2

Use same ingredients as for Indian Curry, only substituting pepper for chillies. Use the method for Country Captain 1.

You can also use ordinary curry powder with chillie flavour.

*Lynn Nakamura-Tengan*

## CRISPY OVEN FRIED DRUMSTICKS

¾ c. dried bread crumbs
2 Tbsp. chopped parsley
½ tsp. paprika

8 drumsticks, skinned
⅓ c. lowfat buttermilk
1 Tbsp. vegetable oil

Preheat the oven to 400°. On a sheet of waxed paper, combine the bread crumbs, parsley, and paprika. Set aside.

Dip each drumstick in buttermilk; dredge in crumb mixture. Arrange the drumsticks on a nonstick baking sheet. Drizzle with oil. Bake chicken 25 to 30 minutes till done. Makes 8 servings.

*Agnes Goo*

## CURRIED PAPAYA CHICKEN BAKE

1 c. flour
1 tsp. seasoned salt
¼ tsp. garlic powder
2 tsp. curry powder
2½ to 3 lb. boneless,
  skinless chicken
  thighs

1 Tbsp. soy sauce
1½ c. orange juice
1 tsp. lemon juice
⅓ c. brown sugar
1 heaping Tbsp. cornstarch
2 tsp. curry powder
2 c. sliced papaya

Combine flour, seasoned salt, and 2 teaspoons curry powder and dredge chicken.

In a large baking dish, arrange chicken. Bake at 400° for 20 minutes; turn and bake 20 minutes longer.

While chicken is baking, in a saucepan, combine sugar, cornstarch, and 2 teaspoons curry powder; mix. Add orange juice, lemon juice, and soy sauce; mix well and cook until slightly thickened. Fold in papaya; spread mixture over chicken and bake 10 to 15 minutes more until chicken is glazed. Yield: Approximately 6 servings.

# DRY CURRY (NORTH INDIAN STYLE)

1 chicken or 2 lb. beef or
    mutton or pork
2 large onions, diced
16 to 20 dried chillies,
    seeded and ground
½ tsp. ground fresh ginger
1½ inch cinnamon

4 cloves
¾ lb. red tomatoes, cut into
    pieces
4 dessert spoons ghee or
    oil
Salt to taste

1. Put ghee in pan.
2. Fry diced onions till a little brown.
3. Add ground chillies and ginger, cinnamon, and cloves.
4. Add meat; stir well.
5. Add tomatoes.
6. Add salt to taste.
7. Allow to cook till curry is dry.

Chicken livers done this way are good. Cut each into two.

*Lynn Nakamura-Tengan*

# GINGER CHICKEN

1 whole chicken, boiled,
    cooled, and cut into
    pieces
½ c. vegetable oil, heated
1 small ginger, minced

2 tsp. sugar
2 cloves garlic, minced
5 stems green onion,
    chopped

Add ginger, onion, sugar, and garlic to the heated oil and cook for a few minutes. Pour over chicken and serve.

*L. Takabayashi*

# GINGER SPICY CHICKEN

2 whole chicken breasts, split, boned, and skinned
Salt as desired
2 Tbsp. vegetable oil
1 medium red pepper, cut into ¼ x 2 inch strips (1½ c.)
1 medium green pepper, cut into ¼ x 2 inch strips (1½ c.)
1 (8 oz.) can juice pack pineapple chunks (undrained)
½ c. picante sauce
2 Tbsp. chopped fresh cilantro or parsley
2 to 3 tsp. grated fresh ginger

Lightly salt chicken. Cook in oil over medium heat until lightly browned and cooked through, about 5 minutes. Remove and reserve. Add peppers, pineapple, picante sauce, cilantro, and ginger to skillet; cook, stirring frequently, 5 to 7 minutes or until peppers are tender and sauce is thickened. Return chicken to skillet; heat through. Makes 4 servings.

*Marion Y. Muraoka*

# GRILLED CHICKEN

4 boneless, skinless chicken breasts
2 cloves garlic
2 limes
2 Tbsp. chopped, fresh cilantro

1. Wash and pat dry chicken. Place in large Ziploc bag.
2. Mince or put garlic through press and put into bag.
3. Squeeze juice from limes into bag.
4. Sprinkle chopped cilantro into bag and close.
5. Massage (lomilomi) bag until chicken is well covered. Marinate at least 1 hour.
6. Grill or broil chicken until done.
7. Serve with rice or pasta. Serves 4.

*Marlene Curtis*

# HOISIN CHICKEN BREAST SUPREME

Marinade Sauce:

½ c. hoisin sauce
2 Tbsp. low sodium soy
    sauce
3 Tbsp. rice wine or sake
2 Tbsp. sugar

2 Tbsp. ketchup
2 Tbsp. minced garlic
2½ lb. chicken breast
    (skinless, boneless)

Combine the marinade ingredients in a bowl. Add the chicken and toss lightly to coat. Cover with plastic wrap and marinate for several hours in the refrigerator.

Cut chicken into strips. Heat a wok; add 1 teaspoon vegetable oil and heat until hot. Add chicken and stir-fry until cooked throughout. Makes 8 servings.

*T. Oki*

# HOT CHICKEN SALAD

2 c. chopped, cooked
    chicken
2 c. chopped celery
½ c. chopped salted
    almonds
⅓ c. chopped green pepper
2 Tbsp. chopped pimiento

2 Tbsp. minced onion
½ tsp. salt
2 Tbsp. lemon juice
½ c. mayonnaise
⅓ c. grated Swiss cheese
1 c. crushed potato chips

Blend chicken, celery, almonds, green pepper, pimiento, onion, salt, lemon juice, and mayonnaise. Turn into buttered 1½ quart casserole. Top with grated cheese and crushed potato chips. Bake in moderate oven at 350°F. for 25 minutes, or until cheese is melted. Makes 6 to 8 servings.

This dish is fine for a covered dish supper. It will hold the heat and remain in excellent condition for several hours. Along with this, it would be nice to serve sliced tomatoes and cucumbers, baking powder biscuits, and ice cream for dessert.

*Green*

# KONBU MAKI CHICKEN

3 lb. chicken thighs
3 pkg. konbu maki

2 pkg. kanpyo
½ block oleo

Sauce:

1 Tbsp. dashi-no-moto
⅓ c. sugar
⅓ c. shoyu

1 c. water
1 Tbsp. cornstarch

Wrap deboned thighs with konbu and tie with kanpyo. Brown chicken in ½ block oleo. Mix and pour sauce over slightly browned chicken and simmer for about 45 minutes or until done.

*Fay F. Abe*

# KOREAN STYLE CHICKEN

Salt and flour chicken (wings or thighs); chop.

Sauce:

½ c. shoyu
5 to 6 Tbsp. sugar
1 clove garlic, crushed

Green onion, chopped fine
1 (or more) chili pepper,
   crushed

Deep-fry chicken and then dip into sauce.

# CHICKEN SALAD PIE

2 c. diced cooked chicken
1½ c. diced celery
1 Tbsp. finely minced onion
⅓ c. chopped pecans
1 c. mayonnaise

¼ tsp. pepper
1 tsp. salt
½ tsp. Accent (optional)
1 Tbsp. lemon juice

Topping:

1 c. finely crushed potato chips

½ c. finely grated sharp cheese

Use 1 (9 inch) deep pie shell, *baked.*

Combine all ingredients, except topping, and put into the *baked* pie shell. Combine potato chips and cheese and spread on top of pie ingredients. Bake 20 to 25 minutes at 350°F. Serves 6.

*Louise Frolich*

# LEMON CHICKEN BREASTS

1 lb. boneless, skinless chicken breast halves
¼ c. all-purpose flour
¼ tsp. dried oregano

⅛ tsp. black pepper
2 Tbsp. margarine or butter
¾ c. clear vegetable or chicken broth
1 to 2 Tbsp. lemon juice

Dip chicken in flour combined with oregano and pepper. In skillet, melt margarine over medium-high heat and cook chicken until browned, turning once. Add broth and lemon juice and simmer 8 minutes or until chicken is done. Serve with cooked carrots and a mixed green salad.

# LINGUINE WITH CHICKEN AND PEANUT SAUCE

1 lb. skinned, boneless
    chicken breast
1 (14½ oz.) can chicken
    broth
2 Tbsp. soy sauce
2 Tbsp. dry white wine or
    water
1 Tbsp. cornstarch
⅛ to ¼ tsp. ground red
    pepper
½ c. peanut butter

1 Tbsp. peanut oil or
    cooking oil
2 cloves garlic, minced
1 tsp. grated ginger root
1 medium onion, thinly
    sliced and separated
    into rings
8 oz. linguine, cooked and
    drained
2 green onions, sliced
Papaya slices (optional)

Cut chicken into bite-size pieces; set aside. For sauce, in a medium mixing bowl, stir together chicken broth, soy sauce, wine or water, cornstarch, and red pepper. Blend in peanut butter. Set aside.

Preheat a large skillet over high heat. Add peanut oil. (Add more oil as necessary during cooking.) Stir-fry garlic and ginger root in hot oil 15 seconds. Add onion; stir-fry 2 to 3 minutes or till onion is crisp-tender. Remove vegetables from skillet. Add half of the chicken to the skillet. Stir-fry about 3 minutes or till done. Remove chicken. Repeat with remaining chicken. Return all chicken to skillet. Push chicken from center of skillet.

Stir sauce; add to center of the skillet. Cook and stir till thickened and bubbly. Cook and stir 2 minutes more. Return vegetables to skillet; stir to coat with sauce. Heat through. Serve atop hot cooked linguine. Sprinkle with sliced green onions. Serve with sliced papaya if desired. Makes 6 servings.

# LUP CHEONG CHICKEN

5 lb. boneless, skinless
  chicken thighs
1 bottle oyster sauce
1 lb. lup cheong (Chinese
  sausage), sliced
1 bunch green onions,
  sliced

Chinese peas
Shiitake mushrooms,
  soaked in water to
  soften

Cut chicken into bite-size pieces and marinate with oyster sauce overnight. Stir-fry chicken until well done. Cook together sliced lup cheong and mushrooms. Add to chicken. Mix in green onions and Chinese peas. Serve with rice or over chow mein noodles.

*Shirley Ann Kimizuka*

# MAYONNAISE BAKED CHICKEN

4 lb. chicken, cut up
½ c. mayonnaise
1½ tsp. water
1½ tsp. salt

½ tsp. garlic salt
Pepper to taste
¾ c. corn flake crumbs

Wash and dry chicken. Thoroughly combine mayonnaise, water, garlic salt, salt, and pepper. Dip chicken in mayonnaise mixture, coating each piece well, then coat with crumbs. Bake for 45 minutes at 400° or until tender. Yield: 6 to 8 servings.

*Gold*

# MISO CHICKEN

4 pieces chicken thighs
2 Tbsp. red miso
2 Tbsp. sugar

3 Tbsp. sake
1 Tbsp. mirin
2 Tbsp. soup stock

Heat oil in pan and fry chicken. Combine all other ingredients; pour over chicken. Cover pan and simmer until done.

*Blue*

# MOCHIKO CHICKEN

2 lb. chicken thighs,
    deboned
4 Tbsp. mochiko
4 Tbsp. cornstarch
4 Tbsp. sugar
5 Tbsp. shoyu

½ tsp. salt
2 eggs
¼ c. green onion, chopped
2 cloves garlic, minced or
    crushed

Debone chicken and cut each thigh into 2 or 3 pieces. Mix together remaining ingredients and pour over chicken. Stir to mix and marinate at least 5 hours. Heat about 1 inch of salad oil in skillet. Fry pieces of chicken taken from marinade in sizzling oil. Turn to brown evenly all sides until chicken is thoroughly cooked. Serve hot or cold.

*Gold*

# MOCK CHICKEN LEGS OR CITY CHICKEN

1 lb. lean veal
1 lb. lean pork
¾ tsp. salt
1 egg
¼ c. bread or cracker
    crumbs

Fat (for frying)
4 to 6 skewers
1 chicken bouillon cube
1 c. hot water
1 c. milk or 1 can
    mushroom soup

1. Wipe meat; cut in 1 inch cubes and sprinkle with salt, pepper, and onion juice.

2. Run sharp end of skewer through each piece of meat, alternating kinds, using 5 or 6 pieces on each skewer.

3. Mold into legs with the fingers.

4. Dip in slightly beaten egg and then in crumb mixture.

5. Brown on all sides in fat over medium heat in skillet.

6. In the meantime, dissolve bouillon cube in water; pour over the meat, adding more water as necessary.

7. Cover and cook slowly on top of stove or in the oven at 325°F. about 1 hour or until tender enough to cut with fork. Add more water if necessary.

8. Remove legs to hot serving platter.

9. Make a medium thick gravy with the remaining liquid and milk or mushroom soup.

10. Garnish sharp end of skewer with mushroom if desired. Yield: 4 to 6 servings.

*Mrs. Mary Bartow*

# MUSHROOM CHICKEN

| | |
|---|---|
| 1 (3½ lb.) chicken, dressed | 1 Tbsp. starch |
| 1 tsp. ginger juice | 1 c. bamboo shoots |
| 2 tsp. wine | 1 c. mushrooms |
| 1 Tbsp. shoyu | |

Cut chicken into 2 inch pieces. Season with ginger juice, wine, shoyu, and starch blended together.

Heat 2 tablespoons peanut oil; fry chicken a short while, or until light brown in color. Cover with cold water and cook slowly until tender.

Cut large, soaked mushrooms into halves; slice the bamboo shoots into pieces the same size as mushrooms. Pan-fry the mushrooms in a tablespoon of hot peanut oil; add a little salt and a tablespoon of water in which the mushrooms were soaked. Cook for about 5 minutes, then add to chicken. Pan-fry bamboo shoots in same manner and add to chicken. Cover and cook over low flame until tender.

When ready to serve, thicken the gravy with a little starch. Season with salt. Garnish with Chinese parsley.

*Yellow*

# OKASAN'S CHICKEN (MOTHER'S)

Sauce:

| | |
|---|---|
| 1 c. raw sugar | 1 Tbsp. grated ginger |
| 1 c. pineapple juice | 1 Tbsp. grated garlic |
| 1 c. shoyu | 5 lb. chicken parts |

In large saucepan, boil sauce ingredients. Add the chicken and bring to a boil, then simmer about 25 minutes or until chicken is tender.

Thicken gravy with 2 tablespoons of corn starch mixed with ⅓ cup water.

Serve garnished with minced green onion.

*Mary Soon*

## ONO CHICKEN-PINEAPPLE

Use 2 packages chicken (preferably thighs).

Dust with:

| | |
|---|---|
| ⅓ to ½ c. flour | ½ tsp. salt |
| ½ tsp. celery salt | ¼ tsp. garlic salt |
| ¼ tsp. nutmeg | |

Put dry ingredients in a paper bag and shake. Add pieces of chicken and shake. Be sure all pieces of chicken are well dusted with the flour-spice ingredients.

Brown chicken in frying pan using frying fat of your choice. Drain frying fat when chicken is brown.

Pour over the combined mixture of:

| | |
|---|---|
| ¾ c. pineapple juice (or syrup of canned chunk pineapple) | 2 Tbsp. shoyu |
| | 2 Tbsp. sugar (omit if syrup is used) |

Cover and simmer until tender. Before serving, add 1 cup or more of canned pineapple chunks.

This chicken-pineapple dish may be served with rice and vegetables or a salad of your choice.

*Ludvina Abrew, Red*

## OVEN FRIED CHICKEN

| | |
|---|---|
| 2 lb. chicken thighs | 1½ c. mayonnaise |
| 1½ tsp. salt | 2 c. corn flakes, crushed |
| ½ tsp. pepper | |

Salt and pepper chicken. Roll pieces in mayonnaise, then roll each piece in the crushed corn flakes. Bake for 1 hour in a 325° oven or until done.

*Gold*

# OVEN FRIED CHICKEN

No watching, no turning, no pan to wash.

Have ready the fryer chicken, cut into pieces. Dip pieces in ½ cup evaporated milk or 1 egg.

Roll in mixture of:

**1 c. corn flake crumbs**          **¼ tsp. pepper**
**1½ tsp. salt**

Place in shallow pan lined with foil. Bake at 350° for 1 hour or until chicken is well done.

*Green*

# ORANGE SESAME CHICKEN

**4 chicken breasts**              **2 tsp. shoyu**
**2 cloves garlic, smashed**       **1 Tbsp. sesame seeds**
**2 fresh oranges**

1. Remove skin from chicken. Wash and pat dry.
2. Smash garlic cloves or put through garlic press. Place chicken and garlic pieces in pan.
3. Slice 1 orange in half. Squeeze juice over chicken. Slice second orange into rounds and set aside.
4. Sprinkle shoyu and sesame seeds over chicken. Cover with orange slices.
5. Bake at 350°F. for 1 hour. Remove orange slices and broil until golden brown. Serves 4.

*Marlene Curtis*

# OYSTER CHICKEN

**⅓ c. mochiko**                 **1 Tbsp. flour**
**⅓ c. shoyu**                   **1 (5 lb.) box chicken**
**⅓ c. sugar**                   **1 Tbsp. sesame seeds**
**⅓ c. cornstarch**             **1 green onion, chopped**
**1 egg**                             **fine**
**1 Tbsp. oyster sauce**

Debone chicken. Soak all ingredients overnight. Place ¼ cup oil in frying pan and fry chicken.

*Betsy Arakawa*

# SEVEN LAYER CHICKEN CASSEROLE

7 to 9 pieces boneless,
  skinless thighs
1 pkg. chopped spinach
1 box Stove Top stuffing
  (chicken flavor)

1 can cream of mushroom
  soup
1 c. mayonnaise
Fresh mushrooms, sliced
1 block Cheddar cheese

Boil chicken; save broth. Shred chicken onto bottom of casserole dish. Grate half of cheese over chicken. Prepare stuffing mix as directed and layer over cheese. Mix together cream of mushroom soup, spinach, and mayonnaise and layer over stuffing. Layer sliced mushrooms and grate remaining cheese. Pour ½ to 1 cup broth over all. Bake at 350° for 30 to 35 minutes.

*Shirley Ann Kimizuka*

# SHOYU CHICKEN

1 (3 lb.) chicken, dressed
1 c. shoyu
1 c. water
1 piece ginger

½ c. brown sugar
2 cloves garlic
1 tsp. wine

In large saucepan, mix sugar with shoyu. Heat about 2 tablespoons oil in frying pan and add ginger and garlic; fry whole chicken till slightly browned. Add wine, then place chicken into the shoyu-sugar mixture. Cover and cook slowly until tender. Turn chicken from time to time to get an even brownness. Cut into 1½ inch pieces and serve.

*Yellow*

# SPICY EGGPLANT WITH CHICKEN OR TURKEY

2 c. ground chicken or
    turkey (may
    substitute ground beef
    or pork)

3 long eggplants, cut in
    halves and broiled
    (then peel skin)
Oil (to fry)

Sauce:

2 tsp. ginger, minced
6 Tbsp. shoyu
2 Tbsp. white vinegar
2 to 3 cloves garlic, minced

2 Tbsp. sugar
1 to 2 chili peppers, minced
2 tsp. cornstarch

Add oil in saucepan and brown meat. Add sauce and chopped eggplants. Serve over rice.

*Sachi Gohara*

# STEWED CHICKEN IN SOY SAUCE
## (Dak Jo Rim)

3½ lb. frying chicken
Salt
Pepper
5 dried mushrooms,
   soaked
1 medium carrot
1 small onion
1 Tbsp. salad oil
2 fresh chili peppers, cut
   into halves

1½ c. water
¼ c. soy sauce
2 Tbsp. sake
2 Tbsp. sugar
2 Tbsp. chopped green
   onion
1½ Tbsp. sliced ginger root
1½ tsp. chopped garlic

Cut chicken into 10 to 12 pieces; sprinkle with salt and pepper. Remove stems from mushrooms; cut caps into halves. Cut carrot and onion in large chunks.

In a large skillet, heat oil. Brown chicken on high heat; remove. Drain oil from skillet. Add mushrooms, carrot, onion, and chili peppers; saute for a few minutes. Return chicken to skillet; add the water.

Combine remaining ingredients to make seasoning mix; add half to the chicken. Cook on high heat for 20 minutes or until liquid is almost evaporated. Add the remaining seasoning mix; simmer chicken until done, stirring occasionally to glaze. Makes 6 servings.

# STIR-FRIED CHICKEN

1 lb. boneless chicken, cut
   into pieces
3 Tbsp. soy sauce (light)
2 Tbsp. dry sherry (mirin)
⅓ c. chicken broth
4 Tbsp. polyunsaturated
   vegetable oil
1 medium clove garlic,
   chopped
1 lb. snow pea pods
1 Tbsp. cornstarch
2 Tbsp. chicken broth
1 Tbsp. walnuts, chopped

Remove skin from chicken and cut into small pieces. Mix the sherry, soy sauce, and ⅓ cup of chicken broth and set aside. Mix the cornstarch and 2 tablespoons of chicken broth and set aside. Heat 3 tablespoons of the polyunsaturated vegetable oil in a wok over high heat and brown the chopped garlic. Remove the garlic and discard. Add the chicken and stir-fry until brown. Remove the chicken with a slotted spoon and set aside in a warm dish. Add the remaining vegetable oil and the soy sauce mixture to the wok with the snow pea pods and stir-fry approximately 2 minutes until tender. Stir in the chicken, the cornstarch mixture, and the chopped walnuts. When the sauce thickens, the dish is complete and can be served over rice. Serves 4.

*Ludvina Abrew*

# SUE'S CHICKEN

Approx. 10 chicken thighs,
   skinned, boned, and
   butterflied
2 cloves garlic, minced
½ tsp. 5 spice
Oyster sauce with a little
   salad oil added
   (enough to coat
   chicken)
Seasoned bread crumbs

Combine garlic, 5 spice, and oyster sauce; coat chicken with mixture and then dredge each piece with bread crumbs. Place in baking pan and bake in 325° oven for 45 minutes.

# SWEET SOUR CHICKEN

5 lb. chicken thighs
½ c. flour

1½ Tbsp. salt
¼ tsp. pepper

Sauce:

1½ c. sugar
1 c. Japanese vinegar

1 piece ginger, mashed

Mix flour, salt, and pepper. Mix in thighs. Shake off excess flour and fry to brown. Drain oil. Add sauce and cook for 45 minutes.

*Tomie Kawawaki*

# SWEET SOUR CHICKEN WINGS

Season chicken:

2 lb. chicken wings (cut into sections)
Garlic salt
Pepper

Salt
Monosodium glutamate (optional)

Dip chicken in egg, then roll in cornstarch and fry in oil to brown.

Sauce:

½ c. sugar
½ c. vinegar
3 Tbsp. ketchup
1 Tbsp. shoyu

1 tsp. salt
¼ c. stock (made from boiling wing tips) or water

Place fried chicken in baking pan and pour sauce over it. Bake in oven at 350° for ½ hour. After first 10 minutes, turn chicken.

Variations: Use any other part of chicken, or shrimp. You may also heat it on top of the stove instead of the oven.

*Blue*

# SWEET-SOUR CHICKEN WINGS

2 lb. chicken wings
Garlic
Salt
Pepper

2 eggs
Cornstarch or mochiko
flour

Sauce:

1 Tbsp. shoyu
3 Tbsp. catsup
⅓ c. sugar

¼ c. vinegar
¾ c. chicken stock

Cut off tips of wings for stock. Boil wing tips and ¾ cup water for ½ hour (use 1½ cups water for 5 pounds chicken). Season chicken with garlic, salt, and pepper. Dip in egg. Roll in cornstarch or mochiko. Fry to brown in oil. Arrange in pan lined with foil (sauce gets very sticky). Pour sauce over chicken. Bake at 350° for 45 minutes to 1 hour; turn every 15 minutes.

*Violet Sakai*

# SWEET-SOUR CHICKEN WITH PINEAPPLE

½ c. vinegar

¼ c. shoyu

Add raw or brown sugar to make 1 cup liquid.

4 large cloves garlic,
chopped
4 lb. skinless, boneless
chicken, cut in quarters

1 can pineapple chunks
2 heaping Tbsp. corn
starch

Add raw or brown sugar to vinegar and shoyu to make 1 cup. Add chopped garlic and stir till sugar dissolves. Wash chicken and dry with paper towel. Cut in quarters. (If pieces are big, cut in eighths.) Put chicken in pot on stove and pour sweet/sour sauce on chicken and mix so chicken is thoroughly soaked. Cook on medium/low heat until it comes to boil. Turn heat down to low and simmer till cooked, ½ hour. Mix corn starch in pineapple juice for thickening for sweet/sour chicken. Turn heat to medium and cook 10 minutes. Add pineapple chunks and stir till comes to boil again. Serve.

*Bea Barboza*

# SWEET SOUR SAUCE FOR CHICKEN

½ c. sugar
½ c. vinegar
½ c. water

4 Tbsp. ketchup
1 dash of salt

Mix sauce well and pour over 5 pounds deep-fried chicken. Put in oven at 350°F. for approximately 35 minutes.

*Natalie Corderio*

# TERIYAKI CHICKEN

2 lb. frozen chicken thighs
½ c. shoyu
½ c. sugar
1 Tbsp. sherry wine

1 Tbsp. sesame oil
1 Tbsp. grated ginger
3 cloves garlic, chopped

Thaw chicken; wash and dry with paper towel. In large bowl, put shoyu, sugar, sherry wine, sesame oil, ginger, and garlic. Mix well. Put chicken in and leave overnight in the refrigerator.

In pan, 16x12 inches, put oil first and put foil. Put chicken with skin side up; don't cover. Bake 1 hour in 350° oven.

*Blue*

# WING DINGERS

3 lb. chicken wing
    drumettes
1 (1¼ oz.) env. onion soup
    mix
½ c. dark molasses

½ c. lemon juice
¼ c. soy sauce
¼ c. hot taco sauce
2 tsp. hot pepper sauce

Thaw chicken; drain well. In a large bowl, combine remaining ingredients. Put chicken into marinade and refrigerate for at least 2 hours, turning occasionally. Place chicken in a single layer in a 15x10x1 inch pan. Pour marinade over all. Bake at 400°F. for about 35 to 45 minutes, turning once. Makes 6 servings.

## YAKIDORI (BROILED CHICKEN)

Breast of young chicken and chicken liver, cut into pieces (mouthful size)

White portion of green onion, cut into 1 inch pieces
½ shrimp, sliced crosswise

Put the ingredients on bamboo stick in the following order: Chicken, onion, liver, onion, chicken, onion, and end with shrimp. Wrap ends with aluminum foil. Place on broiling pan across a rack (use 2 stones or pipe) so that food will not touch the pan. Broil for about 2 minutes.

Dip in the following sauce:

3 Tbsp. shoyu
1 to 3 Tbsp. sake

1 to 2 tsp. sugar

Or, use mirin.

Put back on broiler for 30 seconds; dip again in sauce. Continue this for about 3 times.

## ROAST TURKEY WITH OLD-FASHIONED STUFFING

1 (12 to 14 lb.) turkey
Salt
1 c. butter or margarine
1 c. chopped celery
1½ c. chopped onions
2 (7½ oz.) pkg. seasoned stuffing mix

1 c. broth
1 tsp. salt
¼ tsp. poultry seasoning
¼ tsp. pepper
Shortening or unsalted fat

Rinse and drain turkey. Salt neck and body cavities lightly. In a large saucepan, melt butter. Lightly saute celery and onions. Stir in stuffing mix, broth, the 1 teaspoon salt, poultry seasoning, and pepper. Stuff turkey. Rub skin with shortening. Roast at 325°F. in oven until meat thermometer registers 185°F. about 3½ to 4 hours. Bake extra stuffing in a covered casserole for 30 to 45 minutes or until heated. Pan drippings from turkey may be added to casserole if desired. Makes 8 to 12 servings.

# TURKEY AND ASPARAGUS CASSEROLE

2 (10 oz.) pkg. frozen
asparagus spears
3 c. cooked, sliced turkey
½ tsp. salt
¼ tsp. pepper
1 (10 oz.) can cream of
chicken soup

½ c. mayonnaise
1 tsp. lemon juice
½ tsp. curry powder
1 c. shredded Cheddar
cheese

Preheat oven to 350°F. Cook asparagus according to package directions for 4 minutes; drain. Place asparagus on bottom of an 8 inch square baking dish. Arrange turkey slices on asparagus; season with salt and pepper. Combine soup, mayonnaise, lemon juice, and curry powder; pour over turkey. Sprinkle with cheese. Bake for 30 minutes. Makes 6 servings.

# SPICY TURKEY ROAST

1 (4 lb.) frozen whole
  boneless turkey,
  thawed
8 to 10 large cloves garlic
3 Tbsp. rosemary
1 Tbsp. coarsely ground
  black pepper

1 tsp. coarse kosher style
  salt
2 Tbsp. olive oil
Orange slices for garnish
  (optional)
Rosemary sprigs for
  garnish (optional)

1. Remove mesh from thawed turkey. Lay turkey out as flat as possible on a cutting board, skin side out.

2. Combine garlic, rosemary, pepper, and salt in a blender; add oil and blend until coarsely chopped.

3. Spread half the garlic mixture inside the turkey. Reroll the turkey.

4. Spread outside of roll with remaining garlic mixture. Wrap firmly in microwave-safe plastic. Secure with string. Pierce plastic in 2 or 3 places with fork.

5. Place on microwave-safe rack over microwave-safe pan.

6. Microwave at HIGH power for 10 minutes. Turn roast over.

7. Microwave at MEDIUM for 35 to 40 minutes, turning roast 2 or 3 times while cooking.

8. Thicken pan juices for gravy if desired.

9. Remove from oven. Let stand, covered, for 15 minutes. Cut thin slices to serve. Garnish with orange slices and rosemary if desired.

*Anne Hasegawa*

# TURKEY NOODLE BAKE

8 oz. wide noodles
1 to 1½ lb. ground turkey
2 (8 oz.) cans tomato sauce
½ Tbsp. sugar
¾ tsp. salt
¼ tsp. lite garlic salt
¼ tsp. pepper
1 c. cottage cheese (nonfat)
1 (8 oz.) pkg. fat free cream
   cheese
½ c. lite sour cream
1 c. green onions with tops,
   sliced
½ medium green pepper,
   chopped
½ c. shredded fat free
   Parmesan cheese

Cook noodles; drain. Cook turkey. Stir in tomato sauce, sugar, salt, garlic salt, and pepper. Remove from heat.

Combine cottage cheese, cream cheese, sour cream, green onions, and green pepper.

Spread half of noodles in a 13x9x2 inch baking dish. Moisten noodles with some of the meat sauce. Cover with cheese mixture. Top with remaining noodles, then meat sauce. Sprinkle with Parmesan cheese. Bake, covered, at 375° for 45 minutes. Serves 12.

*Betty Kay Ikeda*

# SEAFOOD

## CODFISH CASSEROLE (BACALHOADA)

1 lb. dried salted codfish
¾ c. olive oil
2 onions, sliced
3 large potatoes, sliced
3 large tomatoes, sliced
¼ c. chopped parsley
1 (8 oz.) can tomato sauce
¼ c. white wine

1 tsp. paprika
½ tsp. salt
½ tsp. ground fresh mild
　red pepper
4 hard cooked eggs,
　quartered
Black and green olives
Parsley

Soak codfish for 24 hours, changing water often if fish is salty. Drain; discard skin and bones. Flake codfish into medium size pieces; set aside.

Pour olive oil into a large casserole dish. Layer onions, potatoes, codfish, tomatoes, and parsley. Repeat layers.

In a bowl, combine tomato sauce, wine, paprika, salt, and red pepper; pour over codfish mixture. Bake, uncovered, at 350°F. in an electric oven for about 1½ hours. Garnish with eggs, olives, and parsley. Makes 6 servings.

# PORTUGUESE COD CASSEROLE - BACALHAU A GOMES DE SA

2 lb. salted cod
2 large onions, sliced
¾ c. olive oil
1 clove garlic, minced
3 large potatoes, cooked

4 hard cooked eggs, sliced
½ c. pitted ripe olives, sliced
⅓ c. chopped parsley

Soak cod in cold water overnight. Drain and rinse with fresh water. Add water just to cover cod and simmer, covered, for 15 minutes. Drain; flake into large pieces. Preheat electric oven to 350°F. Saute onions in olive oil until tender and golden; stir in garlic. Slice the potatoes.

In a 2 quart casserole, layer half of the potatoes, half of the cod, and half of the onions. Repeat layers. Bake for 10 minutes or until lightly browned. Garnish with eggs, olives, and parsley. Provide cruets of wine vinegar and olive oil and freshly ground black pepper so that each diner can add some of each to his serving. Makes 6 servings.

# DILL AND LEMON FISH BAKE

2 tsp. dill weed, divided
1 tsp. grated lemon peel
¹⁄₁₆ tsp. ground black pepper
1½ lb. flounder fillets (6) or another whitefish

1 c. water
½ c. dry vermouth or apple juice
3 Tbsp. fresh lemon juice

Preheat oven to 350°F. Combine 1 teaspoon of the dill with lemon peel and black pepper; rub into both sides of each fillet. Roll up fillets from the narrow ends; secure with toothpicks if needed. Place in a shallow 1½ quart casserole. Combine water, vermouth, lemon juice, and remaining 1 teaspoon dill. Pour over fish. Cover with foil. Bake until fish flakes easily when tested with a fork, 15 to 20 minutes. Serve with sauce spooned over fish. Serves 6.

Nutrients per serving: 49 calories, less than 1 g fat, 37 mg cholesterol.

*Ludvina Abrew*

# EGGPLANT PARMIGIANO

1 lb. semi-thawed minced
    fish
2 cloves garlic, minced
¼ c. tomato paste
1 (16 oz.) can tomatoes
2 tsp. salt
Pepper to taste
2 medium eggplants

2 eggs, slightly beaten
Fine dry bread crumbs
Salad oil
½ lb. Mozzarella cheese,
    sliced
½ c. grated Parmesan
    cheese
Oregano

Cook fish and garlic in a frying pan, stirring until crumbly. Add tomato paste, tomatoes, 1 cup water, 2 teaspoons salt, and pepper to taste. Cook slowly for 25 minutes. Cut eggplant into ½ inch slices; sprinkle with salt. Dip in egg, then into bread crumbs. Fry in a small amount of oil until slightly browned.

In a large shallow casserole, arrange alternate layers of eggplant, Mozzarella, fish sauce, and Parmesan cheese. Sprinkle top with oregano. Bake at 350°F. about 30 minutes. Makes 6 servings.

# FISHBURGER

Basic Mix:

**1 lb. minced fish**
**1 egg**
**1 c. soft bread crumbs**
**¼ c. chopped round or**
    **green onions**

**1 tsp. salt**
**⅛ tsp. pepper**
**2 Tbsp. oil or mayonnaise**

Variations -

Aku-Tofu Patties:

**½ block tofu**
**1 egg**
**¼ c. green beans, finely**
    **chopped**

**¼ c. grated carrot**
**2 Tbsp. sugar**
**2½ Tbsp. shoyu**

Squeeze excess water from tofu well and crumble. Add remaining ingredients and tofu to basic mix. Drop by spoonful onto greased frying pan. When one side is golden brown, flip over till done.

Teri-Fishburgers - To Basic Mix, add:

**¼ c. sugar**
**¼ c. shoyu**

**½ tsp. ginger juice**
**1 small clove garlic**

Korean Fish Patties: To Basic Mix, add ½ package bean sprouts, chopped. Substitute 2 tablespoons sesame oil instead of salad oil or mayonnaise.

Fish Balls with Sweet-Sour Sauce: Good for Pupus!! Shape Basic Mix into 1 inch balls. Fry till brown. Simmer in Sweet-Sour Sauce.

Sweet-Sour Sauce:

**1 c. unsweetened**
    **pineapple juice**
**1 Tbsp. shoyu**
**3 Tbsp. vinegar**
**6 Tbsp. water**

**¼ to ½ c. sugar**
**Chunk pineapple (if**
    **desired)**
**Green pepper (if desired)**

# TUNA BURGERS

1 lb. fresh tuna
1 green pepper, seeded
¾ c. chopped onions
2 c. soft crumbs

¾ tsp. salt
¼ tsp. pepper
1 egg
¼ c. oil

Cut fish in chunks; discard bones. Put fish, green pepper, and onions through food chopper. Add crumbs, seasonings, and egg; mix well. Shape into 4 patties and fry in oil until brown. Makes 4 servings of 3 ounces protein each.

# FRIED AKU PATTIES

2 lb. aku
1 carrot, medium grated
1 large onion, chopped
2 stalks celery, chopped
3 eggs

2 tsp. salt
1 piece ginger, grated
1 clove garlic, grated
¼ tsp. ajinomoto (optional)
Black pepper

Scrape aku meat with spoon and take out bones and skin. Combine other ingredients with aku meat and make patties and fry. Serve hot with relish spread.

*Yellow*

# TUNA OR SALMON PATTIES

1 can tuna or salmon
2 medium potatoes, peeled
  and grated
1 medium onion, sliced thin
1 Tbsp. green onion,
  chopped

½ tofu, squeezed water out
2 eggs
1 Tbsp. flour
½ c. grated carrots
  (optional)
1 tsp. salt

In large bowl, mix all ingredients together. Form into balls and flatten and fry in electric pan with oil until nicely browned on both sides. Makes 1 dozen.

*Su Gushiken*

# TUNA TOFU PATTIES

1 tofu
½ c. dried mushrooms
1 small carrot, chopped
    fine
4 eggs
2 cans tuna

¾ tsp. salt
2 Tbsp. sugar
2½ Tbsp. shoyu
½ tsp. gourmet powder
1 stalk green onion,
    chopped fine

Soak mushrooms in water. When soft, chop fine. Squeeze excess water from tofu and crumble. Add all of the other ingredients and mix thoroughly. Drop by spoonfuls onto a greased frying pan. When one side is golden brown, flip over the patties.

*Blue*

# FISH CAKES

1 lb. fresh or frozen fish
    fillets, finely chopped
1 small onion, chopped
    finely
1 c. dry bread crumbs

1 egg
⅓ c. mayonnaise
3 Tbsp. fresh chopped
    parsley
2 tsp. Dijon style mustard

Preheat oven to 375°. In a large bowl, combine all ingredients. Shape into 4 large patties or 12 small patties. On large baking sheet, lightly sprayed with nonstick cooking spray, arrange patties. Bake for 20 minutes or until golden brown and fish is cooked.

# FISH LOAF

1 lb. semi-thawed minced
    fish
2 Tbsp. oil
¾ c. oatmeal

2 eggs, beaten
1 c. chopped onion
½ pkg. dry onion soup mix
2 tsp. soy sauce

Mix together all ingredients, except 1 teaspoon soy sauce. Put into a greased loaf pan; pour the remaining 1 teaspoon soy sauce over the top. Bake at 350°F. for about 1 hour. Makes 4 to 6 servings.

## SALMON LOAF WITH SAUCE

1 (15½ oz.) can salmon
    bones, removed
1 egg, slightly beaten
½ c. milk
½ c. soft bread crumbs

¼ c. chopped green onions
½ tsp. dried dill weed
1 tsp. dry mustard
Cooked peas (optional)
Pearl onion (optional)

Tomato Dill Sauce:

1 (7¾ oz.) can condensed
    tomato soup

½ tsp. dried dill weed

Flake salmon. In a medium bowl, combine egg and milk. Stir in bread crumbs, green onion, dill weed, and dry mustard. Add salmon and mix thoroughly. Pat salmon into a greased loaf pan, 7½ x 3½ x 2 inches. Bake, uncovered, in 350° oven for 35 to 40 minutes or until done.

In a saucepan, stir the tomato soup and the dry dill weed. Cook and stir until heated through. Spoon the sauce over sliced loaf and garnish with the peas and pearl onion.

*T. Oki*

## FISH-NOODLE CASSEROLE

Cook and drain 1 package chow fun noodles.

1 lb. minced aku
1 medium onion, chopped

¼ c. carrots, grated
¼ c. string beans, chopped

Fry aku for a few minutes; add onion, carrots, and string beans.

Add:

1 can cream of mushroom
    soup

1 can water or milk

Mix till soup is well blended. Add cooked noodles and pour into a casserole dish. Sprinkle with grated cheese and bake in a 350° oven for 30 minutes.

*Ludvina Abrew*

# ONO TUNA CASSEROLE

1 (6½ oz.) can tuna, drained
1 c. shell or elbow
  macaroni, cooked
1 (3 oz.) pkg. cream cheese
¼ c. milk
1 can cream of mushroom
  soup
1 Tbsp. prepared mustard
1 Tbsp. round onion,
  chopped
Crushed potato chips or
  bread crumbs
Butter

Cook macaroni and drain well. Soften cream cheese and blend in the rest of the ingredients. Put in greased baking dish. Top with chips or crumbs and dot with butter. Bake in 375° oven for 25 minutes. Yield: 8 servings.

*Karen Najjar*

# SALMON AND NOODLE CASSEROLE
## (Meal-in-a-dish)

1 (16 oz.) can salmon
Water
2 Tbsp. chopped onion
4 Tbsp. butter
3 Tbsp. flour
2 Tbsp. horseradish
1½ tsp. salt
¼ tsp. pepper
1 can evaporated milk
2 c. cooked noodles
1 c. cooked peas or whole
  kernel corn

Drain and flake salmon. Measure salmon liquid and add enough water to make 1 cup. Cook onion in butter until tender but not browned. Remove from heat. Blend in flour and seasonings. Gradually add milk, mixing until smooth. Add water. Mix well. Cook over low heat, stirring, until thickened and smooth. Arrange alternate layers of noodles, salmon, and peas or corn in greased 1½ quart casserole. Bake in 400° oven for 25 to 30 minutes, or until top bubbles and lightly browned.

*Blue*

# SEAFOOD CASSEROLE

2 cloves garlic, minced
2 cans cream of mushroom
    soup
¼ block butter/margarine
½ lb. fresh mushrooms,
    sliced
Pepper and salt to taste

½ lb. shrimp
½ lb. imitation crab
1 (12 oz.) pkg. spinach
    noodle or eggless
    noodle
8 oz. Mozzarella cheese

1. Cook pasta and lay on bottom of a large casserole pan (9x13 inches).

2. Melt butter and add garlic. Brown shrimp (cut into about ½ inch pieces) and add salt and pepper to taste.

3. Add the rest of the ingredients (imitation crab, mushrooms, and soup) and heat until well blended. If mixture looks too thick, add about ½ cup of milk.

4. Pour mixture over noodles. Sprinkle cheese on top.

5. Bake at 375° for 30 minutes. If you don't like the cheese to be hard, cover with foil while baking and remove foil after about 20 minutes.

Note: You may use any seafood you wish.

*Stella Yamamoto*

# SEAFOOD CASSEROLE

1 (6 oz.) can crab
1 (6 oz.) can shrimp
1 potato, cooked and diced
½ c. celery, minced
½ c. round onion, minced
1 kamaboko, minced
1 c. Chinese cabbage,
    chopped

1 c. mayonnaise
1 egg, slightly beaten
1 stalk green onion
    (optional)
½ c. cracker crumbs
1 Tbsp. melted butter

Combine all ingredients and place in greased casserole. Top with ½ cup cracker crumbs and 1 tablespoon butter, melted. Bake, uncovered, at 350° for 30 minutes.

*T. Oki*

# FISH PARMESAN

¾ c. dry bread crumbs
3 Tbsp. Parmesan cheese,
   grated
2 Tbsp. chopped fresh
   parsley
½ tsp. salt
¼ tsp. paprika

⅛ tsp. pepper
⅛ tsp. oregano
⅛ tsp. basil
6 (3 to 5 oz.) fresh or frozen
   fish fillets
½ c. melted butter

Combine crumbs and seasonings. Dip fish in butter, then in crumbs. Place in a greased 9x13 inch pan. Bake, uncovered, 20 to 25 minutes at 375°.

Halibut is a good fish to use.

*Helen Misner*

# FISH STROGANOFF STYLE

¼ c. chopped onions
2 Tbsp. butter or margarine
1 lb. semi-thawed minced
   fish
1 (3 oz.) can sliced or
   chopped
   mushrooms, drained
   (reserve liquid)

1 can cream of mushroom
   soup
¼ tsp. garlic salt
Salt and pepper to taste
½ c. sour cream (room
   temperature)
Cooked rice or mashed
   potatoes

Saute onion and mushrooms in 2 tablespoons of butter until golden; add semi-thawed fish. Stir until crumbly. Add salt, pepper, mushroom liquid, and soup; simmer gently for 15 minutes. Stir in sour cream and heat, but do not boil. Sprinkle with parsley, if desired, and serve with rice or mashed potatoes. Makes 4 servings.

# FISH WITH LEAF VEGETABLES

**4 fillet pieces, paka, or
moilua
1 Tbsp. shoyu**

**1 Tbsp. mirin
¼ lb. spinach**

Soak the fish in shoyu and mirin mixture. Bring enough water to boil. Soak the spinach. When the spinach has wilted, remove from the pan. Soak in cold water to cool. Drain the water and squeeze the spinach to remove all excess water. Chop into ½ inch long pieces.

**1 egg
½ tsp. shoyu
½ tsp. sugar**

**¼ tsp. salt
⅛ tsp. ajinomoto**

Mix ingredients well. Put preceding mixture in double boiler to make a soft scrambled egg. This scrambled egg should neither be too soft nor too hard. Egg should be sticky soft. Mix the spinach with the scrambled egg. Divide the mix into 4 equal parts and place a paka fillet piece on the top of each spinach mound. Place the fish in a Teflon frying pan. Cover the pan and bake on the top burner at low heat for 10 minutes.

Sauce to pour over the fish:

**½ c. stock
1 Tbsp. cornstarch**

**1 tsp. mirin
Pinch of salt to taste**

Bring to a boil and pour over the fish before serving.

*Ludvina Abrew*

# FISH TERIYAKI

**1 lb. ahi, aku, or mahimahi
filets
½ c. shoyu
¼ c. sugar
1 clove garlic, crushed**

**1 (1½ inch) piece ginger
¼ tsp. monosodium
glutamate (optional)
1 Tbsp. toasted sesame
seed**

Combine teriyaki sauce ingredients and marinate fish 3 to 6 hours. Broil in a broiler 2 to 3 minutes on each side. Yield: 4 servings.

*Green*

# FRESH TUNA (AKU) PORTUGUESE STYLE

½ c. vinegar
½ c. water
1 clove garlic, crushed or
   minced
¼ tsp. monosodium
   glutamate (optional)

1½ lb. fresh tuna (aku)
1 tsp. salt
¼ tsp. pepper
¼ c. oil
Flour (in shaker)

Mix together vinegar, water, garlic, and monosodium gluta-mate. Pour over fish slices and let stand for 1 hour. Spoon marinade over fish occasionally. Remove fish from marinade and pat dry with paper towels. Heat oil in frying pan. Sprinkle filets with salt, pepper, and flour. Cook in oil until lightly browned.

Serve with sourdough French bread. Use stale bread as fresh bread gets soggy.

Pour the remaining oil from frying pan. Add the left over marinade and bring to a boil. Dip pieces of bread in marinade. *Onolicious.*

*Green*

## KAMABOKO SHRIMP TEMPURA

Mix together:

¾ c. flour
¼ c. water
1 egg

½ tsp. salt
1 tsp. sugar

Add:

1 chopped kamaboko
6 shrimp, chopped fine

Green onions, chopped

Drop by teaspoonfuls into hot oil and fry.

*Gold*

# KAMABOKO TEMPURA

1 c. flour
1 tsp. baking powder
¾ tsp. salt
1 tsp. sugar
1 egg, beaten
½ lb. fresh shrimp
¾ c. water

1 kamaboko, cut into ¼
   inch strips
1 piece green onion,
   chopped
5 to 6 pieces string beans
1 medium carrot
Yellow food coloring

Cut the string beans and carrot into strips. Chop the shrimp. Mix egg and water. Add all other ingredients and mix. Drop with tablespoon and deep-fry.

# SHRIMP FRITTERS

Use 1 pound shrimp (cleaned). Salt to slightly salt the shrimp.

Batter:

¼ c. flour
1 egg

Dash of salt
1½ Tbsp. water

Mix well.

Sauce:

⅓ c. catsup
2 tsp. sugar
1 Tbsp. vinegar

1 Tbsp. sesame seed,
   toasted
Dash of Tabasco sauce

Mix well. Dip salted shrimp in the batter and deep-fry until slightly browned. Arrange on platter and serve with the sauce.

*Yellow*

# SHRIMP TEMPURA

30 medium shrimp or  
    prawns  
1 c. flour

1 egg  
1 c. water

Shell shrimp, leaving the tail on. Remove entrails and put in gashes on the back to prevent shrinking. Wipe off water.

Mix flour, egg, and water. Do not overbeat. Dip shrimp in batter and deep-fat fry (in 300°F. to 350°F.). Drain on absorbent paper.

Serve with sauce made of:

4 Tbsp. dashi  
1 Tbsp. shoyu

1 Tbsp. mirin (sweet wine)

Serve 1 tablespoon grated daikon (Japanese radish) and ½ teaspoon grated ginger in a small dish with the sauce. Yield: 6 servings.

# OCTOPUS IN WINE SAUCE
## (Polvo em Molho de Vinho)

1 large (2½ lb.) octopus  
2 c. white wine  
2 c. red wine  
1 (12 oz.) can beer  
3 cloves garlic, minced  
2 tsp. paprika  
2 Tbsp. minced parsley

2 tsp. ground fresh mild red  
    pepper  
1 tsp. salt  
1 large onion, minced  
3 Tbsp. olive oil  
3 potatoes, cubed  
French bread

To clean octopus, turn body inside out. Remove internal organs and sac containing black secretion. Rinse thoroughly; slice.

In a large bowl, combine 1 cup of the red and white wines with 1 cup beer, garlic, paprika, parsley, red pepper, and salt. Add octopus; marinate for 2 hours.

In a large saucepan, saute onion in olive oil until transparent; add octopus and marinade. Cover; cook over medium heat for 45 minutes, stirring frequently. Add potatoes, remaining wine, and beer. Cook for 20 more minutes or until potatoes are done. Serve with French bread and wine. Makes 6 servings.

# PINEAPPLE LOBSTER WITH BLACK BEANS

2 lobster tails
2 Tbsp. oil
1 crushed clove garlic
2 Tbsp. black beans
  (Chinese)
2 Tbsp. soy sauce
1 tsp. green onion

1 tsp. cornstarch
2 Tbsp. water
1 tsp. wine
½ c. pineapple tidbits or
  chunks
1 tsp. sugar

Cut lobster and shell in small pieces (about 1 inch). Wash beans and mash with garlic. Add shoyu, sugar, and green onion. Heat pan with 2 tablespoons oil. Add mixed seasonings of garlic, beans, shoyu, and sugar, then add lobster and stir-fry about 1 minute. Add cornstarch mixed with water and wine; stir continually. When sauce thickens slightly, turn heat low; cover and simmer for 3 minutes. Add pineapple chunks. Garnish with Chinese parsley. *Do not overcook.* Serves 4.

Might be served with hot, fluffy rice, fresh broccoli with sesame seed, a tossed green salad, tea, and Chinese almond cookies.

*Ludvina Abrew*

# LOMI SALMON

1 lb. salted salmon
5 large ripe peeled
  tomatoes
1 medium dry onion, finely
  chopped

1 bunch green onions,
  thinly sliced
  (including green tops)

Soak salmon in cold water for 3 hours. Remove skin and bones and shred finely. Mash tomatoes to a pulp. Combine all ingredients and chill.

Just before serving, add several cubes of crushed ice.

*Yellow*

# ARAIMO (DASHEEN) FISHBALLS

1 lb. minced aku (tuna)
3 small araimo (dasheen),
  cooked and grated
½ c. carrots, grated
½ c. string beans, grated

1 onion, chopped
1 egg
2 tsp. mayonnaise
Salt and pepper to taste

Combine ingredients and pan-fry.

*Ludvina Abrew*

# SPANISH FISH BALLS

1 lb. minced aku
1 medium onion, chopped
1 stalk celery, chopped
1 small green pepper,
  chopped

1 small tomato, chopped
1 potato, grated and excess
  water removed
1 egg
Salt and pepper to taste

Mix the preceding, shaped into round balls, and pan-fry. Set aside.

Sauce:

1 (15 oz.) can whole
  tomatoes
½ c. water
2 stalks celery, sliced

1 medium onion, sliced
3 cloves garlic
2 tsp. brown sugar
Salt and pepper to taste

Break tomatoes in saucepan and add rest of ingredients. Bring to a boil, then simmer 10 to 15 minutes.

Add fish balls to sauce and simmer 10 minutes. Garnish with parsley.

*Agnes Groff, Maui Economic Opportunity Grocery Basket;*
*Ludvina Abrew*

# SQUID AND VEGETABLE STIR-FRY

1 lb. squid, cut in rings
3 Tbsp. salad oil
2 cloves garlic, minced
2 tsp. ginger, minced
1 round onion, sliced

¼ lb. fresh mushrooms, sliced
1 green pepper, sliced
1 c. celery, sliced

Sauce - Mix together:

1½ Tbsp. cornstarch
2 Tbsp. shoyu
1 tsp. sugar

1 tsp. vinegar
½ c. beef broth
Sesame seeds

Heat 2 tablespoons oil; add garlic, ginger, and onion and saute for 1 minute. Add mushrooms; stir and cook until limp. Remove and set aside. Heat 1 tablespoon oil; add squid and cook 1 to 2 minutes. Add celery and pepper; cook 2 more minutes. Return onion mix to pan. Add sauce and cook until thickened. Sprinkle with sesame seeds.

*T. Oki*

# STEAMED FISH

½ lb. fish
1 Tbsp. cornstarch
2 Tbsp. shoyu
1 Tbsp. black beans (dau see)
1 tsp. sugar
½ tsp. salt

1 Tbsp. chung choi
1 tsp. oil
1 piece ginger, crushed and cut fine
1 clove garlic
2 sprigs green onions, cut fine

Clean fish and let dry. Chop chung choi fine; mash black beans. Mix well ginger, starch, sugar, salt, chung choi, dau see, and oil and rub over fish. Arrange fish in dish and sprinkle with onion. Steam 20 to 25 minutes.

*Yellow*

# PASTA AND NOODLES

## BUCKWHEAT NOODLE SUSHI
### (Soba Sushi)

1 c. soup stock (dashi)
¼ c. soy sauce
⅓ c. Japanese sweet
  cooking wine (mirin)
10 oz. green tea buckwheat
  noodles (cha soba)
1 pkg. fresh water eel
  (unagi)

1 roll thick-cooked egg
  (atsuyaki tamago)
Beefsteak leaves (shiso)
2 to 3 sheets nori
Green horseradish
  (wasabi)

In a bowl, combine dashi, soy sauce, and mirin for a dipping sauce; chill. Cook soba according to package directions. Do not overcook. Heat unagi in package in boiling water; cool and cut into 3 long strips. Cut tamago roll into long strips. Finely chop shiso leaves.

Place a sheet of nori, shiny side down, on bamboo mat. Spread a layer of noodles over ¾ of the nori, leaving 1 inch uncovered at the farthest end. Two inches from the nearest edge, arrange unagi, tamago, and shiso leaves crosswise on noodles. To roll, bring the edge of nori up and over the noodles, encasing the center ingredients. Roll like jelly roll, lifting mat until nori completely surrounds roll. Leave in bamboo mat for 2 to 3 minutes to hold shape. Slice each roll into 6 pieces. Serve with wasabi and dipping sauce. Makes 3 servings.

# CHOW FUN

Use ¾ pound pork.

Seasoning for pork:

| | |
|---|---|
| **1 small slice crushed** | **1 Tbsp. shoyu** |
| **ginger** | **½ tsp. sugar** |
| **1 tsp. salt** | |

Remaining ingredients:

| | |
|---|---|
| **1 Tbsp. oil** | **1 (10 oz.) pkg. bean sprouts** |
| **2 rolls look fun** | **1 c. green onion (1 inch** |
| **1 c. finely sliced string** | **pieces)** |
| **beans** | **2 Tbsp. toasted sesame** |
| **1 c. finely sliced celery** | **seeds** |

Seasoning:

| | |
|---|---|
| **1 sliced crushed ginger** | **3 Tbsp. shoyu** |
| **1 tsp. salt** | **¼ tsp. ajinomoto** |
| **1 tsp. sugar** | **Dash of pepper** |

Slice pork into strips and marinate with seasoning. Let stand 15 minutes, then saute in oil until brown. Add look fun which has been cut into ¼ inch strips. Add seasoning and vegetables and stir-fry until done. Add sesame seeds. Garnish with finely sliced ham and egg strips. Top with Chinese parsley. Serves 6.

*Yellow*

# CHOW MEIN

Cook as directed and drain 7 ounces dried saimin (1 package instant saimin).

Marinate:

¼ lb. pork, cut into strips
¼ tsp. garlic salt
¼ tsp. salt
¼ tsp. monosodium
    glutamate (optional)
1 Tbsp. cornstarch

Cut vegetables into thin strips and fry in hot skillet:

2 Tbsp. salad oil
1 c. carrots (1 medium)
1 c. celery (1 stalk)
1 c. green onion (2 stalks)

1 c. green beans (6 to 8)
⅛ tsp. salt
⅛ tsp. monosodium
    glutamate

When vegetables are cooked to desired doneness, remove from skillet into large mixing bowl.

Fry in same skillet:

4 c. bean sprouts
⅛ tsp. salt

⅛ tsp. monosodium
    glutamate (optional)

Combine bean sprouts with rest of vegetables in bowl and toss lightly to mix.

Make sauce:

2 cubes soup base
1½ c. water

2 Tbsp. cornstarch

Fry marinated pork in hot skillet with 2 tablespoons salad oil. When pork is thoroughly cooked, add sauce to make gravy.

To serve: Spread cooked saimin on large platter. Cover saimin with cooked vegetables. Pour pork gravy over entire dish. Garnish with Chinese parsley if desired. Serves 6.

*Blue*

# CHOW MEIN

2 boxes noodles (chow
    mein, precooked
    refrigerated noodles)
½ lb. pork (you may color
    the pork)
4 dried mushrooms,
    soaked in water

2 pkg. bean sprouts
½ lb. Chinese peas
3 stalks green onions
Char siu (optional)
½ c. oyster sauce

Fry pork with a little shoyu and sugar, then add sliced mushrooms. In a large bowl, place noodles, peas, bean sprouts, green onions, cooked pork, and mushrooms. Pour oyster sauce and mix well. Pour the mixture in a cookie sheet and bake it in a preheated oven at 450°F. for 10 minutes. Stir the noodles and leave it in the oven another 10 minutes. Serve in a platter.

# BAKED CHOW MEIN

¼ lb. char siu, sliced thin
2 pkg. chow mein noodles
½ pkg. bean sprouts

Carrots, sliced thin
String beans, sliced thin

Sauce:

2 Tbsp. shoyu
2 Tbsp. oyster sauce

1 tsp. garlic powder
¼ c. peanut oil

Mix in broiler pan all the ingredients and sauce. Bake at 350° for 20 to 25 minutes. May need to add more oyster sauce.

*Violet Sakai*

# EASY PANCIT MIKI (FILIPINO NOODLES)

¼ c. achuete seeds
14 c. water
½ lb. chicken breasts
¼ lb. shrimp
2 Tbsp. oil
½ lb. pork, thinly sliced
2 cloves garlic, minced
1 Tbsp. patis
3 (14½ oz.) cans chicken
   broth

1 (9 oz.) pkg. dry udon
   noodles
1 (4 oz.) pkg. long rice,
   soaked and drained
2 tsp. salt
⅛ tsp. pepper
¼ c. chopped chives

Combine achuete seeds and 1 cup of the water; let stand for about 30 minutes or longer. Rub seeds with fingers to release a rich, red color. Strain; discard seeds and reserve achuete water. Cook chicken in 3 cups of the remaining water for 20 minutes. Shred chicken, reserving broth. Shell and clean shrimp; cut into ½ inch pieces.

In a saucepot, heat oil; saute chicken, shrimp, pork, and garlic. Add achuete water, reserved broth, and chicken broth. Cover; bring to a boil. Lower heat and simmer for 20 minutes.

In a large saucepan, bring 10 cups of the remaining water to a boil; add noodles and cook for 10 minutes. Rinse and drain; add to meat mixture with long rice, salt, and pepper. Cook for 10 more minutes, stirring frequently. Add chives before serving. Serve immediately. Makes 10 servings.

# FRIED SOMEN WITH SAKE-CHILI SAUCE

1 (9 oz.) pkg. somen
3 Tbsp. salad oil
1 tsp. salt
Dash of white pepper
¼ lb. lean pork, cut in thin
    strips
2 cloves garlic, minced
3 c. shredded cabbage
1 Tbsp. soy sauce

¼ tsp. hondashi (fish
    flavored soup
    granules)
2 green onions, cut into 1
    inch lengths
½ c. sake
3 Hawaiian red peppers,
    seeded and minced

Cook somen according to package directions; rinse and drain. In a large skillet, heat 2 tablespoons of the oil. Fry somen; season with ½ teaspoon of the salt and the pepper. Place on a platter. Add the remaining tablespoon oil to the skillet. Lightly brown pork. Add garlic; cook for 30 seconds. Add cabbage, soy sauce, hondashi, and the remaining ½ teaspoon salt; cook for 1 minute. Add green onions; cook for 30 seconds. Arrange pork and vegetable mixture over somen. Combine sake and red peppers; use sparingly on somen. Makes 6 servings.

Note: Sauce is very hot!

# GON LO MEIN - DRIED TOSSED NOODLES

6 lb. ready-to-eat chow
    mein noodles
2¼ c. oyster sauce
6 Tbsp. sesame oil
3 oz. dried mushrooms,
    soaked
18 green onions, chopped
2 lb. bean sprouts
12 stalks celery, slivered
2 lb. green beans, sliced
1½ c. Chinese peas, sliced
1½ tsp. salt
1 Tbsp. monosodium
    glutamate (optional)
2¼ lb. char siu, thinly
    sliced

Preheat oven to 250°F. Place noodles in a large baking pan. Sprinkle with ¾ cup of the oyster sauce and 3 tablespoons of the sesame oil; heat in oven for 15 minutes. Remove stems from mushrooms; slice caps.

In a large saucepot, heat remaining 3 tablespoons oil. Add mushrooms and other vegetables; stir-fry for 2 minutes. Add salt, monosodium glutamate, and the remaining 1½ cups oyster sauce. Stir in char siu and noodles; toss gently. Makes about 50 (1 cup) servings.

# "LOOK FUN" - CHOW FUN

Use 1½ pounds lean pork.

Marinade for pork:

1 (½ inch) slice ginger,
    pressed
¾ tsp. salt

2 tsp. shoyu sauce
1 tsp. sugar

Remaining ingredients:

1 Tbsp. corn oil
2 rolls look fun noodles, cut
    into ¼ inch strips
2 c. string beans, finely
    sliced
1 medium size carrot, finely
    sliced

1 (10 oz.) pkg. bean sprouts
1 stalk celery, sliced
    diagonally
4 stalks green onions, cut
    in 1 inch lengths
Chinese parsley

Seasoning for ingredients:

¼ to ½ c. chicken broth
2 tsp. salt
¼ tsp. white or black
    pepper

1 tsp. oyster sauce
1 tsp. sherry
¼ tsp. monosodium
    glutamate

Slice pork in thin strips and marinate for 15 minutes. Saute pork in oil until brown (pork should be cooked through). While pork is cooking, steam look fun noodle strips in a colander. Add look fun noodles and stir-fry 1 minute. Add vegetables and seasonings and stir-fry for another minute or so. For those who like Chinese parsley, garnish with parsley. Yield: Enough to serve 6 people.

*Blue*

# 3-IN-ONE NOODLE DISH

1 (12 oz.) pkg. noodles
   (wide or thin)
½ c. chopped onion
2 Tbsp. margarine or oil
1 can Cheddar cheese
   soup

1 clove garlic (optional)
½ c. chopped celery
1 can cream of mushroom
   soup

Cook noodles according to package directions. Saute garlic, onion, and celery in oil. Add sauteed vegetables and soups to drained noodles. Divide noodle mixture into 3 equal parts.

To each of these parts, add 1 of the following or make up a combination:

1. Use 1 can tuna, 1 cup frozen peas, ½ cup liquid (milk, chicken broth, or water).

2. Use 1 cup chopped ham, 1 cup peas or broccoli, 1 teaspoon mustard, ½ cup liquid (ham broth, milk, water, or vegetable liquid).

3. Use 2 or 3 chopped boiled eggs and milk.

4. Use 1 cup chopped chicken.

5. Use 1 cup sauteed ground beef.

# SUSHI AND RICE

## SUSHI

Sushi is Japanese food made with vinegar seasoned rice. They are made in different forms with variety of ingredients. Depending on the meats and vegetables used, sushi can be used as the main dish or as the starchy staple food.

When used as main dish, variety of sushi with fish, egg, and shrimp topping are arranged attractively on a plate with slices of ginger in the center and served with a little dish of shoyu.

Menu for sushi meal may be: Soup, tray of sushi, okoko (pickled vegetables), tea, and fruit or senbei may be served for dessert.

The important part of sushi is the rice. It must be cooked properly and seasoned well so that each grain will be separate and shiny.

Sushi Rice:

**5 c. rice**　　　　　　　　　　**5x1 inch konbu (dried**
**5½ c. water**　　　　　　　　　**seaweed kelp)**

Wash rice and add water with konbu in a thick pot. Boil vigorously for about 10 minutes, then cook for about 10 minutes at medium heat, and then lower heat and steam for about 10 minutes. Turn off heat and leave for about 10 minutes more or use automatic rice cooker.

Vinegar Sauce - Mix together:

**½ c. vinegar**　　　　　　　　　**½ tsp. ajinomoto**
**1½ to 2 Tbsp. salt (more or**　　　**(monosodium**
**　less according to**　　　　　　**glutamate, optional)**
**　taste)**
**2½ Tbsp. sugar (more or**
**　less according to**
**　taste)**

When rice is ready, transfer rice into a large shallow rice container, preferably wooden. While still hot, add vinegar sauce; pour over top and leave for a moment and then mix lightly and
*(Continued on next page)*

fan to cool. This method gives the gloss to the rice and the vinegar flavor will penetrate the rice.

*Red*

# INGREDIENTS FOR VARIETY SUSHI

## 1. Matsumae

Aji Kobu-zume:

**Fillet fish (must be fresh fish)**

**Salt (use about 5% by weight of fish)**

Soak for 5 to 6 hours, then soak in vinegar. Roll in konbu.

## 2. Nimono - "gu" (cooked thing):

**1 bundle kanpyo (rub with salt, wash and boil)**
**10 dried mushrooms (soak overnight)**

**1 c. dashi**

For dashi:

**3x1 inch konbu**
**½ c. katsuobushi (dried bonito shavings)**

**1⅔ c. water**

Put konbu in water and boil. When large bubbles appear, take out tangle and put in katsuobushi. When water reaches boiling point, turn off heat. When katsuobushi sinks, use upper clear liquid as stock. Cook kanpyo, mushroom, and dashi together and boil until soft.

Add:

**4 Tbsp. sugar**
**3 Tbsp. shoyu**

**¼ tsp. ajinomoto**

Cover and cook until all sauce is absorbed.

## 3. Aburage (fried bean curd or tofu):

**10 aburage**
**3 Tbsp. shoyu**

**11 tsp. sugar**
**3½ c. dashi**

Cut 5 aburage into halves into triangles. Slice the other 5 to open the triangle into a square. Remove soft inside. Cook in

*(Continued on next page)*

*(Continued from previous page)*

dashi only, then add half of sugar and shoyu. Cook for 20 minutes, then add the remaining sugar and shoyu. Cover and cook until sauce is absorbed. Leave in pan and cool.

### 4. Tamago yaki (Atsuyaki - thick fried eggs):

5 eggs
5 Tbsp. scraped white meat
    fish or grind in suri-
    bachi (Japanese
    mortar)

5 Tbsp. dashi
½ tsp. salt
¼ tsp. ajinomoto
4 Tbsp. sugar

Mix together all ingredients well and fry in greased pan, on slow heat. Use square pan if possible. If bottom is cooked and top is still soft, put under broiler, watching carefully not to overheat.

### 5. Tamago Yaki (Usuyaki - thin sheet of fried eggs):

3 eggs
¼ tsp. salt

½ tsp. oil

Mix together eggs and salt and fry in greased pan as thin as possible in square pan. Makes 2 sheets.

### 6. Ebi Oboro (shrimp flakes):

½ lb. shrimp
Drops of red coloring
    (enough to color
    pink)

¼ tsp. salt
2 Tbsp. sugar

Remove black vein from shrimp and boil for 2 to 3 minutes in salted water. Cool. Remove shell. Grind in suri-bachi or put through meat grinder. Add coloring. Put in double boiler; add sugar and salt, a little at a time, and cook until dry. Ready prepared oboro is available in red, green, or yellow color.

**7. Shibi (Ahi):** Cut fish in ⅓ inch strip, the width of nori. Make a paste of wasabi (horseradish powder) and water.

**8. Noshi Ebi (shrimp topping):** Pierce a bamboo stick through shrimp to keep it straight. Boil in salted water.

**9. Cucumber:** Pour boiling water over cucumber and cool in cold water. Cut into ⅓ inch strips. Sprinkle salt for taste.

**10. Watercress:** Boil in salted water about 3 minutes.

*Red*

# SUSHI VARIATIONS

## A. Norimaki (seaweed roll):
1. Hosomaki or Teppo sushi (small roll):

2 c. seasoned rice
3 nori
Kanpyo
Oboro
Watercress

Atsuyaki tamago, cut in
thin strips
Cucumber strip
Shibi (Ahi)

Cut nori into half. Put sudari (bamboo mat) on a cutting board. Place a layer of rice (about ¼ cup) on nori and put kanpyo and roll. Cut into pieces. Put oboro into the next and roll. Make 4 other rolls with the other ingredients. Skewer 1 piece each of the various rolls together.

2. Norimaki (regular or medium): Place 1 sheet of nori on bamboo mat; spread rice evenly, about ½ inch. Place flavored ingredients (kanpyo, mushrooms, fried eggs, oboro or unagi (seasoned eel), and greens at one end. Roll up tightly. Cut into ¾ inch pieces.

3. Futomaki (fat or large roll):

2 nori
2 c. seasoned rice
Mushroom
Watercress

Atsuyaki tamago
Kanpyo
Oboro

Place 2 nori on sudari (bamboo mat) and spread a layer of rice. Place all 5 ingredients in a row about 1 inch apart and roll. Cut into crosswise slices. Slices will be a pinwheel.

## B. Tamago Maki (egg roll):

1 usuyaki tamago
Flavored rice

1 hosomaki with red or
green filling

Place usuyaki tamago on wax paper; spread out thin layer of rice. Place hosomaki at one end and roll up like jelly roll. Keep wrapped in wax paper until ready to cut. Cut into ¾ inch slices.

*(Continued on next page)*

*(Continued from previous page)*

### C. Chakin Zushi (dishcloth sushi):

Red meat fish
White meat fish

Horseradish paste made
  with water flavored
  rice

Place waxed paper on dishcloth. Place sliced fish on it and the rice, then press into shape. Remove and place horseradish in the impression.

### D. Takara Zushi (treasure sushi):

3 usuyaki tamago
1½ c. seasoned rice
1 Tbsp. kanpyo, chopped
1 Tbsp. mushroom,
  chopped

1 Tbsp. oboro
1 nori
Watercress
2 shrimp, boiled in salt and
  sliced in halves

Mix chopped ingredients into rice; make into 3 balls. Put shrimp on top. Place on fried eggs and wrap. Tie with watercress.

### E. Matsumae Zushi:

2 pieces flavored aji (akule)     2 c. seasoned rice

Remove skin from fish; slice through the thick portion, leaving 1 end attached. Open out into a good size sheet. Soak in vinegar. Place on dishcloth. Put 1 cup seasoned rice on fish and roll. Leave overnight.

### F. Inari Zushi (Shinoda Zushi - cone sushi):

2 c. seasoned rice
Chopped "gu" (flavored
  ingredients)

10 pieces aburage (either
  cone or square)
Seasoned kanpyo

Mix "gu" into the rice, mixing lightly. Fill aburage with the mixture. Tie with kanpyo.

*(Continued on next page)*

232

*(Continued from previous page)*

**G. Chirashi Zushi (scattered sushi):** Use 1¼ cups seasoned rice.

1. Edo Mai (Tokyo rice)

**Noshi ebi**
**Shibi slices**
**Aji (akule) slices**
**White meat fish slices**
**Oboro**

**Atsuyaki tamago**
**Chinese peas, cooked in**
   **salted water**
**Nori (heat over range unit**
   **until crispy)**

Make a mound of seasoned rice in a bowl. Sprinkle pieces of nori on top. Arrange the other ingredients attractively.

2. Osaka Zushi - Chop and add to the seasoned rice the prepared mushroom (shiitake), kanpyo, and carrots. Sprinkle over top the nori, usuyaki tamago (cut in strips), Chinese peas (cooked in salted water and cut into strips), oboro, flavored aji (akule), sliced.

**H. Nigiri Zushi:** Mold seasoned rice into 1x2x1 inch cakes and arrange on plate or sushi tray. Place sliced raw fish with wasabi or mustard paste, tamago yaki, shrimp, etc. Wrap some in 1 inch strip of nori; lay on side and top with suzuko (fish eggs).

**I. Oshi Zushi (pressed sushi):**

1. Press seasoned rice into wooden form and decorate top with pieces of fried eggs, parsley, fish cake, nori, and colored shrimp flakes. The form comes with 3 holes in the shape of a fan, peach blossom, and pine leaves.

2. A large square or rectangular box may be used. Special box is made with removal bottom and lid that slides inside. Arrange banana leaf at the bottom of the box. Spread out about ½ inch of rice; sprinkle or arrange pieces of fried eggs, parsley, fish cake, nori, and colored shrimp flakes. Cover with banana leaf and repeat layer of rice and other ingredients. Repeat as many times as you have ingredients and space in the box. Press down with a lid and lift out the sides. Cut into 2 or 3 inch squares.

# SUSHI RICE

**3 c. rice (either plain, Smith type, or Calrose)**   **3 c. boiling water**

Wash rice gently and quickly, then drain and pour in boiling water. Cook with the cover slightly open so that water will not boil over. After water has receded, turn to low and steam with the cover on tightly until done.

This method prevents rice from getting mushy, and a good sushi can be identified by the grains of rice. These grains should be distinctly apart from each other and sticking. When washing, be careful not to break loose the wheat germ at the end of the kernel. All the nutrients are in the germ.

Vinegar Sauce for Rice:

**½ c. vinegar (Japanese rice vinegar preferably)**   **⅓ c. white sugar**
**1½ tsp. ajinomoto**   **1¼ tsp. salt**

Cook over heat to dissolve sugar and salt. When cool, add sauce to rice which has been taken out of pot into another container (preferably enamel or wooden because of the acid in the vinegar). Stir in sauce.

The common sushi made and eaten in Hawaii are Inari and Maki sushi. Inari sushi, commonly called cone sushi is used for picnics and informal functions. Maki sushi or rolled sushi is usually used at parties. There are other variations in shape and ingredients - sushi as nigiri sushi, chirashi sushi, and oshi sushi.

*Red*

# INARI SUSHI

Iriko Sauce: Make 1½ cups of iriko dashi (you may use dried shrimp). Boil 1½ cups of water with a handful of iriko. Do not boil too long or dashi will become bitter.

Aburage (fried tofu or bean curd): Cut 12 into halves and take excess tofu out of the sack. Pour boiling water over the aburage to remove excess fat. Drain in a sieve.

Stock for Aburage:

**¾ c. iriko dashi (sauce)**
**1 tsp. salt**
**1 Tbsp. shoyu**

**3 Tbsp. brown sugar**
**½ tsp. ajinomoto**

Place ingredients in saucepan; add 24 pieces of aburage (12 aburage, cut in halves) and cook slowly until seasoning is absorbed. Shake pot occasionally to season evenly.

Filling - Vegetables and Stock:

**½ c. mushroom (soak in**
**water to soften**
**before cutting)**
**1 small gobo (burdock**
**root), chopped fine**

**½ c. chopped string beans**
**½ c. chopped carrots**
**(soaked in water with**
**a drop of vinegar until**
**ready to cook)**

Stock:

**½ c. iriko dashi**
**1 tsp. salt**
**½ tsp. ajinomoto**

**2 Tbsp. brown sugar**
**1 Tbsp. shoyu**

Cook all ingredients, except gobo (stock and vegetables). Cook until done and drain, then cook gobo in same stock quickly because long cooking will result in loss of flavor. Drain with the other ingredients.

Other ingredients:

**2 eggs, fried thin and**
**chopped**
**Chopped Kamaboko (fish**
**cake)**

**Minced parsley (optional)**
**Ginger may be added**

*(Continued on next page)*

*(Continued from previous page)*

To 6 cups of cooked and seasoned rice (3 cups uncooked rice), add chopped fried eggs and parsley green; add vegetable and other chopped ingredients.

Put rice into cones gently, filling from the bottom. Do not pack cone with rice. Rice should fall out when cone is turned upside-down. Place on tray or platter for about 3 hours. This way, flavor from the vegetables will blend into rice along with the vinegar sauce.

*Red*

## NORIMAKI (ROLLED SEAWEED RICE)

1 recipe Sushi Rice
10 sheets nori (black
    seaweed)
1 (2 oz.) pkg. kanpyo (dried
    gourd)
2 oz. shiitake (dried
    mushrooms)

2 medium carrots
10 stalks watercress
2 cans boiled eel or
    Hawaiian tuna

*(Continued on next page)*

*(Continued from previous page)*

Kanpyo: Wash and cook in water until soft. Add enough stock to cover and cook until tender. Add 4 tablespoons sugar, 3 teaspoons shoyu, 2 teaspoons salt, and 1 teaspoon gourmet powder and continue cooking for 10 minutes. Cut into the length of nori.

Shiitake: Wash and soak in enough water to cover until soft. Cook in the same water until very tender. Add 3 tablespoons sugar, 4 tablespoons shoyu, and ½ teaspoon gourmet powder and cook until the sauce is well absorbed. Cut into ¼ inch strips.

Carrots: Cut carrots lengthwise into ¼ inch strips. Add 1 cup water and cook for 7 to 10 minutes. Add 2 tablespoons sugar, 1 teaspoon salt, and ½ teaspoon gourmet powder and cook 5 minutes more.

Watercress: Clean and boil 2 minutes in salted water. Drain and squeeze out water.

Hawaiian Tuna: Cook in a saucepan and add 3 tablespoons sugar and 4 tablespoons shoyu.

Method of rolling sushi: Place a sheet of nori on the bamboo mat (square) with the end towards you. Sprinkle some vinegar solution (see sushi rice solution) on the nori and spread sushi rice over ⅔ of the nori to a thickness of about ½ inch. Arrange 5 strands of kanpyo, 1 row of shiitake, carrots, watercress, and eel split lengthwise on the rice about ⅓ from the front edge. Roll away from you, being careful to keep ingredients in place with your fingers. When the edge of the mat touches the rice, lift the mat and finish rolling. Roll again with the mat and apply slight pressure to tighten the roll.

To serve, cut in half and then into fours. Arrange on plate, cut side up.

*Red*

# CONE SUSHI

Sushi Rice:

4 c. rice
¼ c. vinegar
¼ c. sugar
2 tsp. salt

2 tsp. ajinomoto (gourmet
  powder, optional)
¼ c. dried shrimp

Shrimp should be soaked in vinegar, sugar, and salt. Drain shrimp and save liquid. Use this vinegar liquid to pour over cooled rice and toss lightly so rice will not be gummy.

Filling:

12 aburage
2 medium size carrots
10 string beans
A few dried shrimp
1¼ tsp. salt

1 Tbsp. sugar
¾ c. water
½ tsp. ajinomoto (optional)
Small shavings from
  aburage

Chop carrots and beans in long, fine strips. Boil aburage for 10 minutes. Add sugar and salt to taste. Cook a little longer. Drain and cool. Boil chopped shrimp and cook slowly several minutes. Add seasoning and aburage. Drain. Mix vegetables with rice and fill aburage cones.

*Yellow*

# TAMAGO YAKI (USUYAKI - VERY THIN, FRIED EGG)

**4 eggs**
**¼ tsp. salt**
**½ tsp. oil**

**1 tsp. cornstarch**
**1 tsp. water**

Beat together eggs and salt until well blended. Fry in large, greased fry pan in very thin sheets. Trim edges to form a square sheet. Makes 3 to 4 sheets.

To prepare Egg Roll:

1. Place the fried egg skin on doubled waxed paper or on a bamboo mat (sudare).
2. Spread over ⅔ of egg skin a thin layer of flavored rice about ¼ inch thick.
3. Place lengthwise on rice ⅓ in from edge nearest to you a thin line of either: a) cooked spinach or cress, b) cooked carrot sticks, c) cooked shrimp, or d) a combination of these.
4. Now roll egg, rice, and filling away from you like a jelly roll. Roll rather firmly to keep ingredients together.
5. Moisten the far edge of egg skin with crushed rice grains to make a better seal, then reroll to tighten the roll.
6. Store in waxed paper, seam side down, until ready to cut. Cut into 1 inch slices.
7. Makes 3 to 4 rolls about 1 inch in diameter.

# CENTERS FOR EGG ROLL

Cooked Spinach or Watercress:

**3 to 4 sprigs fresh spinach,**     **½ tsp. salt**
  **watercress, or whole**
  **green beans**

Drop into boiling, salted water about 3 minutes. Drain or squeeze slightly to remove excess liquid.

Cooked "Stick" Carrots:

**1 medium carrot, cut into**     **¼ tsp. monosodium**
  **thin sticks**                 **glutamate**
**½ tsp. salt**                **1 tsp. sugar**

Cook carrot in 1 cup water 3 to 5 minutes, then add salt, monosodium glutamate, and sugar and continue cooking 4 to 5 minutes or until carrot is tender but firm. Drain.

Oboro Ebi (shrimp flakes):

**½ lb. shrimp (fresh,**     **¾ tsp. salt**
  **canned, or frozen)***     **1 Tbsp. sugar**
**A few drops of red coloring**
  **(enough to make**
  **pink)**

Remove shell and black vein from shrimp and boil for 2 to 3 minutes in salted water (½ teaspoon salt). Cool, and grind in mortar or in suribachi or put through a meat grinder. Add coloring. Put mixture in top of double boiler; add sugar and remaining ¼ teaspoon salt, a little at a time, and cook until shrimp mixture is dry. Ready-prepared oboro (shrimp flakes) is available in grocery stores in red, green, or yellow color.

* May use canned tuna flakes, drained, and seasoned with sugar; omit salt.

# HAKO ZUSHI (BOX SUSHI)

2 (8x8 inch) pans
3 c. rice
1 egg, fried thin and sliced
   thin in strips

Wax paper
1 pkg. sushi furi
1 sheet nori
Pickled ginger (optional)

Wash rice gently and rinse thoroughly. Let it stand for ½ hour or more. When rice cooker pops, let it stand for 20 minutes to simmer. Rice is very important in sushi making.

1 (7½ oz.) can tuna
1½ Tbsp. brown sugar

1 tsp. shoyu
¼ tsp. salt

In small frying pan, put all the preceding ingredients and cook until almost all the liquid evaporates. Set aside.

Sauce for 3 cups rice:

½ c. sugar
½ c. Japanese vinegar

1 Tbsp. salt

Mix together. Take rice out in large bowl and fold sauce in gradually. Line pan with double layer of wax paper and put 1 sheet of sushi nori. Put in mixed rice about ½ inch thick. Sprinkle tuna mix on top of rice. Put another layer of rice about ½ inch thick. Sprinkle 1 package sushi furi or strips of egg and ginger. Cover with waxed paper and put another pan of same size and press. You may put weight on. Pull out the wax paper and rice together and lay flat on cutting board and cut to desired size. Arrange nicely on tray and serve.

# HIJIKI OR KUROME BARA SUSHI

1 c. mochi rice
3 c. rice
4 c. water
¾ c. sugar
¾ c. vinegar
2 tsp. salt
2 large aburage, finely chopped
½ pkg. kurome, washed, cleaned, soaked 15 minutes in water, drained, and chopped fine

1 or ½ can ajitsuke kogai
¼ c. cooking oil
1 medium carrot, grated like sashimi grass
½ red Kamaboko, chopped fine
¼ c. sugar
¼ c. shoyu

Cook rice and let cool. Heat sugar, vinegar, and salt, then sprinkle over rice. Fry aburage in oil until crisp; add kurome, kogai, carrots, and kamaboko. Add sugar and shoyu. Cook on high until carrots are done. Mix ingredients into rice. Roll into sushi or make rice balls.

*Patsy Nakamura*

# PAN SUSHI

5 c. rice, cooked
½ c. Japanese vinegar
½ c. white sugar
1 Tbsp. salt
1 can tuna

1½ Tbsp. brown sugar
1 tsp. shoyu
¼ tsp. salt
Furikake
Nori

Cook tuna with brown sugar, shoyu, and salt. Mix together vinegar, sugar, and salt. Scoop rice into a large pan. Gradually fold the vinegar sauce into rice.

Line a 9x13 inch pan with doubled wax paper. Line with nori. Spread half of rice on nori. Spread tuna on rice. Spread other half of rice on tuna. Sprinkle furikake. Cover with wax paper. Press down with another pan.

*Helen Kawahara*

# QUICKIE LAYERED SUSHI

3¼ c. rice
3¼ c. water
1 pkg. shiofuke konbu (use
    straight from pkg.)

⅓ c. furikake nori
½ c. takuwan, diced

Cook rice. Line a 13x9 inch cake pan with waxed paper; spread shiofuke konbu and furikake nori evenly on the bottom. While rice is still hot, spread ½ of the rice in pan over the konbu and nori mixture. Pack down slightly. Spread diced takuwan over the rice and cover with the remaining half of rice. Pack rice down so that the layers will stick together and hold its shape. When rice is cool, or when ready to serve, invert pan over a tray or platter. The konbu-furikake part will be on the top. Remove the waxed paper and cut sushi into squares. Yield: Approximately 30 (2 inch) squares.

*Blue*

# TEMAKI OR HAND ROLLED SUSHI

Cook rice as you do for other sushi.

Sauce:

½ c. vinegar
1 Tbsp. salt

¼ c. sugar
Ajinomoto (optional)

Mix with rice. Cut nori into halves or fourths. For filling you can use anything you desire. Some combinations are imitation crab, cucumber, celery, raw fish, cut in strips, thick omelet, cut in ¼ inch or larger size, natto beans mixed with green onion and shoyu or salt, ham, cheese, avocado, kaiware (turnip sprouts), or asparagus cooked in salt.

Put nori in palm of your hand; add a little rice, mayonnaise, and wasabi (horseradish). Put choice of filling. You may add a few drops of shoyu.

This "roll your own sushi" is very refreshing and delightful party dish. Your guests will have fun and there is less fussing for the hostess.

*Ann Arisumi*

# MAZE GOHAN - RICE MIXED WITH VEGETABLES

**3 c. rice**                          **3 c. water**

When steamed and ready, mix in the following:

**½ konnyaku (made from flour of tuber root)**
**1 small carrot**
**6 string beans**
**6 dried mushrooms, soaked in water**

**⅓ kamaboko (fish cake)**
**1 aburage (fried bean curd)**
**1 small gobo (burdock)**

Seasoning:

**2 Tbsp. shrimp flakes**
**3½ Tbsp. shoyu**
**3½ Tbsp. sugar**

**1½ tsp. salt**
**½ tsp. gourmet powder (optional)**

Cut all ingredients into small thin pieces and cook in 1 cup water until vegetables are tender. Add seasoning and cook for 7 to 8 minutes, then mix into the cooked rice. Keep rice flaky. Serve hot.

# PIBIUM PAHB
## (Korean)

4 c. rice, cooked in 4½ c. water
1 bunch watercress, cut 1 inch
1 pkg. bean sprouts
2 Tbsp. shoyu
2 Tbsp. toasted sesame seeds
1 tsp. oil
1 tsp. salt
1 tsp. sugar

Cook watercress and bean sprouts in sauce made of remaining ingredients. Boil 2 minutes and squeeze out excess liquid.

1 c. kim chee, drained and chopped
½ lb. pul kogi, cut in strips

Rice Sauce:

1 Tbsp. sesame seed oil
3 Tbsp. shoyu

Garnish:

Fried egg strips
Finely chopped green onion

In a large bowl, combine hot rice with seasoned watercress, bean sprouts, beef, and kim chee. Pour Rice Sauce mixture over rice and toss gently to blend. Garnish and serve. Yield: 10 to 12 servings.

# SEKIHAN
## (Red Bean Rice)

½ c. azuki (Japanese dried
   red beans)
4 c. water
1 tsp. salt
½ tsp. ajinomoto (optional)

2 c. rice
2½ c. mochi rice
Salt to taste
Sesame seeds, roasted

In a pot, combine azuki with 3 cups water; bring to a boil, then add another cup of cold water. Simmer for about 1 hour until azuki is soft. Do not overcook. Remove from heat; add salt and ajinomoto. Drain, reserving liquid. Add enough water to azuki liquid to measure 4½ cups.

Wash and soak the rice and mochi rice for 1 hour. Drain water and place rice in a rice cooker. Add the 4½ cups reserved liquid to the soaked rice; top with the cooked azuki. Cook according to manufacturer's directions. When rice is done, gently stir to mix rice and azuki.

Just before serving, sprinkle with salt and roasted sesame seeds.

*Janice Toguchi*

## EASY SEKIHAN

¼ c. azuki
4 c. sweet rice
   (mochigome)
1 c. plain white rice

3½ c. azuki liquid
2 tsp. salt
2 drops of red food
   coloring

Evening before, pour ¼ cup azuki in a quart size Thermos bottle. Fill half full with boiling water; drain after 1 hour. Add 3½ cups of boiling water to azuki. Cover and let stand until morning.

Next day: Drain azuki; save liquid. Wash mochigome and plain rice. Add cooked azuki and 3½ cups azuki liquid, salt, and food coloring. Stir until well blended. Cook in automatic rice cooker. May add black goma (sesame seed) over sekihan before serving.

*Ethel Miyahira*

# SPAM MUSUBI

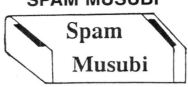

Prepare Spam: Use 1 (7 ounce) can Spam, sliced into 7 pieces lengthwise. Place sliced Spam in a frying pan.

Add:

**2 Tbsp. shoyu**          **1 Tbsp. mirin**
**2 Tbsp. sugar**

Cook Spam in sauce until liquid is reduced and thickened. Set aside.

Prepare 3 cups rice. (Cup equals measuring cup that comes with your rice cooker.)

Nori (use "yaki nori" type): Cut sheets in 2 or 3 pieces.

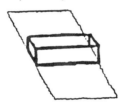

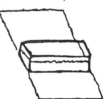

1. Place nori on wax paper. Put mold on center of nori.

2. Fill ¾ of the mold with cooked rice.

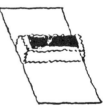

3. Firmly press rice down with cover. Push molded rice out by gently lifting mold off.

4. Place prepared Spam onto rice. (Add a little of the sauce too.) Fold nori over rice. Wrap musubi with wax paper. Let set for 10 minutes.

*Ann Arisumi*

# SPINACH RICE

2 c. cooked rice
2 (10 oz.) pkg. frozen
    chopped spinach,
    thawed and well
    drained
1 medium onion, chopped
¼ c. margarine

⅔ c. milk
2 eggs, beaten
2 c. shredded mild Cheddar
    or American cheese
Pinch of nutmeg
1½ tsp. salt

Combine all ingredients and put in a greased ovenproof bowl or casserole dish. Bake in 325° oven for 1 hour or microwave for 10 minutes. If it is firm, it's done.

# VEGETABLE-RICE SUSHI - YASAI GOHAN

3 dried mushrooms
3 c. water
¼ lb. warabi (fern shoots)
2½ c. rice
1 Tbsp. mirin
3 Tbsp. soy sauce
½ tsp. hondashi (fish
    flavored soup
    granules)

1 tsp. salt
2 tsp. salad oil
½ c. finely diced gobo
½ c. finely diced carrot
4 tsp. sugar
2 tsp. sake
6 sheets sushi nori
Black sesame seed

Soak mushrooms in 1 cup of the water for 20 minutes. Reserve mushroom liquid; remove stems from mushrooms and finely dice caps. Blanch warabi and cut into ¼ inch pieces.

In a rice cooker, wash and drain rice. Add the reserved mushroom liquid, the remaining 2 cups water, the mirin, 1 tablespoon of the soy sauce, the hondashi, and salt. Stir well and cook.

In a skillet, heat the oil. Saute mushrooms, gobo, and carrot for 1 minute. Add the remaining 2 tablespoons soy sauce, the sugar, and sake; cook for 1 minute. Add warabi; cook for 1 more minute. When rice is done, fold in vegetable mixture; cover and let stand for 15 minutes. Cut sheets of nori into halves. Place rectangular musubi mold widthwise in center of nori; fill mold with rice. Using mold press, pack rice into mold; remove mold. Fold nori over rice; seal edges with water. Cut in half diagonally. Sprinkle cut sides with sesame seed. Makes 12 sushi.

# OTHERS

## EGG FOO YONG

6 eggs
1 c. bean sprouts
1 c. canned or fresh shrimp
¼ c. sliced or chopped
    water chestnuts

½ c. finely sliced onions
½ tsp. salt
Dash of pepper

Beat eggs lightly. Add bean sprouts, water chestnuts, shrimp, onions, and seasonings. Mix lightly.

Put vegetable oil into a heavy skillet to a depth of ½ inch and heat. Drop about ½ cup of egg mixture into oil for each patty. Brown both sides, cooking until bean sprouts are tender but still crisp.

After cooking Egg Foo Yong, drain off most of oil. Add ½ cup hot water and 1 chicken flavored bouillon cube and cook till dissolved. Add 1 tablespoon shoyu, ½ teaspoon sugar, and cornstarch to thicken. Cook until thick and smooth.

*Green*

# HILO FRANKS

Franks are seasoned with a tangy apricot sauce. Use sauce for glazing spitted duck or pork roast, too.

1 c. apricot preserves
½ (8 oz.) can (½ c.)
    seasoned tomato
    sauce
⅓ c. vinegar
¼ c. cooking sherry
2 Tbsp. soy sauce
2 Tbsp. honey

1 Tbsp. salad oil
1 tsp. salt
1 tsp. grated fresh ginger
    root or ¼ tsp. ground
    ginger
2 lb. frankfurters
1 (No. 2) can pineapple
    slices, drained

For the sauce, combine first 9 ingredients. Score the frankfurters on the bias and broil slowly, turning and basting often with the sauce, till hot through and glazed.

Last few minutes, grill pineapple rings. Place on grill; brush with basting sauce. Broil and turn. Brush again with sauce. Heat remaining sauce to pass with franks. Goes with a tossed salad. Serves 8 to 10.

*Ludvina Abrew*

# NIKOMI ODEN

½ c. katsuobushi, shaved
    bonito
3 c. water
5 Tbsp. shoyu
4 Tbsp. sugar
1 tsp. salt
12 araimo (dasheen)
1 chikuwa (fish cake)

2 konnyaku (glutaneous
    cake made from
    stants tubrous root)
1 can takenoko (bamboo
    shoots)
2 large daikon (white
    radish)

Parboil araimo and remove skin. Cut chikuwa, daikon, bamboo shoots into thick slices. Cut konnyaku into triangular pieces.

Prepare stock by boiling katsuobushi in water. Add shoyu, sugar, salt, and boil. Add vegetables and chikuwa and simmer for 45 to 60 minutes or until vegetables are cooked and well seasoned. Serves 6.

*Blue*

# ONION CASSEROLE

3 large onions
1 can cream of chicken
   soup
½ lb. Swiss cheese

1 tsp. soy sauce
Dash of pepper
Buttered bread (on top)

Saute onions. Mix soup with soy sauce and pepper. Grate cheese. Put onions on the bottom, then soup, then grated cheese and buttered bread (cut into squares) on top. Bake in 350° oven for 15 to 30 minutes.

*Misae Kameya*

# OVEN BAKED BEANS

½ Portuguese sausage,
   sliced or chopped
¼ c. onion, chopped
2 cans pork and beans

1 Tbsp. brown sugar
1 tsp. prepared mustard
Ketchup to taste

Brown sausage in skillet; add onion and saute with sausage. Mix in other ingredients and simmer 10 minutes. Bake in Pyrex dish at 325°F. for 30 minutes or until brown crust is formed on top.

*Natalie Corderio*

# PORTUGUESE CORN MEAL DISH

2 to 3 leaves kale
4 strips bacon
4 c. water

1 c. corn meal
1 tsp. salt

Chop kale, then parboil. Fry bacon until crisp, then crumble. Combine 1 cup water and 1 cup corn meal; let set for ½ hour. Combine 1 teaspoon salt and 3 cups water; mix with preceding ingredients. Simmer 20 minutes, then pour into pie pan. Let set. Cut into wedges. Can be eaten plain or fried in butter.

*Sharen Cruel*

# TACOS

1 lb. semi-thawed minced
  fish
3 Tbsp. vegetable oil
1 pkg. taco seasoning
½ amount of water called
  for on pkg. of taco
  seasoning

12 tortillas
Shredded lettuce
Shredded cheese
Taco sauce

Cook the fish in the oil until color changes. Add the taco seasoning and water. Cook until nearly dry, stirring occasionally. Heat tortillas as directed on the package. Fill with several spoons of sauce, some shredded cheese, lettuce, and a garnish of taco sauce.

Other additions: Finely chopped onions or sliced scallions, sour cream, and guacamole.

# BAKED TOFU CASSEROLE

1 block tofu
½ c. ground pork
1 can cream of mushroom
  soup
1 small carrot, grated
2 eggs, beaten

½ c. chopped onion
¾ c. bread crumbs
2 Tbsp. shoyu
1 tsp. salt
Dash of ajinomoto

1. Mash tofu and pork in bowl.
2. Add all other ingredients, leaving ¼ cup bread crumbs.
3. Mix the ingredients and place in greased casserole dish.
4. Top with remaining ¼ cup crumbs.
5. Bake in preheated oven at 375°F. for 30 minutes.

*Mitsuko Yamamoto*

## STUFFED A-GE (FRIED TOFU)

1 tofu, drained and mashed
6 mushrooms, soaked and
   chopped
1 lb. ground pork
2 eggs
6 a-ge, each cut into 3
   pieces

2 tsp. salt
2 Tbsp. flour
3 Tbsp. shoyu
Dash of ajinomoto

Mix together all ingredients, except the a-ge. Stuff the a-ge with the pork mixture and place on bowl. Put bowl in steamer and steam for 20 to 30 minutes.

*Red*

## STUFFED TOFU

1 tofu, cut in 1½ x 1½ x ⅜
   inch pieces
1 lb. ground pork
8 water chestnuts,
   chopped
1 stalk green onion,
   chopped
1 egg
1 tsp. shoyu
½ tsp. ajinomoto

1 tsp. salt
1 Tbsp. chung choi,
   chopped
4 small fresh frozen
   shrimp, chopped
1 tsp. salt
1 c. water for steaming
   (boiling)
2 Tbsp. cornstarch
2 Tbsp. oil

Mix pork, chestnut, green onion, egg, shoyu, aji, chung choi, shrimp, and salt. Slit 1 corner of tofu and stuff with pork mixture. Heat oil and brown stuffed tofu on both sides. Leave tofu in pan and pour boiling water and add salt. Simmer for about ½ hour on very low heat. Pour cornstarch and water paste, stirring gravy well. Serve hot with some 1½ inch green onions.

*Red*

# TOFU LOAF

1½ tofu
3 eggs
1 small onion, chopped
1 small carrot, chopped
1 green onion, chopped
1 (10¾ oz.) can cream of
    mushroom soup

⅓ c. bread crumbs
1 Tbsp. sugar
½ tsp. MSG (optional)
½ tsp. salt
2 Tbsp. oil
½ Tbsp. shoyu

Cut tofu into thirds horizontally. Lay on cutting board between paper towels, pressing to remove water, squeeze between palms of both hands to extract remaining water. Combine tofu and all remaining ingredients in a bowl and mix thoroughly. Pour into a 9x13 inch pan and bake at 375° for 90 minutes. Center puffs up when done.

*T. Oki*

# TOFU PATTIES

1 block tofu, mashed
1 can tuna
½ c. thinly chopped carrots
½ c. string beans, chopped
⅓ c. green onions,
    chopped

2 eggs
1¼ tsp. salt
¼ tsp. monosodium
    glutamate
Dash of pepper

Mash the tofu into bowl. Add the tuna and vegetables. Add eggs and seasonings and mix. Make into patties and fry in oil until brown.

*Blue*

# TOFU SQUARES

1 block tofu (squeeze water
    out with cloth)
½ c. grated carrots
½ c. chopped beans
½ c. dried mushrooms
    (shiitake), chopped

½ c. green onion, chopped
½ c. mayonnaise (lite)
2 eggs, beaten
1 tsp. salt

Mix together and bake at 350° for 45 minutes. Cut into tiny squares. Serve with mustard/shoyu or oyster sauce.

Single recipe, use 8x8 inch pan, 45 minutes. Double recipe, use 9x13 inch pan, 1 hour.

*Helen Kawahara*

# ZUCCHINI AND TOFU

3 or 4 zucchini, sliced
½ lb. pork, sliced (or
    chicken may be
    substituted)
2 Tbsp. canola oil

2 eggs, beaten
1 block tofu, drained well,
    dried, and cut into
    bite-size pieces
½ tsp. MSG (optional)

Sauce:

¼ c. shoyu
6 Tbsp. oyster sauce
1 tsp. salt

2 Tbsp. raw sugar
¼ c. mirin

Heat oil. Saute pork well. Add zucchini and cook slightly. Stir in sauce, then the tofu, eggs, and MSG. Mix until zucchini and tofu are cooked.

# DESSERTS

# Common Baking Dishes and Pans

**Spring Form Pan**

**Layer Cake or Pie Pan**

**Ring Mold**

**Baking or Square Pan**

**Loaf Pan**

**Brioche Pan**

**Angel Cake Pan**

**Bundt Tube**

## Equivalent Dishes

**4-CUP BAKING DISH**
= 9″ pie plate
= 8″ x 1¼″ layer cake pan
= 7⅜″ x 3⅝″ x 2¼″ loaf pan

**6-CUP BAKING DISH**
= 8″ or 9″ x 1½″ layer cake pan
= 10″ pie pan
= 8½″ x 3⅝″ x 2⅝″ loaf pan

**8-CUP BAKING DISH**
= 8″ x 8″ x 2″ square pan
= 11″ x 7″ x 1½″ baking pan
= 9″ x 5″ x 3″ loaf pan

**10-CUP BAKING DISH**
= 9″ x 9″ x 2″ square pan
= 11¾″ x 7½″ x 1¾″ baking pan
= 15″ x 10″ x 1″ flat jelly roll pan

**12-CUP BAKING DISH OR MORE**
= 13½″ x 8½″ x 2″ glass baking dish
= 13″ x 9″ x 2″ metal baking pan
= 14″ x 10½″ x 2½″ roasting pan

## Total Volume of Pans

**TUBE PANS**

| | |
|---|---:|
| 7½″ x 3″ Bundt tube | 6 cups |
| 9″ x 3½″ fancy or Bundt tube | 9 cups |
| 9″ x 3½″ angel cake pan | 12 cups |
| 10″ x 3¾″ Bundt tube | 12 cups |
| 9″ x 3½″ fancy tube mold | 12 cups |
| 10″ x 4″ fancy tube mold | 16 cups |
| 10″ x 4″ angel cake pan | 18 cups |

**SPRING FORM PANS**

| | |
|---|---:|
| 8″ x 3″ pan | 12 cups |
| 9″ x 3″ pan | 16 cups |

**RING MOLDS**

| | |
|---|---:|
| 8½″ x 2¼″ mold | 4½ cups |
| 9¼″ x 2¾″ mold | 8 cups |

**BRIOCHE PAN**

| | |
|---|---:|
| 9½″ x 3¼″ pan | 8 cups |

# DESSERTS
## CAKES

### APPLE CAKE

½ c. salad oil
2 c. sugar
2 eggs
2 tsp. vanilla
4 c. chopped apple
2 c. sifted flour

½ tsp. salt
2 tsp. baking soda
2 tsp. cinnamon
1 c. chopped nuts
  (optional)

In a large mixer bowl, combine oil and sugar and beat well. Add eggs, 1 at a time, beating well. Add vanilla and apple. Sift dry ingredients together twice; fold into apple mixture. Fold in nuts.

Pour into a greased and wax papered 9x13x2 inch pan and bake in a preheated oven for about 45 minutes or until done. Set oven at 350°F.

Serve plain with powdered sugar sprinkled on top or with your own favorite icing.

*Blue*

### APRICOT NECTAR CAKE

1 pkg. yellow cake mix
3 Tbsp. flour
½ tsp. baking powder

1 pkg. orange or lemon jello
4 eggs
¾ c. apricot nectar

Mix all ingredients in mixer and beat at moderate speed for 4 minutes. Pour into greased tube pan and bake for 1 hour at 350°. Instead of apricot nectar, 1 cup apricot fruit, chopped and ½ cup syrup from fruit may be used.

Lemon Icing:

1½ c. powdered sugar        Juice of 1 lemon

Combine; mix well and frost cake.

*Red*

# BISCOTTI

1 block butter
1 c. sugar
2 eggs
2 c. + 2 Tbsp. flour
1 tsp. baking powder
    (Rumford)

¼ tsp. salt
1 tsp. vanilla
¼ tsp. anise extract or rind
    of lemon
½ c. nuts

Cream butter and sugar. Add eggs. Add dry ingredients and vanilla, anise, and nuts. Divide dough in half. Put flour on hand and roll into 2 logs to length of cookie sheet. Pat it down to 1½ inch width. Bake in 300° to 325° oven until brown. Slice and turn over slices until all sides are brown and crisp.

*Gerrie Honda*

# BOOZE CAKE

1 box yellow cake mix
1 box instant vanilla
    pudding
4 eggs
½ c. oil

¾ c. water
¼ c. wine, whiskey, or
    vodka
1 tsp. baking powder

Combine all ingredients and mix with mixer 2 to 3 minutes. Pour into greased and floured 9x13 inch pan. Bake in 350° oven for 35 to 40 minutes.

*Betty Yamashiro*

# BROKEN GLASS CAKE

1 cocoa chiffon cake, cut
   into 3 layers
1 pkg. lime Jell-O

1 pkg. strawberry Jell-O
1 pkg. orange Jell-O
1 pkg. unflavored gelatin

Prepare each Jell-O separately by dissolving in 1½ cups of boiling water. Soften the gelatin in ¼ cup water and add ⅓ to each of the Jell-O while hot. Cool and let set in refrigerator. Dice.

Whip Cream Mixture:

1 pkg. gelatin
¼ c. water
¼ c. boiling water

½ c. pineapple juice
1 pt. whipping cream
½ c. sugar

Soften gelatin in water, then add boiling water and stir until gelatin is dissolved. Add pineapple juice. Refrigerate till slightly thickened. Beat whipping cream with ½ cup sugar. Add the pineapple juice mixture. Fold in diced Jell-O. Between each layer of cake, put whipped cream mixture, ending with the whipped cream on top. Keep in refrigerator until ready to serve.

Variation: Cake may be shredded and folded in the whipped cream. Put in mold and refrigerate.

*Red*

# CARROT AND PINEAPPLE CAKE

3 c. flour
2 tsp. soda
2 tsp. cinnamon
½ tsp. salt
2 tsp. vanilla
3 eggs
1½ c. nuts

2 c. sugar
1½ c. oil
2 c. grated carrots
1 (8¼ oz.) can crushed
   pineapple
   (undrained)

Sift flour, soda, cinnamon, and salt together. In large bowl, combine sugar and oil and ½ of flour mixture. Mix well.

Beat in carrots, pineapple, vanilla, and nuts. Add remaining flour mixture and beat well. Add eggs, 1 at a time, and beat well. Pour into 10 inch Bundt pan. Bake at 350° for 60 to 70 minutes.

You can use electric mixer.

*Leo Hubbard*

# CARROT-PINEAPPLE CAKE

Cream:

2 c. sugar

1½ c. corn oil

Add:

4 eggs (1 at a time, beating at high speed)

1 (13½ oz.) can crushed pineapple, drained

Sift:

2¼ c. flour
2 tsp. baking soda

1 tsp. cinnamon
½ tsp. salt

Add slowly to other mixture and beat well.

Add:

2 c. shredded carrots

1 tsp. vanilla

Bake in well greased and floured rectangular pan. Bake at 375° for 50 minutes or until done.

*Mary Soon*

# CHOCOLATE CAKE

1 c. butter
2½ c. sugar
4 eggs
3 c. cake flour

½ tsp. salt
2 tsp. baking soda
2 tsp. baking powder

Melt 4 squares chocolate in 1½ cups hot water until dissolved. *Cool.* Cream butter and sugar; add eggs and beat well. Add sifted dry ingredients and mix well. Add cooled chocolate mixture and blend. Pour into 2 (9 inch) layer pans that have been rubbed with shortening and lined with waxed paper. Bake at 350° for 35 to 40 minutes.

Frosting:

½ tsp. salt
2 sq. chocolate
2 c. water

1½ c. sugar
4 Tbsp. cornstarch
½ tsp. vanilla

Cook together until thick in double boiler. Cool, then spread on cake.

*Kimie Tanaka*

# CHOCOLATE ZUCCHINI CAKE

1 box chocolate cake mix
1½ c. zucchini (grate and
    drain liquid)
2 eggs

¼ c. oil
½ c. sour cream
⅔ c. water

Line a 9x13x2 inch pan with wax paper. Preheat oven to 350°F. Empty mix in a large bowl; add eggs, oil, sour cream, and water and blend on low speed until moistened. Add zucchini; mix well. Pour batter into pan and bake at 350° for 32 to 35 minutes or when toothpick comes out clean. Cool in pan on rack. Frost with your favorite frosting or sprinkle powdered sugar.

*Yoshiko Maeda*

# COCONUTTY CAKE

4 large eggs, separated
1 (13.5 oz.) can coconut
    milk

⅓ c. oil
1 tsp. coconut extract
1 box white cake mix

Topping:

2 c. coconut flakes
½ c. sugar (brown)
½ c. macadamia nuts,
    chopped

1 (4 oz.) block butter,
    melted

Grease and flour a 9x13 inch pan.

Topping: Mix and sprinkle on cake batter before baking.

1. Whip egg whites. Reserve. Beat egg yolks, coconut milk, oil, and extract together.
2. Blend liquids to cake mix gradually.
3. Fold whites gently into batter.
4. Pour batter into pan.
5. Lightly sprinkle the topping.
6. Drizzle melted butter over the topping.
7. Bake at 350° for 30 minutes. Test with toothpick for doneness.

*Maysie Tam*

# COFFEE-ORANGE FUDGE CAKE

This quick cake-mix fix-up turns chocolate cake into an elegant dessert, perfect for special get-togethers.

1 (2 layer size) pkg. devils food or German chocolate cake mix
1 (8 oz.) ctn. dairy sour cream
½ c. cooking oil
½ c. water
4 eggs
¼ c. coffee liqueur

2 Tbsp. finely shredded orange peel
1 tsp. ground cinnamon
1 (12 oz.) pkg. semi-sweet chocolate pieces
Powdered sugar (optional)
1 (4 serving size) pkg. instant chocolate fudge pudding mix

Grease and flour a 10 inch fluted tube pan. In large mixer bowl, combine cake mix, sour cream, oil, water, eggs, pudding mix, liqueur, orange peel, and cinnamon. Beat with an electric mixer on low speed till blended, scraping sides of bowl constantly. Beat on medium speed for 4 minutes. Stir in chocolate pieces. Pour into prepared pan. Bake in 350° oven for 50 to 60 minutes or till a toothpick inserted near the center comes out clean. Cool on wire rack 10 minutes. Remove from pan and cool on rack. Sprinkle with powdered sugar if desired. Makes 12 to 16 servings.

# CRANBERRY APPLE CAKE

1¼ c. all-purpose flour
2 Tbsp. sugar
1 tsp. baking powder
¼ tsp. salt
⅓ c. margarine or butter
1 egg yolk
2 Tbsp. brandy or milk
2 c. sliced peeled apples

1 c. cranberries
¾ c. sugar
¼ c. rolled oats
2 Tbsp. all-purpose flour
½ tsp. ground cinnamon
2 Tbsp. margarine or butter
Dairy sour cream (optional)

In a medium bowl, stir together flour, sugar, baking powder, and salt. Cut in margarine or butter till mixture resembles coarse crumbs. Combine egg yolk and brandy or milk; add to dry ingredients and mix well. Press mixture onto bottom and up sides of a 9 x 1½ inch round baking pan. Arrange apple slices over crust. Sprinkle with cranberries.

In a medium bowl, combine sugar, rolled oats, flour, and cinnamon. Cut in margarine or butter till mixture resembles coarse crumbs. Sprinkle over apples and cranberries. Bake in a 350° oven for 40 to 45 minutes or till apples are tender. Cool slightly; serve warm, dolloped with sour cream if desired. Makes 6 to 8 servings.

Or, place cooled cake in a 350° oven for 5 to 10 minutes or till warm. Serve immediately.

# CREAM PUFF CAKE

1 c. water                          1 c. flour
1 block margarine                   4 eggs

      Topping:

1 (8 oz.) cream cheese              2½ c. fresh milk
2 pkg. instant vanilla
    pudding

Boil water and margarine. Add flour all at once and stir mixture until it comes off the side. Cool 10 to 15 minutes. Add eggs, 1 at a time, beating well. Spoon and spread in 9x13 inch greased pan. Bake at 400° for 30 minutes. Cool.

Topping: Mix preceding topping ingredients together. Wait 18 minutes. Spread on crust, then spread 1 (8 ounce) container Cool Whip on topping. Drizzle chocolate syrup on top and slice chocolate through Cool Whip with knife to give it the marble look. Refrigerate.

*Betsy Nishimura*

# DUMP CAKE

Dump 1 can of cherry pie filling into a rather large cake pan. Dump a Number 2 can of crushed pineapple over this. One package of white cake mix (dry) is dumped over this. Chop into bits, 1 cube of butter or margarine and dump this over it. Hastily sprinkle ½ cup nuts over all. Bake at 350° for 1 hour.

· A real dessert styled cake and easy.

*Blue*

# GERMAN APPLE CAKE

2 c. sugar
¾ c. margarine
2 eggs
1 tsp. cinnamon
3 c. sifted flour

1 tsp. salt
2 tsp. baking soda
1 tsp. vanilla
1 c. walnuts
4 c. chopped apples

Topping:

¼ lb. margarine
8 Tbsp. brown sugar

2 Tbsp. flour

Mix till crumbly.

Cream sugar and margarine well. Add beaten eggs and vanilla and beat well. Add dry ingredients which were sifted together. Mix well. Fold in apples and nuts. Spread in greased 9x12 inch pan. Spread topping on cake and bake at 375° for 35 to 40 minutes. Serves 12.

*Leo Hubbard*

# GERMAN APPLE CAKE

Mix:

1½ c. sugar
3 eggs

1 c. oil
1 tsp. vanilla

Mix together and add to "egg" mixture:

2 c. flour
2 tsp. cinnamon

1 tsp. baking soda
½ tsp. salt

Remaining ingredients:

4 c. apple (fresh tart type), diced or sliced (you can experiment with canned type - maybe even mango)

½ c. chopped nuts (pecans or walnuts)

Add apples and nuts to preceding mixture. Pour into greased and floured 9x13 inch pan or 2 (8x8 inch) pans. Batter is very thick. Bake at 300° for 45 minutes to 1 hour.

Frosting (optional):

1 (8 oz.) pkg. cream cheese
1½ c. powdered sugar (Note: Recommend less, maybe 1 c.)

3 Tbsp. melted butter or oleo
1 tsp. vanilla

Mix or blend well and spread over cooled cake. Cake will keep 2 weeks if refrigerated. Ono - the longer it keeps. *Enjoy!*

# JELLO CREAM CAKE

Crust - Cream:

**1½ blocks butter**　　　　　**½ c. brown sugar**

Add:

**1½ c. flour**　　　　　**1 c. chopped nuts**

Press dough into 9x13 inch buttered pan and bake 15 minutes at 350° or till brown.

Filling: Dissolve 1 box lemon Jell-O in 1 cup hot water. Let cool. Cream 1 (8 ounce) cream cheese. Add ¾ cup powdered sugar. Add cooled Jell-O to mixture. Whip 1 bottle Avoset and fold in.* Pour on top of cooled crust and chill until firm.

Topping: Dissolve 2 boxes or 1 family size Jell-O (cherry or other flavor) in 3 cups hot water and let cool. Pour on top of cooled crust and cream filling and chill until firm.

* May use 1 large box (4½ ounces) Dream Whip, or 2 boxes of Lucky Whip.

# LIGHT FRUIT CAKE
## (First prize cake)

**2 c. sugar**　　　　　**1 box raisins (light)**
**¾ lb. butter**　　　　　**2 boxes fruit mix**
**8 eggs**　　　　　**1 box dates**
**4 c. flour**　　　　　**½ c. sherry wine**
**2 tsp. nutmeg**　　　　　**Rind of 1 lemon**
**½ tsp. soda in 2 Tbsp. hot**　　　　　**1 c. broken walnuts**
**water**

Cream butter and sugar. Add eggs, 2 at a time. Sift flour and nutmeg and add to the creamed ingredients. Add soda mixture, fruits, and nuts and the rind. Pour wine in and mix well. Pour in paper lined pan and bake in 250° oven (1½ hours for loaf pan, 3½ hours for tube pan).

*Yellow*

# MANGO BREAKFAST CAKE

1 c. sugar
3 eggs
½ c. oil
½ c. sour cream or yogurt
½ c. nuts
2 c. flour

1 tsp. cinnamon
2 tsp. baking soda
1 tsp. salt
½ c. dates
2 c. diced mangoes

Beat sugar, eggs, and oil until well blended. Add dry ingredients to oil mixture with sour cream. Stir in nuts and dates. Add mangoes. Pour into greased 9x13 inch pan. Let stand for 15 minutes. Bake at 350° for 40 to 50 minutes or until done.

*Juanita Vierra*

# MANGO CAKE

Mixture 1:

3 eggs, slightly beaten
1 tsp. vanilla
1 c. salad oil
2 c. cubed mango

½ c. coconut
½ c. raisins
¼ c. walnuts

Mixture 2:

2 c. flour
2 tsp. cinnamon
2 tsp. baking soda

1 tsp. baking powder
½ tsp. salt
1½ c. sugar

Combine the 2 mixtures and let stand 20 minutes. Top batter before baking. Bake in 350° oven for 45 minutes for large cake pan and 35 minutes for 8 inch square pan.

Topping:

⅔ c. corn flakes, crushed
¼ c. chopped nuts

¼ c. brown sugar
2 Tbsp. melted butter

*Blue*

# MANGO UPSIDE-DOWN CAKE 1

2 c. sliced ripe mangoes
2 Tbsp. lemon or lime juice
1 Tbsp. margarine
⅓ c. brown sugar
¼ c. shortening
¼ tsp. salt

¾ c. sugar
1 egg
½ c. milk
1¼ c. flour
2 tsp. baking powder

Add lemon or lime juice to sliced mangoes. Melt margarine in 8 inch cake pan; add brown sugar. Place sliced mangoes over margarine and brown sugar.

Cream shortening; add sugar and mix thoroughly. Add well beaten egg. Sift dry ingredients and add alternately with the milk. Pour batter over mangoes. Bake about 1 hour at 375°. When cake is done, remove from oven and turn it upside-down. Serve warm.

*Yellow*

# MANGO UPSIDE-DOWN CAKE 2

1 cube butter
1 c. brown sugar

2 c. mangoes, chopped

Basic Cake Batter:

1 box yellow cake mix
1 box instant vanilla
    pudding

1 c. 7-Up
3 eggs

Preheat oven to 350°. Melt sugar and butter in 9x13 inch pan. Slice mangoes generously over melted butter. Pour Basic Cake Batter over mangoes. Bake for 35 to 45 minutes. Cake is done when toothpick comes out clean. Cool and frost with 1 bottle Avoset; mix into 1 carton Cool Whip.

Variations: You can use the Basic Cake Batter with blueberry pie filling or cherry pie filling.

## MOIST PRUNE CAKE DELIGHT

1 box spice cake mix
1 box instant vanilla
   pudding
1 tsp. baking soda
½ c. melted butter

4 eggs
1 c. cooked and chopped
   prunes
1 c. prune juice
1 tsp. vanilla

Mix all ingredients and beat for 3 minutes. Pour into greased 9x13 inch pan and bake at 350° for 40 to 45 minutes.

*Vicky Malaqui*

## NEW ENGLAND CARROT CAKE

Cream together:

2 c. sugar

4 eggs

Add:

2 junior size jars baby food
   carrots
1 small can crushed
   pineapple, drained
1 c. raisins
1⅓ c. oil

1 tsp. vanilla
2 tsp. cinnamon
2 c. flour
2 tsp. baking soda
1 tsp. salt

Blend well. Bake in ungreased 9x13 inch pan at 375° for 40 minutes.

Frosting - Blend together:

½ pkg. powdered sugar
2 tsp. butter

1 (8 oz.) pkg. cream cheese
1 tsp. vanilla

# OATMEAL CAKE

1¼ c. boiling water
1 c. uncooked oats
½ c. butter or margarine
1 c. sugar
1 c. brown sugar, packed
1 tsp. vanilla
2 eggs

1½ c. flour
1 tsp. baking soda
½ tsp. salt
¾ tsp. cinnamon
¼ tsp. nutmeg
1 tsp. baking powder

Pour water over oats; leave for 20 minutes. Beat butter until creamy. Add sugar. Beat until fluffy. Blend in eggs and vanilla. Add oats and mix well. Sift dry ingredients. Add to mixture. Pour into greased and floured 9x13 inch pan. Bake at 350° for 50 to 55 minutes.

Frosting - Mix:

¼ c. melted butter
½ c. brown sugar
3 Tbsp. half & half (or cream)

⅓ c. nuts
¾ c. coconut

Spread on warm cake. Broil until bubbly.

# ONO CHOCOLATE CAKE

1 box German chocolate cake mix
4 eggs
1½ c. chopped walnuts
½ c. butter or margarine, melted

1 (8 oz.) pkg. cream cheese, softened
1 (1 lb.) box powdered sugar

Combine the cake mix, 1 of the eggs, nuts, and butter and spread in a well greased 9x13 inch pan. Mix the remaining 3 eggs, cream cheese, and powdered sugar and pour over the cake mixture. Bake at 300° for 60 minutes. Do not bake any longer than 60 minutes.

*Jean Okada*

# ORANGE CHIFFON CAKE

2¼ c. sifted cake flour
1½ c. sugar
3 tsp. baking powder
1 tsp. salt
½ c. cooking (salad) oil
5 medium unbeaten egg
    yolks

Juice of 2 medium oranges
    plus water to make ¾
    c.
Grated rind of 2 oranges
    (about 3 Tbsp.)
1 c. egg whites (7 or 8)
½ tsp. cream of tartar

Heat oven to 325°. Sift flour, sugar, baking powder, and salt into bowl. Make a well and add oil, egg yolks, orange juice, and rind. Beat with spoon until smooth.

Beat egg whites and cream of tartar in large bowl until whites form very stiff peaks or 3 to 5 minutes with electric mixer on high speed. *Do not underbeat.* Pour egg yolk mixture slowly over beaten egg whites, folding just until blended. *Do not stir.* Pour into ungreased 10 inch tube pan.

Bake 55 minutes at 325°, then increase to 350° and bake 10 to 15 minutes longer, or until top springs back when lightly touched.

Turn upside-down over neck of funnel or bottle. Hang until cold. Loosen from sides with spatula. Hit edge sharply on table to loosen. Frost or serve (day-old cake is easier to handle).

*Yellow*

# PAPAYA-GINGER DELITE CAKE

1 box white cake mix
1½ tsp. baking powder
½ tsp. baking soda
1½ c. ripe papaya, mashed
¼ c. orange juice

1 Tbsp. candied ginger,
    finely chopped
4 eggs
¾ c. oil

Glaze:

½ c. milk

1 tsp. powdered sugar

Sift together cake mix with baking powder and baking soda in a large bowl. Add eggs and oil and blend. Add the ginger, papaya, and orange juice and beat 2 minutes. Pour into a 9x13 inch pan sprayed with vegetable spray only on the bottom. Bake for 40 minutes in a 350° oven. Poke holes in cake with chopstick when just removed from oven. Spoon glaze evenly over cake. Cool thoroughly before cutting.

*Sally Yoshina*

# PETITE CHERRY CHEESECAKE

2 (8 oz.) pkg. cream cheese
¾ c. sugar
2 eggs
1 Tbsp. lemon juice
1 tsp. vanilla

24 paper muffin cups
24 vanilla wafer cookies
1 (21 oz.) can cherry pie
    filling, chilled

Line muffin tin with 24 paper cups. Put a vanilla wafer cookie in each cup. Beat until light and fluffy cream cheese, sugar, eggs, lemon juice, and vanilla; fill cups ⅔ full and bake at 375° for 15 to 20 minutes or until set. Top each cup with about 3 cherries.

*Gold*

# PINEAPPLE CAKE

1½ c. sugar
¾ c. butter or margarine
3 eggs
2½ c. flour
1 tsp. baking soda
1 tsp. salt

1 c. buttermilk
½ c. crushed pineapple
  (reserve juice)
1 tsp. vanilla
1 c. chopped nuts

Cream butter and sugar until fluffy. Add eggs, 1 at a time, beating well after each addition. Combine dry ingredients and add alternately with milk, beginning and ending with flour. Stir in nuts, pineapple, and vanilla. Pour batter into greased 13x9x2 inch pan. Bake at 350° for 35 to 40 minutes or when tested with toothpick, it comes out clean. Cool cake 10 minutes.

Combine reserved juice with ½ cup powdered sugar. Poke holes on cake and cover with glaze. Serves 12 to 16.

# PINEAPPLE CAKE ROLL

The easiest "jelly" roll we've ever tried! The filling is baked in!

1 (No. 2½) can (3½ c.)
  crushed pineapple
⅔ c. Hawaiian washed raw
  sugar, well packed
4 egg yolks
¼ c. granulated sugar
½ tsp. vanilla

4 egg whites
½ c. granulated sugar
¾ c. sifted enriched flour
1 tsp. baking powder
½ tsp. salt
Sifted confectioners sugar

Drain the pineapple thoroughly. Spread pineapple evenly in bottom of ungreased 15½ x 10½ x 1 inch jelly roll pan; sprinkle with raw sugar. Beat egg yolks till thick and lemon colored; gradually beat in ¼ cup granulated sugar. Add vanilla. Beat egg whites till soft peaks form; gradually add ½ cup granulated sugar, beating till stiff peaks form. Fold yolks into whites. Sift together flour, baking powder, and salt; fold into egg mixture. Spread evenly over pineapple in pan. Bake in moderate oven (375°) about 20 minutes or till done. Loosen sides; turn out on towel sprinkled with confectioners sugar. Let cool 2 or 3 minutes. Roll up, starting at narrow end, using towel as "pusher." Wrap in the sugared towel and cool.

*Ludvina Abrew*

# PINEAPPLE PLANTATION CAKE

3 Tbsp. margarine or butter
½ c. brown sugar
6 slices canned pineapple

10 to 12 maraschino
  cherries
Ginger cake mix*

Melt butter or margarine in an 8x8x2 inch square pan. Add brown sugar and well drained pineapple slices and cherries. Fill ⅔ full with ginger cake batter and bake at 350° for 40 minutes.

* May substitute white or yellow cake mix.

# POPPY SEED COFFEE CAKE

2 c. sifted cake flour
½ c. sugar
2 Tbsp. poppy seeds
2 tsp. baking powder
½ tsp. cinnamon
⅛ tsp. salt
1 (8 oz.) plain nonfat yogurt

¼ c. skim milk
¼ c. vegetable oil
1 egg, beaten
1 tsp. almond extract
Vegetable cooking spray
½ c. sifted powdered sugar
2 tsp. lemon juice

Combine first 6 ingredients in a large bowl; stir well. Combine yogurt, milk, oil, egg, and almond extract. Add to flour mixture, stirring just until dry ingredients are moistened. Pour batter into a 9 inch square baking pan coated with vegetable cooking spray. Bake at 400° for 20 minutes or until done.

Combine powdered sugar and lemon juice; stir well. Drizzle glaze over warm cake. Yield: About 16 servings.

*T. Oki*

# PRUNE CAKE
## (First prize County Fair)

1¾ blocks butter
1 c. sugar
3 c. flour (cake type
    preferred)
3 tsp. baking powder
5 eggs (2½ whites for
    frosting, 5 yolks and
    2½ whites for cake)
1 c. stewed and sieved
    prunes

¾ c. juice (half prune juice
    and half milk - keep
    separate)
2 tsp. baking soda
    dissolved in a little
    prune juice
½ tsp. nutmeg
¼ tsp. cloves
1 tsp. cinnamon
Pinch of salt

Cream butter and sugar; add slightly beaten egg yolks and whites. Add prune juice, alternating with milk and dry ingredients. Add baking soda and juice last. Bake in 2 (9 inch) greased and paper lined pans for 35 minutes at 375° or until done. Frost with boiled frosting mixed with prune pulp.

*Yellow*

# PUMPKIN CAKE AND FROSTING

Beat together:

**2 c. sugar**
**1 c. oil**

**2 c. pumpkin (16 oz. can)**
**4 eggs**

Sift together, then mix with preceding:

**2 c. flour**
**2 tsp. baking powder**
**1 tsp. baking soda**

**1½ tsp. cinnamon**
**½ tsp. nutmeg**
**½ tsp. allspice**

Bake at 350° for about 50 minutes in 9x13 inch cake pan, greased and floured.

Frosting:

**1 (3 oz.) pkg. cream cheese**
**¾ stick butter**
**1 Tbsp. cream or milk**

**1 tsp. vanilla**
**1¾ c. powdered sugar (sift**
**  if lumpy)**

Cream together and frost.

# RED VELVET CAKE

| | |
|---|---|
| 1 c. butter or margarine | ½ tsp. salt |
| ½ c. sugar | 2 Tbsp. cocoa |
| 1½ Tbsp. red food coloring | 2½ c. cake flour |
| 2 eggs | 1½ tsp. baking soda |
| 1 tsp. vanilla | 1½ tsp. vinegar |
| 1 c. buttermilk | |

Cream butter and sugar until light and fluffy. Add coloring. Add eggs, one at a time, beating well after each addition. Add vanilla to buttermilk. Sift together salt, cocoa and cake flour. Alternately blend dry ingredients and buttermilk into creamed mixture, beginning and ending with the flour mixture. Mix baking soda and vinegar and fold into mixture. Pour into 2 lightly greased 8 or 9 inch layer pans. Bake in 350° oven for 30 to 35 minutes.

Frost with Butter Cream Frosting:

| | |
|---|---|
| ⅓ c. butter | 1½ tsp. vanilla extract |
| 4 c. sifted powdered sugar | 2 Tbsp. evaporated milk |
| 1 egg yolk | |

Cream butter and half the sugar, blending well. Add egg yolk and vanilla. Gradually blend in remaining sugar. Add enough milk to make it of spreading consistency.

For a festive touch, garnish with toasted coconut, chopped nuts, or cinnamon candy bits.

# STRAWBERRY SENSATION

1 pkg. white cake mix
1 (3 oz.) pkg. vanilla
    pudding

1 c. mayonnaise
1 c. water
3 eggs

Frosting:

1 (3 oz.) pkg. vanilla instant
    pudding
Liquid from frozen
    strawberries and milk to
    make 1 c.

8 oz. cream cheese
1 (16 oz.) frozen
    strawberries
1 (8 oz.) Cool Whip

Mix cake ingredients. Pour into 9x13 inch greased pan. Bake at 350° for 30 to 35 minutes or until done. Cool.

Frosting: Mix together instant pudding and 1 cup liquid; add ½ container of strawberries and cream cheese. Mix until smooth. Fold in Cool Whip.

Frost cake and decorate with remaining ½ container of strawberries.

*Sharon Cruel*

# SUNSHINE CAKE

1½ c. sugar
½ c. water
1 tsp. cream of tartar
6 eggs, separated

1 stick butter, melted
1 tsp. lemon extract
1 c. flour

Mix sugar, water, and cream of tartar; boil until syrupy. Beat egg whites until stiff; pour syrup over whites, beating constantly. Combine cool butter, egg yolks, and lemon extract; add to egg whites. Fold in flour. Pour into an ungreased tube pan. Bake at 325° for 30 minutes. Place pan upside-down until cake is cooled.

# YUMMY CAKE

**1 box pound or butter recipe cake mix**
**½ c. butter**
**4 eggs**
**1 (8 oz.) pkg. cream cheese, softened**

**1 (16 oz.) box powdered sugar**
**1 c. chopped walnuts**

Mix the cake mix, butter, and 2 eggs and spread in a greased 9x13 inch pan. Mix the cream cheese, 2 eggs, and the powdered sugar. Leave out ½ cup of the sugar. Spread the cream cheese mixture over the first mixture. Sprinkle nuts and then the ½ cup sugar on the top. Bake at 325° for 45 to 50 minutes. Cool before cutting.

*Jean Okada*

# BARS AND COOKIES

## CANDIED FRUIT BARS

2 eggs
1 c. brown sugar
2 tsp. vanilla
1 c. flour
1 tsp. baking powder

½ tsp. salt
1 c. chopped candied fruits
⅔ c. chopped nuts
½ c. raisins
Powdered sugar

Preheat oven to 350°F. Grease an 11x7x2 inch pan; line with waxed paper. In a large bowl, beat eggs until thick. Gradually add sugar and beat well; stir in vanilla. Sift flour with baking powder and salt; add to sugar mixture. Fold in fruits, nuts, and raisins. Pour into prepared pan. Bake for 30 minutes or until lightly browned. Remove from pan while warm; cool. Cut into bars and roll in powdered sugar. Makes 48 bars.

## CHESS BARS

Crust:

1 box yellow cake mix
½ c. butter or margarine,
    softened

1 egg

Topping:

1 (8 oz.) pkg. cream cheese,
    softened
1 (1 lb.) pkg. powdered
    sugar

2 eggs
1 tsp. vanilla

Combine all crust ingredients in a bowl until crumbly. Press mixture into a greased and floured 12x9x2 inch pan. Combine all topping ingredients in a mixing bowl, mixing well. Pour over crust layer. Bake at 350° for 35 minutes or until golden brown. Let cool.

# CHEWY BUTTERSCOTCH BARS

½ c. undiluted evaporated
   milk
½ c. chopped dates
½ c. raisins
½ c. soft butter
¼ c. confectioners sugar
1 c. flour

1 egg
¼ c. granulated sugar
1 (4 oz.) pkg. butterscotch
   pudding and pie
   filling mix
½ tsp. baking powder
1⅔ c. small flake coconut

Combine milk, dates, and raisins. Allow to stand. Cream butter with confectioners sugar until light and fluffy. Blend in flour. Press evenly into buttered 8 inch square pan. Bake in moderate oven at 350° about 20 minutes or until lightly browned. Beat egg; gradually add granulated sugar. Stir in pudding mix, baking powder, coconut, and milk-fruit mixture. Spread over crust. Bake 40 minutes longer or until browned. Cool and cut in bars. Yield: 16 bars.

# CHOCOLATE CHIP BARS

Crust:

½ c. margarine
½ c. brown sugar

1 c. flour

Topping:

2 eggs
2 c. brown sugar
2 Tbsp. flour

½ tsp. salt
1 tsp. vanilla
1 c. chopped nuts

Optional:

Coconut
Raisins

Macadamia nuts

Mix crust ingredients and press into baking pan and bake at 350° for 10 minutes. Cool.

Mix together topping ingredients and spread over crust. Sprinkle 12 ounces chocolate chips and bake at 350° till lightly browned (25 minutes).

# CREAM CHEESE BROWNIES

1 (1 lb. 7 oz.) pkg. brownie
    mix
1 (8 oz.) pkg. cream cheese,
    softened

⅓ c. sugar
1 egg
½ tsp. vanilla

Preheat oven to 350°F. Grease a 13x9x2 inch pan. Prepare brownie mix as directed on package. In a small bowl, mix cream cheese with sugar until well blended. Stir in egg and vanilla. Spread half of brownie batter in prepared pan. Cover with cream cheese mixture. Spread remaining brownie batter on top. Cut through batter with a knife several times for marble effect. Bake 20 to 25 minutes. Makes 24 brownies.

# ENERGY BARS

Combine in pan and heat for 7 to 10 minutes:

2 c. uncooked quick oats
2½ c. Rice Krispies
1½ c. raisins

1 c. unsalted peanuts
¼ c. sesame seeds, toasted
¼ c. sunflower seeds

Melt in pot:

½ block oleo
½ c. peanut butter

1 (10 oz.) pkg.
    marshmallows

Pour melted ingredients over dry mixture. Mix quickly and spread into 9x13 inch pan. Cool and cut into bars. Wrap individually in waxed paper.

# ENERGY BARS

2½ c. crisp rice cereal
1 c. quick oats
¾ c. toasted sesame seed
1 (10 oz.) pkg.
    marshmallows

½ c. creamy peanut butter
¼ c. butter or margarine
¼ c. peanuts
½ c. raisins

Grease a 13x9x2 inch pan with butter. In a saucepan, combine rice cereal, oats, and sesame seed; toast over medium heat for a few minutes.

In a large saucepan, combine marshmallow, peanut butter, and butter; melt over low heat. Stir in cereal mixture, peanuts, and raisins. Press firmly into prepared pan. Cool; cut into bars. Makes 36 bars.

*Kimiko Anzai, Stella Yamamoto*

# PINEAPPLE BARS

2 c. granulated sugar
½ c. butter
4 eggs
1 (No. 2) can crushed
    pineapple, well
    drained

1 can chopped walnuts
1½ c. flour
½ tsp. salt
½ tsp. baking soda

Put sugar in mixing bowl. Melt butter and add to sugar. Beat eggs well and add to mixture. Sift dry ingredients together and add to butter-sugar mixture. Add pineapple and nuts and mix. Pour into greased pan, 10½ x 15 x 2 inches. Bake in 350° oven 30 to 35 minutes.

*Green*

# PINEAPPLE-FILLED COCONUT BARS

Filling:

¾ c. granulated sugar
3 Tbsp. cornstarch
¼ tsp. salt
1 c. crushed pineapple (not
    drained)

1 Tbsp. lemon juice
1 Tbsp. margarine or butter

Mix first 4 ingredients together in a small saucepan; bring to a boil. Continue cooking until thickened and clear, about 5 minutes, stirring constantly to prevent sticking. Remove from heat and blend in lemon juice and margarine or butter. Cool slightly while preparing crumb mixture.

Crumb Mix:

1 c. brown sugar, firmly
    packed
¼ c. margarine or butter
1 c. sifted all-purpose flour

½ tsp. salt
1½ c. shredded coconut
    (do not use fresh)

Cream margarine and sugar together. Add flour, salt, and coconut; mix until well distributed and crumbly. Press ½ crumb mixture *firmly* into a greased and floured 9 inch square baking pan. Spread pineapple filling evenly over surface. Cover with remaining crumbs and press top layer down firmly. Bake in preheated moderate oven, 350°, for 35 minutes or until golden brown. Cut into 24 bars.

*Ludvina Abrew*

# CEREAL CRISPIES

1 c. butter or margarine
1 c. white sugar
1 c. brown sugar
2 eggs
2 c. flour
2 c. rolled oats

2 c. Rice Krispies
1 tsp. baking powder
1 tsp. baking soda
1 tsp. vanilla
½ tsp. salt

Cream sugar and butter or margarine till light and fluffy. Add eggs, 1 at a time, beating well. Sift flour, baking powder, baking soda, and salt. Add gradually to egg and sugar mixture. Add cereals and vanilla. Spoon onto slightly greased cookie sheets. Bake at 325° for 12 to 15 minutes. Remove from pan when out of the oven.

*Green*

# CHINESE ALMOND COOKIES

1½ c. shortening
1 c. sugar
1 egg
1 Tbsp. almond extract

3 c. flour
¼ tsp. baking soda
¼ tsp. salt
Red food coloring

Cream sugar and shortening. Add egg and almond extract. Add flour, salt, and baking soda. Shape into balls. Place on ungreased cookie sheet. Using thumb, press center of balls. Using the end of a chopstick, dot dough with red food coloring. Bake at 350° for 15 to 20 minutes.

# CHOCOLATE CRISP COOKIES

Cream:

**1 c. butter**                    **1½ c. sugar**

Add to creamed mixture:

**1 tsp. vanilla**                  **1 c. chocolate chips**
**1 c. All-Bran or Bran Buds**

Add last:

**2¼ c. flour**                     **½ tsp. salt**
**½ tsp. baking soda**

Drop by teaspoon on greased baking sheet. Bake at 375° for 12 minutes.

*Green*

# CHRISTMAS CONFETTI COOKIES

**1 c. butter or margarine**        **¾ c. finely chopped red and**
**1 c. sugar**                          **green candied**
**2 Tbsp. milk**                        **cherries**
**1 tsp. vanilla or rum extract**   **½ c. finely chopped pecans**
**2½ c. flour**                      **¾ c. flaked coconut**

In a large bowl, cream butter and sugar. Add milk and vanilla; beat well. Stir in flour, candied cherries, and pecans. Form into 2 rolls, 1½ inches in diameter. Roll in coconut. Wrap and chill several hours or overnight.

Preheat oven to 375°. Slice rolls ¼ inch thick and place on ungreased baking sheets. Bake for 12 minutes or until edges are golden brown. Makes 5 dozen.

# CORN FLAKE BUTTER COOKIES

Sift together:

**1½ c. flour, sifted (all-**            **½ tsp. salt**
**purpose)**

Cream together ½ cup butter with ⅓ cup sugar. Blend in 1 egg (unbeaten), then add half of the dry ingredients and mix well. Add 2 tablespoons orange juice and 1 teaspoon orange rind and blend well, then add remaining dry ingredients and mix well. Stir in 1 cup corn flakes (crushed). Drop by teaspoon on the ungreased cookie sheets. Bake at 350° for 9 to 12 minutes. While cookies are still hot, roll in powdered sugar. Makes about 3 dozen.

Note: You may substitute lemon rind and juice for the orange. You may also add ½ cup nuts or substitute 1 cup of nuts for the corn flakes.

# CORN MEAL COOKIES

**¾ c. margarine or butter**        **1 tsp. baking powder**
**¾ c. sugar**                      **¼ tsp. salt**
**1 egg**                           **1 tsp. vanilla**
**1½ c. flour**                     **½ c. raisins (if you like)**
**½ c. corn meal**

Mix fat and sugar in a large bowl. Add egg and beat well. Add rest of ingredients and mix well. Drop dough from a teaspoon on a greased baking pan. Bake at 350° (moderate oven) about 15 minutes until lightly browned. Makes about 3 dozen cookies.

Variation: Chocolate Corn Meal Cookies - Mix ¼ cup cocoa into cookie dough with rest of dry ingredients. Add ¼ cup fluid milk.

# GARBAGE COOKIES

2 blocks butter
1 c. sugar
½ c. brown sugar
2 eggs
2 c. flour
1 tsp. baking soda

½ tsp. baking powder
2 c. oatmeal
2 c. Rice Krispies
2 c. chopped nuts
1 (12 oz.) chocolate chips

Cream butter and sugar. Add eggs, then dry ingredients. Stir in oats, Rice Krispies, nuts, and chips. Form into balls and press lightly onto ungreased cookie sheet. Bake at 350° for about 12 to 15 minutes or until done.

*Janice Toguchi*

# GINGERBREAD COOKIES

1 c. butter or margarine
1½ c. dark brown sugar
2 eggs
½ c. dark molasses
5 c. flour

1 Tbsp. baking powder
2 tsp. ground ginger
1½ tsp. ground cinnamon
1 tsp. ground cloves
½ tsp. salt

In a large bowl, cream butter and sugar. Add eggs and molasses; beat well. Sift remaining ingredients and add to creamed mixture; mix well. Chill dough until easy to roll.

Preheat oven to 350°F. Grease baking sheets. On a lightly floured board, roll dough ¼ inch thick. Cut into desired shapes. Place on prepared baking sheets. Bake 10 to 12 minutes; cool. Decorate cookies as desired. Makes about 7 dozen 3 inch cookies.

# MELTING MOMENTS

1 c. butter or margarine
½ c. powdered sugar
1½ tsp. vanilla

1½ c. chopped nuts
2¼ c. cake flour
Powdered sugar

Preheat oven to 350°F. In a large bowl, cream butter and sugar. Add vanilla and nuts; beat well. Stir in flour; mix well. Form into 1 inch balls. Place on ungreased baking sheets. Bake for 15 minutes or until lightly browned. Remove from baking sheets and immediately roll in powdered sugar. Cool and roll in powdered sugar again. Makes 5 dozen.

# MORNING COOKIES

¼ c. margarine or butter
½ c. packed brown sugar
¾ c. whole wheat flour
¾ c. applesauce
½ c. rolled oats
⅓ c. wheat bran
⅓ c. nonfat dry milk powder
1 egg white
½ tsp. baking soda

½ tsp. ground cinnamon
¼ tsp. baking powder
½ tsp. salt
⅛ to ¼ tsp. ground cloves
½ c. raisins
¼ c. chopped walnuts
½ c. soft style cream
  cheese or peanut
  butter

In a mixer bowl, beat margarine or butter and brown sugar with an electric mixer till well combined. Add whole wheat flour, applesauce, oats, bran, milk powder, egg white, soda, cinnamon, baking powder, salt, and cloves. Beat on low speed just till combined. Stir in raisins and nuts. Spray a baking sheet with nonstick spray coating. Drop rounded tablespoons of dough, 2 to 3 inches apart, onto baking sheet. Spread dough so each cookie is about 2 inches across. Bake in a 375° oven 10 minutes or till set. Cool on a wire rack. Spread bottoms of half of the cooled cookies with a tablespoon of cream cheese or peanut butter; top with remaining unfrosted cookies. Chill till serving or wrap and freeze. If frozen, let thaw in refrigerator overnight. Makes 8 sandwich cookies.

# OATMEAL COOKIES

¾ c. shortening
1 c. brown sugar
½ c. granulated sugar

1 egg
¼ c. water
1 tsp. vanilla

Place preceding ingredients in mixing bowl; beat thoroughly.

1 c. sifted enriched flour
½ tsp. soda

1 tsp. salt
3 c. oatmeal

Sift together and add to creamed mixture and mix well. Blend in 3 cups oats, uncooked. Drop by teaspoon onto greased cookie sheets. Bake in moderate oven at 350° for 12 to 15 minutes.

Chocolate Chip Cookies: Add 1 (6 ounce) package semi-sweet chocolate pieces and ½ cup chopped nutmeats with the oats.

Raisin-Spice Cookies: Sift 1 teaspoon cinnamon and ¼ teaspoon nutmeg with the flour. Add 1 cup raisins with the oats.

*Red*

# PEANUT BUTTER COOKIES

1 c. white sugar
1 c. brown sugar
1 c. shortening
2 eggs

1 c. peanut butter
1 tsp. vanilla
1 tsp. soda
2½ c. flour

Cream first 3 ingredients; add eggs, peanut butter, and vanilla and mix well. Sift dry ingredients and add to batter. Shape into balls and flatten with fork. Bake on ungreased sheets in 375° oven until done.

*Yellow*

# PECAN TART COOKIES

3 oz. cream cheese      1 c. flour
1 stick butter (less 1 inch
   to be used for filling)

Mix preceding ingredients and make 24 balls. Place balls in miniature muffin pans and press dough to form cups for filling.

Filling:

½ c. sugar              1 tsp. vanilla
1 egg                  ¾ c. pecans, chopped
1 inch butter

Mix ingredients and place in molded muffin cups ¾ full. Bake for 30 minutes in 350° oven. Cool in pan for 15 minutes before removing.

*Shirley Ann Kimizuka*

# POTATO CHIP COOKIES

1 c. shortening        1 c. chopped nuts
1 c. white sugar       2 c. crushed potato chips
1 c. brown sugar      1 tsp. salt
2 c. sifted flour        2 eggs
1 tsp. baking soda

Cream shortening and sugar; add eggs and mix well. Mix flour, salt, and soda and add to batter. Add crushed chips and nuts. Shape into small balls. Press down on ungreased cookie sheets with a floured fork. Bake in moderate oven at 325° for 10 to 15 minutes.

*Red*

# RITZ CRACKER DROPS

3 egg whites, beaten stiff
½ tsp. baking powder
½ tsp. cream of tartar
1 tsp. vanilla

1 c. white sugar
¾ c. crushed Ritz crackers
(about 20 crackers)
1 c. nuts, chopped fine

Beat egg whites and sprinkle baking powder and cream of tartar. Fold in vanilla and sugar, then crushed crackers and nuts. Drop by spoonful on greased cookie sheet. Bake at 300° for 35 to 40 minutes.

*Jean K. Okada*

# SNOWBALLS

1 c. butter (2 sticks)
1½ c. sifted confectioners
sugar
1 egg
1 tsp. vanilla
2½ c. sifted all-purpose
flour

1 tsp. baking soda
1 tsp. cream of tartar
¼ tsp. salt
¾ c. chopped walnuts
Confectioners sugar (to
roll cookies in)

Cream butter; add confectioners sugar gradually. Cream until fluffy. Add unbeaten egg and vanilla. Beat well. Sift together dry ingredients. Blend into creamed mixture. To cookie dough, add chopped walnuts and chill.

Roll chilled dough into large size marbles and bake 8 to 10 minutes at 350°. Roll at once in confectioners sugar. Cool on rack and roll again in sugar. Makes about 2½ dozen or more.

# SPONGE DROPS

3 eggs
1 c. sugar
½ tsp. cream of tartar

¼ tsp. baking soda
1 c. flour plus 2 Tbsp. (cake flour)

Beat eggs well; add sugar slowly and beat some more. Sift flour; measure flour, soda, and cream of tartar and sift again. Add into your egg mixture and beat well. After beating, leave the mixture alone for about 15 to 20 minutes. Drop dough from teaspoon on oiled cooky sheet and bake until brown, about 5 minutes, at 350° to 375°. Bake cookies 1 day before filling cream.

Sprinkle powdered sugar on cookies. Add 2 tablespoons powdered sugar and 1 teaspoon vanilla to whip cream and beat. Top cookies with whipped cream.

*Yellow*

# STUFFED DATE DROPS

1 lb. pitted dates
¼ lb. pecan halves
¼ c. shortening
¾ c. brown sugar
1 egg
1¼ c. flour
½ tsp. baking powder

½ tsp. baking soda
¼ tsp. salt
½ c. sour cream
½ c. butter or margarine
3 c. sifted powdered sugar
¾ tsp. vanilla
3 Tbsp. water

Stuff dates with pecan halves. Preheat oven to 400°. Grease baking sheets. In a small bowl, cream shortening and brown sugar. Beat in egg. Sift flour with baking powder, baking soda, and salt. Add alternately with sour cream to creamed mixture. Dip each date into dough, making sure date is evenly covered. Place on prepared baking sheets and bake for 8 to 10 minutes; cool.

In a small saucepan, melt butter and brown lightly; cool. In a small bowl, beat butter with powdered sugar and vanilla. Slowly beat in water until frosting is of spreading consistency. Spread on cookies. Makes 6 dozen.

# SUGAR COOKIES

1 c. sugar
½ c. salad oil
½ c. margarine
½ tsp. cream of tartar

1 tsp. vanilla
2 c. flour
½ tsp. salt
1 egg

Mix all ingredients and chill overnight. Roll into small balls and place on ungreased cookie sheets. Flatten into thin cookies. Sprinkle with sugar. Bake at 350° for 10 to 12 minutes.

*Patsy Takushi*

# PIE CRUSTS

Plain Pastry - Single Crust:

1 c. enriched flour
⅓ c. shortening
¾ tsp. salt

2 to 3 Tbsp. cold water or
cold milk

Rich Pastry - Double Crust:

2 c. sifted flour
1 tsp. salt
1 c. shortening

5 to 6 Tbsp. ice cold water
or milk

Sift flour and salt. Add shortening and cut it until the size of rice grain. Add enough water to moisten the flour mixture. Make 2 balls and roll 1 at a time on a floured board. While rolling the crust, fold in half twice. This will make the crust flaky. Roll out with rolling pin and shape into pie pan.

Crust - First Prize:

1½ c. flour
6 Tbsp. Crisco
¼ tsp. salt

½ tsp. baking powder
About 4 Tbsp. water

Sift dry ingredients; cut in Crisco until crumbly in appearance. Add water, a tablespoon at a time, until mixture is moistened just enough to hold together. Chill 10 minutes before rolling out. Bake for 10 minutes at 450°F.

Pie Crust:

1 c. sifted flour
1 tsp. baking powder
1 Tbsp. granulated sugar

⅛ tsp. salt
½ c. shortening
1 Tbsp. cold water

Bake at 450°F. for 10 minutes.

# PIES

## BERRY AND FRUIT PIES
### (Recipes for Fillings)

Apple:

**3½ c. apples, sliced**
**1¼ c. sugar**

**4 Tbsp. flour (maximum)**

Blueberry:

**3 c. berries**
**⅔ to ¾ c. sugar**
**2 Tbsp. flour and 2 Tbsp.**
   **cornstarch (or 4**
   **Tbsp. flour)**

Cherry:

**3½ c. pitted fresh cherries**
**⅔ to ¾ c. sugar**
**2 Tbsp. flour and 2 Tbsp.**
   **cornstarch (or 4**
   **Tbsp. flour)**

Rhubarb:

**3½ c. rhubarb**
**1½ c. sugar**
**2 Tbsp. flour and 2 Tbsp.**
   **cornstarch (or 4**
   **Tbsp. flour)**

# AVOCADO CHIFFON PIE

1 c. strained avocado
3 egg yolks
1½ Tbsp. butter
½ tsp. nutmeg
1 tsp. cinnamon
¼ c. sugar

1 pkg. plain gelatin
¼ c. water
3 egg whites
½ c. sugar
Juice of ½ lemon
Whipped cream (if desired)

Cook avocado, egg yolks, butter, nutmeg, cinnamon, ½ cup sugar, and lemon juice together. Dissolve gelatin in water and add to hot mixture. Cool and fold in 3 egg whites, beaten with ½ cup sugar. Chill in refrigerator. Top with whipped cream.

*Red*

# BETSY'S COCONUT HAUPIA DESSERT

First layer - Crust:

2 c. flour
1 block butter

1 block margarine
2 Tbsp. sugar

Bake at 325° until golden brown in 9x13 inch pan. (I like macadamia nuts, so add.)

Second layer - Cook over medium heat in Teflon pan:

2 cans coconut milk
¾ c. sugar

1 c. water

Add:

7 Tbsp. cornstarch
1 pkg. gelatin

⅓ c. water

Third layer - Beat until thick:

2 boxes vanilla instant
    pudding

3 c. milk

Fourth layer: Use Cool Whip topping.

Fifth layer: Sprinkle coconut or nuts.

# BLUEBERRY CREAM CHEESE PIE

1 (8 oz.) pkg. cream cheese,
   softened
1 bottle whipping cream
¾ c. powdered sugar
   (unsifted)

1 tsp. vanilla
1 can blueberry pie filling
1 (9 inch) baked pie shell

Whip cream till it stands in peaks. Cream cheese with sugar; add vanilla. Fold whipped cream into cheese mixture. Pour into baked crust and top with blueberry filling. Chill for at least 4 to 5 hours or overnight.

Hint: One-half can blueberry pie filling is enough for 1 pie. Blueberry filling can be thickened more by adding 1 teaspoon cornstarch and bringing to a boil, stirring constantly.

*Green*

# NO-ROLL COCONUT CRUST

1⅓ c. flaked coconut
   (canned, frozen, or
   fresh)
2 Tbsp. butter or
   margarine, melted

¼ c. graham cracker
   crumbs
2 Tbsp. sugar

Combine coconut and butter; mix well. Add crumbs and sugar, mixing thoroughly. Press firmly on bottom and sides of 8 inch pie pan. Bake in 375° oven 10 to 12 minutes or until lightly browned. Cool. Fill with softened ice cream and freeze, or other favorite filling. (We use Crystal Passion Fruit Pie Filling.) Makes 8 inch pie.

# CRYSTAL PASSION FRUIT PIE

Gelatin:

**1 Tbsp. unflavored gelatin**
**¼ c. water**
**1 c. boiling water**

**¼ c. sugar**
**½ c. passion fruit juice**

Pudding:

**½ c. sugar**
**¼ c. cornstarch**
**¼ tsp. salt**
**1 c. milk**

**½ c. passion fruit juice**
**2 eggs**
**1 Tbsp. butter or margarine**

Soften gelatin in ¼ cup water; dissolve in boiling water. Add sugar; stir until dissolved. Add juice. Pour into flat pan and chill until set. Cut into small squares and fold into cooled pudding.

Combine sugar, cornstarch, and salt in heavy saucepan. Blend in milk, passion fruit juice, eggs, and butter. Cook until thick and smooth, stirring constantly. Cool. Fold gelatin into pudding and pour into *No-Roll Coconut Crust*. Chill.

## GUAVA CHIFFON PIE

**1 Tbsp. gelatin**
**¼ c. water**
**1 c. sugar**
**⅔ c. strained guava pulp**
   **(unsweetened)**
**4 eggs, separated**

**¼ c. guava juice**
**⅛ tsp. salt**
**¼ tsp. lemon extract**
**1 baked 9 inch pie shell**
**½ c. unsweetened whipped**
   **cream**

Soak gelatin in water, then place over hot water until it melts. Combine ½ cup of the sugar, guava pulp, and egg yolks. Beat until well mixed. Cook in double boiler, stirring constantly, until it thickens. Add gelatin; remove from heat and stir thoroughly. Cool and add fruit juice and extract. Beat egg whites and salt until stiff. Add ½ cup sugar and beat until mixture is glossy. Gently fold the guava mixture into beaten egg whites; pour into pie shell and place in refrigerator to chill.

Before serving, the filling may be spread with whipped cream sweetened to taste.

*Green*

# HARVEST PUMPKIN PIE

Crust:

**40 vanilla cookies**  **4 Tbsp. butter, melted**

Filling:

**4 eggs, lightly beaten**
**1 (12 oz.) can evaporated**
    **milk**
**1 tsp. lemon extract**
**1 (29 oz.) canned pumpkin**

**1 c. brown sugar**
**1 tsp. cinnamon**
**¼ tsp. cloves**
**¼ tsp. nutmeg**
**½ tsp. salt**

Topping:

**Lemon cake mix**  **½ lb. butter**
**1 c. macadamia nuts,**
    **chopped**

Crust: Crush cookies and mix with melted butter. Press into 9x13 inch pan.

Filling: Beat eggs. Add evaporated milk and lemon extract. Add pumpkin, brown sugar, and spices. Blend well. Pour onto crust.

Topping: Layer dry cake mix over pumpkin mixture. Sprinkle nuts on top. Melt ½ pound butter. Drizzle melted butter over cake mix.

Bake at 350° for 55 to 60 minutes. Test with butter knife.
*Maysie Tam, Hanalima Club*

# LATTICE PINEAPPLE PIE

½ c. sugar
2 Tbsp. cornstarch
¼ tsp. salt
2½ c. crushed pineapple
(not drained, No. 2
can)*

1 Tbsp. butter
1 Tbsp. lemon juice
Pastry for 2 crust, 8 inch
pie

Line an 8 inch pan with pastry. Mix sugar, cornstarch, and salt; add to pineapple in saucepan. Heat, stirring constantly, until mixture boils, then boil, stirring, about 2 minutes, until clear and thickened. Remove from heat and stir in butter and lemon juice. Pour into pastry lined pan; weave pastry strips across top. Bake at 425°F. for 25 to 35 minutes, or until crust is done and nicely browned.

You may also use the new canned Hawaiian pineapple pie filling; just turn contents of No. 2 can into pastry shell. Cover with top crust and bake as preceding. Serves 6.

* Fresh, shredded pineapple may be used if precooked to the consistency of canned, crushed pineapple.

# LEMON MERINGUE PIE

½ c. cold water
7 Tbsp. cornstarch
1½ c. hot water
1¼ c. sugar

3 egg yolks, slightly beaten
Juice of 2 lemons
Grated rind of 1 lemon
1 Tbsp. butter

Mix cold water and cornstarch until smooth. Combine hot water and sugar in top of double boiler; bring to a boil over direct heat. Add cornstarch mixture; cook until it begins to thicken. Return to double boiler and cook until thick and smooth (15 minutes). Stir a small amount of mixture into beaten yolks; return to double boiler and cook a few minutes longer. Add lemon juice and rinds and butter and blend. Cool, stirring occasionally. Pour into baked pie shell, topped with meringue.

*Yellow*

# LEMON MERINGUE PIE

1½ c. sugar
8 Tbsp. cornstarch
¼ tsp. salt
1½ c. boiling water
3 egg yolks, beaten

¼ c. lemon juice
1 tsp. grated lemon rind
2 Tbsp. butter
1 (9 inch) baked pie shell

Combine dry ingredients. Add water slowly, stirring constantly. Cook on low heat until thick. Add egg yolks, juice, and rind, continuing cooking 2 minutes until thick and smooth. Add butter; cool. Pour into baked pie shell. Top with meringue and brown in oven.

Meringue:

3 egg whites
6 Tbsp. sugar

¼ tsp. cream of tartar

Beat egg whites and cream of tartar until stiff. Gradually beat in sugar. Spread on pie and bake at 325° for 15 minutes.

*Shirley Ann Kimizuka*

# LUDY'S MULBERRY PIE

3 c. ripe mulberries,
    stemmed
1 c. sugar*
3 Tbsp. Minute tapioca
2 Tbsp. butter

Dash of salt
Milk
Enough pastry for a 2 crust
    9 inch pie

Combine mulberries, sugar, tapioca, and salt. Put combined mixture in pie crust pan. Dot with butter. Put top crust on; cut steam vents and crimp or flute crust edge. Brush on milk for a shiny pie top. Bake at 425° for 40 to 50 minutes.

Hint: Place crimped strips of foil around edge of pie crust to prevent it from burning. Remove foil last 10 minutes to brown crust even.

* For a sweeter filling, add 3 more tablespoons of sugar.

*Blue*

# MANGO CREAM CHEESE PIE

Crust:

| | |
|---|---|
| **2 c. flour** | **2 blocks margarine** |
| **½ c. powdered sugar** | |

Optional: Add ½ cup chopped macadamia nuts; omit sugar.

Cheese Filling:

| | |
|---|---|
| **8 oz. cream cheese** | **1 tsp. vanilla** |
| **½ c. white sugar** | **8 oz. Cool Whip** |

Topping:

| | |
|---|---|
| **2 pkg. unflavored gelatin** | **Few drops of yellow** |
| **1 c. cold water** | **coloring** |
| **1 c. hot water** | **4 c. diced mangoes** |
| **1 c. sugar** | **(peaches may be** |
| **¼ tsp. salt** | **substituted)** |
| **1 Tbsp. lemon juice** | |

Crust: Mix flour, powdered sugar, and margarine well together as you would for pie crust. Press into 9x13 inch pan. Bake 20 to 25 minutes at 350°.

Cheese Filling: Mix cream cheese till soft. Add sugar and vanilla. Fold in Cool Whip and spread over crust. Refrigerate.

Topping: Sprinkle gelatin in cold water to soften. Add hot water, sugar, and salt. Cool and add lemon juice, coloring, and mangoes. Pour over cream cheese filling and refrigerate.

*Mabel Ito*

# MANGO PIE

**1 (8 oz.) pkg. cream cheese, softened**
**3 c. mangoes, sliced**

**1 c. dairy sour cream**
**2 Tbsp. sugar**

Blend cream cheese and sour cream. Add sugar to cream mixture. Add mangoes. Pour into graham cracker crust. Freeze firm. Remove from freezer 5 minutes before serving. Cut in wedges.

Graham cracker crust: Combine 1 cup fine graham cracker crumbs, 2 tablespoons sugar, and 3 tablespoons melted butter or margarine. Press firmly into unbuttered 9 inch pie plate. Chill till firm, about 45 minutes.

*Green*

# MANGO PIE

Filling:

**4 c. mango slices**
**¾ c. sugar**
**¼ tsp. cinnamon**

**Dash of nutmeg**
**1 Tbsp. lime or lemon juice**
**3 Tbsp. flour**

Line pie pan with pastry; put in mango slices and sprinkle sugar, flour, spices, and lemon juice. Cover with pastry. Bake in hot oven at 425°F. for 15 minutes, then reduce heat to 350° for 30 minutes.

*Yellow*

# ORANGE CREAM DESSERT

Crust:

¾ c. margarine (1½ blocks)          1½ c. flour
¼ c. firmly packed brown          ½ c. chopped nuts
   sugar

Filling:

2 pkg. (8 oz.) cream cheese          1 (8 oz.) ctn. Cool Whip
1½ c. sugar or 2 c.
   powdered sugar

Topping:

1 env. unflavored gelatin          1 pt. sherbet
1 c. cold water          2 cans mandarin oranges,
1 (6 oz.) pkg. orange jello          drained
2 c. hot water

Crust: Cream margarine and sugar. Add flour and nuts; mix well. Spread dough in 9x13 inch pan and bake at 375° for 10 minutes. Cool.

Filling: Beat cream cheese and sugar. Fold in Cool Whip. Spread filling evenly on the crust. Chill ½ hour.

Topping: Soften unflavored gelatin in ¼ cup water and set aside. In a large bowl, dissolve jello with hot water; add softened gelatin and remaining water and stir until dissolved. Stir in sherbet and mix until dissolved. Fold in mandarin oranges. Pour jello mixture over cream cheese and refrigerate.

*Karen Nemoto*

# PEACH PARFAIT PIE

Easy Crust:

**2 c. flour**
**¼ c. sugar**

**¾ c. margarine**

Cut margarine into dry ingredients. Spread in 9x13 inch pan and pat down. Bake at 350° for 20 minutes or golden brown. Cool completely before filling.

Filling:

**1 large can or 2 medium**
**cans sliced peaches**
**2 (3 oz.) pkg. lemon jello**

**1 c. cold water**
**1 qt. vanilla ice cream**

Topping: Use 1 (8 ounce) tub Cool Whip.

Drain peaches, reserving syrup. Add water to syrup to make 2 cups. Heat till boiling. Add jello and stir till dissolved. Add cold water. Cut ice cream into pieces and add to hot liquid. Stir till melted. Chill till mixture thickens slightly, about 2 hours. Fold in peaches. Pour into cooled crust. Chill till firm. Top with Cool Whip.

Make sure to let jello mixture thicken to consistency of whipped cream before pouring over crust; otherwise, the crust will become soggy.

# PEACH TOFU PIE

**½ block tofu, drained well**
**1 c. boiling water**
**1 (3 oz.) pkg. peach jello**
**½ pkg. Knox gelatine**

**¼ c. cold water**
**1 graham cracker pie crust**
**Whipped cream**

Combine jello and hot water. Combine Knox gelatine and the water. Blend tofu in blender until smooth. Add the jello and gelatine mixture in the tofu and blend again. Pour into graham cracker pie crust and refrigerate until firm. Top with whipped cream. Arrange peach, strawberry, or other fruit slices over it.

*T. Oki*

## PECAN MERINGUE PIE

3 egg whites
1 c. sugar (white)
1 tsp. baking powder
1 tsp. vanilla

12 soda crackers,
    crumbled
1 c. chopped pecans

Beat egg whites until very stiff; add sugar, baking powder, and vanilla. Fold in 12 soda crackers. Add pecans. Put in buttered pie pan. Bake at 350° for 30 minutes. Let stand until cool.

*Virginia M. Newgent*

## PERFECT APPLE PIE
### (First prize County Fair)

5 to 7 tart apples (green)
¾ to 1 c. sugar
2 Tbsp. enriched flour
⅛ tsp. salt

1 tsp. cinnamon
¼ tsp. nutmeg
2 Tbsp. butter
1 recipe Plain Pastry

Mix sugar, flour, salt, and spices; sprinkle half over 9 inch pastry lined pie pan. Heap apples into pastry shell. Sprinkle with remaining sugar mixture. Dot with butter. Adjust top crust. Brush with top milk; sprinkle with sugar. Bake in hot oven (450°F.) 10 minutes, then in moderate oven (350°F.) about 40 minutes.

*Yellow*

# PINEAPPLE CARAMEL PIE
## (First Place Senior Division)

¾ c. Hawaiian washed raw brown sugar
2 Tbsp. Minute tapioca
¼ tsp. salt
¼ tsp. grated orange peel
2½ c. canned crushed Hawaiian pineapple, drained

2 Tbsp. of the drained syrup
1 Tbsp. butter

Mix brown sugar, tapioca, salt, and grated orange peel. Add 2 tablespoons of the drained syrup to crushed pineapple. Mix and place in unbaked pie shell. Dot with butter. Cover with top crust. Flute and bake at 400° for 15 minutes. Reduce temperature to 375° and continue baking for 30 minutes. If a glaze is desired, brush pie top with milk before baking.

Pie Crust:

2 c. sifted flour
1 tsp. salt

¾ c. shortening
4 to 6 Tbsp. water

Mix flour and salt in bowl. Cut shortening into flour with pastry blender or 2 knives until the pieces are the size of peas. Sprinkle water over this mixture, tossing lightly. Work dough into firm ball and divide in half. Roll dough about ⅛ inch thick on lightly floured surface. Place in pie plate and trim even with edge of plate. Add filling. Roll other half of dough in same manner and place over filling.

Trim edges to about ½ inch beyond edge of plate. Fold under edge of bottom crust and flute to seal. Cut small steam vents in top of crust. Vents may be cut before placing over filling.

*Ludvina R. Abrew*

# PINEAPPLE-CHEESE ICEBOX PIE

Filling:

| | |
|---|---|
| 1 Tbsp. plain gelatin | ¼ c. sugar |
| ¼ c. cold water | 1 c. soft cottage cheese |
| 3 egg yolks | 3 egg whites |
| 1 c. crushed pineapple | ¼ tsp. salt |
| 1 tsp. grated lemon peel | ½ c. sugar |
| 2 Tbsp. lemon juice | |

Add gelatin to cold water and set aside. In cold double boiler, beat 3 egg yolks slightly; add crushed pineapple (syrup and all), lemon peel, lemon juice, and ¼ cup sugar. Cook over hot water, stirring, until thick; add gelatin. Stir until melted; remove from heat. Put cottage cheese through wire strainer; add to hot mixture. Cool until beginning to thicken. Beat 3 egg whites with salt; when stiff, gradually beat in ½ cup sugar and fold into pineapple-cheese mixture. Heap in chilled crust; sprinkle with reserved crumbs, and chill 3 hours or longer.

Crumb Crust:

| | |
|---|---|
| 4 c. corn flakes, crushed (makes 1 c.) | 4 Tbsp. melted margarine or butter |
| 2 Tbsp. sugar | |

Mix crushed flakes, sugar, and melted margarine. Press into 9 inch pie pan, reserving 3 tablespoons crumbs for topping. Chill thoroughly in refrigerator. Serves 6.

# PINEAPPLE MERINGUE PIE

3 c. fresh pineapple
½ c. sugar
3 Tbsp. cornstarch
¼ tsp. salt

3 egg yolks
2 Tbsp. butter or margarine
1 Tbsp. lemon juice
1 baked 9 inch pie shell

Meringue:

Dash of salt
3 egg whites

6 Tbsp. sugar

Heat pineapple in saucepan. Mix sugar thoroughly with cornstarch and salt; add all at once to hot pineapple and cook, stirring briskly, until thick and clear. Beat egg yolks in bowl; stir in a little of the hot mixture, then return all to saucepan and cook, stirring 1 minute. Remove from heat; stir in butter and lemon juice. Pour into baked pie shell.

Spread roughly with this meringue: Add dash of salt to 3 egg whites; beat stiff, then beat in, gradually, 6 tablespoons sugar. Bake about 8 minutes at 400°. Serve cold.

*Katsuko Enoki*

# PINEAPPLE WHIPPED CREAM PIE

1 pkg. coconut or
    butterscotch nut cookie
    dough
2 Tbsp. cornstarch
2 Tbsp. sugar
¼ tsp. salt

¼ c. water
2 c. chopped fresh
    pineapple *or* 1 (20 oz.)
    can crushed
    pineapple, drained
1 c. whipping cream

Slice cookie dough in ¼ inch slices. Arrange slices in 9 inch pie pan, first lining bottom of pan, then sides. (Let side slices rest on bottom layer to make higher sides.) Bake in 375°F. oven until lightly browned, 9 to 12 minutes. Cool. Combine remaining ingredients, except cream, in saucepan. Cook and stir over medium heat until thickened. Cool. Fold into whipped cream. Pour into cooled crust. Chill or serve immediately. Makes 9 inch pie.

# PUMPKIN PIE

1 (1 lb.) can pumpkin
2 eggs, slightly beaten
¾ c. sugar
½ tsp. salt
1 tsp. cinnamon

½ tsp. ginger
¼ tsp. cloves
1 (13 oz.) can evaporated
   milk
1 unbaked 9 inch pie shell

Preheat oven to 425°F. Combine pumpkin and eggs. Stir in sugar, salt, spices, and milk. Pour into pie shell. Bake for 15 minutes; lower heat to 350°F. and bake about 45 more minutes or until filling is set. Makes 8 servings.

This pie may be made with 1½ to 1¾ cups mashed cooked pumpkin.

## SHORTBREAD PUMPKIN PIE

3 c. all-purpose flour
½ c. sugar
1 c. butter or margarine
2 (No. 2½) cans pumpkin (1
   large 29 oz.)
4 eggs, slightly beaten
1½ c. sugar

1 tsp. salt
1 tsp. cinnamon
1 tsp. nutmeg
½ tsp. pumpkin pie spice
2 large cans evaporated
   milk

Sift flour; add sugar and butter and mix well. Press in 9x13 inch pan and bake at 375° for 20 minutes or until golden brown. Cool. Mix the rest of the ingredients together and pour into baked crust. Bake at 350° for about 1 hour.

*Gold*

# SHORTBREAD PUMPKIN PIE

1 c. butter or margarine          3 c. flour
½ c. sugar

Mix preceding ingredients until well blended. Press down firmly into a 9x13 inch or 10x16 inch pan. Spread evenly.

Filling:

4 eggs, beaten                    1 tsp. ginger
3½ c. pumpkin (large can)         ½ tsp. ground cloves
1½ c. sugar                       3½ c. evaporated milk (2
1 tsp. cinnamon                     large cans)
1 tsp. salt

Mix preceding together and pour over shortbread crust and bake at 425°F. for 15 minutes. Reduce heat to 350°F. and bake for 55 minutes or until knife inserted in middle comes out clean. Makes 20 servings.

# SWEET POTATO PIE

1½ c. boiled sweet                2 Tbsp. butter, melted
   potatoes                       1 tsp. nutmeg or cinnamon
2 eggs, separated                 ½ tsp. baking powder
¾ c. brown sugar                  Pinch of salt
2 c. milk

Mash boiled potatoes. Beat egg yolks with sugar; add to potatoes with milk, melted butter, and spice. Fold in well beaten egg whites, baking powder, and salt. Pour into a pastry-lined pie pan. Bake until a knife inserted in center comes out clean, about 45 minutes, in a 350° oven. Serves 8.

# WIKI WIKI DESSERT

Crust:

**3 c. sifted all-purpose flour**      **½ c. sugar**
**2 sticks butter**

Remaining ingredients:

**2 (3 oz.) boxes instant**            **1 (8 oz.) pkg. cream cheese**
**vanilla pudding**                     **4½ oz. Cool Whip (use only**
**3 c. milk**                           **¾ of container)**
**1 c. crushed pineapple**

Mix crust ingredients well and press in 9x13x2 inch pan. Bake in 400° oven until brown. Mix pudding and milk; add softened cream cheese and mix well. Add pineapple; mix and spread on crust. Top with Cool Whip; chill. Cut into squares.

*Gold*

# OTHERS

## BANANA ICE CREAM

Scald in top of double boiler 1 cup milk.

Meanwhile, combine:

**2 eggs, slightly beaten**          **¼ tsp. salt**
**¾ c. sugar**

Mix well. Blend in a small amount of the hot milk and then slowly add to milk in double boiler, while stirring. Cook, while stirring, until mixture coats a silver spoon, or until it reaches 176°F. on a candy thermometer. Remove from heat. Cool thoroughly.

When cool, stir in:

**⅓ c. light corn syrup**          **1½ c. mashed ripe banana**
**2 c. heavy cream**          **¼ c. lemon juice**

Mix well. Freeze in crank freezer (hand turned or electric) according to manufacturer's directions. Makes about 2 quarts.

*Ludvina Abrew*

# FRESH STRAWBERRY ICE CREAM

Combine in a bowl:

**2 c. crushed fresh**        **1 c. sugar**
   **strawberries**

Mix well. Set aside.

Place in top of a double boiler, 1¼ cups half & half. Cook over boiling water until scalded. Meanwhile, beat slightly 4 egg yolks.

Add:

**⅔ c. sugar**        **Dash of salt**

Mix well. Blend in a small amount of the hot cream and then slowly add to cream in double boiler, while stirring. Cook, while stirring, until mixture coats a silver spoon, or until it reaches 176°F. on a candy thermometer. Remove from heat. Cool thoroughly.

When cool, stir in:

**1 c. heavy cream**        **1 tsp. vanilla**
**Sweetened crushed**
   **strawberries**

Freeze in crank freezer (hand turned or electric) according to manufacturer's directions. Makes about 2 quarts.

*Ludvina Abrew*

# GREEN MANGO SAUCE ICE CREAM PIE

**1 pt. vanilla ice cream**
**1½ to 2 c. partially frozen**
    **Green Mango Sauce**

**½ c. whipped cream**
**½ tsp. cinnamon**

Line an 8 or 9 inch aluminum foil pie tin with soft vanilla ice cream. Place in freezer until firm. When ice cream crust is firm, add slightly thawed Green Mango Sauce as pie filling; decorate with whipped cream as an all-over or crisscross topping. Sprinkle with cinnamon and return to freezer. When solidly frozen, cut into pie shaped slices and serve for dessert. Yield: 8 small slices.

Green Mango Sauce:

**4 c. mango slices (1½ lb.)**
**1½ c. water**

**½ c. sugar**

Place the mangos and water in a heavy saucepan; the lower part of the pressure saucepan with an ordinary lid does very well. The amount of stirring necessary to prevent burning is minimized by using a heavy-bottomed pan. Mango sauce spatters during cooking, therefore a large pan is more satisfactory than a small one.

Cook the mango slices in the water until they are tender, about 15 minutes. Stir in the sugar and bring the mixture to a full boil. Puree the sauce. Chill the sauce quickly; package and freeze.

The waste in pureeing is slight, less than 0.5 percent, and consists chiefly of the hairy residue from near the seeds and coarse strings near the outside of the fruit. Sauce which is pureed before the sugar is added tends to be thinner and more watery than that pureed after the sugar has been added. It also requires more handling.

# ICE CREAM JELLO

1 (6 oz.) pkg. lemon
flavored gelatin
1 (3 oz.) pkg. orange,
lemon, lime, or
pineapple-orange
flavored gelatin

¼ c. sugar (optional)
⅛ tsp. salt
2½ c. water
1 Tbsp. unflavored gelatin
¼ c. cold water
1 pt. vanilla ice cream

Fill large measuring cup to the 2½ cup mark with water. Bring to a boil in microwave oven for 2 minutes. Combine flavored gelatin with sugar and salt in 9x9 inch pan. Soften gelatin in cold water. Pour 1 cup of the boiling water over flavored gelatin. Stir to dissolve. Stir softened unflavored gelatin into remaining boiling water. Combine with flavored gelatin mixture. Place ice cream on paper towel in oven and soften for 30 seconds. Stir into hot gelatin until smooth. Chill until set. Cut in serving pieces. Makes about 45 slices.

*Gold*

# ORANGE ICE CREAM

Scald in top of double boiler 2 cups milk.

Meanwhile, combine:

1 c. sugar
2 Tbsp. flour

Dash of salt

Mix well. Blend in small amount of the hot milk and mix to a paste. Gradually stir into milk in double boiler. Cook, stirring constantly, until mixture begins to thicken.

Beat slightly 2 eggs. Blend in a small amount of hot milk mixture and then slowly add to mixture in double boiler and cook, while stirring, until thickened. Cool.

When cool, add:

1 (6 oz.) can frozen orange
juice concentrate,
thawed

1 Tbsp. grated orange peel
1 c. heavy cream

Mix well. Freeze in crank freezer (hand turned or electric) according to manufacturer's directions. Makes about 2 quarts.

*Ludvina Abrew*

## PINEAPPLE SHERBET

1 qt. buttermilk
1 (20 oz.) can crushed
   pineapple, drained

1⅓ c. sugar
½ c. chopped walnuts
1 tsp. vanilla extract

In a bowl, combine all ingredients and mix well. Cover and freeze for 1 hour. Stir and return to freezer for at least 2 hours before serving. Yield: About 6 servings.

*Mary Soon*

## PINEAPPLE SHERBET

½ Tbsp. (½ env.) gelatin
2 Tbsp. cold water
2 c. buttermilk
1 c. sugar

1 c. (9 oz. can) crushed
   pineapple
1 tsp. vanilla
1 egg white, beaten stiff

Soften gelatin in cold water; dissolve over hot water. Thoroughly combine buttermilk, sugar, pineapple and syrup, vanilla, and gelatin. Pour mixture into freezer tray; freeze firm. Beat with an electric beater (or hand beater) until smooth. Add stiffly beaten egg white. Refreeze until firm. Serves 5 to 6.

## SOUR SOP MOUSSE

20 marshmallows
¼ c. water
2 Tbsp. sugar

1 c. sour sop puree
1 c. whipping cream

Add sugar and marshmallows to the water. Place over low heat until marshmallows are softened and a smooth mixture is obtained. Cool. Add sour sop puree. Mix and let stand in cool place until partially congealed. Add whipped cream. Pour into freezing tray and freeze.

# SOUR SOP SHERBET

1 c. sugar
2 c. water
2 c. sour sop puree

1 Tbsp. lemon juice
1 egg white

Combine sugar and water. Boil 5 minutes. Cool to lukewarm. Add puree; freeze in ice tray. When partially frozen, beat egg white and add to puree. Mix well and freeze.

# VANILLA ICE CREAM

Scald in top of double boiler:

2 c. heavy cream

2 c. milk

Meanwhile, combine:

4 eggs, slightly beaten
1½ c. sugar
½ c. sweetened condensed
    milk

¼ tsp. salt

Mix well. Blend in a small amount of the hot cream and then slowly add to mixture in double boiler, while stirring. Cook, while stirring, until mixture coats a silver spoon, or until it reaches 176°F. on a candy thermometer. Remove from heat. Cool thoroughly.

When cool, stir in:

6 c. heavy cream

1 Tbsp. vanilla

Freeze in crank freezer (hand turned or electric) according to manufacturer's directions. Makes about 1 gallon.

*Ludvina Abrew*

# ALMOND FLOAT

| | |
|---|---|
| 1 env. unflavored gelatin | 2 tsp. almond extract |
| ½ c. water | Fruit (grapes, mandarin |
| 1½ c. milk | oranges, pineapple, |
| ½ c. sugar | lichee, etc.) |

Dissolve gelatin in water. Heat milk and sugar; add gelatin. Stir until sugar and gelatin are completely dissolved. Cool and add almond extract. Pour into mold and refrigerate until set. Unmold in attractive deep dish; pour chilled fruits with syrup over and add a few maraschino cherries.

*Blue*

# AVOCADO MOLD

| | |
|---|---|
| 1 large pkg. lime Jell-O | 1½ c. sugar |
| 3 pkg. gelatin | 4 c. water |
| ½ c. evaporated milk | 1 c. avocado |
| ½ c. mayonnaise | |

1. Boil 2 cups water with sugar till sugar is dissolved.
2. Mix gelatin with ½ cup water.
3. Add Jell-O and gelatin to sugar and water mixture.
4. Add rest of water to Jell-O mixture.
5. Mix mayonnaise and milk, then add the mashed avocado and mix well.
6. Add to Jell-O mixture and refrigerate.

*Helen Kawahara*

# BROKEN GLASS DESSERT

| | |
|---|---|
| 1 pkg. lime gelatin | 1 pkg. raspberry gelatin |
| 1 pkg. orange gelatin | |

Dissolve gelatin separately in 1½ cups hot water. Chill. Dissolve 1 tablespoon unflavored gelatin in ¼ cup cold water; add ¼ cup hot water. Add ¼ cup pineapple juice. Whip 1 pint whipping; add ¼ cup sugar. Add gelatin mixture to cream. Dice chilled gelatin and add to creamed mixture. Line 2 loaf pans with slices of pound cake. Pour gelatin mixture over cake and chill.

*Green*

## FRESH CRANBERRY RELISH MOLD

1 (3 oz.) pkg. strawberry
   gelatin
1 c. boiling water
¾ c. cold water

1 apple
1 orange
2 c. fresh cranberries
3 Tbsp. sugar

Dissolve gelatin in boiling water; add cold water. Chill until slightly thickened. Cut unpeeled apple and orange into sections, removing seeds. Put ¼ of the berries, apples, and orange pieces into blender. Cover and blend only until fruit is coarsely ground. Empty into a bowl and repeat until all fruit is ground. Mix in sugar. Fold fruit mixture into gelatin; pour into a 4 cup mold. Chill until firm. Makes 8 servings.

## GELATIN CREAM CHEESE DESSERT

1 (6 oz.) pkg. lemon gelatin
2 qt. boiling water
2 (6 oz.) pkg. strawberry
   gelatin
1 c. butter or margarine
½ c. light brown sugar

2 c. flour
1 c. chopped nuts
2 (8 oz.) pkg. cream cheese
1½ c. sugar
2 (8 oz.) bottles heavy
   cream, whipped

Preheat oven to 375°F. Dissolve lemon gelatin in 2 cups of the boiling water. Dissolve strawberry gelatin in the remaining 6 cups boiling water; set both aside to cool. Cream butter and brown sugar. Gradually stir in flour; mix in nuts. Spread evenly in a 20x12x4 inch pan. Bake for 15 to 18 minutes; cool. Chill for 15 minutes. Beat cream cheese with sugar. Fold in whipped cream. Gently stir in cooled lemon gelatin. Pour onto crust; refrigerate until firm. Pour strawberry gelatin over cheese mixture and chill again until strawberry layer is firm. Cut into 2 x 2½ inch pieces. Makes 48 servings.

# GUAVA KANTEN

**2 sticks red kanten**
**2½ c. water**

**1 c. sugar**
**1 can frozen guava nectar**

Cook kanten in water until melted. Add sugar and cook for 15 minutes. Add guava nectar (thawed). Strain for clearer kanten. Pour into mold.

*Green*

# HAUPIA DELIGHT

Crust:

**1 c. butter**
**2 c. flour**

**½ c. chopped nuts**
**⅓ c. sugar**

Filling:

**2 cans coconut milk**
**1½ c. water**

**9 Tbsp. sugar**

Blend:

**7 Tbsp. cornstarch**

**½ c. water**

Crust: Blend together in large bowl with pastry blender. Spread evenly in 9x13 inch pan. Press down with waxed paper and back of soup spoon. Bake 15 minutes at 350°. Cool.

Filling: Put together in pot the coconut milk, water, and sugar. Cook on medium heat. When all are blended and very hot, add cornstarch mixture. Cook until thickened and slight boil. Cool until warm. Pour filling onto cooled crust and level off. Chill about 2 hours to set. Spread 1 medium size Cool Whip evenly and sprinkle 1 (3½ ounce) package sweet coconut flakes.

# KANTEN

**4 pkg. gelatin**
**2 c. sugar**

**1 or 2 pkg. Kool-Aid**
**2½ c. hot water**

Soak gelatin in 1 cup cold water for 10 minutes. Dissolve well and add the rest of the ingredients. Pour in 9x9 inch pan and refrigerate. If sweetened Kool-Aid is used, do not add sugar.

*Thelma Oshiro*

# MIZU YOKAN

4 sticks red kanten    2½ c. sugar
5 c. water        1 can tsubushi an

Wash kanten and tear into pieces and cook with 5 cups water. When kanten is dissolved, add sugar and cook about ½ hour. Pour into 9x13 inch pan. When cool, add tsubushi an and mix well. Chill until set. Cut into pieces and serve.

*Green*

# CASCARON
## (Mochi Flour-Coconut Confection)

2 c. mochi flour     Deep fat (for frying)
1¼ c. coconut milk    1 c. sugar
½ c. shredded coconut  2 Tbsp. water

Mix flour with coconut milk and coconut. Shape into balls, 1¼ inches in diameter. If dough will not shape easily, add more coconut milk. Heat deep fat to 350°F. Fry cascaron for 4 to 5 minutes or until golden brown. Drain.

In a saucepan, combine sugar and water. Cook to 236°F. (soft ball stage). Put cascaron into syrup and stir lightly until each is dried and coated with sugar. Makes 2 dozen.

# CASCARON

1 grated coconut (2½ c.)
1 long (10 oz.) pkg. mochi
   flour
1 tsp. baking powder
½ tsp. salt

½ c. sugar
1 c. undiluted evaporated
   milk (or enough to
   moisten)

Mix coconut with dry ingredients. Stir in milk until very moist. Roll dough into a ball or drop by teaspoonfuls in hot fat (280°F. to 300°F.). Fry until light brown. Drain. Either drop into a bag of sugar and shake, or use the Sugar Syrup following.

Sugar Syrup:

2 c. sugar ¾ c. water

Cook until light caramel in color. Pour over deep-fried Cascaron that has been placed in a bowl. Toss quickly with 2 forks to coat each piece, then separate on a platter.

# AN (BLACK BEAN PASTE)

1 (12 oz.) pkg. azuki (black
   beans)
6 c. water

2 c. sugar
½ tsp. salt

Soak the beans in water overnight and drain. Add fresh water to generously cover; cook, adding water as necessary.

When very tender, add the sugar and salt. Bring to a boil, then simmer while you continue to stir until mixture is thick. Cool or chill. Shape into balls the size of walnuts. Fills 24 mochi.

*Green*

# MANJU

4 c. flour
3 Tbsp. white sugar

1 lb. butter or margarine
½ c. evaporated milk

Cut butter or margarine into dry ingredients like pie crust. Add milk and mix lightly. Break into 60 balls slightly smaller than golf balls. Fill with An balls. Brush with evaporated milk. Bake for 15 to 20 minutes at 375° to 400°.

*Mabel Ito*

# DORAYAKI MANJU

1 c. sugar
2 c. flour
3 tsp. baking powder
4 eggs

2 tsp. honey
½ c. water
2 tsp. shoyu

Mix water, honey, and shoyu. Beat eggs. Combine flour, baking powder, sugar, and pinch of salt. To dry ingredients, add preceding liquid and beaten eggs. Fry like small pancakes. Azuki An can be put between 2 pancakes. Pinch all sides.

*Kiyome Ito*

# LAYERED MANJU

5 c. flour
1 lb. butter
½ c. sugar
½ tsp. salt

¾ c. condensed milk
1 can koshian
1 can tsubushian
1 egg

Cream butter and sugar. Add milk and salt. Add flour and mix well. Spread half of dough in 9x13 inch pan. Mix the cans of An and spread on the dough. Spread the rest of the dough on the An. Pat gently. Beat the egg and brush on top. Bake at 375° for 35 to 40 minutes or until golden brown. Cool. Cut into squares.

*Rosalind Ishisaka, Hawaii*

# STEAMED MANJU

3½ c. flour
3 tsp. baking powder
½ c. oil

1½ c. sugar
3 egg whites
⅓ c. milk

Sift flour, baking powder, and sugar. Add egg whites and oil to dry ingredients and mix well. Add milk while stirring. Make a ball of prepared An the size of a walnut and cover each ball with dough. Place them on 2x2 inch wax paper and steam for 15 minutes.

Coloring may be added to the dough by mixing food coloring in the milk.

*Mabel Ito*

# STEAMED WHITE MANJU

3½ c. flour
3 tsp. baking powder
½ c. sugar
½ c. milk

½ c. salad oil
2 egg whites
1 can "An" (bean paste)

Sift together flour and baking powder. Mix sugar, milk, and salad oil. Beat egg whites gently. Add to sugar mixture. Add this mixture to flour. Mix gently until thoroughly blended. Roll batter into 1 inch balls. Flatten and place spoonful of "An" in center. Pull edges together to the center. Close opening with a pinch. Steam about 10 minutes.

*Namie Honda*

# YAKI MANJU

5 c. flour
1 tsp. salt
¾ c. water

1¾ c. salad oil
1 can tsubushi or koshi-an

Sift the flour and salt together. Make a well and add the water and oil and mix. Flatten each dough about the size of a walnut, and place teaspoonful of An on it, and pinch. Place on ungreased cookie sheet and brush milk on top. Bake at 425° for 20 to 25 minutes.

# BUTTER MOCHI

½ c. butter
1 (1 lb.) pkg. Mochiko
2½ c. sugar
1 tsp. baking powder

3 c. milk
5 eggs, beaten
1 tsp. vanilla
1 c. flaked coconut

Preheat electric oven to 350°F. Melt butter; cool. Combine Mochiko, sugar, and baking powder. Combine remaining ingredients and stir into Mochiko mixture; mix well. Pour into a 13x9x2 inch pan. Bake for 1 hour; cool. Makes 24 pieces.

*Gold*

# CHOCOLATE MOCHI

2 c. mochi flour
2 c. white granulated sugar
1 Tbsp. baking soda
½ c. melted margarine
1 c. semi-sweet chocolate
  chips

2 (12 oz.) cans evaporated
  milk
2 tsp. vanilla extract
2 beaten eggs

Sift dry ingredients (mochiko, sugar, and baking soda) in a large bowl. Melt margarine and chocolate chips together and combine with evaporated milk, vanilla extract, and eggs. Mix well and stir into dry ingredients until it becomes a smooth batter. Pour into greased 9x13 inch pan. Bake in 350° preheated oven for 45 to 55 minutes. Cool, then serve. No need to refrigerate.

# CUSTARD MOCHI

Cream together:

½ c. butter                    1¾ c. sugar

Beat in, 1 at a time, 4 eggs.

Add:

4 c. milk
2 tsp. vanilla extract

2 c. mochiko
2 tsp. baking powder

Grease and flour a 9x13 inch pan. Bake at 350° for 1 hour and 20 minutes.

# EASY MOCHI

1 c. sugar
2½ c. water
1 (1 lb.) box mochiko (3½
    c.), sifted

¼ to ½ tsp. coloring
(optional)

Boil together sugar and water. Lower heat and add the mochiko, all at once; constantly mix well so it will not get lumpy. If it gets hard, add a little hot water and mix until shiny. Turn off heat and start pounding. Spread out on cutting board covered with Katakuri. When cool, cut into desired size and shape.

If doubling the recipe, add less water. If needed, add hot water, a little at a time, while mixing or pounding. Get mochi the texture of your ear lobe.

*Mabel Ito*

# QUICKY MOCHI

3 c. water
1 c. light corn syrup

1 box mochiko (3 c.)

Bring water and syrup to a boil. Lower heat; gradually pour in mochiko, stirring constantly. Mix hard and well. Mixture will harden rapidly. Form into small patties. If desired, "An" can be filled into each patty. To add color, add a few drops of food coloring to the syrup before adding the mochiko.

*Green*

# SWEET POTATO MOCHI

1 lb. mochiko
1¼ c. brown sugar
1 tsp. baking soda
⅛ tsp. salt
1 (13½ oz.) can coconut
  milk

1¼ c. water
2 c. cooked and diced
  sweet potatoes
1 Tbsp. black sesame seed
Kinako (yellow soy bean
  powder)

Preheat electric oven to 350°F. Grease a 13x9x2 inch baking pan. In a large bowl, sift mochiko, brown sugar, baking soda, and salt. Add coconut milk and water; mix well. Fold in sweet potatoes; pour into prepared pan. Sprinkle with sesame seed. Bake for 1 hour. Cool; cut into 2x1 inch pieces. Coat each piece with kinako. Makes 54 pieces.

# TRI-COLORED MOCHI

Mix:

1 (1 lb.) box mochiko
2 c. sugar

1 tsp. baking powder

Gradually add:

2 c. water
1 can coconut milk

1 tsp. vanilla

Divide into 3 parts (2 cup portions): 1) Green (add 12 drops of food coloring), 2) leave white, 3) red (add 12 drops of food coloring).

Heat oven to 350°. Spray 9x13 inch pan with Pam. Place green colored portion into pan. Cover with foil. Bake for 15 minutes. Remove foil and add white portion. Cover and bake 20 minutes. Remove foil and add red colored portion. Cover and bake 30 minutes. Remove foil after baking and let cool thoroughly. Cut with plastic knife and roll in potato starch or kinako.

*Janet Shiratori*

# YOMOGI MOCHI

1 c. sugar
1 box mochiko (3½ c.),
    sifted

2½ c. yomogi water
Kinako

For Yomogi Water:

1 handful young shoots of
    yomogi

2 c. water
1 tsp. baking soda

Boil together until tender. Blend or grind. Prepare easy mochi. Spread on Kinako. Break off pieces and fill with An. Makes approximately 36 An filled mochi.

Azuki An: Use canned An. Heat. May add a little more sugar. Stir constantly until thickened. Cool. Make balls of 1 teaspoon or 1 tablespoon size. The An balls may be prepared ahead and kept in an airtight container for a few days in the refrigerator or longer in the freezer. Thaw before using.

May be made from scratch by soaking and cooking dried Azuki.

*Mabel Ito*

# APPLE CRISP

4 c. peeled and sliced tart
    apples
½ tsp. salt

½ tsp. cinnamon
¼ c. sugar
¼ c. water

Topping:

⅓ c. butter
¾ c. flour

¾ c. sugar

Combine first ingredients and place in shallow casserole or deep pie plate. Combine topping ingredients and sprinkle over apple mixture. Bake in a 350° oven for 40 to 45 minutes. Serve plain or with ice cream.

*Mary Soon*

# BREAD PUDDING

1 block butter
1 (1 lb.) loaf sweet bread
6 eggs, beaten
1 (12 oz.) can evaporated
   milk
1 tsp. vanilla extract

⅔ c. sugar
1 tsp. cinnamon
1 c. raisins
2 c. diced apples, baked (or
   canned fruit, like
   peaches)

Melt butter in 9x13 inch pan. Break or cut sweet bread into cubes in a large mixing bowl. Mix wet ingredients (eggs, milk, vanilla) together. Add dry ingredients (sugar, cinnamon) to wet mixture and beat lightly. Pour over bread cubes. Mix to moisten.

Hydrate raisins, covered with water, by microwaving for 1 minute on HIGH power or setting in hot water. Add to mixture. Add sliced apples, or canned fruit like peaches, to mixture. Pour into buttered pan.

Bake at 325° for 40 to 45 minutes. Test for doneness by inserting a knife blade into center. If the knife is clean, the pudding is ready. Cool on rack.

*Maysie Tam, Hanalima Club*

# BREAD PUDDING

3 c. milk
3 large eggs
½ tsp. salt
½ tsp. cinnamon
½ tsp. vanilla
3 Tbsp. honey
2 Tbsp. brown sugar
Juice of ½ lemon (sprinkle
   on grated apple)

1 freshly grated apple
   (large)
¾ c. raisins (and/or other
   dried fruits, chopped)
½ c. nuts
4 c. coarsely crumbled
   bread (any kind - whole
   wheat, plain, banana,
   sweet bread, etc.)

Put first 7 ingredients in blender or mixer and mix well. Mix together in a 9x13 inch baking pan the crumbled bread and cake, grated apple, dried fruits, and nuts. Pour liquid mixture into pan and stir together with the second mixture. Bake for 35 minutes or until slightly firm and brown on top. Test with toothpick or knife in the center (should come out clean).

*Mabel Ito*

# BREAD PUDDING

1 can condensed milk
3 c. hot water
15 slices cubed bread
3 eggs, slightly beaten

1 Tbsp. melted butter
½ tsp. salt
1 tsp. vanilla

Combine milk and hot water. Pour over bread and let stand till lukewarm. Stir in eggs, butter, salt, and vanilla. Pour into greased 1½ quart casserole or baking dish. Set in shallow pan of hot water. Bake at 350° until knife comes out clean, approximately 1 hour. Serve hot or cold.

*Leo Asuncion*

# BREAD PUDDING

1 loaf bread
6 eggs
2 large cans evaporated
   milk

3 c. water
1½ c. sugar
2 tsp. vanilla
1 cube melted butter

Preheat oven to 350°. Grease a 9x13 inch pan. Slice bread into cubes and place in pan. Beat eggs. Add milk, water, sugar, vanilla, and butter. Pour over bread and sprinkle with cinnamon. Bake for 1 hour or until brown. Bread will rise.

Optional: May add raisins and/or finely chopped fresh fruit (apple or pear) to bread cubes.

# CHINESE LYCHEE ALMOND PUDDING

1 (20 oz.) can Lychee
½ c. water
½ c. sugar
1½ pkg. unflavored gelatin
Maraschino cherries (to garnish)

Mint leaves (to garnish)
Dash of salt
1 c. fresh milk
1 c. water
1½ tsp. almond extract

Add sugar, gelatin, and salt to ½ cup water and stir to dissolve ingredients. In saucepan, bring to a boil 1 cup water and 1 cup fresh milk. Add almond extract and dissolved ingredients. Cook and stir for 5 minutes. Cool and pour in a small square pan and refrigerate until firm.

To serve, cut pudding in half inch squares and gently spoon into dessert serving dishes.

Save Lychee syrup. Cut each Lychee in fourths and place on the top of the cubes. Pour on chilled Lychee syrup and garnish with a maraschino cherry and mint leaves.

Suggestions: Canned mandarin oranges, sliced peaches, pears, and fruit cocktail may be used in place of Lychee.

*Blue*

# FRENCH TOAST STRATA

1 (1 lb.) loaf unsliced
   French bread
1 (8 oz.) pkg. cream cheese,
   cubed
8 eggs
2½ c. milk, light cream, or
   half & half

6 Tbsp. margarine or
   butter, melted
¼ c. maple syrup or maple
   flavor syrup
Cider Syrup

Cut French bread into cubes. (You should have about 12 cups bread cubes.)

Grease a 3 quart rectangular baking dish. Place *half* of the bread cubes in the dish. Top with cream cheese cubes and remaining bread cubes.

Combine eggs, milk, melted margarine or butter, and maple syrup in a blender container or a mixing bowl. Process or beat with a rotary beater till well combined. Pour egg mixture evenly over bread and cheese cubes. Using a spatula, slightly press layers down to moisten. Cover with plastic wrap and refrigerate for 2 to 24 hours.

Remove plastic wrap from baking dish. Bake, uncovered, in a 325° oven for 35 to 40 minutes or till the center appears set and the edges are lightly golden. Let stand about 10 minutes before serving. Serve with Cider Syrup. Makes 6 to 8 servings.

Cider Syrup:

½ c. sugar
4 tsp. cornstarch
½ tsp. ground cinnamon
1 c. apple cider or apple
   juice

1 Tbsp. lemon juice
2 Tbsp. margarine or butter

Combine sugar, cornstarch, and cinnamon in a small saucepan. Stir in apple cider or apple juice and lemon juice. Cook and stir the mixture over medium heat till thickened and bubbly. Cook and stir for 2 minutes more. Remove saucepan from heat and stir in margarine or butter till melted. Makes about 1½ cups.

Note: This recipe is equally as good using sweetbread.

# CREAM PUFFS

| | |
|---|---|
| 1 c. water | 1 pt. whipping cream |
| 1 c. flour | Sugar to taste |
| 1 cube margarine | Powdered sugar |
| 4 eggs | |

Combine water and margarine in pan and bring to rolling boil. Lower heat and add flour, beating vigorously, using wooden spoon, until it forms a ball and leaves pan clean. Remove from heat and add eggs 1 at a time. Beat each egg into mixture until the egg disappears. Spoon on baking sheet (ungreased) forming 8 large puffs. Bake at 425° for 30 to 45 minutes. Cool slowly in oven with door open or puffs will collapse.

When cool, cut off the top of each puff and remove any remaining egg mixture in puff. Whip cream, adding sugar to taste, and fill puffs; put the top back on and sprinkle with powdered sugar.

*Blue*

# CRUNCHY APPLE COBBLER

| | |
|---|---|
| ½ c. uncooked rolled oats | 1 tsp. cinnamon |
| 6 c. thin sliced apples | ¼ tsp. cloves |
| 1 c. apple juice | ⅓ c. crunch cereal such as |
| 2 Tbsp. raisins | Grape-Nuts |

Layer the oats in the bottom of an 8 inch square nonstick pan. Add the apple slices. Pour the apple juice on top and sprinkle with raisins, cinnamon, and cloves. Cover with foil and bake in a 350° oven for 1 hour. Remove the foil. Cover the top of the apples with crunchy cereal and bake an additional 15 minutes. Serves 6.

*Ludvina Abrew*

# HALO HALO
## (Filipino Dessert)

Shaved or crushed ice
Assorted condiments such
as kaong (sugar palm),
macapuno (grated
coconut in syrup), yam
yam (yam paste),
sweet beans, or
sweetened garbanzo
beans

Light cream, coconut milk,
or evaporated milk

For each serving, half fill a 12 ounce glass with shaved ice. Top with 1 or 2 tablespoons of 1 or more condiments. Lightly mix in ⅓ to ½ cup light cream. Sweeten if desired. Makes 1 serving.

# HAUPIA WITH FRUIT

1½ c. commercial coconut
milk
1½ c. water
½ c. plus 2 Tbsp. sugar
½ c. plus 2 Tbsp.
cornstarch

1 c. crushed pineapple,
peach slices, or
mango slices

Combine coconut milk, cornstarch, sugar, and water. Stir until smooth. Stir over medium heat until thickened. Lower heat and continue cooking for 10 minutes. Pour half into flat pan; spread fruit evenly, then pour remaining haupia. Refrigerate until set. Cut into 1½ inch squares. Serves 10 to 12.

# HAWAIIAN PINEAPPLE CRISP

⅔ c. sugar
1 Tbsp. cornstarch
1 tsp. finely shredded
   lemon peel
¾ tsp. ground cinnamon
¼ tsp. ground nutmeg
4 medium baking apples,
   peeled, cored, and
   sliced (4 c.)

1 (20 oz.) can pineapple
   chunks, drained
¾ c. rolled oats
¼ c. all-purpose flour
¼ c. packed brown sugar
¼ c. margarine or butter
¾ c. chopped macadamia
   nuts (3.5 oz. jar) or
   almonds

In a 1½ quart casserole, combine sugar, cornstarch, lemon peel, cinnamon, and nutmeg. Add apples and pineapple; toss to coat.

For the topping, in a medium mixing bowl, stir together rolled oats, flour, and brown sugar. With a pastry blender, cut in margarine or butter till thoroughly combined (the mixture should be dry). Stir in nuts. Sprinkle topping over fruit mixture. Bake in a 375° oven for 30 minutes. Cover loosely with foil to prevent overbrowning. Bake about 15 minutes more or till apples are tender. Serve warm. Makes 6 to 8 servings.

# LEMON DEE-LITE

First layer - Crust:

**2 c. all-purpose flour, sifted**    **½ c. nuts, chopped**
**2 blocks margarine**

Mix ingredients together and press into greased 9x13 inch pan. Bake in 350° oven about 25 minutes. Cool.

Second layer:

**1 (8 oz.) pkg. cream cheese**    **1 (9 oz.) Cool Whip**
**½ c. powdered sugar**

Mix together and spread over crust. Chill.

Third layer:

**2 (3 oz.) boxes instant**    **3 c. skim milk**
   **lemon pudding**

Mix together and spread over second layer. Chill for a few minutes.

Fourth layer: Use 1 (4½ ounce) Cool Whip. Spread Cool Whip on top. Chill before serving.

*Gold*

# MINIATURE CREAM CHEESE TARTS

**2 (8 oz.) pkg. cream cheese**    **Cherry or blueberry pie**
**¾ c. sugar**                **filling (Comstock**
**1 tsp. vanilla**              **brand)**
**2 eggs**                  **24 paper cupcake liners**
**1 box vanilla wafers**

Combine cream cheese, sugar, vanilla, and eggs. Beat until fluffy. Place liners in muffin pans. Place a vanilla wafer into each cup. Pour cream cheese mixture into cups. Bake at 350° for 15 to 20 minutes. Cool, then top with pie filling.

*Sylvia Sakaki, Maui*

# MINIATURE TARTS

Crust:

**2 (3 oz.) pkg. cream cheese**　　**2 c. sifted all-purpose flour**
**2 blocks butter, melted**

Filling:

**2 eggs, separated**　　　　　　**1 c. dates or raisins,**
**¾ c. sugar**　　　　　　　　　　**chopped**
**1 block butter, melted**　　　　**1 c. nuts, chopped**

Mix crust ingredients together; chill for easy handling. Divide into 48 pieces and fill in miniature muffin pans. Beat egg yolks; add the rest of the ingredients and fold in well beaten egg whites. Fill crust and bake at 350° for 20 to 25 minutes.

*Gold*

# MITSUMAME (FRUIT, BEAN, AND KANTEN DESSERT)

1. One cup saru-endo (brown peas) or green peas or azuki may be used. Cook with care so as not to break the skin. Simmer long instead of boiling.

2. Use 1 red kanten, 1¾ cups water, and 1 tablespoon sugar. Boil together and pour into flat pan. When jelled, dice into ½ inch cubes. Do the same with 1 white kanten.

3. To 1 cup of mochiko, add ½ cup water and mix into paste. Roll into balls the size of marbles and drop into boiling water. Cook until they rise to the top. Put in syrup and cool.

4. Use 1 can fruit salad. Drain and save syrup. Prepare fresh fruits of pineapple and papaya.

5. Syrup: Use 1½ cups sugar and 1 cup water. Boil together and cool.

Place the prepared food in layers in a large glass bowl. Pour syrup over all.

# PRETZELS

Dry ingredients:

**1 c. cornstarch**
**½ c. sugar**

**1 c. flour**
**⅛ tsp. salt**

Milk Mixture:

**¼ c. evaporated milk**
**1¼ c. water**

**1 egg, beaten**

Need oil for deep-frying.

1. Heat oil for deep-frying, 385°F.
2. Sift dry ingredients.
3. Combine milk mixture.
4. Add milk mixture to dry ingredients and blend until smooth.
5. Heat rosette iron in oil until hot.
6. Dip hot iron into batter and return to oil.
7. Cook until golden brown, turning once
8. Drain on paper towels. Makes 6 dozen.

# ROYAL HAWAIIAN DELIGHT

**1 c. whipping cream**
**¼ c. powdered sugar**
**8 large or 32 miniature**
**  marshmallows**

**½ c. shredded coconut**
**1½ c. ripe papaya cubes**
**½ c. diced orange**
**2 tsp. lemon juice**

Chill cream and whip. Add sugar and marshmallows, cut into quarters (if large size). Fold in papaya, lemon juice, orange, and coconut. Pour into serving dish or individual glass dishes. Chill before serving. Garnish with coconut and maraschino cherry.

# SEX IN A PAN

Step 1:

**1 c. chopped walnuts**               **½ c. butter**
**1 c. flour**

Cream butter; add flour and nuts. Press into 9x13 inch pan. Bake 30 minutes at 300°F. Cool.

Step 2:

**1 (8 oz.) cream cheese**          **1 c. white powdered sugar**

Cream and spread over the crust.

Step 3: Use ½ tub Cool Whip (large size). Spread over cream cheese layer.

Step 4:

**1 (3 oz.) pkg. instant**               **3 c. milk**
    **chocolate pudding**
**1 (3 oz.) pkg. instant vanilla**
    **pudding**

Mix each pudding with 1½ cups milk and let set. Spread over Cool Whip layer the chocolate pudding first.

Step 5:

**½ tub Cool Whip**
**Plain chocolate bar or**
    **chopped walnuts**

Spread remaining Cool Whip. Grate chocolate or walnuts and sprinkle over the top. Refrigerate.

*Ruth Mari Balderas*

342

# TRIFLE

1 (9 inch) round white pudding cake (½ recipe)
¾ c. jam (red preferred, 8 oz.)

2 c. canned pears (29 oz.)
1 c. whipping cream (½ pt.)

Custard - Mix well in 2 quart saucepan:

¾ c. sugar
2 Tbsp. cornstarch
⅛ tsp. salt

3 eggs (or 3 egg yolks and 1 egg)

Slowly blend in 2 cups milk. Cook, stirring constantly, until thick. Cool. Stir in 1½ teaspoons vanilla and 1 cup whipped cream.

Split round cake and put ½ cut side up in 3 quart dish. Spread cake with ½ of jam. Cut pears into 1 inch pieces and spread ½ of pear and juice on top. Spread ½ of custard mix as next layer. Repeat layers with the rest of the ingredients. Top with whipped cream and custard mix and dot with jam for color. Keep refrigerated.

Lowfat variation: Use ½ angel food cake, skim milk for custard, "Cool Whip" instead of whipped cream, and fresh strawberries may be used instead of jam.

*Mabel Ito*

# Notes

# MICROWAVE

# MICROWAVE HINTS

1. Place an open box of hardened brown sugar in the microwave oven with 1 cup hot water. Microwave at high for 1½ to 2 minutes for ½ pound or 2 to 3 minutes for 1 pound.
2. Soften hard ice cream by microwaving at 30% power. One pint will take 15 to 30 seconds; one quart, 30 to 45 seconds; and one-half gallon, 45 seconds to one minute.
3. One stick of butter or margarine will soften in 1 minute when microwaved at 20% power.
4. Soften one 8-ounce package of cream cheese by microwaving at 30% power for 2 to 2½ minutes. One 3-ounce package of cream cheese will soften in 1½ to 2 minutes.
5. Thaw frozen orange juice right in the container. Remove the top metal lid. Place the opened container in the microwave and heat on high power 30 seconds for 6 ounces and 45 seconds for 12 ounces.
6. Thaw whipped topping...a 4½ ounce carton will thaw in 1 minute on the defrost setting. Whipped topping should be slightly firm in the center but it will blend well when stirred. Do not overthaw!
7. Soften jello that has set up too hard - perhaps you were to chill it until slightly thickened and forgot it. Heat on a low power setting for a very short time.
8. Dissolve gelatin in the microwave. Measure liquid in a measuring cup, add jello and heat. There will be less stirring to dissolve the gelatin.
9. Heat hot packs in a microwave oven. A wet fingertip towel will take about 25 seconds. It depends on the temperature of the water used to wet the towel.
10. To scald milk, cook 1 cup milk for 2-2½ minutes, stirring once each minute.
11. To make dry bread crumbs, cut 6 slices bread into ½-inch cubes. Microwave in 3-quart casserole 6-7 minutes, or until dry, stirring after 3 minutes. Crush in blender.
12. Refresh stale potato chips, crackers, or other snacks of such type by putting a plateful in the microwave oven for about 30-45 seconds. Let stand for 1 minute to crisp. Cereals can also be crisped.
13. Melt almond bark for candy or dipping pretzels. One pound will take about 2 minutes, stirring twice. If it hardens while dipping candy, microwave for a few seconds longer.
14. Nuts will be easier to shell if you place 2 cups of nuts in a 1-quart casserole with 1 cup of water. Cook for 4 to 5 minutes and the nut meats will slip out whole after cracking the shell.
15. When thawing hamburger meat, the outside will many times begin cooking before the meat is completely thawed. Defrost for 3 minutes, then remove the outside portions that have defrosted. Continue defrosting the hamburger, taking off the defrosted outside portions at short intervals.
16. To drain the fat from hamburger while it is cooking in the microwave oven (one pound cooks in 5 minutes on high), cook it in a plastic colander placed inside a casserole dish.
17. Cubed meat and chopped vegetables will cook more evenly if cut uniformly.
18. When baking large cakes, brownies, or moist bars, place a juice glass in the center of the baking dish to prevent a soggy middle and ensure uniform baking throughout.
19. Since cakes and quick breads rise higher in a microwave oven, fill pans just half full of batter.
20. For stamp collectors: Place a few drops of water on stamp to be removed from envelope. Heat in the microwave for 20 seconds and the stamp will come right off.
21. Using a round dish instead of a square one eliminates overcooked corners in baking cakes.
22. When preparing chicken in a dish, place meaty pieces around the edges and the bony pieces in the center of the dish.
23. Shaping meatloaf into a ring eliminates undercooked center. A glass set in the center of a dish can serve as the mold.
24. Treat fresh meat cuts for 15 to 20 seconds on high in the microwave oven. This cuts down on meat-spoiling types of bacteria.
25. A crusty coating of chopped walnuts surrounding many microwave-cooked cakes and quick breads enhances the looks and eating quality. Sprinkle a layer of medium finely chopped walnuts evenly onto the bottom and sides of a ring pan or Bundt cake pan. Pour in batter and microwave as recipe directs.
26. Do not salt foods on the surface as it causes dehydration (meats and vegetables) and toughens the food. Salt the meat after you remove it from the oven unless the recipe calls for using salt in the mixture.
27. Heat leftover custard and use it as frosting for a cake.
28. Melt marshmallow creme in the microwave oven. Half of a 7-ounce jar will melt in 35-40 seconds on high. Stir to blend.
29. Toast coconut in the microwave. Watch closely because it browns quickly once it begins to brown. Spread ½ cup coconut in a pie plate and cook for 3-4 minutes, stirring every 30 seconds after 2 minutes.
30. Place a cake dish up on another dish or on a roasting rack if you have difficulty getting the bottom of the cake done. This also works for potatoes and other foods that don't quite get done on the bottom.

# MICROWAVE

## APPETIZER PIE

1 (8 oz.) pkg. cream cheese, softened
2 Tbsp. milk
1 (1½ oz.) jar sliced dried beef (about ¾ c. snipped)
2 Tbsp. instant minced onion
2 Tbsp. finely chopped green pepper
½ c. sour cream (real or imitation)
⅛ tsp. pepper
¼ c. chopped nuts (optional)

Mix together all but the nuts in a casserole. Microwave on MEDIUM for 5 minutes, or until warm. Sprinkle nuts on top and heat 1 more minute. Let stand to heat through. Serve with crackers.

*Virginia M. Newgent*

## CHILI DIP

2 cans (12 or 16 oz.) chili
1 small can diced green peppers
1 (8 oz.) pkg. cream cheese

Put in microwave-safe bowl and mix. Microwave 3 to 4 minutes. Stir and microwave 1 to 2 minutes. Serve with chips.

*Kathleen Mumford*

# FLORENTINE CRAB DIP

1 (10 oz.) pkg. frozen
  chopped spinach
2 Tbsp. chopped onion
1 (3 oz.) pkg. cream cheese
1 (7.04 oz.) pkg. imitation
  crab, shredded
½ c. shredded Swiss
  cheese

¼ c. mayonnaise
¼ c. chopped water
  chestnuts
¼ c. milk
½ tsp. salt
⅛ tsp. ground nutmeg
⅛ tsp. pepper

Unwrap spinach; place on a glass plate. Cover and microwave at HIGH power for 5 minutes or until defrosted, turning spinach over and breaking apart once during cooking time. Drain well and set aside.

In a 1 quart casserole, cover and cook onion on HIGH power for 1 minute. Add spinach and the remaining ingredients; mix well. Cover and microwave for 2 minutes at 70% power; stir and microwave for 2 more minutes or until mixture is hot and cheese is melted. Serve with assorted crackers or chips. Makes 2 cups.

# NUTS AND BOLTS

¼ c. margarine or butter
1 tsp. Worcestershire
  sauce
¼ tsp. garlic powder
¼ tsp. celery salt
½ c. salted peanuts

2 c. bite-size Shredded
  Wheat biscuits
  (Wheat Chex)
1 c. O-shaped puffed oat
  cereal
1 c. pretzel sticks

Put butter in an 8 inch square heat-resistant baking dish; heat in microwave oven 30 seconds. Stir in Worcestershire sauce, garlic powder, and celery salt. Lightly mix in remaining ingredients. Microwave for 1½ minutes; stir well and microwave for 1½ more minutes. Makes 4½ cups.

# MICROWAVE ROASTED PEANUTS

Fill turntable, single layer, with peanuts; microwave 6 minutes on HIGH. Let cool.

For microwave without turntable: Single layer of peanuts on 9 inch flat pan; microwave 3 minutes on HIGH. Rotate when halfway done and microwave another 3 minutes.

# BRAN MUFFINS

4 eggs
1 qt. buttermilk
5 c. flour
2½ c. sugar
5 tsp. baking soda

2 tsp. salt
1 c. oil
1 (15 oz.) box raisin bran cereal

In a large bowl, beat eggs and blend with buttermilk. Add flour, sugar, soda, and salt. Mix in oil and bran flakes. Allow batter to set for 24 hours. Keep covered in refrigerator up to 6 weeks.

Spoon out muffin batter as needed. Cook in plastic cupcake utensil or custard cups, filling cups half full of batter. If custard cups are used, place cups in a circle on a large plate. Because batter is cold, timings are slightly longer than usual.

To make 2 muffins: Cook on MEDIUM for 2 to 2½ minutes. To make 4 muffins: Cook on MEDIUM for 2½ to 3½ minutes. To make 6 muffins: Cook on MEDIUM for 3½ to 4½ minutes. Remove muffins from utensil immediately after baking to cool. Makes 6 to 8 dozen muffins.

*Mabel Ito*

# HONEY MICROWAVE MUFFINS

1 (8 oz.) can crushed
   pineapple
1½ c. whole bran cereal
⅔ c. buttermilk
1 egg, slightly beaten
⅓ c. chopped walnuts

3 Tbsp. vegetable oil
½ c. honey, divided
⅔ c. whole wheat flour
½ tsp. baking soda
⅛ tsp. salt

1. In a large mixing bowl, combine undrained pineapple, bran, and buttermilk. Let stand 10 minutes until bran has absorbed the liquid. Stir in egg, nuts, oil, and ¼ cup honey. Combine flour, soda, and salt; stir into bran mixture.

2. Line 6 cup microwave muffin pan with double thickness paper baking cups.

3. Fill muffin cups to top with batter. Microwave on HIGH 3½ to 4 minutes, rotating pan ½ turn, if necessary, after 1½ minutes. Muffins are done when they look dry and set on top.

4. Remove from oven; spoon 1 teaspoon honey over each muffin. Repeat for remaining 6 muffins.

*T. Oki*

# BEEF BOURGUIGNONNE

1½ to 2 lb. sirloin steak, cut
   into 1½ inch cubes
¼ tsp. salt
2 Tbsp. flour
½ c. dry red wine
½ c. water
1 c. sliced fresh
   mushrooms or 1 c.
   canned, sliced
   mushrooms, drained

1 green pepper, cut in 1
   inch pieces
1 c. chopped onions

In 2 quart casserole, combine steak, salt, flour, wine, and water. Blend well. Cook, covered, in microwave oven for 9 minutes. Stir once. Stir in mushrooms, green pepper, and onions. Cook, covered, 6 minutes or until meat is tender and sauce is thickened. Yield: 6 to 8 servings.

Tested for use in a 600 to 650 watt microwave oven.

# BEEF, NOODLE, AND SOUR CREAM CASSEROLE

3 c. cooked noodles
1 medium onion, grated
1 lb. ground beef
1 tsp. salt
¼ tsp. pepper

1 (7½ oz.) can tomato
   sauce
½ c. sour cream
½ c. grated Cheddar
   cheese

Saute onions and ground beef in medium size casserole dish in microwave oven for 3 minutes. Stir tomato sauce, sour cream, and noodles into beef and onion mixture. Cook in microwave oven 8 minutes. Stir; sprinkle cheese on top and cook another 2 to 3 minutes until cheese melts. Let stand 2 to 3 minutes. Yield: 4 servings.

Tested for use in 600 to 650 watt microwave oven.

# MEAT LOAF

2 beaten eggs
¾ c. milk
½ c. fine bread crumbs
¼ c. chopped onion
2 Tbsp. chopped parsley

1 tsp. salt
¾ tsp. ground sage
⅛ tsp. black pepper
1½ lb. ground beef

In a bowl, combine beaten eggs, milk, dry bread crumbs, onion, parsley, salt, sage, and pepper and mix well. Add ground beef; combine thoroughly.

In a 9 inch glass pie plate, shape meat mixture into a ring about 1 inch high around a small juice glass having a 2 inch diameter. Microwave, covered, until meat is done about 12 to 13 minutes, giving dish ¼ turn every 3 minutes. Let meat loaf stand 5 minutes.

*T. Oki*

# OYSTER SAUCE MEATLOAF

2 c. ground meat (turkey, chicken, or beef)
3 slices bread, moistened and torn
1 medium carrot, grated
1 medium onion, minced
⅓ c. celery, chopped
⅓ c. oyster sauce
2 heaping tsp. minced ginger
1 egg
Oyster sauce (for topping)

Combine all ingredients until well mixed. For microwave cooking: Press mixture firmly into a 9 inch microwave-safe tube pan sprayed with Pam. Cover lightly with plastic wrap. Microwave on MEDIUM HIGH for 20 minutes. Remove from oven and spread oyster sauce over meat mixture. Microwave at MEDIUM HIGH for another 5 minutes or until done. Let stand for 5 minutes before serving.

*Ethel Miyahira*

# MEXICAN LASAGNA

1 pkg. corn tortillas
1 lb. lean ground beef
1 large onion, chopped
1 pkg. taco seasoning mix
1 (4 oz.) can diced green
   chilies
1 (16 oz.) ctn. cottage
   cheese

2 c. shredded Monterey
   Jack cheese
1½ c. shredded Cheddar
   cheese
1 can chopped olives
1 c. sour cream
1 can enchilada sauce

Mix beef and taco mix in a medium glass mixing bowl. Microwave for 4 minutes on HIGH. Drain.

In a 9x13 inch glass casserole dish, layer 3 tortillas on the bottom. Spread ½ of the beef mixture on top of tortillas. In separate layers, sprinkle a handful of onions, then green chilies. Spread half of cottage cheese over onion and chilies. Sprinkle ⅓ of Monterey Jack and Cheddar cheese. Repeat tortillas, beef, onion, and chilies, cottage cheese layers. Microwave on HIGH 5 minutes. Reduce power to 50% (MEDIUM) for 10 minutes. Combine remaining cheeses and sour cream. Spread over casserole. Sprinkle with chopped olives. Pour can of enchilada sauce over casserole and microwave for 2 to 3 minutes on HIGH or until cheese is melted. Let stand for 10 minutes before serving.

# ONE DISH MACARONI BEEF

½ lb. ground round
1 small onion, finely
   chopped
1 c. uncooked macaroni
1 (8 oz.) can tomato sauce
1½ c. water
⅓ c. catsup

1 (7 oz.) can whole kernel
   corn (undrained)
1 Tbsp. brown sugar
½ tsp. salt
¼ tsp. pepper
¼ tsp. chili powder

Crumble ground round in 2 quart casserole. Stir in onion. Cover with glass lid or plastic wrap. Microwave on HIGH for 3 minutes. Drain and stir in remaining ingredients; recover. Microwave on DEFROST for 30 to 35 minutes or until macaroni is tender. Let stand, covered, 5 minutes before serving.

# TACO CASSEROLE

½ lb. ground beef
1 pkg. taco seasoning mix
1 (15 oz.) can chili with
  beans
1 (16 oz.) can stewed
  tomatoes

1 onion, chopped
1 pkg. corn chips
1 c. grated American
  cheese
1 c. shredded lettuce

In a large 3 quart glass bowl, microwave beef on HIGH for 4 minutes. Add chili with beans, stewed tomatoes, and seasoning mix; heat for 4 minutes more on HIGH.

Just before serving, stir in corn chips and top with grated cheese. Serve with shredded lettuce. May garnish with additional corn chips. Serves 4.

# TERIYAKI MEATBALLS

1½ lb. ground beef
¼ c. finely chopped onion
1 egg
½ tsp. salt

2 Tbsp. soy sauce
½ tsp. grated fresh ginger
1 clove garlic, grated

Combine ingredients together and mix well. Shape into 1 inch meatballs and place it in a glass baking dish. Cover with plastic wrap.

Sauce:

½ c. soy sauce
1 Tbsp. sake
3 Tbsp. sugar
1 tsp. ginger, grated

1 clove garlic, grated
1 tsp. cornstarch, mixed
  with water

Combine all the ingredients for the sauce in a glass bowl. Microwave on HIGH until sauce boils. Microwave meatballs on ROAST for 5 to 6 minutes or until piping hot.

# VEAL PARMIGIANA

1 Tbsp. olive oil
¼ c. chopped onion
1 (8 oz.) can tomato sauce
½ tsp. basil leaves
¾ c. shredded Mozzarella
    cheese

1 lb. veal cutlets
1 egg, beaten
⅓ c. finely crushed corn
    flake crumbs
1 Tbsp. Parmesan cheese

In 4 cup measure, combine oil and onion. Microwave at HIGH for 1 minute or until onion is tender. Stir in tomato sauce and basil. Microwave at HIGH for 3 to 5 minutes or until sauce is hot and somewhat thickened. Dip veal pieces in egg; dredge in crumbs. Place in 12x8 inch dish. Cover with wax paper. Microwave at HIGH 3½ to 5 minutes or until veal is fork tender. Pour sauce over veal; sprinkle with Mozzarella and top with Parmesan. Microwave, uncovered, at 50% (MEDIUM) 2 to 3 minutes or until cheese melts.

# VEGETABLE MEAT LOAF

1 lb. ground beef
1 medium onion, finely
    chopped
½ c. chopped green pepper
1 c. grated carrot
¾ c. fine bread crumbs
1 egg, lightly beaten
1 c. grated potatoes

1 tsp. salt
¼ tsp. pepper
½ tsp. dry mustard
⅛ tsp. cayenne
1 Tbsp. Worcestershire
    sauce
1 (10 oz.) can tomato soup
    (undiluted)

Combine all ingredients, blending thoroughly. Press in greased 1½ quart casserole. Microwave 10 minutes. Stir. Microwave 5 more minutes or until set and vegetables are tender. Yield: 4 servings.

Tested for use in a 600 to 650 watt microwave oven.

# BEACHCOMBER CHICKEN

3 lb. chicken thighs or 1 (3
   to 3½ lb.) fryer
1 clove garlic
¾ c. sugar
1 Tbsp. minced ginger

2 Tbsp. sherry
½ c. shoyu
½ c. catsup
1 tsp. salt

Crush ginger and garlic. Combine with rest of the ingredients into a sauce. Marinate chicken for an hour. Drain the chicken from all excess marinade, reserving liquid. Microwave on HIGH for 12 minutes, skin side down if using thighs, breast side down for whole chicken. Cover. Turn chicken pieces or chicken and baste with marinade. Microwave on HIGH for 13 minutes; cover. If desired, thicken marinade with a little cornstarch and use it as gravy. Makes 4 to 6 servings.

# BROCCOLI AND CHICKEN CASSEROLE

5 chicken breasts,
   precooked in
   microwave 15 minutes
   and cubed

2 pkg. frozen broccoli,
   thawed and drained

Sauce:

2 cans cream of chicken or
   mushroom soup

1 c. mayonnaise
¼ tsp. garlic powder

Need Parmesan cheese.

Place broccoli on bottom of casserole container. Place chicken cubes evenly over broccoli. Mix sauce together and pour evenly over chicken. Sprinkle with Parmesan cheese. Microwave, uncovered, on HIGH 9 minutes.

# CHICKEN RELLENO (STUFFED CHICKEN)

3 larp chong
1 medium carrot
¼ lb. green beans
12 boneless chicken thighs

1 tsp. salt
½ tsp. pepper
1 (8 oz.) can tomato sauce

Cut each larp chong into quarters lengthwise, then into 2½ inch pieces. Cut carrot into ¼ inch strips, then into 2½ inch lengths. Cut green beans into 2½ inch lengths. Place chicken, skin side down, on a cutting board; flatten slightly. Season with salt and pepper. Place 2 pieces of larp chong, carrot, and green beans on each piece of chicken; roll and fasten with foodpick. Place in microwave dish, cut side down. Pour tomato sauce over chicken rolls; cover. Rotating dish several times, microwave on HIGH power for 20 to 25 minutes. Remove foodpicks and arrange chicken on a serving platter. Makes 6 servings.

# CHICKEN SALAD

½ lb. chicken breast
1 Tbsp. sake
½ tsp. salt
1 (12 oz.) pkg. bean sprouts

1½ c. water
1 bundle long rice
1 cucumber, shredded

Sauce:

2 Tbsp. white sesame
 seeds, toasted
2 Tbsp. shoyu
1 tsp. salt
2 Tbsp. sugar
¼ c. vinegar

2 Tbsp. chopped green
 onion
2 Tbsp. sesame seed oil
2 tsp. slivered ginger
 (optional)

Combine first 3 ingredients in a bowl. Microwave, covered, for 2 to 2½ minutes. Cool, then shred.

Microwave bean sprouts for 3 minutes. Rinse; cool. Microwave about 1½ cups of water in a medium size mixing bowl. Place long rice into the heated water; microwave 1½ minutes. Set aside for several minutes. Drain long rice and cut into 2 to 3 inch lengths.

Arrange shredded chicken, bean sprouts, long rice, and cucumber on a platter. Chill. Pour sauce over just before serving. Makes 6 servings.

# MICROWAVE CHICKEN BREAST

4 pieces boneless chicken
    breasts
½ tsp. salt
¼ tsp. black pepper
2 Tbsp. salad oil
2 Tbsp. margarine
2 Tbsp. chopped green
    onions

Juice of ½ lemon
2 Tbsp. sherry
2 Tbsp. chopped parsley
2 tsp. Dijon mustard
¼ c. chicken broth

Place chicken breasts between plastic wrap and pound slightly. Sprinkle with salt and pepper. In a microwave dish, melt margarine and mix with oil. Place chicken breasts and coat both sides.

Microwave at HIGH power for 3 minutes. Turn breasts over and microwave again at HIGH for 3 minutes until chicken breasts are done. Set aside.

Prepare sauce by mixing green onions, lemon juice, sherry, parsley, and mustard in a microwave dish. Microwave at HIGH for 1 minute. Add juices from chicken and broth. Stir and pour sauce over chicken breasts.

*T. Oki*

# MUSHROOM CHICKEN

3 lb. chicken, cut into
    pieces
3 Tbsp. soy sauce
½ tsp. salt
¼ tsp. pepper
1 tsp. sugar
1 (15 oz.) can bamboo
    shoots, cut into
    pieces

1 medium can button
    mushrooms
2 stalks green onion, cut
    into 1 inch pieces

Combine soy sauce and sugar; mix with chicken in a glass casserole. Salt and pepper. Cover chicken with glass lid or plastic wrap. Microwave on HIGH for 15 minutes. Mix in the remaining ingredients with the chicken. Recover and microwave 10 minutes or until chicken is cooked. Let stand 5 minutes before serving.

# OVEN FRIED CHICKEN FOR TWO

¼ c. dry bread crumbs
1 Tbsp. Parmesan cheese
1 tsp. parsley flakes
¼ tsp. salt
¼ tsp. paprika
Dash of garlic powder

Dash of thyme
1 Tbsp. milk
1 lb. chicken pieces (legs, thighs, and/or breasts)

Combine all ingredients, except milk and chicken, in plastic storage bag. Dip chicken pieces into milk, then place pieces in plastic bag and coat with crumb mixture.

Arrange coated pieces, skin side up, on roasting rack in 12x8 inch glass baking dish or instead of rack on heavy paper plate. Microwave with FULL power, covered with paper towel, 10 to 12 minutes or until done. Rotate dish once.

*Virginia M. Newgent*

## POOKIE MICRO CHICKEN

3 to 4 lb. fryer chicken
4 Tbsp. oyster sauce
1 Tbsp. sugar
1 tsp. Chinese five spice
1 Tbsp. minced garlic

4 Tbsp. chopped green onions
4 Tbsp. chopped Chinese parsley
1 Tbsp. shoyu

Combine all ingredients for sauce. Rub sauce inside and outside of chicken. Let stand in refrigerator for a couple of hours or overnight. Place chicken on microwave roasting pan. Cover loosely with waxed paper. Microwave on HIGH for 25 minutes. Let stand for 5 minutes. Cut into serving pieces.

*Ethel Miyahira*

# STEAMED CHICKEN AND LUP CHEONG

2 lb. chicken
2 tsp. soy sauce
1 tsp. sugar
1 tsp. salt
1 Tbsp. cornstarch
1 tsp. sherry

½ tsp. ginger juice
4 dried mushrooms,
   soaked
4 larp chong (Chinese
   sausage), thinly
   sliced

Chop chicken into 1½ x 2 inch pieces. In a large bowl, mix chicken with soy sauce, sugar, salt, cornstarch, sherry, and ginger juice. Remove stems from mushrooms; slice caps. Stir mushrooms and lup cheong into chicken. Put mixture into a 9 inch glass pie plate. Steam over boiling water for 25 minutes or cover with plastic wrap and microwave on HIGH power for 13 to 16 minutes. Makes 6 servings.

# CHINESE SWEET ROAST PORK
## (Char Siu)

4 lb. pork butt
½ c. honey
1 Tbsp. red food coloring
1 tsp. Five Spices
   (Chinese)
¼ c. thick red soy sauce

1 tsp. salt
1 Tbsp. oyster sauce
2 Tbsp. red bean curd
¼ c. sherry
3 cloves garlic, minced
2 c. brown sugar

Slice pork into 2x5 inch pieces. Combine all of the preceding ingredients together. Marinate the pork for several hours or overnight. Place 6 pieces of pork, fat side down, on microwave roasting rack, in a 2 quart (12x7 inch) or 3 quart (13x9 inch) baking dish. Microwave on HIGH for 10 minutes. Turn pork, fat side up, and baste. Microwave on ROAST for 12 to 15 minutes or until done. Let stand 5 minutes before slicing.

# HAWAIIAN ROAST PORK

1 Tbsp. rock salt
¼ c. soy sauce
1 tsp. Worcestershire
   sauce
1 clove garlic, crushed
1 (½ inch) piece ginger
   root, crushed

Few drops of liquid smoke
3 lb. boneless shoulder
   pork roast
4 large ti leaves

In a small bowl, combine salt, soy sauce, Worcestershire sauce, garlic, ginger root, and a few drops of the liquid smoke. Place roast into a plastic bag; set in a bowl. Pour in the marinade and close bag tightly. Marinate overnight in refrigerator. Occasionally distribute marinade evenly.

Wash ti leaves; remove fibrous part of veins. Place 2 ti leaves vertically and the third leaf horizontally in the center between the other 2 leaves. Place the fourth leaf horizontally next to the third leaf. Place roast in center of leaves. Baste with marinade. Wrap and secure with string. Place pork, fat side down, on a trivet in a 9 inch square baking dish. Cook in microwave oven for 24 minutes. Turn pork over and cook 12 minutes longer. Cool and slice pork. Heat remaining marinade and baste sliced pork. Makes 6 servings.

# KALUA PIG

3 lb. pork butt
6 Tbsp. liquid smoke
3 Tbsp. Hawaiian salt

½ banana leaf
5 ti leaves

Wipe pork with paper towel; score ¼ inch around pork. Rub with Hawaiian salt and liquid smoke. Wrap in banana leaf and tie. Wrap again with ti leaves and tie securely. Place in a 3 quart casserole; cover.

Microwave on HIGH for 20 minutes. Turn pork butt over and cover again. Microwave on ROAST for 40 minutes or until internal temperature is 170°F. Let Kalua Pig stand for 10 minutes or until internal temperature reaches 185°F. Shred pork and serve with poi, lomi salmon, or poki, etc.

## MICROWAVE BAKED HAM
## WITH PINEAPPLE SAUCE

5 lb. canned ham
1 (8¼ oz.) can crushed
    pineapple

¼ c. brown sugar
½ tsp. dry mustard

Place ham, fat side down, in glass baking dish. Cover with vented plastic wrap. Cook in microwave oven at 50% power for 15 minutes. Combine remaining ingredients. Turn ham over and spread with sauce. Cook at 50% power for 10 to 15 more minutes. Tent with foil and let stand about 15 minutes before serving. Makes about 25 (3 ounce) servings.

## MICROWAVE MIXED VEGETABLE-HAM BAKE

2¼ c. beef broth
¾ c. uncooked rice
½ c. chopped onion
⅓ c. chopped green pepper
¼ c. chopped celery

1 tsp. curry powder
2 c. fully cooked ham
1 (10 oz.) pkg. frozen mixed
    vegetables

In a 2 quart casserole, combine the preceding 6 ingredients and mix well. Microwave, covered, 8 minutes, stirring after 4 minutes. Stir in 2 cups chopped fully cooked ham and the frozen vegetable mix, partially thawed. Microwave, covered, 12 minutes more, stirring every 3 minutes. Transfer mixture to serving bowl. Makes 4 to 5 servings.

*T. Oki*

# PORK HAWAIIAN
## (You'll like the quick preparation of this exotic dish)

3 c. cubed cooked pork
  (about 1½ lb.)
⅓ c. packed brown sugar
2 Tbsp. cornstarch
½ tsp. ground ginger
¼ tsp. garlic powder
¼ c. soy sauce
2 Tbsp. ketchup
1 onion, cut in chunks
1 green pepper, cut in ½
  inch squares

1 (20 oz.) can pineapple
  chunks packed in
  juice
⅓ c. wine vinegar
¼ c. soy sauce
1 Tbsp. cornstarch
1 (8 oz.) can water
  chestnuts, drained
1 (3 oz.) jar sliced
  mushrooms, drained
4 to 6 c. hot cooked rice

Place pork cubes in a 2½ quart casserole dish; set aside. In a 2 cup measure, combine brown sugar, 2 tablespoons cornstarch, ginger, and garlic powder. Stir in ¼ cup soy sauce and ketchup. Pour over pork. Stir to coat evenly. Cook on HIGH 3 minutes. Add onion and green pepper. Cook on HIGH 4 minutes. Drain pineapple, reserving juice in a 2 cup measure. Add water to juice to make 1 cup liquid. Stir in vinegar and ¼ cup soy sauce. Stir in 1 tablespoon cornstarch until blended. Pour over pork. Stirring twice, cook on HIGH 6 to 7 minutes until sauce is thickened. Stir in reserved pineapple chunks, water chestnuts, and mushrooms. Cook on HIGH 2 to 3 minutes. Serve over hot rice. Makes 6 to 8 servings.

# RIO GRANDE PORK ROAST

An unusual flavor blend gives this pork roast pizzaz. It's excellent served with rice.

½ tsp. salt
½ tsp. garlic salt
½ tsp. chili powder
¼ tsp. liquid smoke
1 (5 lb.) pork loin roast
  (boned and tied)

½ c. apple jelly
½ c. ketchup
1 Tbsp. vinegar
½ tsp. chili powder
1 c. crushed corn chips

Combine salt, garlic salt, and ½ teaspoon chili powder. Rub liquid smoke over roast, then sprinkle with salt mixture. Shield ends of roast by covering with small, smooth pieces of foil. Place roast, fat side down, on a rack in a 12 x 7½ inch baking dish. Cook on LOW 48 minutes. While roast cooks, combine jelly, ketchup, vinegar, and ½ teaspoon chili powder in a 2 cup measure. Heat on HIGH 3½ to 4½ minutes or until mixture comes to a boil. Stir and set aside.

Remove foil; turn roast fat side up. Brush generously with jelly glaze. Sprinkle with corn chips. Cook on LOW 35 to 45 minutes. Internal temperature should register 160°F. immediately after cooking. Temperature increases to 170°F. after standing time. Roast may be *browned* during part of standing time. Makes 8 to 10 servings.

# GON LO MEIN

1 pkg. soft fried noodles
1 medium stalk celery, cut
   into slivers
2 stalks green onion, cut
   into 1 inch pieces
1 carrot, cut into slivers
1½ c. green beans, slivered

¼ lb. char siu (Chinese
   sweet roast pork)
2 tsp. sesame oil
3 Tbsp. oyster sauce
½ tsp. salt
¼ tsp. pepper
½ pkg. bean sprouts

Combine sesame oil and oyster sauce; marinate noodles in a 2 quart casserole. Add the remaining ingredients, except the bean sprouts. Microwave on HIGH (6) for 5 minutes, covered. Stir; add the bean sprouts. Recover and microwave on HIGH (6) for another 2 to 2½ minutes or until bean sprouts are wilted but crisp. Serves 6 people.

Note: This recipe may be doubled; adjust the time to 8 minutes on the first setting and 3 minutes on the second.

*Gold*

# CRAB REGAL

¾ to 1 c. (6 to 8 oz.) drained
   and flaked cooked
   crabmeat
¼ to ½ c. shredded
   Cheddar or Swiss
   cheese
2 Tbsp. dry bread crumbs
2 Tbsp. chopped celery
2 Tbsp. salad dressing or
   mayonnaise

2 Tbsp. milk or cream
1 Tbsp. chopped pimiento
   (if desired)
½ tsp. minced onion
½ tsp. lemon juice
Dash of salt
Dash of pepper

In 1 quart casserole or mixing bowl, combine all ingredients. Spoon into 2 individual casseroles. Microwave on HIGH for 1 minute and 30 seconds or until edges bubble.

# POACHED FISH

**2½ lb. fish fillets**
**¼ c. chopped onion**
**Butter or margarine**

**1 c. dry white wine**
**Salt and pepper**

Butter a shallow microwave baking pan lightly. Place fish fillets. Salt and pepper and sprinkle with onions. Pour wine over fish. Cover with plastic wrap in microwave oven on MEDIUM-HIGH for 8 to 10 minutes, or until fish flakes easily. Baste fish with wine and onions a couple of times during cooking.

*T. Oki*

# STEAMED FISH

**1 medium size moana,**
**   weke, or mullet**
**1 Tbsp. salad oil**
**2 tsp. soy sauce**
**1 tsp. sugar**
**1 tsp. cornstarch**
**Salt**

**1 stalk green onion, cut into**
**   pieces**
**1 inch piece ginger root,**
**   cut into slivers**
**1 Tbsp. chung choy**
**   (Chinese salted turnip)**

Combine oil, soy sauce, cornstarch, and sugar in a glass dish, mixing it into a sauce. Sprinkle fish with salt and marinate with sauce. Sprinkle with green onions, chung choy, and ginger over fish. Cover dish with plastic wrap or glass cover. Microwave on HIGH for 4 minutes or until done. Let stand 3 minutes before serving. Makes 2 servings.

Note: Cooking time for 2 fish is 6 minutes.

# SALMON LOAF WITH CAPER SAUCE

1 (1 lb.) can salmon
¼ c. butter or margarine
¼ c. flour
½ tsp. salt
Dash of pepper
2 c. milk
2 eggs, beaten
1 Tbsp. lemon juice

1 Tbsp. minced onion
1 tsp. Worcestershire
  sauce
2 c. soft bread crumbs
1 egg yolk, beaten
1½ Tbsp. capers
½ lemon, thinly sliced

Grease an 8½ x 4½ x 2½ inch loaf pan. Drain salmon, reserving liquid. Remove skin and bones from salmon. In a saucepan, melt butter. Stir in flour and seasonings until mixture is smooth. Remove from heat; stir in milk. Bring to a boil, stirring constantly. Set aside 1 cup of the sauce. Slowly stir remainder into eggs. Mix in salmon, lemon juice, onion, and Worcestershire sauce. Fold in crumbs. Pour into prepared baking dish; bake at 350°F. for 40 to 45 minutes.

Mix egg yolk with reserved salmon liquid; stir into the remaining 1 cup sauce. Heat slowly, stirring constantly. Remove from heat and stir in capers and lemon slices. Serve with salmon loaf. Makes 6 servings.

Place salmon loaf in a glass baking loaf pan. Cover with plastic wrap or wax paper and microwave for 9 to 11 minutes. Let stand 5 minutes before serving.

Tuna may be substituted for salmon.

# SALMON WITH HONEY-MUSTARD SAUCE

4 (4 oz.) salmon steaks (½ inch thick)
1 Tbsp. lemon juice
¼ c. Dijon mustard

3 Tbsp. honey
2 Tbsp. plain nonfat yogurt
Green onion (optional)

Brush salmon steaks with lemon juice. Arrange salmon in an 8 inch square baking dish with thickest portions toward outside of dish. Cover with heavy-duty plastic wrap and microwave at HIGH 4 minutes. Turn salmon over; cover and microwave at HIGH 2 to 4 minutes, or until fish flakes easily. Place in platter.

Combine the mustard, honey, and yogurt in microwave dish and microwave on HIGH 1 minute. Spoon sauce evenly over salmon. Garnish with green onion.

*T. Oki*

# SHRIMP CREOLE

1 medium onion, chopped
¾ c. chopped green pepper
¼ c. chopped celery
3 Tbsp. margarine
1 (16 oz.) can whole tomatoes
1 (6 oz.) can tomato paste
1 c. water
2 Tbsp. all-purpose flour

2 Tbsp. dried parsley flakes
1½ tsp. sugar
1 tsp. salt
½ tsp. chili powder
⅛ tsp. black pepper
⅛ tsp. dried thyme leaves
⅛ tsp. red pepper sauce
12 oz. raw shrimp, shelled and deveined

1. Combine onion, green pepper, celery, and margarine in 3 quart casserole. Microwave at HIGH until vegetables are tender, 3 to 6 minutes. Add tomatoes, tomato paste, water, and flour, stirring to break up tomatoes. Mix in remaining ingredients, except shrimp. Cover.

2. Microwave at HIGH until mixture is bubbly, 8 to 10 minutes, stirring twice during cooking. Stir in shrimp; cover. Microwave at HIGH until shrimp is cooked and tender. (Do not overcook or shrimp will become tough), 4 to 6 minutes, stirring once or twice during cooking. Serve with rice. Makes 4 servings.

*T. Oki*

2821-95

**367**

# SHRIMP CREOLE

2 Tbsp. margarine
¾ c. chopped green pepper
1 c. chopped onion
1 c. chopped celery
1½ Tbsp. flour
1 (14 oz.) can tomatoes
1 tsp. sugar
5 to 6 drops of Tabasco
    sauce

1 tsp. salt
⅛ tsp. pepper
Dash of powdered bay leaf
    (optional)
1 lb. fresh or frozen shrimp,
    cleaned and shelled

In a 1½ to 2 quart casserole, melt margarine (approximately 1 minute). Stir in green pepper, onion, and celery. Cook 5 to 6 minutes or until vegetables are barely tender. Stir vegetables at least once during this time. Sprinkle vegetables with flour. Stir well to blend. Add tomatoes. Cook 4 minutes. Stir well. Cook 4 minutes longer. Add sugar, Tabasco, bay leaf, salt, and pepper. Blend well. Add shrimp. Heat about 8 minutes, stirring lightly at 2 minute intervals. Correct seasoning if necessary. Serve over cooked rice. Yield: 4 servings.

Tested for use in a 600 to 650 watt microwave oven.

# SHRIMP SCAMPI

1 lb. fresh jumbo shrimp
½ c. butter or margarine
2 Tbsp. lemon juice
2 Tbsp. dried parsley flakes

1 to 2 cloves garlic,
    crushed
½ tsp. salt
Paprika (optional)

Remove shells from the shrimp, leaving just the tail section. Slit the back of the shrimp and wash out the sand vein.

In a shallow microwave baking pan, place butter, lemon juice, parsley flakes, garlic, and salt to taste. Heat, uncovered, in microwave oven 2 to 2½ minutes. Add shrimp and stir. Sprinkle with paprika. Heat, uncovered, 4 to 6 (5 to 8) minutes. Stir occasionally. Cook just until shrimp are pink and tender. Do not overcook shrimp, or it will be tough.

*T. Oki*

# MICRO STEAMED FISH WITH CHUNG CHOI

Fish Mixture:

**1½ lb. fish**
**1 inch piece gow pi, soaked**
**Hawaiian salt to taste**

**1 roll chung choi, finely**
  **chopped**

Garnish:

**6 slices ginger, slivered**
**¼ c. soy sauce**
**Dash of black pepper**

**½ c. green onions, finely**
  **cut**
**½ c. Chinese parsley**

Hot Oil Mixture:

**6 Tbsp. oil**

**2 cloves garlic, mashed**

1. Wash and soak chung choi and gow pi in separate bowls. Scrape off white area of gow pi. Combine chung choi and gow pi and chop fine.

2. Rub salt on fish and sprinkle chung choi and gow pi over fish.

3. Cover fish with plastic wrap and microwave fish on HIGH power for 6 to 7 minutes.

4. Remove plastic wrap and garnish fish.

5. Heat oil in a pan till oil smokes. Brown garlic in oil.

6. Pour oil over fish and serve hot.

# MEETING NIGHT TUNA CASSEROLE

**1 (3 oz.) pkg. potato chips,**
  **crushed**
**1 (9 oz.) can tuna**

**4 slices American cheese**
**1 (10 oz.) can cream of**
  **mushroom soup**

Place layer of potato chips in a 1½ quart casserole. Add ½ of the tuna. Add 2 slices of cheese. Cover with ½ of the soup. Repeat layers. Cover with paper plate to avoid splatters. Bake in microwave oven 10½ to 13 minutes. Turn dish twice during the baking time, until heated thoroughly. Yield: 4 servings.

Tested for use in a 600 to 650 watt microwave oven.

# TUNA AND EGG CASSEROLE

1 (10¾ oz.) can condensed
   cream of mushroom
   soup
1 (6½ oz.) can chunk tuna,
   drained
¼ c. finely chopped onion
1 Tbsp. chopped pimento

1 (4 oz.) can mushroom
   stems and pieces,
   drained
2 hard cooked eggs,
   chopped
1 (10 oz.) pkg. potato chips,
   crumbled

Combine all ingredients, except potato chips, in 1½ quart casserole. Mix well. Cover with glass lid or plastic wrap. Microwave for 10 minutes or until hot. Let stand, covered, 5 minutes. Sprinkle potato chips on top and serve. Yield: 4 servings.

Tested for use in a 600 to 650 watt microwave oven.

# TOFU CASSEROLE

1 block tofu
½ c. fine bread crumbs
½ c. grated carrots
½ c. chopped green onion
1 tsp. minced ginger
2 Tbsp. soy sauce

½ tsp. salt
¼ tsp. ajinomoto
2 eggs, beaten
1 can cream of mushroom
   soup

Grease a 1½ quart glass casserole. Place tofu in a cloth and squeeze out the water. Mix the tofu and other ingredients together in a large bowl. Place in dish. Microwave on ROAST for 15 minutes. Let stand for 10 minutes before serving.

# STUFFED ABURAGE

1 (8 piece) pkg. aburage
   (rectangular shape)
1 lb. ground pork
1 egg
1 Tbsp. shoyu
⅓ c. chopped green onion
6 water chestnuts,
   chopped

6 fresh shrimp, chopped
1 (14½ oz.) can chicken
   broth
1 Tbsp. shoyu
1½ Tbsp. katakuriko
   (potato starch)
½ c. water

Cut each aburage piece in half, across the width. In a small bowl, combine pork, egg, shoyu, green onion, water chestnuts, and shrimp; mix thoroughly. Stuff aburage with this mixture. Set aside.

In 3½ quart casserole, cook chicken broth and 1 tablespoon shoyu, covered, on HIGH for 5 minutes. While broth is heating, dissolve katakuriko in water. Add katakuriko mixture to hot soup; stir well. Cook, covered, on HIGH for 2 minutes.

Add stuffed aburage to gravy mixture. Cook, covered, on MEDIUM for 12 minutes; stir. Let stand 5 minutes before serving.

# ALMOND FLOAT

2 Tbsp. unflavored gelatin
3 c. milk
⅔ c. sugar

½ tsp. almond extract
1 (No. 2½) can fruit
   cocktail, chilled

In mixing bowl, combine unflavored gelatin and 1 cup of milk; stir until dissolved. Scald remaining milk in microwave oven for 3 minutes. Add sugar to hot milk and cook 2½ minutes longer, stirring constantly. Add almond extract. Pour into an 8 inch square pan and chill until firm. Cut into 1 inch squares.

To serve, put 8 pieces to a dish. Add fruit cocktail. Garnish with a sprig of mint. Makes 8 servings.

Note: Other canned fruit such as lychee, longan, pineapple tidbits, mandarin oranges, or sliced peaches, and fresh fruits such as mango, tangerine, banana, or papaya may be used.

# BUTTER MOCHI BARS

2 Tbsp. margarine or
  butter, melted
1 c. mochiko (glutinous
  rice flour)
½ c. sugar

½ tsp. baking powder
¼ tsp. vanilla
1 c. milk
2 Tbsp. kinako (roasted soy
  bean flour)

Microwave oven: Put butter in 8 inch square glass baking dish. Heat 30 seconds or until butter melts. In a mixing bowl, combine sugar, mochiko, and baking powder. Add milk, vanilla, and butter and mix thoroughly. Return to baking dish and cook 4 minutes on HIGH; turn the dish and microwave additional 3 minutes. Cool and cut into squares. Sprinkle with kinako. Makes 8 servings.

Or: Preheat oven to 350°F. and pour mochi mixture into a greased 8 inch square baking dish. Bake for 30 minutes. Sprinkle with kinako. Makes 8 servings.

# CHERRY CRUMBLE

1 (18½ oz.) pkg. yellow
  cake mix
1 (21 oz.) can cherry pie
  filling

1 c. water
1 tsp. lemon juice
½ tsp. cinnamon

Sprinkle half of the cake mix into a 13x9 inch baking dish. Pour pie filling over cake mix. Sprinkle remaining cake mix over pie filling. Combine water and lemon juice. Pour evenly over mixture. Sprinkle with cinnamon. Microwave on SIMMER 7 minutes. Microwave on HIGH for 3 to 4 minutes or until topping is set like streusel.

# COPYCAT POPPY COCK

2 qt. popcorn
2 c. slivered almonds
1 c. butter or margarine

½ c. light corn syrup
1½ c. sugar
1 tsp. vanilla

In a buttered 5 quart container, combine popcorn and nuts. In a saucepan, combine butter, syrup, and sugar. Boil until mixture reaches 300°F. or hard crack stage. Stir in vanilla; immediately pour over popcorn, stirring lightly until popcorn mixture is evenly coated. Spread on a large sheet of foil and immediately separate into smaller pieces with 2 forks. Cool and store in an airtight container. Makes about 2½ quarts.

To cook syrup in microwave oven: Combine butter, syrup, and sugar in a 2½ quart heat-resistant mixing bowl. Cook on HIGH until brittle threads form when a small amount of syrup is dropped into cold water, about 9 to 15 minutes, stirring every 3 minutes.

# CREAMY LIGHT CHEESECAKE
## (Microwave oven)

3 Tbsp. margarine
1 c. graham cracker
   crumbs
2 Tbsp. sugar
2 c. lowfat cottage cheese
1 c. lowfat vanilla yogurt

½ c. egg substitute or 3 egg
   whites
¼ c. sugar
½ tsp. almond extract
Fresh or frozen fruit

Put margarine in an 8 inch round microwave-safe baking dish. Microwave on HIGH for 45 to 60 seconds, or until margarine is melted. Stir in crumbs and sugar. Press firmly into bottom and ½ inch up sides of dish. Microwave on HIGH 45 to 60 seconds, or until firm. Set aside.

In a blender, blend cottage cheese and yogurt until smooth. Add egg substitute, the ¼ cup sugar, and almond extract; blend until mixed. Transfer to a microwave-safe bowl. Microwave on HIGH 5 to 7 minutes or until slightly thickened, stirring several times. Beat until smooth. Pour into crust. Microwave on 50% power 6 to 14 minutes or until edges are set, rotating dish several times during cooking. Chill for at least 4 hours. Serve with fruit. Makes 8 servings.

# EASY CHOCOLATE CAKE

1 pkg. fudge or chocolate
   cake mix
2 eggs
1 tsp. vanilla

⅓ c. salad oil
1 c. water
1 (6 oz.) pkg. semi-sweet
   chocolate morsels

Combine chocolate cake mix with eggs, vanilla, oil, and water; beat for 2 minutes until smooth. Pour into ungreased dish. Sprinkle with semi-sweet chocolate morsels. Microwave on HIGH 7 to 9 minutes. Serve warm or cool with ice cream or frost with favorite frosting. Makes 12 servings.

Note: Rotate a quarter turn 4 times for even baking if you do not have a carousel turntable.

# ENERGY BARS

2½ c. toasted rice cereal
2 c. oats
1 c. raisins
½ c. roasted peanuts
¼ c. toasted sesame seeds

¼ c. butter or margarine
½ c. peanut butter
1 (10½ oz.) pkg. miniature
   marshmallows

In medium casserole, mix rice cereal, oats, raisins, peanuts, and sesame seeds. Cook, covered, on HIGH for 2 minutes. Stir and set aside.

In large casserole, combine remaining ingredients. Cook, covered, on HIGH for 2 minutes; stir until smooth. Quickly stir in cereal mixture; mix thoroughly. Press evenly into buttered 9x13 inch pan. Cut into bars while warm. When cool, wrap individual pieces in waxed paper.

# EVERBEST FRUIT COBBLER

1 (22 oz.) can prepared pie
   filling
1 (9 oz.) yellow cake mix
¼ c. thinly sliced butter

2 Tbsp. brown sugar
1 tsp. cinnamon
3 Tbsp. finely chopped
   walnuts

In 8 inch square or round baking dish, arrange pie filling evenly. Sprinkle evenly with cake mix. Dot butter slices evenly over mixture. Combine sugar, cinnamon, and nuts and sprinkle over top. Microwave on HIGH for 9 to 11 minutes. Let dish rest for 10 minutes before serving. Serves 6 to 8.

# FLAN

⅓ c. sugar
1 tsp. water
2 (13 oz.) cans evaporated
   milk

6 eggs
½ c. sugar
2 tsp. vanilla

In a 2 cup glass measure, combine the ⅓ cup sugar and the water. Cook at HIGH for 1¾ minutes or until sugar is caramelized. Quickly pour syrup into bottom of 4 (6 ounce) custard cups. In a 4 cup glass measure, cook milk at HIGH for 4 to 5 minutes or until very hot.

In a mixing bowl, combine eggs, remaining sugar, and vanilla. Gradually stir in the hot milk. Pour over syrup in cups. Place cups in an 8x8x2 inch glass baking dish. Pour hot water into dish to 1 inch deep. Microwave on MEDIUM (50%) 14 minutes or until custard is nearly set and knife inserted off-center comes out clean. Chill flan. Carefully loosen custard from sides and invert onto dessert plates.

## MICROWAVE JELLO MOCHI

1 c. boiling water
1 (3 oz.) Jell-O (any flavor)
1 c. sugar

1 c. mochiko
1 tsp. vanilla
½ c. potato starch

Dissolve Jell-O in boiling water. Stir well. Add sugar and mochiko. Mix well. Add vanilla. Pour into 12 inch microwave Bundt pan which has been sprayed with Pam. Cover pan with plastic wrap. Microwave 5 minutes on HIGH. Remove plastic wrap carefully. Cool thoroughly. Take out from pan and place on potato starch dusted board. Slice with plastic knife and coat pieces with potato starch.

*Janet Shiratori*

# MICRO OVEN NANTU (OKINAWA MOCHI)

2 c. mochiko
¾ to 1 c. white sugar
⅛ tsp. salt
2 c. water

¼ tsp. red food coloring
1 tsp. vanilla or lemon
    extract (optional)

1. Mix together dry ingredients.

2. Mix coloring, vanilla, and water. Add ⅔ of the water to dry ingredients. Mix well and add rest of the water. Mix.

3. Spread mayonnaise or Pam on pan, then pour mixed dough into pan. (Use a microwave Bundt pan.)

4. Wet sides of pan and cover with plastic wrap to seal pan.

5. Microwave on MEDIUM HIGH for 9 minutes and 5 seconds.

6. Spread potato starch (katakuriko) or soy bean flour (kinako) on flat surface (cookie sheet works fine) and invert the cooked nantu.

7. Cool and cut with plastic knife to your desired pieces.

8. Before cutting, dab kinako or potato starch and as you cut, roll nantu in potato starch or kinako.

*Helen Kawahara, Patsy Nakamura*

## PINEAPPLE HAUPIA

1 (12 oz.) can frozen
    coconut milk
4 to 6 Tbsp. cornstarch

4 to 6 Tbsp. sugar
1 (8½ oz.) can crushed
    pineapple

Microwave coconut milk on MEDIUM-LOW (30%) 8 to 10 minutes to defrost. Combine sugar and cornstarch. Microwave mixture on HIGH 12 to 15 minutes, stirring with wire whisk 3 times. Cook until thickened and fat melts. Stir in pineapple. Pour into 8 inch square pan. Cool until firm. Cut into squares. Makes 6 servings.

# PINEAPPLE CAKETTES

2 Tbsp. butter or margarine
2 Tbsp. brown sugar

4 Tbsp. undrained crushed
   pineapple

Cake:

½ c. unsifted all-purpose
   flour
⅓ c. sugar
½ tsp. baking powder
¼ c. milk

⅛ tsp. salt
½ tsp. vanilla
2 Tbsp. oil
1 egg

Prepare 4 (6 ounce) custard cups by melting ½ tablespoon butter in each cup (30 seconds). Stir ½ tablespoon brown sugar and 1 tablespoon pineapple into each cup. Prepare cake batter in a small bowl by combining all ingredients and mixing well. Spoon onto pineapple mixture, filling cups about half full. Cook, uncovered, 3 minutes and 30 seconds or until toothpick comes out clean. Makes 6 cupcakes.

# MICROWAVE PEANUT BUTTER COOKIES

| | |
|---|---|
| 1 c. butter or margarine | 2 eggs, beaten |
| ¾ c. brown sugar | 1¼ c. all-purpose flour |
| ¾ c. granulated sugar | 1 c. bran |
| 1 tsp. vanilla | ¾ c. rolled oats |
| 1 c. peanut butter (creamy or chunky) | 2 tsp. baking soda |

1. Place butter in microwave-safe bowl, breaking it up in pieces.

2. Microwave at HIGH power for 45 seconds. Cover with wax paper to prevent spattering.

3. Beat in sugars, vanilla, peanut butter, and eggs.

4. Combine flour, bran, oats, and baking soda. Stir into butter mixture.

5. Press out ½ of dough into an 8x8 inch microwave-safe dish.

6. Shield corners of dish with foil to prevent overcooking.

7. Microwave at HIGH power for 4 to 5 minutes, turning a quarter 3 times during baking.

8. Cool before cutting into bars.

9. Repeat with second batch of dough.

Microwave setting — HIGH 100%. Microwave cooking time — 4 to 5 minutes. Yield: 32 bars.

*Anne Hasegawa*

# BEAN SPROUTS NAMASU

1 medium cucumber, cut
   lengthwise, seeds
   removed, and sliced
½ tsp. salt
1 (12 oz.) pkg. bean sprouts
1 Tbsp. roasted sesame
   seeds

½ (7 oz.) pkg. kamaboko,
   cut into ¼ inch strips
1 c. Awasezu (recipe
   follows)

Wash and drain bean sprouts. Place into a glass casserole. Microwave on HIGH for 1 minute and 30 seconds or until wilted. Drain liquid from bean sprouts and chill for at least 1 to 2 hours. Add the salt to the cucumbers and let stand 10 minutes. Squeeze cucumbers to remove excess liquid. Toss chilled bean sprouts with remaining ingredients. Makes 4 to 6 servings.

Awasezu - Sauce:

2 c. sugar
2 c. rice vinegar or white
   vinegar

2 Tbsp. salt

Mix all the ingredients in a 4 cup measuring cup. Microwave on HIGH for 2 to 4 minutes or until mixture boils and sugar dissolves. Stir and chill. This can be used for namasu or as a salad dressing.

# BROCCOLI AND CAULIFLOWER
## WITH MUSTARD SAUCE

3 c. fresh broccoli
   flowerets
3 c. fresh cauliflowerets
¾ c. milk

1 Tbsp. prepared mustard
1½ Tbsp. flour
½ tsp. salt
¼ tsp. onion powder

Combine broccoli and cauliflower in a baking dish. Cover and microwave on HIGH power for 8 to 12 minutes or until tender, stirring once. Drain. In a medium bowl, combine remaining ingredients. Microwave on HIGH power for 3 to 4 minutes or until thickened, stirring after each minute. Pour over vegetables. Makes 6 servings.

# BROCCOLI SURPRISE

2 pkg. (10 oz.) frozen
    broccoli spears
1 (10¾ oz.) can condensed
    cream of chicken
    soup
½ c. real or imitation sour
    cream
¼ c. finely shredded
    carrots

1 Tbsp. flour
1 Tbsp. instant minced
    onion
¼ tsp. salt
⅛ tsp. pepper
2 Tbsp. butter or margarine
¾ c. herb seasoned
    stuffing cubes

Microwave frozen broccoli in package 3 to 4 minutes or until thawed; drain. Cut broccoli spears into 1 inch pieces.

Combine soup, sour cream, carrot, flour, onion, salt, and pepper in 1 quart glass casserole. Add broccoli; mix lightly.

Microwave butter in glass dish ½ to 1 minute or until melted. Stir in stuffing cubes. Spoon over broccoli. Microwave, uncovered, 9 to 10 minutes or until bubbly in center.

Note: May use chopped broccoli instead of broccoli spears.

*Virginia Newgent*

# CAULIFLOWER PICK-UPS

1 small head cauliflower
⅓ c. butter or margarine
¼ c. dry bread crumbs
¼ c. grated Parmesan
    cheese

1 tsp. tarragon leaves,
    crushed
1 tsp. paprika
½ tsp. salt
Dash of pepper

Wash cauliflower and pat dry. Separate into flowerettes; cut larger flowerettes into bite-size pieces. Microwave butter in small glass dish 1 to 1½ minutes or until melted. Combine remaining ingredients in plastic bag. Dip several pieces cauliflower at a time in butter. Add to crumbs and shake to coat evenly. Repeat with remaining cauliflower. Arrange in single layer in 12x8 inch glass baking dish. Microwave, covered with paper towel, 4½ to 5½ minutes or until tender. Serve warm on toothpicks.

*Virginia M. Newgent*

# CRUMB-TOPPED TOMATOES

5 tomatoes
¼ c. dry bread crumbs
2 Tbsp. Parmesan cheese

¼ tsp. garlic salt
¼ tsp. leaf basil

Cut tomatoes in half horizontally. Arrange, cut side up, on glass serving plate. Combine remaining ingredients; spoon onto tomato halves.

Microwave, uncovered, 3 to 5 minutes or until heated, rotating plate once. This makes 10 servings.

*Virginia M. Newgent*

# EGGPLANT PARMESAN

2 small (about 1 lb. each)
   eggplants
2 Tbsp. mayonnaise
¼ c. dried bread crumbs
½ tsp. oregano
1 (14 to 16 oz.) jar spaghetti
   sauce

1 (8 oz.) pkg. (2 c.)
   shredded Mozzarella
2 Tbsp. grated Parmesan
   cheese

Cut eggplants crosswise into slices ¾ inch thick. Mix bread crumbs and oregano in small bowl. Brush eggplant on one side with mayonnaise and coat that side with crumb-oregano mixture. In shallow casserole, arrange eggplant, crumb side up, overlapping slices. Cover with waxed paper and cook in microwave oven on HIGH for 12 to 15 minutes or until tender.

Heat spaghetti sauce 1 to 3 minutes on HIGH until hot. Sprinkle 1½ cups Mozzarella over eggplant and spoon sauce over all. Top with rest of Mozzarella and then Parmesan. Microwave on HIGH 2 to 4 minutes until cheese melts. Yield: 6 servings.

Substitutions: Six small zucchini (about 6 ounces each) can be substituted for eggplant. Cut zucchini in halves lengthwise. Prepare as for eggplant and cook on HIGH 8 to 10 minutes; drain liquid if necessary. Continue as with eggplant.

Meat addition: Place ½ pound ground meat in colander placed in a dish which will collect the fat from the meat. Microwave on HIGH 2½ to 3½ minutes. Pour over eggplant before adding cheese.

# FRIED TARO

1 lb. raw taro
3 to 4 Tbsp. butter or
   margarine

2 to 3 Tbsp. sugar
   (optional)

Microwave taro on HIGH for 10 to 12 minutes per pound. Peel skin off taro when cool. Rinse and pat dry with paper towels. Preheat browning dish for 4 to 6 minutes or according to manufacturer's instructions. Cut taro in half lengthwise. Cut into ½ inch slices (half moon shapes). Place butter or margarine in browning dish. Place taro in browning dish. Stir quickly to brown. Microwave 2 to 3 minutes. Turn taro over. Microwave on HIGH for 1 to 2 minutes. Place taro on serving dish.

Optional: Sprinkle taro with sugar before serving. Makes 4 to 6 servings.

# LIMA BEANS AN

Use 1 package (1 pound) large lima beans. Soak overnight or several hours. Take outer skin off. Add water and cook until soft. Squeeze out as much of the water as possible, using rice bag or dish cloth.

Add 2½ to 2¾ cups granulated sugar. Mix well. Microwave, mixing every few minutes, for 25 minutes (may set microwave for 5 minutes at a time). May be ready to stop after 20 minutes of cooking at HIGH, if water had been squeezed out well.

Cool and make into balls. The size depends on size of manju you want to prepare. Will freeze well and may be kept for several months. Thaw before filling the manju or mochi. Yield: Approximately 60 balls.

*Mabel Ito*

# QUICK CHOW MEIN

2 pkg. chow mein noodles
½ lb. char siu, sliced
½ bunch watercress,
    washed, drained, and
    cut into 1 inch lengths

½ pkg. bean sprouts,
    washed and drained
½ bunch green onion, cut
    in 1 inch lengths
1 small onion, sliced

Sauce:

½ c. peanut oil
2 Tbsp. soy sauce

2 Tbsp. oyster sauce
½ tsp. garlic powder

Combine chow mein noodles and remaining ingredients in a glass casserole dish and mix lightly together. Combine sauce ingredients in a jar and shake thoroughly. Pour over chow mein ingredients and mix lightly. Cover dish with plastic wrap and micro-wave on HIGH for 6 to 8 minutes or until heated through. Makes 4 to 6 servings.

# STUFFED EGGPLANT

3 medium size round
  eggplants
1 lb. lean pork, ground
1 (5 oz.) can water
  chestnuts, chopped

1 tsp. soy sauce
1½ tsp. cornstarch
1 Tbsp. minced green
  onion

Cut the eggplants in halves lengthwise. Scoop out the pulp from the center, leaving a ½ inch of pulp around the shell. Chop pulp and combine with the meat mixture. Combine with the remaining ingredients; mix well. Fill the halved eggplants with the meat mixture. Place the filled shells, meat side up, in a 13x9 inch glass baking dish. Pour Teriyaki Sauce over the eggplants. Cover with plastic wrap. Microwave on HIGH for 20 minutes or until done. Let stand, covered, 5 minutes before serving.

Teriyaki Sauce:

⅓ c. soy sauce
2 Tbsp. sugar

1 Tbsp. water
2½ tsp. cornstarch

Combine ingredients in a glass measuring cup. Microwave on HIGH for 3 minutes, stirring occasionally until thick. Pour over stuffed eggplants. Serves 4 to 6 people.

# SPECIAL DIETARY NEEDS

# HEART HEALTHY TIPS
## Substitutions, Modifications and Equivalents

| Instead of | Use | Instead of | Use |
|---|---|---|---|
| 1 c. butter<br>498 mg cholesterol | ⅞ c. polyunsaturated oil-0 mg cholesterol<br>1 c. tub margarine- 0 mg cholesterol<br>2 stks margarine- 0 mg cholesterol | 1 c. whole milk yogurt, plain- 250 calories | 1 c. part skim milk yogurt, plain- 125-145 calories |
| | | 1 c. sour cream- 416 calories | 1 c. blended low-fat cottage cheese- 208 calories |
| 1 c. heavy cream- 832 calories, 296 mg cholesterol | 1 c. evap. skim milk- 176 calories 8 mg cholesterol | 1 oz. baking chocolate 8.4 gm sat. fat | 3 Tbsp. cocoa powder- 1.7 gm sat. fat PLUS |
| 1 md whole egg- 274 mg cholesterol | ¼ c. egg sub- 0 mg cholesterol* | | 1 Tbsp. polyunsaturated oil - 1.1 gm sat. fat TOTAL: 2.8 gm sat. fat |

*Some egg substitutes do contain cholesterol. Check label to be sure.

## To Reduce Cholesterol or Saturated Fats:

1. Select lean cuts of meat.
2. Serve moderate portions.
3. Replace animal fats with appropriate substitutes.

### Examples

| Instead of | Use |
|---|---|
| Butter, lard, bacon or bacon fat, and chicken fat | Polyunsaturated margarine or oil |
| Sour cream | Low-fat yogurt |
| Whole milk | Skim milk |
| Whole milk cheeses | Low-fat cheeses |
| Whole eggs | Egg whites or egg substitutes |

## To Reduce Calories or Fats:

1. Brown meat by broiling or cooking in non-stick pans with little or no oil.
2. Chill soups, stews, sauces, and broths. Lift off congealed fat (saves 100 calories per Tbsp. of fat removed).
3. Trim fat from meat. Also remove skin from poultry.
4. Use water-packed canned products (canned fish, canned fruits).
5. In recipes for baked products, the sugar can often be reduced ¼ to ⅓ without harming the final product. Cinnamon and vanilla also give the impression of sweetness.
6. Use fresh fruit whenever possible. If canned fruit must be used, select water-packed varieties, fruit in own juice, or drain heavy syrup from canned fruit.
7. For sauces and dressings, use low-calorie bases (vinegar, mustard, tomato juice, fat-free bouillon) instead of high calorie ones (creams, fats, oils, mayonnaise).

## Equivalents for Sugar Substitutes

| Brand Name | Amount | Substitution for Sugar |
|---|---|---|
| Adolph's Powder | 1 tsp. | = ¼ c. |
| | 4 tsp. | = 1 c. |
| Equal Powder | 1 pkt. | = 2 tsp. |
| Sweet N'Low Powder | 1 pkt. | = 2 tsp. |
| | 1 tsp. | = ¼ c. |
| | 4 tsp. | = 1 c. |
| Sweet N'Low Brown | 4 tsp. | = 1 c. brown sugar |
| Sugar Twin Powder | 1 tsp. | = 1 tsp. |
| Sugar Twin Brown Powder | 1 tsp. | = 1 tsp. brown sugar |
| Sweet-10 Liquid | 10 drops | = 1 tsp. |
| | 2 Tbsp. | = 1 c. |

# SPECIAL DIETARY NEEDS

## LEAN-EATING HINTS

1. Brighten and add spice to your meals and parties: Select a variety of vegetables and fruits to add color and spunk to your meals. Fresh herbs and seasonings like parsley, Chinese parsley, basil, ginger, green onions, and lemon juice add zest to your dishes; use them whenever you can.

2. Be selective and try these lower fat alternatives:

**Nonfat yogurt (in place of mayonnaise and sour cream)**
**Mock sour cream (see recipe in this booklet)**

**Whipped evaporated skim milk (in place of regular whipped cream - see recipe in this booklet)**

3. Remember these dietary guidelines: *30% or less* of your calories should come from fat. Keep your cholesterol intake *below 300 ml* per day. *Choose lean!*

| Food | Measure | Weight grams | Cholesterol milligrams |
|---|---|---|---|
| **Bread** | | | |
| Bread, white | 1 slice | 25 | 1 |
| Biscuit, baking powder (VF) | 2 (2" diameter) | 70 | 3 |
| Coffeecake, rich (VF) | | | |
|     Butter and sugar topping | 4½" x 4½" | 70 | 21 |
| Doughnut (VF), fried in (L) | 1 | 32 | 27 |
| French toast | | | |
|     Grilled, 1 teaspoon butter | 1 slice | 55 | 144 |
|     Grilled, 1 teaspoon margarine | 1 slice | 55 | 130 |
| Muffin (MF) | 2" diameter | 35 | 19 |
| Pancake (VF) | 2 (4" diameter) | 90 | 110 |
| Sweet roll (L) | 1 average | 55 | 38 |
| Waffle (VF) | 5½" diameter | 75 | 128 |
| **Dairy Products** | | | |
| Cheese | | | |
|     American processed | 1 slice (3½" square) | 30 | 44 |
|     Cheddar | 1 cubic inch | 30 | 30 |
|     Cottage cheese, creamed | ½ cup | 50 | 8 |
|     Cream | 2 tablespoons | 30 | 36 |
| Cream | | | |
|     Light, 20% | 2 tablespoons | 30 | 20 |
|     Heavy, 35%, whipped | 2 tablespoons | 15 | 18 |
| Egg | 1 medium | 50 | 225 |
| Milk | | | |
|     Skim | 1 cup | 240 | 7 |
|     Whole | 1 cup | 240 | 26 |
| Yogurt | 1 cup | 240 | 27 |
| **Seafoods** | | | |
| Crab, meat only | ¼ cup | 42 | 55 |
| Fish (cod, flounder, haddock, | | | |
|     halibut, mackerel, salmon) | 4 ounces | 120 | 76 |
| Frog | 2 to 3 large legs | 100 | 40 |
| Lobster | ¼ cup | 42 | 84 |
| Oysters | 5 medium | 90 | 294 |
| Sardines, canned | 1 (3"x1½"x1") | 50 | 35 |
| Shrimp, canned, dry pack | 4 to 6 shrimps | 50 | 75 |
| Tuna, canned, drained solids | ¼ cup | 50 | 30 |
| **Meat and Poultry** | | | |
| Beef, round, medium fat | 4 ounces | 120 | 150 |
| Brains, all kinds | 3 ounces | 90 | 2012 |
| Chicken, fryer | | | |
|     Breast (without bone) | 4 ounces | 120 | 108 |
|     Leg (without bone) | 4 ounces | 120 | 72 |

| Food | Measure | Weight grams | Cholesterol milligrams |
|---|---|---|---|
| **Meat and Poultry,** *continued* | | | |
| Duck | 4 ounces | 120 | 84 |
| Ham, pan broiled | 4 ounces | 120 | 84-126 |
| Heart, raw | 4 ounces | 120 | 180 |
| Kidneys, raw | 4 ounces | 120 | 450 |
| Lamb | 4 ounces | 120 | 84 |
| Liver, beef | 4 ounces | 120 | 384 |
| Liver, calves | 4 ounces | 120 | 432 |
| Pork | 4 ounces | 120 | 72 |
| Prem (canned luncheon meat) | 4 ounces | 120 | 140-210 |
| Rabbit | 4 ounces | 120 | 96 |
| Sweet breads | 4 ounces | 120 | 336 |
| Turkey, dark meat | 4 ounces | 120 | 19-31 |
| Turkey, light meat | 4 ounces | 120 | 10-18 |
| Tripe, beef | 1 piece (5"x2½") | 85 | 128 |
| Veal leg | 4 ounces | 120 | 168 |
| | | | |
| **Desserts** | | | |
| Cake, white, plain (VF) | 1 piece (3"x3"x1") | 60 | 41 |
| Cake, fudge (VF) | 1 piece (3"x2"x2") | 45 | 34 |
| Cake, if fudge frosted, add | | 10 | 2 |
| Cookies, sugar (B) | 3" diameter | 20 | 23 |
| Cookies, sugar (VF) | 3" diameter | 20 | 10 |
| Custard, baked | ½ cup | 126 | 151 |
| Ice cream, vanilla | ½ cup | 70 | 30 |
| Pie, cream filling (B), crust (VF) | One-sixth of 8" | 160 | 131 |
| Pie, fruit filling (B), crust (VF) | One-sixth of 8" | 160 | 13 |
| | | | |
| **Fats** | | | |
| Butter | 1 teaspoon | 5 | 14 |
| Bacon, cooked | 2 slices | 16 | 16 |
| Bacon, fat | 1 tablespoon | 14 | 26 |
| Hydrogenated vegetable shortening | 1 tablespoon | 13 | ... |
| Lard | 1 tablespoon | 14 | 15 |
| Margarine | 1 teaspoon | 5 | 3 |
| Mayonnaise (cottonseed oil) | 1 tablespoon | 14 | 11 |
| Vegetable oils (coconut, corn, cottonseed, olive, peanut, soybean) | 1 tablespoon | 14 | ... |
| White sauce, medium (B) | ¼ cup | 66 | 28 |
| White sauce, medium (M) | ¼ cup | 66 | 8 |

Abbreviations:

MF — Mixed hydrogenated animal and vegetable shortening
VF — Hydrogenated vegetable shortening
B — Butter
L — Lard
M — Margarine

# 15 METHODS OF PREPARING FOOD
# TO REDUCE CHOLESTEROL

1. Steam, boil, or bake vegetables, or for a change, stir-fry in a small amount of vegetable oil.

2. Season vegetables with herbs and spices rather than with sauces, butter, or margarine.

3. Try lemon juice on salads or use limited amounts of oil-based salad dressing.

4. To reduce saturated fat, use margarine instead of butter in baked products and when possible, use oil instead of shortening.

5. Try whole grain flours to enhance flavors of baked goods made with less fat and cholesterol-containing ingredients.

6. Replace whole milk with skim or lowfat milk in puddings, soups, and baked products.

7. Substitute plain lowfat yogurt, blend-whipped lowfat cottage cheese, or buttermilk in recipes that call for sour cream or mayonnaise.

8. Choose lean cuts of meats.

9. Trim fat from meats before and/or after cooking.

10. Roast, bake, broil, or simmer meat, poultry, or fish.

11. Remove skin from poultry before cooking.

12. Cook meat or poultry on a rack so the fat will drain off. Use a nonstick pan for cooking so added fat will be unnecessary.

13. Chill meat or poultry broth until the fat becomes solid. Spoon off the fat before using the broth.

14. Limit egg yolks to 1 per serving when making scrambled eggs. Use additional egg whites for larger servings.

15. Try substituting egg whites in recipes calling for whole egg. For example, use 2 egg whites in place of each whole egg in muffins, cookies, and puddings.

# GUIDELINES FOR LOW CHOLESTEROL, LOW TRIGLYCERIDE DIETS

Foods to use -

Meat, fish: Choose lean meats (chicken, turkey, veal, and nonfatty cuts of beef with excess fat trimmed (1 serving equals 3 ounces of cooked meat). Also fresh or frozen fish, canned fish packed in water, and shellfish (lobster, crab, shrimp, oysters). Limit use to no more than 1 serving of these per week. Shellfish are high in cholesterol but low in saturated fat and should be used sparingly. Meats and fish should be broiled (pan or oven) or baked on a rack.

Eggs: Egg substitutes and egg whites (use freely). Egg yolks (limit 2 per week).

Fruits: Eat 3 servings of fresh fruit per day (1 serving equals ½ cup). Be sure to have at least 1 citrus fruit daily. Frozen or canned fruit with no sugar or syrup added may be used.

Vegetables: Most vegetables are not limited (see *Foods to avoid*). One dark green (string beans, escarole) or 1 deep yellow (squash) vegetable is recommended daily. Cauliflower, broccoli, and celery, as well as potato skins, are recommended for their fiber content. (Fiber is associated with cholesterol reduction.) It is preferable to steam vegetables, but they may be boiled, strained, or braised with polyunsaturated vegetable oil. (See following.)

Beans: Dried peas or beans (1 serving equals ½ cup) may be used as a bread substitute.

Nuts: Almonds, walnuts, and peanuts may be used sparingly (1 serving equals 1 tablespoonful). Use pumpkin, sesame, or sunflower seeds.

Breads, grains: One roll or 1 slice of whole grain enriched bread may be used, or 3 soda crackers, or 4 pieces of Melba toast as a substitute. Spaghetti, rice, or noodles (½ cup), or ½ large ear of corn may be used as a bread substitute. In preparing

*(Continued on next page)*

*(Continued from previous page)*

these foods, do not use butter or shortening; use soft margarine. Also use egg and sugar substitutes. Choose high fiber grains, such as oats and whole wheat.

Cereals: Use ½ cup of hot cereal or ¾ cup of cold cereal per day. Add a sugar substitute, if desired, with 99% fat free or skim milk.

Milk products: Always use 99% fat free or skim milk, dairy products such as lowfat cheeses (Farmers, uncreamed diet cottage), lowfat yogurt, and powdered skim milk.

Fats, oils: Use soft (not stick) margarine, vegetable oils that are high in polyunsaturated fats (such as safflower, sunflower, soybean, corn, and cottonseed). Always refrigerate meat drippings to harden the fat and remove it before preparing gravies.

Desserts, snacks: Limit to 2 servings per day; substitute each serving for a bread/cereal serving - ice milk, water sherbet (¼ cup), unflavored gelatin or gelatin flavored with sugar substitute (⅓ cup), pudding prepared with skim milk (½ cup), egg white souffles, unbuttered popcorn (1½ cups). Substitute carob for chocolate.

Beverages: Fresh fruit juices (limit 4 ounces per day), black coffee, plain or herbal teas, soft drinks with sugar substitutes, club soda (preferably salt free), cocoa made with skim milk or nonfat dried milk and water (sugar substitute added if desired), clear broth. Alcohol - limit 2 servings per day (see *Foods to avoid.*)

Miscellaneous: You may use the following freely - vinegar, spices, herbs, nonfat bouillon, mustard, Worcestershire sauce, soy sauce, flavoring essence.

Foods to avoid -

Meats, fish: Marbled beef, pork, bacon, sausage, and other pork products, fatty fowl (duck, goose), skin and fat of turkey and chicken, processed meats, luncheon meats (salami, bologna), frankfurters and fast food hamburgers (they're loaded with fat), organ meats (kidneys, liver), canned fish packed in oil.

*(Continued on next page)*

*(Continued from previous page)*

Eggs: Limit egg yolks to 2 per week.

Fruits: Coconuts (rich in saturated fats).

Vegetables: Avoid avocados. Starchy vegetables (potatoes, corn, lima beans, dried peas, beans) may be used *only* if substitutes for a serving of bread or cereal. (Baked potato skin, however, is desirable for its fiber content.)

Beans: Commercial baked beans with sugar and/or pork added.

Nuts: Avoid nuts. Limit peanuts and walnuts to 1 tablespoonful per day.

Breads, grains: Any baked goods with shortening and/or sugar. Commercial mixes with dried eggs and whole milk. Avoid sweet rolls, doughnuts, breakfast pastries (Danish), and sweetened packaged cereals (the added sugar converts readily to triglycerides).

Milk products: Whole milk and whole milk packaged goods, cream, ice cream, whole milk puddings, yogurt, or cheeses, nondairy cream substitutes.

Fats, oils: Butter, lard, animal fats, bacon drippings, gravies, cream sauces, as well as palm and coconut oils. All these are high in saturated fats. Examine labels on "cholesterol free" products for "hydrogenated fats." (These are oils that have been hardened into solids and in the process have become saturated.)

Desserts, snacks: Fried snack foods like potato chips, chocolate, candies in general, jams, jellies, syrups, whole milk puddings, ice cream, and milk sherbets, hydrogenated peanut butter.

Beverages: Sugared fruit juices and soft drinks, cocoa made with whole milk and/or sugar. When using alcohol (1 ounce liquor, 5 ounces beer, or 2½ ounces dry table wine per serving), 1 serving must be substituted for 1 bread or cereal serving (limit of 2 servings of alcohol per day).

*(Continued on next page)*

*(Continued from previous page)*

Special notes:

1. Remember that even nonlimited foods should be used in moderation.

2. While on a cholesterol-lowering diet, be sure to avoid animal fats and marbled meats.

3. While on triglyceride-lowering diet, be sure to avoid sweets and to control the amount of carbohydrates you eat (starch foods such as flour, bread, potatoes).

4. Buy a good lowfat cookbook, such as the one published by the American Heart Association.

5. Consult your physician if you have any questions.

## ASPARAGUS CHICKEN

12 oz. chicken breast
  (boneless and
  skinless)
2 lb. fresh asparagus
1 c. Island fresh onion
1 (8 oz.) ctn. fresh
  mushrooms
2 Tbsp. oil
3 Tbsp. oyster sauce

1. Clean and parboil asparagus. Cut into 1 inch pieces.

2. Remove any visible fat from chicken and cut into bite-size pieces.

3. Heat oil and brown chicken.

4. Add onions and stir-fry for 2 to 3 minutes.

5. Add mushrooms and asparagus and stir-fry for 2 to 3 minutes.

6. Add oyster sauce and mix well. Makes 8 servings.

*Patricia Kubo*

# CHICKEN AND BROWN RICE TOSS

¼ c. reduced calorie
   mayonnaise
¼ c. reduced calorie Italian
   dressing
3 c. cooked brown rice
12 oz. cooked skinless,
   boneless Island
   Fresh chicken, cubed
   (2 c.)

½ c. Island fresh celery,
   sliced
2 Tbsp. Island Fresh green
   onion, sliced
Lettuce leaves

1. Thoroughly mix mayonnaise and Italian dressing.
2. Toss together rice, chicken, celery, green onion, and mayonnaise mixture.
3. Cover and chill.
4. Serve in a lettuce-lined salad bowl. Makes 5 servings.

*Michelle Saladino*

# WHERE'S THE BEEF STEW

1½ lb. turkey tenderloin, cubed
3 medium cooking potatoes, peeled and cut into bite-size pieces
1 large carrot, cut into bite-size pieces
1 stalk celery, cut into bite-size pieces
1 small onion, peeled and chopped
1 (14½ oz.) can stewed tomatoes, chopped (reserve liquid)
½ c. ketchup
½ tsp. Island Fresh basil
½ tsp. Island Fresh tarragon
½ tsp. Island Fresh cinnamon
1 medium bay leaf
1 Tbsp. Island Fresh chopped parsley
Salt and pepper to taste
Garlic powder to taste

1. Brown turkey in a nonstick pan coated with cooking spray.
2. Combine with potatoes, carrot, celery, onion, and tomatoes in a 5 quart crock pot.
3. Combine reserved tomato liquid, ketchup, herbs, and spices.
4. Pour over contents in a crock pot. Add water to barely cover vegetables and meat. Stir thoroughly.
5. Cook on HIGH heat for 2½ hours, then on LOW for 5 hours or until tender, stirring occasionally.
6. Serve alone or on rice. Makes 6 servings.

*Christine Grear*

# TURKEY POT ROAST

2 turkey thighs or 2
   hindquarters (about 2
   to 3 lb.)
1 tsp. salt
1¼ tsp. pepper
½ c. chopped round onions
2 cloves garlic, minced
½ tsp. dried basil leaves

1 can chicken broth
3 medium potatoes, pared
   and cut into halves
6 medium carrots, pared
   and cut into chunks
1 Tbsp. cornstarch
¼ c. water
2 Tbsp. chopped parsley

1. Preheat oven to 450°F.
2. Remove skin from turkey. Sprinkle with salt and pepper.
3. Place turkey in pan and roast for 25 minutes.
4. Drain off fat.
5. Add onions, garlic, basil, and broth.
6. Lower oven temperature to 375°F.
7. Cover and roast for 30 minutes.
8. Add potatoes and carrots; cook for 20 more minutes or until vegetables are tender.
9. Remove turkey and vegetables.
10. Skim fat from pan juices. Discard fat.
11. Mix cornstarch and water; stir into pan juices.
12. Cook, stirring constantly, until sauce is thickened.
13. Pour over sliced meat and vegetables.
14. Sprinkle with chopped parsley

# FISH SABAW

4 c. water
1 medium Island Fresh
  onion
1 large tomato
1 inch piece Island Fresh
  ginger root
1 stalk Island Fresh lemon
  grass
1 tsp. patis (Filipino fish
  sauce, optional)

½ tsp. (red rock) salt
1 akule, opelu, or any
  Island Fresh fish
Green onion or marungay
  leaves
Chili pepper leaves or
  spinach leaves
  (optional)

1. Bring water, onion, tomato, ginger, and lemon grass to a rolling boil.

2. Reduce heat to low and simmer until vegetables are tender.

3. Add patis, rock salt, and fish; cook on medium heat until fish is done.

4. Reduce heat and simmer 2 minutes. Remove from heat and, if desired, add green onion or marungay leaves or chili pepper leaves or spinach leaves.

*Josephine Endrina*

# LASAGNA SEAFOOD ROLL-UPS

**6 lasagna noodles**
**1 (15 oz.) bottle spaghetti**
   **sauce without meat**

    Filling:

**8 oz. imitation crab flakes**
**1 c. lowfat Ricotta cheese**
**¼ c. grated Parmesan**
   **cheese**

**1 egg**
**1 Tbsp. Island Fresh fresh**
   **or dried parsley**
**¼ tsp. onion powder**

1. Cook lasagna noodles according to package directions; rinse in cold water and drain well.

2. Thoroughly combine filling ingredients. Spread ⅓ cup of filling on each noodle; roll tightly and place, seam side down, in a 9 inch square baking pan.

3. Pour prepared spaghetti sauce over roll-ups; bake covered in 375° oven for 30 minutes.

*Erinn Morishita*

# SIMMERED ONAGA WITH SOMEN NOODLES

2½ lb. red or pink snapper
    fillets
2 c. water
½ c. low salt shoyu
⅓ c. shoyu
2½ Tbsp. sake
¼ c. sugar
1 Tbsp. shredded bonito
    flakes

3 Tbsp. Island Fresh green
    onion, chopped
2 tsp. Island Fresh ginger
    root, minced
1 tsp. garlic powder
2 tsp. rice vinegar
5 c. cooked somen noodles
1 Tbsp. diluted cornstarch

1. Prepare somen noodles as directed. Cool in ice water.
2. In a large skillet, combine all ingredients, except fish.
3. Bring the sauce to a boil.
4. Reduce the heat to a low simmer and add the fish fillets.
5. Cover the skillet and simmer for 15 minutes or until fish is done.
6. Remove the fish and continue to cook the sauce.
7. Add cornstarch paste to slightly thicken sauce.
8. Place fish over somen noodles and pour some sauce over noodles and fish.

Reduce the fat by simmering fish instead of frying in oil. Makes 6 servings.

*Claire Doi*

# TOFU-TUNA SPREAD

1 (20 oz.) block tofu,
    drained
1 can water packed tuna,
    well drained
¼ c. pickle relish

1 stalk celery, chopped
1 stalk green onion,
    chopped
2 Tbsp. mustard
Salt and pepper to taste

1. Mash tofu with fork.
2. Mix in other ingredients.

Serve on whole grain bread, crackers, flour tortillas, or in pita bread with vegetables such as lettuce, tomatoes, and alfalfa sprouts. Add salsa for spicier flavor. Makes approximately 4 cups.

# TOFU, TUNA, TOMATO DELIGHT

1 block tofu
1 can tuna
1 large Island Fresh
    tomato, diced

1 small Island Fresh onion,
    chopped
½ c. Island Fresh green
    onion, chopped

Dressing:

1 Tbsp. salad oil
⅓ c. low sodium soy sauce

¼ tsp. garlic powder

1. Place tofu in a large platter, cut into cubes.
2. Top with tuna, tomato, onion, and green onion.
3. Combine dressing ingredients and mix well. Pour over salad just before serving. Makes 8 servings.

*Kimberly Hew*

# TUNA-TOFU PATTIES

1 (20 oz.) block firm tofu,
    drained
1 can water packed tuna
1 egg

¼ c. carrots, grated
¼ c. green onion, chopped
Salt and pepper to taste

1. Mash tofu with fork.
2. Add all other ingredients.
3. Shape into 1½ inch diameter patties.
4. Heat nonstick pan well. Add 1 tablespoon oil. Heat.
5. Fry patties until brown and firm.
6. Serve on bed of shredded leaf lettuce.

To add zest, add 1 teaspoon finely grated ginger.

# BANANA BREAD - FAT FREE

½ c. applesauce
¾ c. sugar
2 eggs
1 c. all-purpose flour
1 tsp. baking soda
½ tsp. salt
1 c. whole wheat flour
3 large ripe bananas, mashed
1 tsp. vanilla extract
½ c. walnuts, coarsely chopped

Preheat oven to 350°. Spray a 9x5x3 inch bread pan with vegetable spray. Beat applesauce and sugar until light. Add eggs, 1 at a time, beating well after each addition. Sift all-purpose flour, baking soda, and salt together. Stir in whole wheat flour and add to first mixture, mixing well. Fold in mashed bananas, vanilla, and walnuts. Pour mixture into the prepared pan. Bake for 50 to 60 minutes or until a cake tester inserted in the center comes out clean. Cool in pan for 10 minutes, then turn onto rack.

*Marlene Curtis*

# ZUCCHINI BREAD - FAT FREE

3 eggs
1¼ c. applesauce
1½ c. sugar
1 tsp. vanilla
2 c. grated raw zucchini
2 c. all-purpose flour
2 tsp. baking soda
1 tsp. baking powder
1 tsp. salt
1 tsp. ground cinnamon
1 tsp. ground cloves
1 c. walnuts, chopped

Preheat oven to 350°F. Spray a 9x5 inch loaf pan with vegetable spray. Beat eggs, applesauce, sugar, and vanilla until light and thick. Fold grated zucchini into mixture. Sift dry ingredients together. Stir into zucchini mixture until just blended. Fold in the walnuts.

Pour batter into loaf pan. Bake on middle rack of the oven for 1 hour and 15 minutes, or until a cake tester inserted in the center comes out clean. Cool slightly; remove from pan and cool completely on a rack.

*Marlene Curtis*

# FRUIT COMPOTE FOR THE CAJUN VEAL LOIN AND YAM PANCAKES

Fruit Compote:

4 large Island Fresh guavas
1 yellow Island Fresh
　papaya
2 ripe Island Fresh
　mangoes
3 oz. Island Fresh honey
1 tsp. white wine vinegar or
　juice from 1 whole
　lemon

1 Tbsp. coarsely ground
　black pepper
4 pieces Island Fresh green
　onion, thinly sliced
Salt to taste

1. Peel and remove seeds from guava, papaya, and mango; dice into medium size cubes. Set aside.

2. In a heavy saucepan, bring the honey and white wine vinegar to a boil, then add the diced fruits.

3. Bring to a boil again and turn off the heat and transfer the mixture into a mixing bowl.

4. Add the black pepper and mix until combined; cool bowl over ice.

5. When mixture is cooled, add green onion and season to taste. Set aside until ready to serve. Makes 3 servings.

# OAT BRAN APPLESAUCE MUFFINS

2¼ c. oat bran
¼ c. chopped nuts
¼ c. raisins
1 Tbsp. baking powder
1 Tbsp. cinnamon
½ c. skim milk

1½ c. unsweetened
  applesauce
2 Tbsp. oil
2 egg whites
¼ c. brown sugar or honey

1. Combine oat bran, nuts, raisins, baking powder, and cinnamon. Set aside.
2. Mix milk, applesauce, egg whites, and oil together.
3. Stir in brown sugar or honey. Mix well.
4. Combine with dry ingredients and mix.
5. Pour into individual muffin tins.
6. Bake at 425° for 15 to 17 minutes. Makes 12 muffins.

Note: Pumpkin may be substituted for applesauce.

# APPLE CRISP IN A JIFFY

8 Granny Smith apples,
  peeled, cored, and
  cut into 1 inch pieces
¼ c. fresh lemon juice
1 Tbsp. cornstarch
3 Tbsp. frozen apple juice
  concentrate, thawed
¼ tsp. ground nutmeg

¼ tsp. ground allspice
¼ tsp. ground cinnamon
⅔ c. dark raisins
3 Tbsp. vegetable oil
1⅓ c. 100% bran
⅔ c. walnuts
½ c. brown sugar

1. Toss apple pieces with lemon juice in microwave-safe and ovenproof 13x9 inch rectangular dish. Set aside.

2. Mix cornstarch and apple juice concentrate until smooth.

3. Gradually mix in nutmeg, allspice, and cinnamon until mixture is smooth.

4. Pour over reserved apples. Stir in raisins. Mix well.

5. Cover tightly with microwave-safe plastic wrap. Microwave at FULL power (100%) for 15 minutes, stirring twice during the cooking time.

6. Pierce plastic wrap to release steam. Carefully uncover.

7. Combine oil, bran, walnuts, and sugar in food processor. Whirl until nuts are coarsely chopped.

8. Sprinkle nut mixture evenly over apples.

9. To serve, broil Apple Crisp 5 to 6 inches from source of heat for 2 to 3 minutes or until lightly browned. Makes 18 servings.

# APRICOT TOFU PIE

Crust:

5 (2½ x 5 inch) whole wheat graham crackers
3 Tbsp. whole wheat flour
3 Tbsp. wheat germ

½ tsp. ground cinnamon
2 Tbsp. oil
1½ Tbsp. Island Fresh honey

Filling:

1 (6 oz.) pkg. dried apricot halves
2½ c. cold water
1 lb. soft tofu (about 1½ c.)

1 tsp. vanilla extract
½ c. Island Fresh honey
1 tsp. powdered sugar (or kanten)

Glaze:

1 Tbsp. Island Fresh honey
1 Tbsp. water or white wine vinegar

Few drops of almond extract or peach or apricot brandy

To make crust:

1. In a food processor, process graham crackers, flour, wheat germ, and cinnamon until crackers are ground finely.

2. Add oil and honey during last stages of processing to make a dough.

3. Press dough into well greased 9½ inch pie pan.

4. Bake at 375° for 8 minutes or until edges turn slightly browned.

To make filling:

1. Cook dried apricots in 1½ cups of the water until soft but not mushy.

2. Reserve 9 apricot halves for garnish. Continue simmering remaining ingredients until all water is absorbed.

3. With electric or rotary beater, blend tofu, half at a time, with vanilla.

4. In a small saucepan, combine remaining 1 cup of water and ½ cup honey; mix well and sprinkle powdered agar over mixture.

*(Continued on next page)*

*(Continued from previous page)*

5. Let agar soften; bring mixture to a rolling boil and cook for 30 seconds.

6. Remove agar mixture from heat and cool 5 to 8 minutes.

7. Place apricots and tofu in food processor. Process while slowly adding agar mixture; process a few seconds longer.

8. Refrigerate filling 15 to 20 minutes. Pour filling into cooled crust and chill until firm.

To garnish:

1. Place 9 reserved apricot halves in small saucepan with glaze ingredients.

2. Heat for a few minutes.

3. Garnish pie with glazed apricots and mint leaves for color. Makes 16 servings.

*Gladys Horner*

# STRAWBERRY PIE

Crust:

**1½ c. flour**
**6 Tbsp. margarine**

**6 Tbsp. sugar**

Filling:

**2 (3 oz.) boxes strawberry
  flavored gelatin**
**2½ c. boiling water**
**1 lb. frozen or whole
  strawberries**

**3 (8 oz.) ctn. unflavored
  lowfat yogurt**

1. Mix ingredients for crust with a fork until crumbly.
2. Press into a 9x13 inch pan.
3. Bake at 350° for 10 to 15 minutes.
4. Dissolve gelatin in 2½ cups boiling water and chill until slightly thickened.
5. Measure ¾ cup of gelatin and fold into yogurt.
6. Spread this mixture over baked and cooled crust. Chill until firm.
7. Add strawberries on top of yogurt mixture and pour remaining gelatin over strawberries.
8. Refrigerate until set.

Reduce fat content by reducing the amount of margarine. The whipped cream for the filling was replaced with lowfat yogurt. Makes 24 servings.

*Erinn Morishita*

# CUBAN CARAMEL FLAN

1 (8 oz.) container
   refrigerated or frozen
   egg product, thawed
1 (14 oz.) can lowfat
   sweetened
   condensed milk

1 (12 oz.) can evaporated
   skim milk
½ c. skim milk
8 tsp. dark corn syrup

Whisk together egg product, condensed milk, evaporated milk, and skim milk in a bowl. Pour *1 teaspoon* of corn syrup into each of 8 individual ramekins, 6 ounce custard cups, or disposable foil cups to coat the bottom. Pour about *1/2 cup* egg mixture into each. Place cups in a large baking pan; fill pan with 1 inch of water. Place entire dish in a 325° oven and bake about 50 minutes or till a knife inserted near center comes out clean. Remove cups from baking pan; cool. Refrigerate for at least 1 hour before serving. Serve in cups. Or run a knife or spatula around edge of cups or ramekins to loosen; invert onto serving plates. Makes 8 servings.

For 1 large flan, pour all of dark corn syrup (about 3 tablespoons) into the bottom of a 9 x 1½ inch round baking pan. Place pan inside a large rectangular baking pan or roasting pan. Pour egg mixture into round pan. Fill rectangular pan with 1 inch of hot water. Bake in a 325° oven for 50 to 55 minutes or till a knife inserted near center comes out clean. Chill and serve as preceding.

# RICH MOIST FRUIT CAKE

½ c. grated apples
1 c. grated carrots
1 c. raisins (may use part
    prunes)
½ c. honey
½ c. chopped dates
1 tsp. cinnamon
1 tsp. allspice

½ tsp. nutmeg
¼ tsp. ground cloves
1½ c. water
1½ c. whole wheat flour
1 tsp. baking soda
½ c. bran (Miller's
    unprocessed bran)
½ c. chopped walnuts

1. Cook apples, carrots, raisins, dates, honey, and spices in water for 10 minutes. Cool.
2. Mix together flour, baking soda, bran, and walnuts.
3. Add to carrot mixture. Mix together well.
4. Pour into lightly oiled or nonstick loaf pan or 9x9 inch baking dish.
5. Bake at 325° for 45 minutes. Makes 16 servings.

# STRAWBERRY AND BANANA FREEZE

1 c. frozen whole
    unsweetened
    strawberries

2 small ripe bananas
½ c. evaporated skim milk
½ tsp. vanilla

1. Peel ripe bananas and wrap in plastic and freeze until firm.
2. Slice frozen bananas into ½ inch pieces.
3. Combine evaporated skim milk and banana in a blender. Add frozen strawberries, 1 at a time, and blenderize.
4. Spoon into dessert dishes. Serve immediately. Makes 5 (½ cup) servings.

# FRENCH DRESSING (LOW SALT)

⅓ c. lite mayonnaise
3 tsp. vinegar
1½ c. Saffola salad oil
½ c. lite ketchup
1 tsp. mustard (prepared)

½ c. sugar
1 tsp. Mrs. Dash steak
    sauce
1½ tsp. pepper
2 tsp. lemon juice

Combine all ingredients and refrigerate.

# MOCK SOUR CREAM

**1 c. lowfat cottage cheese**     **2 Tbsp. skim milk**
**1 Tbsp. lemon juice**

1. Mix in blender until smooth.
2. Use as substitute for sour cream in all of your favorite recipes. Goes well with baked potatoes too! Makes 1¼ cups.

# WHIPPED EVAPORATED SKIM MILK

**1 c. evaporated skim milk**     **2 tsp. lemon juice**

1. Chill 1 cup of evaporated skim milk in a metal bowl until ice crystals begin to form.
2. Whip milk with lemon juice at high speed until tripled in volume. Makes 3 cups.

# VEGETARIAN

## BRAZILIAN BLACK BEANS

Each serving of this full-flavored combo provides ¼ of the fiber, ½ of the vitamin C, and ¾ of the vitamin A you need for the day, plus enough protein to make it a main dish. *Now that's nutritious!*

8 oz. dry black beans (1⅛ c.)
3 c. water
½ c. chopped onion
2 cloves garlic, minced
1 bay leaf
¼ c. snipped parsley
½ tsp. salt
½ tsp. crushed red pepper
3 c. water
1 medium sweet potato, halved lengthwise and sliced ¼ inch thick

1 (16 oz.) can diced tomatoes
½ tsp. finely shredded orange peel
3 c. hot cooked rice
Shredded kale, spinach, or flat-leaf parsley (optional)

Rinse beans. In a large saucepan, combine beans and enough water to cover. Bring to boiling; reduce heat. Simmer for 2 minutes. Remove from heat. Cover; let stand for 1 hour. (Or, soak beans in water in a large saucepan. Cover; set in a cool place for 6 to 8 hours or overnight.)

Drain beans in a colander; rinse. Return beans to the saucepan. Stir in onion, garlic, bay leaf, parsley, salt, and red pepper. Stir in 3 cups fresh water. Bring to boiling; reduce heat. Cover and simmer about 1½ hours or till beans are tender, adding more water, if necessary, and stirring occasionally.

Meanwhile, cook sweet potato in boiling salted water to cover for 15 to 20 minutes or till tender; drain.

Remove bay leaf from beans; discard. Add tomatoes to bean mixture. Uncover and simmer for 15 to 20 minutes more or till a thick gravy forms.

# EGGPLANT APPETIZER

3 medium, long eggplants
½ c. chopped onion
¼ c. chopped parsley or
   cilantro
1 clove garlic, pressed or
   minced

1 tsp. shoyu
½ tsp. freshly ground black
   pepper
2 Tbsp. olive oil
2 tsp. fresh lemon or lime
   juice

1. Prick eggplants several times with fork. Place on double thickness paper toweling. Microwave at 100% power for 12 minutes until soft. Remove from oven. Let cool.

2. When eggplant is cool enough to handle, halve lengthwise and scoop out flesh. Place in bowl of food processor or in blender. Add remaining ingredients. Process until coarsely chopped.

3. Serve at room temperature with vegetable dippers.

*Marlene Curtis*

# JAI (MONK'S FOOD)

5 dried mushrooms
¼ c. dry lily flowers
4 water chestnuts (ma tai)
1 c. Chinese cabbage
¼ c. dried fungus
½ c. black seaweed (fat
   choy)
½ small bundle long rice

2 c. (or more) water
1 tsp. gourmet powder
2 cloves garlic
3 Tbsp. Chinese bean curd
   (narm yue)
1 tsp. salt
3 Tbsp. shoyu
2 Tbsp. sugar

Soak and wash mushrooms, lily flowers, and fungus. Drain well and fry in oil and garlic. Add long rice which has been soaked in water and softened for at least 30 minutes and cut into 3 inch lengths. Add the rest of ingredients. Cover pan and simmer for 20 to 30 minutes.

*Red*

# LOWFAT HUMMUS

1 (16 oz.) can garbanzo
   beans (drain and
   save liquid)
2 Tbsp. tahini (sesame
   paste)
2 cloves garlic
Juice of 1 lime
Juice of ½ lemon

⅓ c. coarsely chopped
   parsley
⅓ c. coarsely chopped mint
¼ tsp. dried rosemary
⅛ tsp. cayenne
Salt and fresh ground
   pepper to taste

1. Blend garbanzos, tahini, garlic, and lime and lemon juices. Pulse on and off until coarsely chopped. With processor running, slowly pour enough garbanzo bean liquid to make mixture thick, but spreadable.

2. Add parsley, mint, rosemary, cayenne, and salt and pepper. Pulse until herbs are finely chopped and well distributed. Serve with pita bread wedges, crackers, or vegetable dippers.

*Marlene Curtis*

## NO-EGG VEGETARIAN MAYONNAISE

½ block soft tofu
3 Tbsp. olive oil
Juice of ½ lemon
Pinch of salt
2 cloves fresh garlic,
   pressed or minced
   (optional)

1 tsp. finely minced ginger
   (optional)

1. Process all ingredients in food processor until smooth. Use as you would any mayonnaise.

2. Flavors may be varied by adding mustard, onion, dill, or shoyu to seasonings.

*Marlene Curtis*

# PASTA SALAD

2 heads broccoli
1 bell pepper, chopped
2 stalks green onion
1 carrot, grated

1 bunch parsley, finely
   chopped
1 pkg. rotelle pasta

Dressing:

¼ c. wine vinegar
⅓ c. olive oil

⅔ c. low calorie Italian
   dressing

1. Cook pasta as specified on package. Rinse in cold water. Drain. Place in large bowl.
2. Combine all dressing ingredients in separate bowl.
3. Pour dressing over pasta. Toss.
4. Place pasta in refrigerator.
5. Chop broccoli into bite-size pieces. Dip broccoli into boiling water for 1 minute. Drain and set aside.
6. Chop green pepper in ¾ inch squares. Add to broccoli.
7. Add broccoli, green pepper, and all remaining vegetables to pasta.
8. Toss to coat with dressing.
9. Cover and refrigerate for at least 1 hour before serving.

# PILAF

2 tsp. olive oil
½ c. broken very thin pasta
   (angel hair)
⅔ c. chopped onion
1 c. bulgur
2 c. vegetable broth

¼ tsp. salt (optional)
Black pepper to taste
1 Tbsp. dried basil
¾ c. garbanzo beans
   (about ½ can),
   drained

1. Heat oil in deep saucepan with tight fitting cover. Add pasta and cook over medium heat until golden brown; stir to prevent burning.
2. Add onion and bulgur and cook mixture for 2 minutes. Stir to prevent sticking.
3. Add remaining ingredients; bring pilaf to a boil. Reduce heat to very low. Cover pan and simmer for 20 minutes.

*Helen Tamashiro*

# SHIRA AE - TOFU SAUCE

1 Tbsp. toasted sesame
   seeds
1 Tbsp. miso
1 Tbsp. sugar
½ block tofu

½ tsp. monosodium
   glutamate (optional)
2 konyaku
1 large carrot

Place tofu in a cloth or clean dish towel and squeeze out excess water. Set aside.

Crush sesame seeds in suribachi. Add miso, sugar, tofu, and monosodium glutamate, 1 at a time, blending thoroughly before adding the next ingredient. Cut the konyaku and carrots into fine pieces and boil until tender. Drain. Cool, then add the preceding mixture.

*Green*

# SPICY EGGPLANT

1 lb. eggplant
½ Tbsp. minced garlic
1 Tbsp. minced ginger
½ Tbsp. dry wine or sake
1 Tbsp. hot bean paste
½ Tbsp. chile pepper paste
   (for *hot* recipe)
1 Tbsp. soy sauce

½ tsp. sugar
1 Tbsp. vinegar
2 Tbsp. chopped scallion
½ c. stock
1 tsp. cornstarch in 1 Tbsp.
   water
1 tsp. sesame oil

Microwave eggplant, after cutting into ¾ x ¾ x 4 inch strips, until soft.

Set a wok or skillet to high flame or heat. Pour in about 2 tablespoons oil. When hot, add garlic and ginger and stir-fry 1 minute. Add eggplant, wine, hot bean paste, chile pepper paste, soy sauce, sugar, vinegar, chopped scallion, and stock. Blend everything and cook for 2 minutes. Add cornstarch paste and cook until sauce is thick. Add sesame oil.

# SPINACH HERB DIP

1 (10 oz.) pkg. frozen
    chopped spinach
1½ c. 2% lowfat cottage
    cheese
2 Tbsp. mayonnaise
½ c. plain yogurt
2 Tbsp. lemon juice
⅓ c. chopped onion

Pepper to taste
Salt to taste (optional)
¼ tsp. basil
¼ tsp. dill weed
¼ tsp. oregano
¼ tsp. tarragon
¼ tsp. thyme

1. Thaw frozen spinach and squeeze out all water.
2. Whirl all ingredients in blender until smooth.
3. Chill thoroughly.
4. Thin with more yogurt if necessary. Makes 2½ cups.

Can also be used as sauce on vegetables.

Note: Do not prepare more than 24 hours ahead as color will change.

# SPINACH ROLL-UPS

1 (10 oz.) box frozen
    chopped spinach
¼ c. chopped round onion
1 can water chestnuts,
    chopped

¼ c. plain lowfat yogurt
¼ c. light mayonnaise
Garlic powder to taste
Large flour tortillas (whole
    wheat if available)

1. Cook spinach until slightly tender by parboiling, steaming, or microwaving.
2. Squeeze to drain water.
3. Combine all ingredients.
4. Spread filling evenly on tortillas.
5. Starting from 1 end, roll into cylindrical shape.
6. Cut into 1 inch bite-size pieces. Makes 5 rolls.

# STRING BEANS WITH MISO SAUCE

1 lb. string beans, julienned
2 Tbsp. sugar
2 Tbsp. miso

⅔ to ½ c. mayonnaise
2 Tbsp. sesame seed,
   toasted

Steam string beans until crisp tender; cool. Mix together sugar, miso, and mayonnaise. When it's blended, mix into beans. Sprinkle sesame seed and serve.

*Yoshiko Maeda*

# SZECHUAN EGGPLANT

1 lb. eggplant (long works
   well)
½ c. oil (canola oil is
   healthy as is olive oil)
½ Tbsp. minced garlic
1 Tbsp. minced ginger
½ Tbsp. sherry or sake
   (optional)

½ Tbsp. mirin
1 Tbsp. hot bean paste
1 Tbsp. shoyu
½ Tbsp. oyster sauce
1 Tbsp. vinegar
½ Tbsp. sesame oil
1 tsp. corn starch
⅔ c. stock or water

Wash and trim eggplant and cut into thin slices. Toss quickly in hot oil, then turn fire low; cover and simmer till soft, stirring occasionally, 5 to 10 minutes. Mix all remaining ingredients and add to eggplant, stirring well, with fire on medium. Cook till bubbling, adding a little more water if necessary. Garnish with scallions or cilantro.

*Becky Lau*

# TABBOULI SALAD

1 c. bulgur wheat
2 c. boiling water
1 green pepper, chopped
  (may use less)
2 tomatoes, diced
4 stalks green onion, finely
  chopped
2 stalks celery, finely
  chopped

½ round onion, chopped
1 sweet red pepper or
  pimento, diced
1 c. corn, well drained
1 can water chestnuts,
  coarsely chopped
Sliced olives or chopped
  walnuts (for garnish)

Pour boiling water over bulgur wheat. Let stand 1 to 2 hours. Drain well. Add remaining ingredients: Green and red peppers, tomatoes, green onion, celery, round onion, corn, and water chestnuts. Garnish with sliced olives or chopped walnuts. Serve with low calorie Italian dressing. Yields 8 servings.

# TOMATOES

1 tsp. salt
1 tsp. pepper
3 cakes tofu
3 Island Fresh tomatoes
    (ripe)
1 clove garlic
3 shallots
1 Island Fresh onion
1 Tbsp. tomato paste

½ c. dry white wine
½ c. water
2 cubes bouillon (low salt)
1 bay leaf
Flour (for dusting)
Island Fresh parsley,
    minced (for
    garnishing)

1. Sprinkle salt and pepper over tofu and let stand until water comes out.

2. Drain in colander.

3. Peel tomatoes; cut in halves. Squeeze firmly to remove the seeds. Dice.

4. Peel garlic and shallots; mince, keeping them in separate piles.

5. Cut onion into thin slices.

6. Fry the onion and shallots until golden (with vegetable cooking spray).

7. Stir in the garlic and tomato paste and cook for several more minutes. Add wine and bring to a boil.

8. Add ½ cup water, the bouillon cubes, bay leaf, and tomatoes.

9. Cut the tofu into ½ inch slices; dust with flour.

10. In another pan, saute the tofu until golden brown, again using vegetable cooking spray.

11. Slide the tofu into the tomato sauce and simmer over low heat until sauce thickens.

12. Add seasonings to taste. Serve sprinkled with minced parsley. Makes 6 servings.

*Christine Beck*

# VEGETABLE LAULAU

1 lb. Island Fresh sweet
  potatoes, peeled
1 lb. Island Fresh taro,
  peeled
8 to 12 Island Fresh ti
  leaves

1 lb. Island Fresh taro
  leaves
1 Tbsp. lowfat coconut milk

1. Clean and slice sweet potatoes and taro into desired pieces.

2. Place in taro (luau) leaves and add coconut milk and, if desired, salt to taste.

3. Wrap laulau-style in ti leaves and steam for 20 to 25 minutes or until done. Makes 4 servings.

*Herman Ling, Stephen Garcia*

# VEGETABLE WITH TOFU DRESSING

1 carrot
30 string beans
½ tsp. salt

½ c. dashi
1 Tbsp. sugar
1 Tbsp. shoyu

Slice the carrots into rectangular shape. Cut string beans into 1 inch lengths. Boil carrots in salted water, then add beans and dashi, sugar, and shoyu.

For dressing:

4 Tbsp. sesame seed
8 oz. tofu
4 Tbsp. sugar

1 tsp. salt
1 tsp. shoyu

Prepare sesame seed by heating and grinding. Press out water from tofu and add to sesame seed and grind with sugar, salt, and shoyu. Mix with carrot and beans.

# VEGETARIAN CHILI

1 c. raw bulgur
12 oz. tomato sauce
3 Tbsp. olive oil
4 cloves garlic, crushed
1 large onion, chopped
3 stalks celery, chopped
1 large carrot, shredded
2 medium zucchini, sliced
2½ c. cooked kidney beans
16 oz. whole kernel corn
    with liquid

2 c. whole tomatoes
16 oz. tomato sauce
Juice from ½ lemon
1 tsp. ground cumin
1 tsp. basil
2 tsp. chili powder (or
    more, to taste)
Dash of cayenne pepper
Finely chopped hot chili
    pepper (optional)
Salt (optional)

1. Heat 12 ounces tomato sauce to a boil and pour over raw bulgur.
2. Cover and let stand for 15 minutes.
3. Saute garlic and onion in olive oil.
4. Add celery, carrots, zucchini, and spices.
5. Cook until tender.
6. Combine remaining ingredients.
7. Bring to a boil and simmer for 1 hour. Makes 10 (1½ cup) servings.

# VEGETARIAN MINESTRONE

2 Tbsp. olive oil
3 cloves garlic, pressed or
  minced
1 medium onion, diced
2 large stalks celery, diced
2 medium carrots, diced
8 c. vegetable broth
1 (14 oz.) can Italian plum
  tomatoes or stewed
  tomatoes, chopped
1 Tbsp. Italian spice

2 c. coarsely chopped
  cabbage
1 (14 oz.) can red kidney
  beans, rinsed and
  drained
1 c. uncooked elbow
  macaroni or shells
Pinch of hot, red pepper
  flakes (optional)
Grated Romano or
  Parmesan cheese

1. In large pot, heat oil. Add garlic and saute 30 seconds, until fragrant.

2. Add onion, celery, and carrots. Cook 5 minutes until onions are soft.

3. Add broth, tomatoes, and spice; bring to a boil. Add cabbage and beans. Reduce heat to low; partially cover pot and cook 20 to 30 minutes.

4. Add pasta. Simmer 3 to 5 minutes. Add hot pepper flakes if desired. Pass a bowl of Romano or Parmesan cheese on the side. Serve with any hot, crusty bread and *enjoy!*

*Marlene Curtis*

# VEGETARIAN SPAGHETTI SAUCE

2 Tbsp. olive oil
5 cloves garlic, pressed or
  minced
1 medium onion, diced
1 green pepper, diced
  (optional)
1 small zucchini, diced
2 c. sliced mushrooms

2 tsp. dried Italian spices
1 (28 oz.) can Italian plum
  or stewed tomatoes
4 (8 oz.) cans tomato sauce
1 small can tomato paste
1 c. water (or flat beer or
  red wine)
1 block tofu, cubed

1. In large pot over medium heat, warm olive oil. Saute garlic in oil for 30 seconds. Add onion and green pepper. Cook until onions are translucent, about 5 minutes.

2. Add zucchini, mushrooms, and spices. Cook additional 5 to 7 minutes, until vegetables are wilted.

3. Add tomatoes, sauce, paste, and water (beer or wine). Bring to a slight boil; reduce heat and simmer 15 minutes.

4. Add tofu and continue simmering additional 45 minutes, until sauce is thick and flavors are blended.

5. Serve sauce over cooked spaghetti noodles with Parmesan or Romano cheese if desired.

*Marlene Curtis*

# WATERCRESS SHIRA AE - TOFU DISH

½ block tofu
2 Tbsp. toasted sesame
  seed

3 Tbsp. miso
2 Tbsp. sugar
1 bunch watercress

Clean and wash watercress. Boil and drain. Cut into 1½ inch lengths. Squeeze out excess liquid; cool. Slice tofu and drain between paper towels.

Grind sesame seeds in suribachi or use a blender. Add tofu and mix until smooth. Add miso and sugar. Mix until well blended. In a bowl, mix watercress and tofu mixture and serve.

Won bok, head cabbage, or other leafy vegetables may be used in place of watercress.

# YASAI AMAZU (VEGETABLE DISH)

4 medium daikon (turnips)    1 (3 inch) piece konbu
1 section lotus root         (seaweed)
1 medium carrot

    Peel daikon, carrot, and lotus root. Slice turnips thin; cut 5 shallow wedges lengthwise in carrot and slice thin, forming flower-shaped slices. Slice lotus root thin; pour hot water over it and drain. Wash seaweed; cut into strips, 1 x ¼ inch. Combine vegetables; add 2 teaspoons salt. Mix and let stand 10 to 15 minutes. Drain off liquid; add ¼ cup vinegar, 2 tablespoons sugar, ¼ teaspoon gourmet powder, and seaweed and mix. Soak several hours before serving.

*Yellow*

# Notes

426

# MISCELLANEOUS

# EQUIVALENT CHART

| | |
|---|---|
| 3 tsp. ..................... 1 Tbsp. | ¼ lb. crumbled Bleu cheese ..................... 1 c. |
| 2 Tbsp. ..................... ⅛ c. | 1 lemon ..................... 3 Tbsp. juice |
| 4 Tbsp. ..................... ¼ c. | 1 orange ..................... ⅓ c. juice |
| 8 Tbsp. ..................... ½ c. | 1 lb. unshelled walnuts ..... 1½ to 1¾ c. shelled |
| 16 Tbsp. ..................... 1 c. | 2 c. fat ..................... 1 lb. |
| 5 Tbsp. + 1 tsp. ..................... ⅓ c. | 1 lb. butter ..................... 2 c. or 4 sticks |
| 12 Tbsp. ..................... ¾ c. | 2 c. granulated sugar ..................... 1 lb. |
| 4 oz. ..................... ½ c. | 3½-4 c. unsifted powdered sugar ..................... 1 lb. |
| 8 oz. ..................... 1 c. | 2¼ c. packed brown sugar ..................... 1 lb. |
| 16 oz. ..................... 1 lb. | 4 c. sifted flour ..................... 1 lb. |
| 1 oz. ..................... 2 Tbsp. fat or liquid | 4½ c. cake flour ..................... 1 lb. |
| 2 c. ..................... 1 pt. | 3½ c. unsifted whole wheat flour ..................... 1 lb. |
| 2 pt. ..................... 1 qt. | 4 oz. (1 to 1¼ c.) uncooked |
| 1 qt. ..................... 4 c. | macaroni ..................... 2¼ c. cooked |
| ⅝ c. ..................... ½ c. + 2 Tbsp. | 7 oz. spaghetti ..................... 4 c. cooked |
| ⅞ c. ..................... ¾ c. + 2 Tbsp. | 4 oz. (1½ to 2 c.) uncooked |
| 1 jigger ..................... 1½ fl. oz. (3 Tbsp.) | noodles ..................... 2 c. cooked |
| 8 to 10 egg whites ..................... 1 c. | 28 saltine crackers ..................... 1 c. crumbs |
| 12 to 14 egg yolks ..................... 1 c. | 4 slices bread ..................... 1 c. crumbs |
| 1 c. unwhipped cream ..................... 2 c. whipped | 14 square graham crackers ..................... 1 c. crumbs |
| 1 lb. shredded American cheese ..................... 4 c. | 22 vanilla wafers ..................... 1 c. crumbs |

# SUBSTITUTIONS FOR A MISSING INGREDIENT

1 square **chocolate** (1 ounce) = 3 or 4 tablespoons cocoa plus ½ tablespoon fat
1 tablespoon **cornstarch** (for thickening) = 2 tablespoons flour
1 cup sifted **all-purpose flour** = 1 cup plus 2 tablespoons sifted cake flour
1 cup sifted **cake flour** = 1 cup minus 2 tablespoons sifted all-purpose flour
1 teaspoon **baking powder** = ¼ teaspoon baking soda plus ½ teaspoon cream of tartar
1 cup **sour milk** = 1 cup sweet milk into which 1 tablespoon vinegar or lemon juice has been stirred
1 cup **sweet milk** = 1 cup sour milk or buttermilk plus ½ teaspoon baking soda
¾ cup **cracker crumbs** = 1 cup bread crumbs
1 cup **cream, sour, heavy** = ⅓ cup butter and ⅔ cup milk in any sour milk recipe
1 teaspoon **dried herbs** = 1 tablespoon fresh herbs
1 cup **whole milk** = ½ cup evaporated milk and ½ cup water or 1 cup reconstituted nonfat dry milk and 1 tablespoon butter
2 ounces **compressed yeast** = 3 (¼ ounce) packets of dry yeast
1 tablespoon **instant minced onion, rehydrated** = 1 small fresh onion
1 tablespoon **prepared mustard** = 1 teaspoon dry mustard
⅛ teaspoon **garlic powder** = 1 small pressed clove of garlic
1 lb. **whole dates** = 1½ cups, pitted and cut
3 medium **bananas** = 1 cup mashed
3 cups **dry corn flakes** = 1 cup crushed
10 **miniature marshmallows** = 1 large marshmallow

# GENERAL OVEN CHART

| | |
|---|---|
| Very slow oven ..................... | 250° to 300°F. |
| Slow oven ..................... | 300° to 325°F. |
| Moderate oven ..................... | 325° to 375°F. |
| Medium hot oven ..................... | 375° to 400°F. |
| Hot oven ..................... | 400° to 450°F. |
| Very hot oven ..................... | 450° to 500°F. |

# CONTENTS OF CANS

*Of the different sizes of cans used by commercial canners, the most common are:*

| Size: | Average Contents |
|---|---|
| 8 oz. ..................... | 1 cup |
| Picnic ..................... | 1¼ cups |
| No. 300 ..................... | 1¾ cups |
| No. 1 tall ..................... | 2 cups |
| No. 303 ..................... | 2 cups |
| No. 2 ..................... | 2½ cups |
| No. 2½ ..................... | 3½ cups |
| No. 3 ..................... | 4 cups |
| No. 10 ..................... | 12 to 13 cups |

# MISCELLANEOUS

## A HAPPY HOME

4 qt. love
2 c. loyalty
3 c. forgiveness
1 large pinch of smiles
5 spoons of hope

2 spoons of tenderness
4 qt. faith
1 barrel of laughter
3 pt. consideration for
others

Take love and loyalty; mix them thoroughly with faith. Blend them with tenderness, kindness, and understanding. Add friendship and hope; sprinkle abundantly with laughter. Top freely with smiles and consideration for others. Bake with sunshine. Serve daily with generous helpings.

*Dorothy Haitsuka*

## GRANDFATHER'S SALT MIX

2 c. Hawaiian salt
2 c. raw brown sugar
(Turbinado)
1 heaping Tbsp.
peppercorns (coarse
grind)

1 heaping tsp. garlic
powder
1 tsp. MSG (optional)

Combine ingredients. Store in a covered jar in a cool place (never in the refrigerator). Use to season meats, fish, etc. Broil or bake. Do not fry because the meats or fish stick to the pan.

## SEASONED SALT

5 c. Hawaiian salt
¼ c. celery powder
¼ c. onion powder
¼ c. chili powder

2 Tbsp. garlic powder
¼ c. MSG (optional)
1 Tbsp. paprika

Combine ingredients. Store in a covered jar in a cool place. Use to season steaks, chicken, fish, etc. Rub inside and outside of a turkey before baking. Excellent for baking, broiling, or frying.

# HIJIKI

1 (3 oz.) pkg. dried hijiki
  (seaweed)
2 aburage (you can also
  add about 2 konyaku)
¼ c. chopped dried shrimp,
  soaked in ½ c. water
1½ Tbsp. salad oil

¾ c. brown or raw sugar
¾ c. shoyu
1 tsp. salt
1 tsp. monosodium
  glutamate (optional)
1 Tbsp. sesame seed

Soak hijiki in lukewarm water for ½ hour; wash and drain. Cut aburage thin and 1½ inches long, also konyaku if added.

Heat frying pan; add oil, hijiki, and aburage or konyaku and fry 3 to 4 minutes, mixing so that it won't burn. Add shrimp and water and keep on cooking another 3 or 4 minutes, then season with sugar, shoyu, salt, and monosodium glutamate. Cook until quite dry, mixing slowly; last, add sesame seed.

*Green*

# KONBU

1½ pkg. kiri konbu
½ c. chirimen iriko
2 c. water
2 Tbsp. vinegar
Iri goma (last)
½ c. brown sugar

½ c. shoyu (put less
  according to taste
  preferred)
1 tsp. monosodium
  glutamate (optional)

Put konbu in colander and wash. Cook konbu, iriko, and vinegar in 2 cups of water for 15 to 20 minutes. Add brown sugar and shoyu and cook a little while longer, then add monosodium glutamate and iri goma.

*Green*

# LUMPIA WRAPPERS

**2 c. flour**                           **2 c. water**

     Combine flour and water; blend until smooth. Heat a Teflon skillet on low heat. Using a clean 3 inch paint brush, quickly dip brush into batter and paint onto skillet with very light even strokes, repeating until bottom of skillet is covered with a paper thin layer.

     As wrapper cooks, it will begin to flake away from the skillet. Lift wrapper gently from skillet and place on a piece of foil; cool slightly. Clean skillet to remove extra flakes of cooked batter. Repeat until all of batter is used.

     If made ahead, keep refrigerated. Wrapper will keep 1 week. Makes 24 wrappers.

# WUN TUN WRAPPERS

**1½ c. flour**                          **¼ c. water**
**½ tsp. salt**                          **1 egg (unbeaten)**

     Sift flour and salt into a bowl. Add water and egg; mix well. Knead dough until smooth and not sticky. Roll out dough paper thin on a floured board. Cut into 3 inch squares. Makes about 50 wrappers.

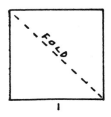
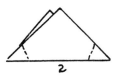

# POI, OPAI, OPIHI, LIMU

Poi: Put poi in large bowl. Mix with hand, adding a little water at a time. Continue mixing and adding water until of desired consistency. To store in refrigerator, add thin layer of water over the poi to prevent drying. To freeze, put in containers and freeze. When ready to use, place in open foil package and steam. Mix more water into poi for proper consistency. *Strain poi.*

Opai: Gather river shrimp. Wash. Put in pot and place on medium heat. When liquid comes out, add Hawaiian salt to taste (about 1 teaspoon for 2 cups of opai). Lower heat and continue cooking until dry.

Opihi: Gather. Either pry out with spoon or another opihi shell or pour boiling water over and let stand ½ minute. Drain and shell. Toss generously with Hawaiian salt. Let stand 1 to 2 hours. Rinse and drain. Bottle and refrigerate. If desired, just toss with Hawaiian salt to taste.

Opihi Limu: Gather and clean limu. Pour boiling water over limu; rinse with cold water after ½ minute. Squeeze and drain. Toss with salted opihi.

Chop Chop Limu: Gather and clean limu; chop in ½ inch pieces. Toss with salted opihi.

# FRESH SALSA

2 (4 oz.) cans green chilies
   or jalapenos,
   chopped
2 (4 oz.) cans ripe olives,
   chopped

1 medium onion, chopped
2 large tomatoes, chopped
3 Tbsp. olive oil
1½ Tbsp. vinegar
1 tsp. garlic powder

Combine first 4 ingredients. Toss with oil, vinegar, and garlic powder. Refrigerate at least 2 hours.

# PAPAYA-CARAMBOLA (STARFRUIT) SALSA

½ medium papaya, peeled
  and cubed (1 c.)
½ medium carambola,
  diced (½ c.)
3 Tbsp. pineapple juice

1 tsp. dark rum
2 Tbsp. thinly sliced green
  onion
1 Tbsp. snipped fresh
  cilantro

Combine the papaya, carambola, pineapple juice, rum, green onion, and cilantro in a small bowl; toss well. Cover and refrigerate at least 1 hour. Serve with grilled or baked shrimp, pork, chicken, or fish. Makes 1½ cups.

# HAWAIIAN PUNCH FOR 40

½ gal. guava nectar
1 large can pineapple juice
1 can frozen passion fruit
  juice, diluted
3 cans orange base, diluted

1 large bottle ginger ale
Ice cubes
Guava, lime, lemon, or
  orange sherbet

Combine all juices and chill. Just before serving, add ice and ginger ale. Pour punch in a punch bowl and float squares or scoops of sherbet on top.

*Blue*

# ISLAND FRUIT PUNCH

2 (46 oz.) cans pineapple
  juice
2 (12 oz.) cans frozen
  lemonade, thawed
2 (12 oz.) cans frozen guava
  juice, thawed

2 (12 oz.) cans frozen
  orange-passion fruit
  juice, thawed
9 qt. water
1 Tbsp. red food coloring

Combine ingredients; pour over ice in a punch bowl. Makes 75 (6 ounce) servings.

# PINE-TEA PUNCH

4 c. boiling water
1 c. tea leaves
4 c. sugar
4 c. cold water
12 c. pineapple juice (fresh,
  frozen, canned)

2 c. tart juice (guava,
  lemon, lime, passion
  fruit)

Add boiling water to tea leaves; let stand 5 minutes, then strain. Add sugar and stir until dissolved. Cool. Add other ingredients; chill. Serve in punch bowl with block of ice. Makes about 6 quarts, or 50 (½ cup) servings.

# PUNCH FOR 80

1 gal. guava nectar
2 large cans pineapple
  juice
3 cans frozen lilikoi juice,
  diluted
6 cans orange base,
  partially diluted

2 large bottles ginger ale
Lots of ice
Guava, lime, lemon, or
  orange sherbet

Combine all juices and chill. Just before serving, add ice and ginger ale. Float squares or scoops of sherbet on top.

# WATERMELON PUNCH - SUBAK HWACHAE

1 c. sugar
1 c. water
½ small evenly shaped
    watermelon
¼ c. brandy

1 (12 oz.) can lemon-lime
    soda
Ice cubes
1 tsp. shelled pine nuts

In a saucepan, bring sugar and water to a boil; cool. Scoop watermelon flesh with a melon baller. Pour sugar syrup over watermelon balls. Scoop remaining watermelon flesh; squeeze in a clean cloth to extract juice. Combine watermelon balls, watermelon juice, and brandy; chill. Cut the upper edge of the watermelon shell in a saw-tooth design and use as a punch bowl.

Just before serving, add watermelon mixture, soda, and ice cubes to watermelon shell. Sprinkle with pine nuts. Makes 10 to 12 servings.

# YASAI MAGIC

*Courtesy of Mrs. T. Kaneo, U.E. member, Mrs. Sachiko Matsumoto, Mrs. Mabel Ito, Extension Home Economists and Cooperative Extension Service Home Economics Circular #288.*

"Yasai" is a Japanese word meaning "vegetable." The Japanese have been, for many years, well known for their unusual vegetable creations for the table. It seems almost unbelievable that some of the most common vegetables can be converted into very attractive table decorations. However, the decorations described here are American adaptations, and not necessarily "authentic Japanese" creations.

"Yasai Magic" is the art of turning a humble turnip into a delicate camellia, a carrot into a bright chrysanthemum, or a long, slender, gracefully curved daikon into a demure bride. With a slight difference in the method of carving and with the use of food coloring, beautiful peonies can be made. With a little practice, other more intricate flowers, fowl, and animals can be made out of the eggplant, cucumber, beet, and other similar vegetables.

An arrangement of vegetable "flowers" may be used for any occasion. It will brighten a tray of food or give that final festive touch to a party table. These vegetable "flowers" may be made days ahead and placed in plastic containers or bags and kept in the refrigerator.

Materials needed are:

Vegetable peeler with one scalloped edge       Teriyaki sticks
Very sharp French knife                        Food coloring
Toothpicks

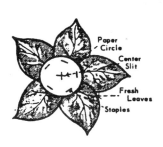

When only vegetable flowers are used for a decoration, they will be more effective if framed with clean green leaves. Cut a 1½ to 2 inch circle of heavy paper and make two ¼ inch criss-crossed slits in the center. Staple several leaves onto the paper circle. Insert the teriyaki stick with the flower on it through the center of the paper base. The little paper bases may be purchased ready-made from florist supply shops who sell them for camellia and gardenia corsages.

DAIKON CAMELLIAS — Use medium-size daikons or Chinese-type turnips.

1. Cut into 3 inch sections; peel if desired.

2. Round off ends and one side of each piece as shown by dotted lines.

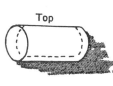

3. Cut thin slices from end to end forming two connected petals.

4. Assemble five or six slices, criss-crossing them as shown to make petals appear to go around. Stab a daikon stick through the center at x.

5. Make a rosette, like a radish rose, by cutting thin V-shaped slashes around a small piece of daikon as shown by dotted lines. Place it in the center of the flower on the end of the teriyaki stick.

6. Place the flower in ice water. It will crisp and shape itself beautifully, like nature's own.

CARROT CHRYSANTHEMUM — Use large-size carrots. They will be easier to work with if allowed to wilt a little by keeping them unrefrigerated for a day or two.

1. Cut carrot sections about 4 inches long and round off ends as for the camellia. Score one side with the scalloped vegetable peeler as shown.

2. Slice and assemble petals the same as for the camellia.

3. For the center, cut a slice of the carrot about ¼ inch thick; score it diagonally with a knife as shown. Place in center of flower.

4. Place in ice water to crisp and curl.

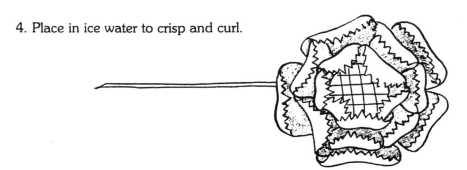

PEONIES — Use extra large daikons. Cut sections of different lengths, such as five inches, three inches and one and three-fourths inches to be used in making a large flower, a medium size one, and a bud. These three sizes of peonies are ordinarily used for Japanese arrangements.

1. Peel and round off sections as for camellia. Score with a knife as shown.

2. Slice petals as for the camellias.

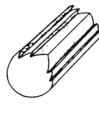

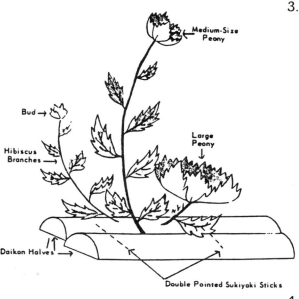

Medium-Size Peony

Bud →

Large Peony ↓

Hibiscus Branches →

Daikon Halves →

Double Pointed Sukiyaki Sticks

3. Assemble these petals as for the camellia. Use 5 of the longest slices for the LARGE FLOWER. Use a round, scored slice for the center as shown for the chrysanthemum. Assemble the MEDIUM - SIZE FLOWER in the same way, using smaller petals towards the center. Use only two or three smaller slices for the BUD and center it with a rosette made as shown for the camellia.

4. Place in ice water to crisp and curl.

5. To tint petals: Place a small amount of food coloring in a small dish. With a wide lettering brush dipped into the food coloring, lightly tint the edges of the petals. Let the color run, forming lighter veins as it travels downward on its own. Give a strong professional brush stroke from top to bottom and deepen the color toward the center, if desired.

TO MAKE THE JAPANESE ARRANGEMENT: Select clean hibiscus branches, shaped with a slight curve as shown in the diagram on page 106. Make a base for the arrangement of two large daikon slices held together invisibly with double pointed sukiyaki sticks as shown. Attach the stick of each blossom to the hibiscus branches with corsage wire. Stab branches into base to make a graceful arrangement similar to that shown here.

FISH NET: It may be placed over a baked fish or crab, or used as a bridal veil for the daikon bride. First cut off both ends of carrot or daikon; pare until a smooth, even cylinder is obtained.

1. Starting at one end, make a straight row of one-inch slits, one eighth of an inch apart and about one-half inch deep. The second row of slits is made half way between those in first row and overlapping the slit length half-way.

2. Make the third row of slits the same as the first, and the fourth row, the same as the second. Continue around until the last row overlaps and fits between the first row of slits.

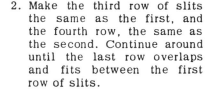

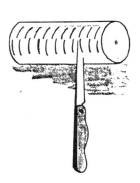

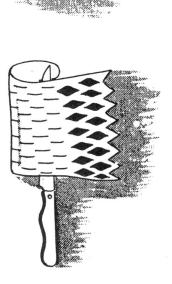

3. The net is now ready to be cut. Place the knife along-side the carrot or daikon and peel around very thinly to any desired length. Sprinkle lightly with salt, and let stand a few minutes to wilt. Wash off salt and spread the net.

DAIKON BRIDE: Select a medium-size daikon with a slight outward curve for the bosom part. The length of the daikon determines the height of the bride. Peel the daikon to give it a clean look and round the top. For the skirt, cut thin slices upward around the daikon starting about two inches from the bottom and cutting almost to the waistline, being careful not to cut right through. Make another row of slices up from the bottom in the same way as for the rosette center of the camellia. With a toothpick invisibly fasten a radish at the top for the head. When crisped in ice water the petal-like skirt flares out attractively. Stand her on a large daikon half using a double pointed teriyaki stick. Drape a long, narrow veil made of daikon net as described on the previous page over the radish head so the blushing bride will peek through.

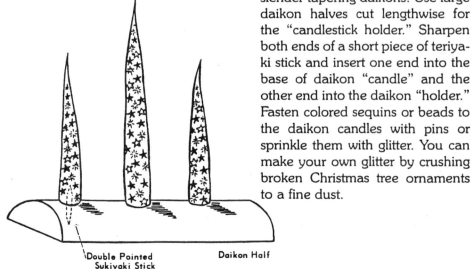

DAIKON CANDLES: Select long, slender tapering daikons. Use large daikon halves cut lengthwise for the "candlestick holder." Sharpen both ends of a short piece of teriyaki stick and insert one end into the base of daikon "candle" and the other end into the daikon "holder." Fasten colored sequins or beads to the daikon candles with pins or sprinkle them with glitter. You can make your own glitter by crushing broken Christmas tree ornaments to a fine dust.

Double Pointed
Sukiyaki Stick

Daikon Half

438

# JAPANESE FLOWER ARRANGEMENT WITH VEGETABLES

The Orientals are noted for their ability to bring natural beauty into the home and recreating color rhythm through the intelligent use of flowers and foliage. Their artistic arrangement with vegetables also shows their technique and originality.

Remember that these arrangements may be used for home decorations and other party decorations.

## Kiku or Chrysanthemum Arrangement

Materials needed:
>    1 small round onion
>    1 stalk green onion
>    ½ green papaya or turnip for base
>    1 chopstick
>    yellow food coloring

To make the kiku:

1.    Make ¼ - ⅜ inch cuts into the round onion from the top to the root of the round onion about ¾ to 1 inch apart (diagram 1). These will form the petals for the flowers (diagram 2). Color the flower with yellow food coloring.

For the stem:

1.    Place the chopstick through the green onion leaf being sure that the stick is covered well. Cut off the green leaf from the center (diagram 3). Leave ¾ inches of the chopstick uncovered on the top and bottom (diagram 4). Put the round onion on the stick and place the whole arrangement on the turnip or papaya which is used for the base (diagram 5).

## Ayame or Iris Arrangement

Materials needed:
>    1 turnip (narrow end of the turnip about 3 inches long)
>    1 green onion stalk
>    yellow and blue food coloring
>    1 chopstick
>    ½ green papaya or turnip for the base

To make the ayame:

1.    Cut four slits on the turnip about ¾ of the way as shown in diagram 6.

2.    Leave cut turnip in cold water to make the petals curl a little and also to make it look fresh. Wipe the turnip with a dishtowel to remove excess water and color the petals blue and the center (bulb) yellow (diagram 7). For stem, refer to diagrams 3, 4 and 5.

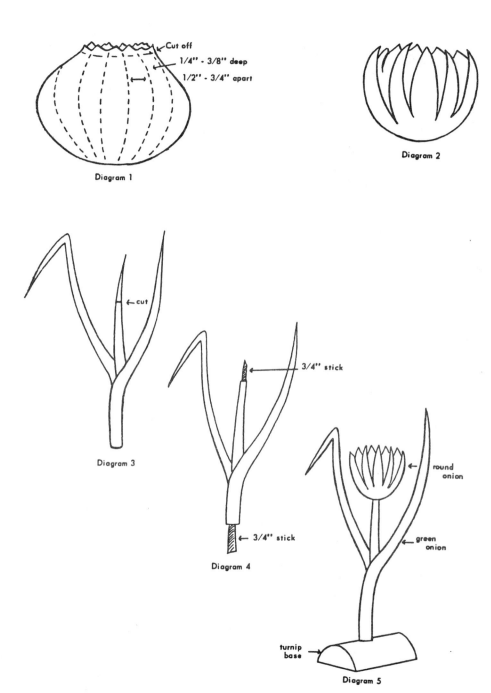

Cut off

1/4" - 3/8" deep

1/2" - 3/4" apart

Diagram 1

Diagram 2

← cut

Diagram 3

3/4" stick

← 3/4" stick

Diagram 4

round onion

green onion

turnip base

Diagram 5

440

Diagram 6

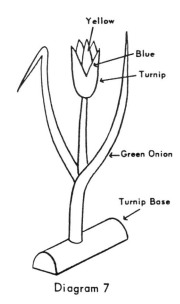

Yellow

Blue

Turnip

Green Onion

Turnip Base

Diagram 7

## *GARNISHES*

### *Onion Lilies*

Cut a small, peeled onion into 16 pie-shaped wedges to within ½ inch of the bottom. Crisp lilies for at least 1 hour in ice water tinted with food coloring; drain. Cut a green pepper in half, saw-tooth fashion, to hold lily. Keep in ice water until serving time.

### *Cucumber Ruffles*

Slice off one end of the cucumber; hold cuke upright. With vegetable peeler at a right angle to it, pare around on top of cut end, turning cucumber carefully to keep strip in one thin spiral. Your salad will taste extra good if you keep pieces sizeable and coat them lightly with creamy dressing.

Lilies

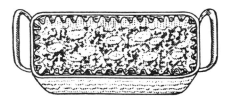

Ruffles

### *Sho-Chiku-bai*

Materials needed:
    1 branch of bamboo
    1 branch citrus with thorns
    1 branch pine
    ½ green papaya or turnip for base
    white popped corn or small carrot

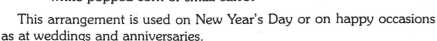

This arrangement is used on New Year's Day or on happy occasions as at weddings and anniversaries.

1. Trim and shape branches. Remove most leaves from citrus branch. Keep this the tallest. Cut pine needles into fan shape.

2. Arrange branches with citrus branch in the middle

3. Cut carrot into flowers
    scrape or peel carrots
    cut a 2 inch piece
    cut grooves for petals
    slice cross wise

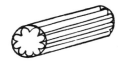

4. Place carrot flower or popped corn on thorns of citrus branch to represent plum blossoms.

5. Place arrangement on platter with morimono — fruits, fish cakes, yokan, kanten. Or — place stork and turtle for wedding arrangement.

### *Stork and Turtle*
### *(Symbol of long life)*

Materials needed:

Stork:
    1 shaped egg plant
    1 small chili pepper
    chopsticks
    shaped daikon
    2 match sticks
    ti-leaves
    2 bamboo branches,
       10 to 11 inches

Turtle:
    ½ small green papaya
    1 shaped dasheen
    1 green papaya
    2 match sticks
    5 small nails

6"

10" –11"
Bamboo

Stork:

1. Cut daikon for body, shaping thigh, neck and head.
2. Pierce match head into head for eyes.
3. Cut slit on side for wings.
4. Cut 2 slits on the back for tail "feathers."
5. Cut ti-leaves for wings and tail and stick into slits.
6. Pierce bamboo or chopstick for legs.
7. Stick legs into ½ papaya to have stork stand.
8. Arrange ti-leaves around stork.

Turtle:

1. Cut green papaya in half.
   Cut grooves on one for turtle back.
2. Cut the other ½ papaya for 4 legs and head.
3. Cut match stick to ¼ inch and stick into head for eyes.
4. Arrange with stork on platter or tray with daikon flowers.

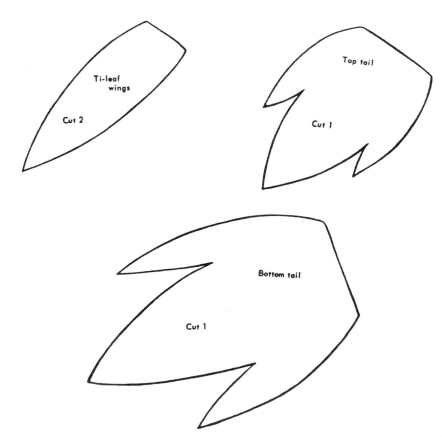

Ti-leaf wings
Cut 2

Top tail
Cut 1

Bottom tail
Cut 1

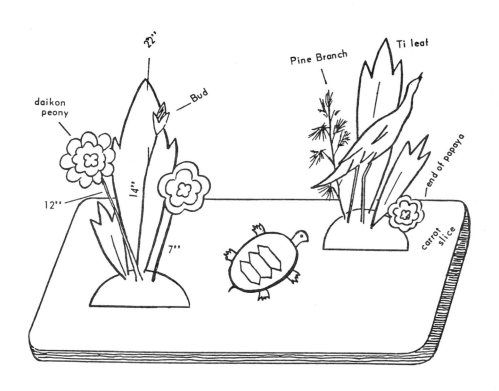

WEDDING ARRANGEMENT

# CUTTING OF MORIMONO FOODS

Oranges

A. Cut oranges into eighths
   Peel almost to end and roll peel under segment

B. Cut orange into fourths
   Slice from both sides to center
   Slide slices to side

Yokan
1. Slice ¾ - 1 inch pieces
2. Cut diagonally along one side half way of slice
3. Turn slice and cut diagonally along other side
4. Stick knife in center of yokan slice between the two slanting slits
5. Pull apart to get 2 pieces

Yokan, Eggs, or Kamaboko
1. Cut yokan or kamaboko into thick slices
2. Holding one end of thread tightly, zigzag thread in the middle of slice of egg all around. Pull apart to get two interestingly cut pieces.

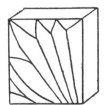 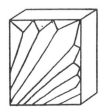 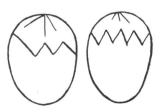

# GLOSSARY

C-Chinese   F-Filipino   H-Hawaiian   J-Japanese
K-Korean   P-Portuguese   PR-Puerto Rican

## A

| | | |
|---|---|---|
| Adobo | **F** | Seasoned meat |
| A-ge or Aburage | **J** | Deep fried tofu (bean curd) slices |
| Ajinomoto | **J** | Monosodium glutamate |
| Ajitsuke | **J** | Seasoned |
| Ahi | **H** | Yellowfin tuna, or shibi **J** |
| Aku | **H** | Bonito, shipjack tuna, or katsuo **J** |
| Akule | **H** | Big-eyed scad or aji **J** |
| Ampalaya | **F** | Bitter melon |
| An | **J** | Paste made from beans, used to fill confections |
| Achuete seeds | -- | Seeds from lipstick pods.  Also known as annatto or achiote |
| Andagi | **J** | Okinawan doughnut |
| Araimo | **J** | Dasheen, Japanese taro.  May substitute with Irish potato or other taro |
| Azuki | **J** | Small red beans |

## B

| | | |
|---|---|---|
| Bagoong | **F** | Salted fish sauce made of shrimp or various small fish, allowed to ferment. Used uncooked or as seasoning for meat, fish and vegetable dishes. |
| Black beans | **C** | Dau see - fermented black beans used for seasoning |
| Bao | **C** | Name for bun |
| Barazushi | **J** | Sushi mixed with seasoned vegetables |

## C

| | | |
|---|---|---|
| Cascaron | **F** | Fried mochi-coconut balls |
| Chuk | **C** | Rice gruel or Jook |
| Char Siu | **C** | Red roast pork |
| Chawan Mushi | **J** | Custard steamed in bowl |
| Chayote | -- | Pipinella **P** or squash |

| Chichi | J | Milk |
| Chirashizushi | J | Sushi with topping sprinkled on it |
| Chow Mein | C | Noodle dish |
| Cilantro | P | Chinese parsley, coriander, Corintigo **PR** |
| Chung Choy, or Chung Choi | C | Salted turnip |

## D

| Daikon | J | White radish or turnip |
| Dashi | J | Soup stock |
| Dashi Konbu | J | Dried seaweed (kelp) used for soup stock |
| Dashi-no-moto | J | Soup stock base (powder) |
| Dango | J | Dumpling |
| Dau See | C | Fermented black beans used for seasoning |

## E

| Ebi | J | Shrimp |
| Five Spice | -- | Mixture of spices - fennel, anise, pepper, clove and cinnamon, Heong Liu Fun **C** |

## F

| Fu | J | Dried gluten cakes |

## G

| Ginko Nuts | C | Edible white or green nuts, Ginnan **J** Available canned, in oriental food section |
| Gobo | J | Burdock root |
| Goma | J | Sesame seed |
| Gow Pi | C | Dried tangerine peel |
| Gulaman | F | Agar agar, Kanten **J** |
| Gum Choy | C | Dried lily flower |
| Gu | J | Flavored rice filling for sushi |

## H

| Hasu | J | Lotus root |
| Hau Yau | C | Oyster sauce |
| Haupia | H | Coconut cornstarch pudding |
| Hawaiian salt | -- | Coarse salt, evaporated from sea water. May substitute rock salt or regular salt |
| Heong Liu Fun | C | Five spice powder |
| Hibachi | J | Charcoal braiser |
| Hi-me | J | Flavoring powder |
| Hokki or Hokkigai | J | Clam |

# I

| | | |
|---|---|---|
| Inamona | H | Roasted kukui nut, pounded and salted, served as relish or mixed with seaweed |
| Iriko | J | Small dried fish |

# J

| | | |
|---|---|---|
| Japanese vinegar | -- | Rice vinegar |

# K

| | | |
|---|---|---|
| Kamaboko | J | Steamed fish cake |
| Kampyo or Kanpyo | J | Dried strips of gourd |
| Kang kong | F | Swamp cabbage |
| Kanten | J | Agar agar, made of seaweed that jells at room temperature |
| Katakuri or Katakuriko | J | Potato starch |
| Katsuobushi | J | Steamed and dried bonito, slivered and used for seasoning |
| Kim Chee | K | Peppery pickled vegetables, usually of celery cabbage, cucumber or daikon |
| Kinako | J | Ground roasted soybean flour |
| Kiri-konbu | J | Seaweed strips |
| Ko Choo Jung | K | Korean hot sauce |
| Kock Chai | C | Steamed filled dumpling |
| Kogai | J | Small clam |
| Konbu | J | Dried kelp, seaweed |
| Konnyaku | J | Geletinous square cake made from flour of tuber root, also known as Devil's tongue jelly |
| Koshi-an | J | Smooth bean paste |
| Kukui nut | H | Candle nut |
| Kumu | H | Fish belonging to the goat fish species |
| Kurome | J | Dried black seaweed |

# L

| | | |
|---|---|---|
| Larm See | C | Salted black olives |
| Lau lau | H | Bundle of meat, steamed in ti leaves |
| Li Hing Mui | C | Preserved Chinese seeds |
| Lilikoi | H | Passion fruit |
| Limu | H | Seaweed |
| Limu Koku | H | Variety of seaweed |
| Limu Manauea | H | Seaweed, ogo J |

| Linguisa | P Portuguese sausage |
|---|---|
| Long Rice | -- Bean thread, Saifun  C |
| Lup Cheong or | C Chinese sausage |
| Larp Cheong | |
| Lomi | H Massage, rub or crush ingredients with fingers |
| Look Fun | C Rice noodles made in wide sheets |
| Luau | H Taro leaves or Hawaiian feast |
| Lumpia | F Fried rolls with filling |

# M

| Mahimahi | H Common dolphin |
|---|---|
| Maki | J Roll |
| Malasada | P Yeast doughnut without hole.  Served on Shrove Tuesday |
| Manju | J Bun with bean filling |
| Marungay | F Horseradish tree.  Young beans, leaves and flowers used in salads and soups.  Used as flavoring in fish and meat dishes |
| Matsutake | J Long stemmed mushrooms, available in cans |
| Meonapua'a | H Chinese pork buns |
| Mirin | J Sweet rice wine |
| Miso | J Paste of fermented rice and soybeans |
| Mitsuba | J Trefoil, leaves used as garnish in soups |
| Mochi | J Pounded rice cake |
| Mochiko | J Glutinous rice flour or sweet rice flour |
| Monosodium Glutamate | Gourmet powder,ajinomoto J, Vetsin C |
| MSG | -- Monosodium glutamate |
| Mongo | C Small green beans used for bean sprouts, Mung beans |
| Moyashi | J Bean sprouts |

# N

| Nam Yue | C Fermented red bean curd |
|---|---|
| Namasu | J Vinegar flavored food with seafood |
| Narazuke | J Pickled melon |
| Nishime | J Cooked vegetable dish |
| Nishime konbu | J Narrow kelp, seaweed used in Nishime |
| Nomei Fu | C Glutinous rice flour, Mochiko J |
| Nori | J Dried seaweed in sheets |
| Norimaki | J Sushi rolled in nori |

# O

| | | |
|---|---|---|
| Oboro | **J** | Shrimp flakes |
| Ogo | **J** | Seaweed, Limu Manauea **H** |
| O'io | **H** | Bonefish, lady fish, or banana fish |
| Okara | **J** | Tofu residue, also known as Kirazu **J** |
| Opihi | **H** | Shell fish, baby abalone served shelled and salted |
| Okinawa | **J** | Ryukyu Islands |
| Opai | **H** | Small shrimp |
| Oama | **H** | Small fish that come in school |

# P

| | | |
|---|---|---|
| Pancit | **F** | Fish sauce, clear liquid pressed out when making bagoong. Used on salad or for seasoning |
| Pohole | **H** | Fern shoot, fiddlehead, Warabi **J** |
| Poi | **H** | Staple starch food, steamed and mashed taro |
| Pul Kogi | **K** | Barbequed chicken or beef with marinade |
| Pupu | **H** | Hors d'oeuve or appetizer |

# R

| | | |
|---|---|---|
| Renkon | **J** | Lotus root |
| Rafute | **J** | Pork prepared Okinawa style |

# S

| | | |
|---|---|---|
| Sai fun | **C** | Bean thread or long rice |
| Saimin | **C** | Noodle soup |
| Sake | **J** | Rice wine |
| Sanbaizuke | **J** | Vegetables pickled with shoyu and sugar sauce |
| Sekihan | **J** | Mochi rice with red bean |
| Senbei | **J** | Wafers, usually served with tea |
| Shibi | **J** | Tuna |
| Shiitake | **J** | Black mushrooms, usually available dried |
| Shoyu | **J** | Soy bean sauce, soyu **C** |
| Shiofuke Konbu | **J** | Chopped salted sea kelp |
| Shiso | **J** | Parilla or beef steak plant, leaves used for flavoring or for color |
| Shira-ae | **J** | Vegetables with mashed tofu sauce |
| Somen | **J** | Fine wheat flour noodles |
| Sukiyaki | **J** | Vegetable and meat dish, usually cooked at the table, sometimes called Hekka in Hawaii |

| Suribachi | J | Mortar or bowl for grinding |
| Sushi | J | Rice seasoned with vinegar sauce |
| Sushi meshi | J | Prepared sushi rice |
| Sushi-no-moto | J | Powdered sushi flavoring |

**T**

| Taegu | K | Spiced codfish |
| Takenoko | J | Bamboo shoot |
| Tahini | -- | Sesame seed paste |
| Takuwan | J | Pickled turnip |
| Taro | H | Corm of tropical plant, steamed or boiled and eaten like potato. When pounded, it is called poi, staple food of Hawaiians |
| Tempura | J | Fritters |
| Ti | H | Cordyline termenalis, broad leaved plant. Large oblong leaves are used in Hawaiian cooking |
| Tofu | J | Soybean curd |
| Tsubushi an | J | Coarsely ground red bean paste |

**U**

| Udon | J | Flat noodles |
| Unagi | J | Eel |
| Un Choi | C | Swamp cabbage |

**V**

| Vetsin | C | Monosodium glutamate |

**W**

| Warabi | J | Fern shoot, Pohole H, Zenmai J, or Fiddlehead |
| Wok | C | Chinese frypan |
| Won Bok | C | White or celery cabbage, Makina J |
| Wun tun chips | C | Deep fat fried small pieces of Wun tun pi |
| Wun Tun Pi | C | Thin squares of dough made of flour and eggs |

**Y**

| Yaki | J | Fried, broiled or baked |
| Yakiniku | J | Broiled beef |
| Yokan | J | Sweet bean confection |
| Yomogi | J | Magwort, dark green leaves used to color and flavor mochi or used as herb |

By
COOKBOOK PUBLISHERS, INC.
P.O. Box 15920
Lenexa, Kansas 66285-5920

# Notes

# INDEX OF RECIPES

458

## VEGETARIAN

## SPECIAL DIETARY NEEDS

## MISCELLANEOUS

Family & Community Education

# JOIN US!

Family and Community Education (FCE) provides learning opportunities. Members share or participate in programs on how to protect the environment, improve family living, develop leadership, and promote global learning through small club meetings or larger association meetings.

Involvement in FCE club and association activities will help you to refine or learn new skills to improve the quality of life through programs such as:

| | |
|---|---|
| Food and Fitness | Public Speaking |
| Travel | Recycling |
| Financial Planning | Home Safety |
| Healthy Foods | Goal Setting |
| Parenting | Coping with Age |
| Making New Friends | Cultural Diversity |
| Cottage Industries | Building Self Esteem |
| Marketable Skills | Serving on Boards |
| Volunteer Opportunities | and Committees |

Membership is offered to any person regardless of race, color, sex, religion, age or national origin. Membership dues are paid annually, which includes a subscription of **FCE TODAY**, the official publication of the National Association of Family and Community Education.

FCE is in cooperation with the University of Hawaii, College of Tropical Agriculture and Human Resources (CTAHR) Extension Service.

Say *"YES"* to Family Community Education by calling, or mailing information about yourself to one of the addresses.

Maui FCE
P.O. Box 1784
Kahului, HI 96733
Ph:  244-3242
Fax: 244-7089

Kauai CTAHR Extension Service
State Office Building
3060 Eiwa St. Room 210
Lihue, HI 96776
Ph: 274-3471   Fax: 274-3474


Hilo FCE
P.O. Box 4203
Hilo, Hawaii 96720
Ph: 959-9155

Kona CTAHR Extension Service
P.O. Box 208
Kealekekua, HI 96750
Ph: 322-2718   Fax: 322-2493

Molokai CTAHR Extension Service
Hoolehua Community Center
P.O. Box 317
Hoolehua, HI 96720
Ph: 567-6833   Fax: 567-6818

Kaneohe CTAHR Extension Service
45-260 Waikalua Road
Kaneohe, HI 96744
Ph: 247-0421   Fax: 247-1912

✂ - - - - - - - - - - - - - - - - - - - - - - - - - - - - - - - - - - - - -

*Yes, I would like to join FCE!*

Name _____

Address _____

_____ Zip Code _____

Phone _____

*This Cookbook is a perfect gift for Holidays, Weddings, Anniversaries & Birthdays.*

*To order extra copies as gifts for your friends, please use Order Forms on reverse side of this page.*

\* \* \* \* \* \* \* \* \* \*

# ORDER FORM

Use the order forms below for obtaining
additional copies of this cookbook.

Fill in Order Forms Below - Cut Out and Mail

**Maui Association for Family and
Community Education
P.O. Box 1784
Kahului, HI   96733**

Please mail _____ copies of your Cookbook @ _____ each, plus shipping/
handling of $3.00 book rate (Hawaii) or $4.00 priority mail (Continental USA) per book
ordered.

**Mail books to:**

Name _____

Address _____

City, State, Zip _____

---

**Maui Association for Family and
Community Education
P.O. Box 1784
Kahului, HI   96733**

Please mail _____ copies of your Cookbook @ _____ each, plus shipping/
handling of $3.00 book rate (Hawaii) or $4.00 priority mail (Continental USA) per book
ordered.

**Mail books to:**

Name _____

Address _____

City, State, Zip _____

# Publish
# Your Own Cookbook
## And
## Profit

*It's as easy as pie!*

Order your own FREE no-obligation Cookbook Instruction Kit today!

**Fast**     Fill out and mail the postage-paid card below.

**Faster**    Fax a copy of you completed postage-paid card to 913-492-5947. Any time of the day.

**Fastest**   Call our Toll-Free Number 800-227-7282. Any time of the day.

Cook Up A Fundraising Success   With Cookbook Publishers, Inc.!

You collect the recipes and we do the rest. We even supply you with FREE recipe forms! We have helped thousands of groups like yours, so let us show you how easy it is to create a successful cookbook.

☐   Yes, please rush me a FREE no-obligation Personalized Cookbook Instruction Kit.
☐   I am also interested in other fundraising ideas.

PLEASE SEND MATERIALS TO:

Organization_____

Name _____

Address _____

City/State _____ Zip_____

Home Phone (   ) _____ Work Phone (   )_____

Previous Correspondent, if any _____

We plan to complete our project by the following date:_____

Cookbook Publishers, Inc.

# Why is a personalized cookbook the right fundraiser for you?

*It's. . . .*

*Easy to put together*
▼
*Self-financing*
▼
*Easy to sell*
▼
*Highly profitable*
▼
*Exciting!*

Request your FREE Step-by-Step Cookbook Instruction Kit Today!

1-800-227-7282
http://www.cookbookpublishers.com

*Interested in additional fundraising ideas? Ask us about our other fundraising programs when you call, or simply check the appropriate box on the opposite side of the business reply card shown below.*
▼ *Drop the card in the mail today!* ▼

---

Cookbook Publishers, Inc.

TEAR ALONG PERFORATION